Understanding Early Modern Primary Sources

Understanding Early Modern Primary Sources is an introduction to the rich treasury of source material available to students of early modern history. During this period, political developments, economic and social change, rising literacy levels, and the success of the printing press ensured that the State, the Church, and the people generated texts and objects on an unprecedented scale. This book introduces students to the sources that survived to become indispensable primary material studied by historians.

After a wide-ranging introductory chapter, Part I of the book, 'Sources', takes the reader through seven key categories of primary material, including governmental, ecclesiastical and legal records, diaries and literary works, print, and visual and material sources. Each chapter addresses how different types of material were produced, whilst also pointing readers towards the most important and accessible physical and digital source collections. Part II, 'Histories', takes a thematic approach. Each chapter in this section explores the sources that are used to address major themes in early modern history, including political and popular cultures, the economy, science, religion, gender, warfare, and global exploration.

This collection of chapters by leading historians in their respective fields showcases how practitioners research early modern history, and is an invaluable resource for any student embarking on their studies of the early modern period.

Laura Sangha is Lecturer in British History 1500–1700 at the University of Exeter. Her publications include *Angels and Belief in England, 1480–1700* (2012).

Jonathan Willis is Lecturer in Early Modern History at the University of Birmingham. His publications include *Church Music and Protestantism in Post-Reformation England* (2010).

Routledge Guides to Using Historical Sources

How does the historian approach primary sources? How do interpretations differ? How can such sources be used to write history?

The *Routledge Guides to Using Historical Sources* series introduces students to different sources and illustrates how historians use them. Titles in the series offer a broad spectrum of primary sources and, using specific examples, examine the historical context of these sources and the different approaches that can be used to interpret them.

Reading Primary Sources
Miriam Dobson and Benjamin Ziemann

History Beyond the Text
Sarah Barber and Corinna Penniston-Bird

History and Material Culture
Karen Harvey

Understanding Medieval Primary Sources
Joel Rosenthal

Memory and History: Understanding Memory as Source and Subject
Joan Tumblety

Understanding Early Modern Primary Sources
Laura Sangha and Jonathan Willis

Understanding Early Modern Primary Sources

Edited by Laura Sangha and
Jonathan Willis

Routledge
Taylor & Francis Group

LONDON AND NEW YORK

First published 2016
by Routledge
2 Park Square, Milton Park, Abingdon, Oxon OX14 4RN

and by Routledge
711 Third Avenue, New York, NY 10017

Routledge is an imprint of the Taylor & Francis Group, an informa business

British Library Cataloguing in Publication Data
A catalogue record for this book is available from the British Library

Library of Congress Cataloguing in Publication Data
Names: Sangha, Laura, editor, author. | Willis, Jonathan P., editor, author.
Title: Understanding early modern primary sources / edited by
Laura Sangha and Jonathan Willis.
Description: London: Routledge, 2016. |
Series: The Routledge guides to using historical sources |
Includes bibliographical references and index.
Identifiers: LCCN 2015047038 | ISBN 9781138823631 (hardback : alk. paper) |
ISBN 9781138823648 (pbk. : alk. paper) | ISBN 9781315622101 (ebook)
Subjects: LCSH: Europe–History–1492–1648–Sources. |
Europe–History–1492–1648–Historiography. | History–Methodology.
Classification: LCC D228.U53 2016 | DDC 940.2072–dc23
LC record available at http://lccn.loc.gov/2015047038

ISBN: 978-1-138-82363-1 (hbk)
ISBN: 978-1-138-82364-8 (pbk)
ISBN: 978-1-315-62210-1 (ebk)

Typeset in Times New Roman
by Out of House Publishing

Contents

Figures

Tables

Contributors

Helen Cowie is Lecturer in History at the University of York. Her research focuses on the history of animals and on natural history. She is author of *Conquering Nature in Spain and Its Empire, 1750–1850* (2011) and *Exhibiting Animals in Nineteenth-Century Britain: Empathy, Education, Entertainment* (2014). She is currently writing a cultural history of the alpaca.

Janet Dickinson specializes in the history of early modern England and Europe, with particular interests in cultural and political history. Her first book, *Court Politics and the Earl of Essex*, was published in 2011. Current projects include work on the Elizabethan nobility and the last years of Elizabeth I's life, as well as court history in general. She has held lectureships at a number of English universities and currently works for the University of Oxford's Department for Continuing Education and New York University in London.

Henry French is Professor of History at the University of Exeter, specializing in the social and economic history of early modern England. His books include *Man's Estate: Masculinity and the English Landed Elite, c. 1680–1900* (with Mark Rothery, 2012), *The Middle Sort of People in Provincial England, 1600–1750* (2007), and *The Character of English Rural Society, 1550–1750: Earls Colne Revisited* (with Richard Hoyle, 2007).

Ian Green is an honorary professorial fellow of the School of History, Classics and Archaeology at the University of Edinburgh. He is the author of *The Christian's ABC: Catechisms and Catechizing in England c. 1530–1740* (1996), *Print and Protestantism in Early Modern England* (2000), and *Humanism and Protestantism in Early Modern English Education* (2009). He is currently working on a volume entitled *Word, Ritual and Image in Early Modern England*.

Mark Hailwood is Associate Research Fellow in History at the University of Exeter. He is a social historian of England in the period 1500–1700, with particular interests in the histories of drinking, work, and popular culture. He is the author of *Alehouses and Good Fellowship in Early Modern England* (2014), and has published articles on occupational identity in *Cultural and Social History* and *Transactions of the Royal Historical Society*.

Tara Hamling is Senior Lecturer in History at the University of Birmingham. Trained as an art historian, she is author of numerous publications on the visual and material culture of early modern Britain. Her books include *Decorating the Godly Household: Religious Art in Post-Reformation Britain* (2010), *Everyday Objects: Medieval and Early Modern Material Culture* (edited with Catherine Richardson, 2010), and *Art Re-Formed: Reassessing the Impact of the Reformation on the Visual Arts* (edited with Richard L. Williams, 2007). Her next book, *A Day at Home in Early Modern England: The Materiality of Domestic Life* (with Catherine Richardson) is forthcoming.

Natalie Mears is Senior Lecturer in Early Modern History at the University of Durham. She worked as a voluntary archive assistant at Hatfield House in Hertfordshire, home of the Cecil Papers, before going to university. She liked it so much that she not only went back every vacation but also completed her undergraduate dissertation on Sir Robert Cecil and became an early modernist. She is the author of *Queenship and Political Discourse in the Elizabethan Realms* (2005, 2009) and a number of essays on Elizabethan politics and religion. She is also lead editor of *National Prayers: Special Worship since the Reformation*, Vol. I: *Special Prayers, Fasts and Thanksgivings in the British Isles, 1533–1688* (2013).

Alec Ryrie is Professor of the History of Christianity in the Department of Theology and Religion at Durham University. His books include *The Age of Reformation* (Routledge, 2009) and *Being Protestant in Reformation Britain* (2013). His interests in religious change in early modern Britain focus on Protestant cultures and experience in the sixteenth and seventeenth centuries.

Laura Sangha is Lecturer in British History 1500–1700 at the University of Exeter. She is a historian of English religious cultures in the 'long' Reformation, focusing on processes of religious change in their social and political contexts. She is particularly interested in the 'social history of theology' – that is to say, the relationship between beliefs and practice. Laura is the author of *Angels and Belief in England, 1480–1700* (Routledge, 2012), and is currently researching the life and times of the puritan antiquarian and diarist Ralph Thoresby (1658–1725).

Margaret Small is Lecturer in Europe and the Wider World at the University of Birmingham, where she teaches courses on European and English exploration, conquest and colonization, and European ideas about 'the nature of the native in the early modern period'. She is a specialist in the sixteenth century and is particularly interested in the role the Renaissance revival of classical knowledge played in the interpretation of empirical information from exploration. She has written on the history of geography and history of ideas in the period, and is currently completing a monograph on classical theory and sixteenth-century geography.

Ceri Sullivan is a Reader at Cardiff University, specializing in the narratives that people tell about themselves in their daily lives, be they religious, mercantile or administrative. Her books include *The Rhetoric of Credit: Merchants in Early Modern Writing* (2002), *The Rhetoric of the Conscience: Donne, Herbert, and Vaughan* (2008), and *Literature in the Public Service: Sublime Bureaucracy* (2013). She is currently completing a book finding out whether private prayer can be seen as the most widespread form of creative writing in the early modern period.

Brodie Waddell is a lecturer at Birkbeck, University of London. His research primarily focuses on how people have interpreted and responded to socio-economic change and crisis. He has published on various aspects of early modern England, including popular preaching, rural landscapes, and manor courts. His first book was entitled *God, Duty and Community in English Economic Life, 1660–1720* (2012). He is currently completing a book on the social and economic turmoil in the aftermath of the Glorious Revolution, having recently published an article on the politicization of economic hardship in the 1690s in *English Historical Review* (May 2015).

Merry E. Wiesner-Hanks is Distinguished Professor at the University of Wisconsin-Milwaukee. She is Senior Editor of the *Sixteenth Century Journal*, an editor of the *Journal of Global History*, and Editor-in-Chief of the nine-volume *Cambridge World History* (2015). She is an author or editor of more than 30 books and nearly 100 articles that have appeared in English, German, French, Italian, Spanish, Greek, Chinese, Turkish, and Korean. These include *A Concise History of the World* (2015), *Early Modern Europe 1450–1789* (2nd edn 2013), *Women and Gender in Early Modern Europe* (3rd edn 2008), *Christianity and Sexuality in the Early Modern World: Regulating Desire, Reforming Practice* (Routledge, 2nd edn 2010), and *Gender in History: Global Perspectives* (2nd edn 2010).

Jonathan Willis is Lecturer in Early Modern History at the University of Birmingham. His research interests focus on the English Reformation and the relationships between culture, theology, religious belief, practice, and identity. He is author of *Church Music and Protestantism in Post-Reformation England* (2010), co-editor (with Elizabeth Tingle) of *Dying, Death, Burial and Commemoration in Reformation Europe* (2015), editor of *Sin and Salvation in Reformation England* (2015) and is currently preparing a monograph entitled *The Reformation of the Decalogue: The Ten Commandments in England, c. 1485–1625.*

Neil Younger studied history at the University of Birmingham and has been a lecturer in History at the Open University since 2014. His doctoral research assessed the national war effort during the Elizabethan wars against Spain; this research appeared as *War and Politics in the Elizabethan Counties* (2012) and in a number of articles. He is presently researching Elizabethan politics and government in the context of post-Reformation religious division, and as part of this project is working on a book on the career of Sir Christopher Hatton and his connections to Elizabethan Catholics.

Acknowledgements

The publishers would like to thank the following for granting permission to reproduce copyright material: The British Library Board; Devon Heritage Centre; English Heritage; Folger Shakespeare Library; University of Glasgow Library; Huntington Library; Lambeth Palace Library; University of Leeds, Brotherton Library Special Collections; London Metropolitan Archives; Mary Rose Trust; National Portrait Gallery, London; National Trust; Norfolk Record Office; Victoria and Albert Museum.

Abbreviations

AHR	*American Historical Review*
BCP	Book of Common Prayer
BL	The British Library
EBBA	*English Broadside Ballad Archive*, http://ebba.english.ucsb.edu
ECCO	*Eighteenth-Century Collections Online*, http://gale.cengage.co.uk product-highlights/history/eighteenth-century-collections-online. aspx
EEBO	*Early English Books Online*, http://eebo.chadwyck.com/home
HMC	Historical Manuscripts Commission
JP	Justice of the Peace
MLA	*Modern Language Association International Bibliography*
RSTC	A. W. Pollard and G. R. Redgrave, *A Short-Title Catalogue of Books Printed in England, Scotland, & Ireland and of English Books Printed Abroad, 1475–1640*, 2nd edn, rev. and enlarged by W. A. Jackson, F. S. Ferguson and K. F. Pantzer, 3 vols (London: Bibliographical Society, 1976–91)
STC	British Library, *English Short Title Catalogue*, available at http://estc.bl.uk
TNA	The National Archives, Kew
USTC	*Universal Short Title Catalogue*, http://ustc.ac.uk
YWES	*The Year's Work in English Studies*

Introduction

Understanding early modern primary sources

Laura Sangha and Jonathan Willis

The 'stuff' of early modern history

Jan Lievens (1607–74) was a Dutch painter who collaborated with Rembrandt in the first half of the seventeenth century. His oil painting *Still Life with Books* (*c.* 1630, reproduced on the cover of this book) is full of early modern 'stuff', or 'different varieties of artefact that can be used in practising history'.[1] In other words, the painting depicts a rich range of early modern primary sources; thus, it is an excellent starting point for this volume. What can it tell us?

Foremost in the painting are several chunky, bound volumes, heaped haphazardly on top of one another. The breathtaking realism of Lievens' image means that we can virtually smell the leather wrappers of the books and feel the sharp edges of the bindings under our fingertips. Anyone who has seen early modern documents in the flesh will recognize the uneven and irregular edges of the yellow paper; they might notice from the ends of the books that the pages are gathered into quires, and perhaps would be interested to see that they are secured with leather straps or tied with lengths of fraying ribbon. These volumes represent the chief type of early modern primary source: texts. In the early modern period literacy was steadily increasing, and as a result handwritten manuscript documents proliferated as never before.[2] The State, the Church and the people each created records that have subsequently become indispensable primary sources for later historians. The business of government produced reams of correspondence; law and Church courts generated depositions by their thousands; bishops penned reports on the condition of their dioceses; individual clergymen scribbled notes on their sermons; merchants recorded accounts of their fortunes; ordinary folk kept track of their experiences in commonplace books and diaries. These written manuscripts are the life blood of early modern history.

Some of the books in the painting may have been printed texts. After Johannes Gutenberg (*c.* 1398–1468) combined mechanical moveable type, a new oil-based ink and a wooden hand press to create the printing press in the mid fifteenth century, this new technology spread rapidly across Europe. The dynamism of early modern print culture was astonishing: it has been estimated that there were perhaps 20 million books in circulation before 1500; by the end of the sixteenth century this had dramatically increased to between 150 and 200 million.[3] Though it represents only a small proportion of the original volume of early modern printed material, the variety of surviving printed sources is staggering. It includes scholarly works of history; treatises on religion, philosophy and literature; practical guides for legal and medical professionals; early writings of eminent reformers; innumerable editions of scripture; liturgies, psalters and devotional aids; copies of sermons; yearly almanacs; chapbooks, newsbooks and popular 'cheap print' such as pamphlets, ballads and broadsheets on a bewildering range of topics. Such printed material is an indispensable primary source for historians. Though manuscript (and oral) culture remained vital to networks of early communication the proliferation of print meant that the distribution and accessibility of textual material increased enormously Europe-wide from the fifteenth century onwards.

In the lower left-hand side of Lievens' painting, a pewter jug, a wine glass and a pewter plate with a piece of bread can be seen. The highly reflective surfaces of the polished jug and plate have allowed the artist to demonstrate his prodigious skill in rendering textures and reproducing the play of light in the room. These everyday objects also suggest another vital type of early modern primary evidence: material culture. For the 'stuff' that survives from the early modern period includes a lot more than just written and printed texts, since any physical remnant of the past is a primary source. Surviving material culture is too various to mention, but it includes ornaments, buildings, landscapes, clothes, furniture, dishes and drinking vessels, each a vital source of evidence about life in the past. Historians are becoming increasingly aware of the value of sources beyond texts, a process that is opening the discipline up to new approaches and encouraging a more rigorous engagement with objects as historical sources.[4] The dish, jug and wine glass also alert us to the centrality of food and drink to a growing consumer culture that promoted the production of such everyday objects. Indeed, the painting itself was part of a thriving Dutch art market, where demand for pictures came from all quarters, but particularly from the expanding middling sorts of people. Household inventories suggest that many Dutch families commonly invested between 3 and 10 per cent of their capital in paintings, whilst artists often produced work serially to improve efficiency and reduce costs.[5]

Still-life paintings, often depicting internationally traded goods, were central to the Dutch art market. They represented not only the wealth of the United Provinces, but also the extent to which Europe was beginning to be integrated with the wider world. In Lievens' painting, the two globes in the shadows on the right remind us that early modern people were increasingly exposed to a flood of information about the world beyond Europe. Travellers, merchants, missionaries and conquistadors encountered peoples and places in the Americas, Africa and Asia, and they wrote and published accounts of their experiences for audiences back home. Texts, maps, charts and globes help us to understand how contemporaries interpreted and perceived the societies they encountered, as well as the often devastating impact they were to have upon them. Alongside new horizons and landscapes, other objects in Lievens' painting eloquently evoke the age. The lute is a reminder that early modern Europe rang with music of many sorts, produced by professional musicians, city waits, ballad singers, local players, bell ringers, alehouse fiddlers, parishioners and Psalm-singing sermon gadders. As with material culture, historians are just beginning to explore the aural soundscapes of early modern life, bringing a new dimension to our appreciation of the period.[6]

Finally, we should not forget that as an example of visual culture, Lievens' painting can be interpreted as a source in itself. Whilst we have noted that the painting summons up a series of worldly pleasures – enjoyment of reading, the feeling of leather, eating and drinking, hearing and playing music – there is an argument to be made that the artist wishes us to recognize these earthly delights as transitory and hollow. The sharp-eyed amongst you may have noticed that the lute is in fact only an old wooden case, not the instrument itself. The books are rather battered, and the artist's palette hanging in the gloom is devoid of paint and colour. Might this be an example of a *vanitas* painting, a type of symbolic work of art designed to convey the ephemerality of sensory pleasures and to call to mind the certainty of death? Hence, might the painting's ultimate purpose be religious – a plausible conclusion given the centrality of the spiritual to the early modern world?

Whatever the intended function of Jan Lievens' *Still Life with Books*, it has served as a worthy introduction to the enormous variety of early modern primary sources available to the student of early modern history. The aim of this book is much the same: it is an introduction to the main types of source material available to those researching the early modern period. It is a survey of the 'stuff' of early modern history – the raw elements that, once chopped, stirred, seasoned and stewed, form the basis of our understanding of the past. Unlike the painting, this collection will also provide guidance on how to identify and locate primary sources, and things to consider when trying to contextualize and interpret them. In doing so, it demonstrates how primary sources can be deployed to produce very different histories, and illustrates why the early modern period remains such a vibrant field of study.

'Sources' and 'Histories'

The volume is divided into two sections – 'Sources' and 'Histories' – each designed for anybody beginning to study or research the early modern period.[7] Part I, 'Sources', takes the reader through seven key categories of primary source material. Each chapter addresses how and why different genres of primary material were produced, providing information that will allow readers properly to understand primary sources in their early modern context. These chapters are not simply step-by-step guides on how to analyse source material; they point readers towards the types of questions that they need to ask of particular genres, highlighting aspects that might reward further investigation. 'Sources' chapters also provide practical research advice, highlighting finding aids, and pointing readers towards some of the most accessible physical and digital editions of texts, artefact collections and archives.

While Part I focuses on the types of materials we use to write history, Part II, 'Histories', takes a thematic approach. Each chapter here explores a major theme of early modern studies, explaining what types of sources have been and can be used to address these different historical themes. To give a few examples, we want to give readers a sense of what sources historians deploy to write about gender, where to turn to research religious belief and practice, and what the richest sources are for writing a history of economic change. In each case, we will see that contemporary historians tend to combine and draw on many different source types when they research and write about a single topic or theme.

A note on practicalities

Given the strength and dynamism of early modern history, it would be impossible to cover every source type or every historical theme in this volume, and we do not make any claim to comprehensive coverage. This collection is written with an eye to the needs of undergraduate and taught postgraduate history students, therefore we intentionally prioritize those primary materials that are most readily accessible to them. This means that English-language materials tend to dominate, although readers will also find plenty of references to increasingly available sources in translation as well as non-English-language databases and collections. Since lengthy and expensive archival trips are usually out of the question for such students, we have also concentrated particularly on printed and digital resources.

However, many of our contributors do point readers towards archival materials, and students are strongly encouraged to dip their toe into the archives if they have the opportunity. A short trip to a local record office or to a university's special collections, or even a decision to look at digitized manuscript material, brings the 'stuff' of early modern history to life in a way that modern published editions or online transcriptions cannot. This raises the issue of early modern handwriting – at first glance, many contemporary handwritten documents will look illegible to the modern reader, a fact that deters many researchers from delving into the archive. However, we would like to emphasize that the quality and style of handwriting varies widely, and that some hands are far more recognizable and readable than others. It is always worth checking with an archivist or calling up items that you are interested in to scan and test for legibility. The other point about handwriting is that a little training can go a long way, and there are many printed guides and excellent, free online palaeographical courses available (palaeography is the study of old handwriting).[8] The tutorials offer practical tips to teach researchers how to decipher more difficult hands. As with any new skill, the secret is to practise, and these online courses provide a variety of documents that allow users to do just that. Even if the bulk of your sources are available elsewhere, there is no substitute for getting your hands on original documents and artefacts.

'Early modern'

This guide to 'understanding early modern primary sources' forms part of a series of Routledge Guides to Using Historical Sources. It sits neatly between Joel T. Rosenthal (ed.), *Understanding Medieval Primary Sources* (2011) and Miriam Dobson and Benjamin Ziemann (eds), *Reading Primary Sources* (2008), which focuses on texts relating to nineteenth- and twentieth-century history.[9] As historians who teach and write early modern history, it is easy for us to take for granted that something called the early modern period existed, and that it was important. However, the more we question the label 'early modern', the more problematic this seemingly innocuous term becomes; Phil Withington has described it as 'a confusing concept – one that promises the presciently familiar but increasingly delivers the perplexingly foreign'.[10] Some of the historical labels historians use, such as 'renaissance' and 'reformation', date in one form or another from the periods they describe. 'Early modern', on the other hand, is quite different; it was a term invented by historians for historians, and it wasn't until the 1970s that 'early modern history' had become established as an academic field.[11] No contemporaries used the term. How could they? For 'early modern' to make any sense at all, it needed to be linked to a sense of the 'modern', and to a historical metanarrative called 'modernity'. Only when historians decided they were living in a 'modern' age, and that the passage of humanity through history should be described in terms of a journey towards 'modernity', could the early stages of that journey be retrospectively labelled *early* modern. As one textbook puts it, '"Early modern" is a description born of hindsight. It assumes that European culture was travelling towards something called "modernity", but had not yet reached its goal: that the journey was begun, but not finished.'[12] While the term 'early modern' might seem merely descriptive, therefore, it is actually far from neutral. It implies some sort of belief, however implicit, that this was the period that witnessed the origins of many of the developments that gave shape and meaning to the modern world.

Many historians writing today find that kind of teleology – or 'present-mindedness', by which we mean viewing the past with one eye on the present – at best a questionable way to approach history, and at worst a downright unproductive way of thinking about the past. Most historians who use the term 'early modern' – ourselves included – would absolutely argue that we need to view this period on its own terms, not just as a precursor to full-blown modernity (whatever that is), and we would encourage you to do the same. Historians also now generally reject simplistic notions of 'progress' centred around justifying a specific Western European and North American model of development, a model that entailed the exploitation of large parts of the rest of the world through imperial and colonial ventures. Because it charts a particular western model of progress, furthermore, 'early modern' is not necessarily the most helpful framework with which to approach the histories of non-European cultures, such as the Indian subcontinent, or the Chinese empire. As another early modern textbook puts it, 'such linear and uniform models are now viewed with considerable scepticism, partly because of the experience of multiple pathways to modernity pursued in different areas of the globe, but also due to contrasting evidence within Europe itself'.[13]

Why then do historians still use the term 'early modern', and why have we chosen to use it in this guide? As Merry E. Wiesner-Hanks has noted, 'even historians who emphasize that these terms are problematic continue to use them because they are convenient and meaningful'.[14] First and foremost, we are talking about a couple of centuries where quite a lot happened, and we need to call them something. In North America, the term 'renaissance' has a lot more currency as a model of periodization than it does in Europe, but renaissance is a slippery beast; it happened at different times in different places, and tends to place an emphasis on cultural, intellectual and artistic developments. We could speak of an 'age of reformation', but similarly, there are substantial disagreements over when the reformation began, and especially when it came to an end. As a method of periodization, furthermore, 'reformation' also prioritizes the consideration of religious history. 'Early modern' is therefore a useful label precisely because it is arbitrary; it allows us to package the sixteenth and seventeenth centuries, and (maybe) most of the eighteenth, and describe them relatively neutrally. And there is more to it than that. The early modern period does represent a period of dramatic change, during which many medieval certainties collapsed, new discoveries were made, and structures and systems developed in areas such as politics, religion, science and warfare that then held sway for a significant period of time – indeed, some of them persist to this day.

We should always bear in mind that many continuities lingered on from the medieval world into the early modern world, and many more stretched from the early modern into the modern. Neither should we consider the Middle Ages a period of timeless continuity; it wasn't. Nevertheless, Europe probably witnessed more rapid, profound and lasting change in more spheres during the decades between 1500 and *c.* 1750 than at any other time, either before or since. Historians therefore continue to use the label 'early modern', and we are confident enough about its usefulness to include it in the title of this book, and this introduction. But words have power, and we must handle them with care. The early modern period is a useful designation, but we think that you need to be aware of why we describe it as we do, and of the dangers as well as the advantages of such an appellation. With that brief note of caution in mind, let's turn to the issue of primary sources.

Primary sources

As we have seen, primary sources are the very stuff of history: the raw material, if you like. Without them, history would be impossible to write. Of course anybody can make up whatever they like about the past – it is hardly in a position to stand up and defend itself. But most historians aspire to understand the past, not to misrepresent it. We don't often say so explicitly, and it's a difficult idea to back up with intellectual or theoretical justifications, but the vast majority of historians feel a moral obligation to treat the lives of the dead – and in the case of early modernists, the very dead! – with a degree of honour and respect. That doesn't mean glamorizing or valorizing the past, but it does mean trying to represent it honestly, accurately and fairly: to try to get as close to the 'truth' as possible. Modern social theory has done much to undermine the idea that historical writing can ever truly and accurately represent the reality of past societies and human experiences. What distinguishes historians is that, while they accept that is probably the case, they nevertheless still try to do so. In this sense, primary sources are our evidence; they are how we justify our interpretations of the past. These interpretations are inevitably subjective, and a wry observer might remark that each new generation of historians keeps itself in work by challenging the views of the previous one. But our sources help to keep us rooted in a past reality, however tenuous, fleeting and subjective that connection might be.

There are different ways of working with sources. One is to decide what you want to say, and then try to find a few pieces of evidence to include in your argument in order to back it up. This is not the ideal way to approach writing history. Primary sources should not be the intellectual equivalent of a sprig of parsley or a few chopped chives. They are not there to provide garnish; rather (to use a stew-based metaphor) they should form the main sources of protein and carbohydrate in your nourishing historical broth, bound together with and indistinguishable from the rich stock of your analysis. The garnish is certainly part of your meal, but it is not representative of it. Leaving both food and metaphors aside, a better way is to start with one or more research questions, then to analyse a body of relevant material, and to let the sources speak for themselves in providing an answer. The process of historical research is very often a surprising one, as we come across things that we didn't expect, and revise our initial ideas accordingly. The historian therefore needs to approach his or her sources with an open mind. Don't cherry-pick them, or misrepresent them in order to support a pre-existing theory; see what the sources have to say, and then form your conclusions accordingly. History is occasionally likened to a science. In one sense this is just plain daft; there are no 'rules of history' in the same way as there are predictable scientific laws governing, for example, the movement of objects as a result of the application of force. But historical method *is* scientific, insofar as it begins with a research question or hypothesis, which is tested by experimentation, and results in a series of preliminary conclusions, which may themselves be modified by additional experimentation or if new evidence comes to light further down the line.

The early modernist is in a somewhat privileged position. We have a wealth of information available to us compared to our medievalist colleagues. The growth of print in our period, of literacy, of the use of vernaculars, and also in the number and sophistication of public and private archives, means that when it comes to source material we have, comparatively, an embarrassment of riches at our disposal. And, unlike modern and contemporary historians, we are not drowning in an unmanageable sea of evidence, although at certain times it might feel that way. The biggest problems facing the early modernist are probably knowing how and where to find relevant material, and this book is designed to help minimize those problems by giving you a working insight into where particular sources can be found, how best to approach them, and the different questions they can help you to answer.

Historians and their sources

Before explaining the content of the volume's chapters, it will be useful to refer briefly to the development of history as an academic discipline, to explain how, and more importantly *why*, particular sources came to be the chief primary materials drawn on by historians.

History had been around for a very long time before it began to be professionalized in the nineteenth century. Then, rather than being seen as a diverting pastime, history began to be perceived of as a science, with particular methods. The chief theory supporting professional historical research was empiricism. This resulted in a desire for documentary accuracy, and for historical narratives to be firmly based on 'evidence' – i.e. primary sources. Many nineteenth-century historians aimed to be 'objective': to analyse primary documents carefully, subjecting them to scientific scrutiny in order to tell the 'truth' about the past. During this phase of its development, this approach produced histories that were usually political – the subjects of scrutiny were policymakers, monarchs, courtiers, governments, aristocrats and peers, and the institutions they were found in. Often this type of history is referred to as 'great men' history, since this type of 'high' political history deals almost exclusively with men: Holy Roman Emperors, military generals, prime ministers, popes, bishops and lords. To write this sort of political history, researchers turned to the primary sources that dealt with government: the correspondence and documents generated as political elites went about the business of ruling the people.

In the 1880s, new trends in history were beginning to emerge, and as a result historians began to cast their net wider in their search for primary sources. Contemporary students of history will know that in many cases wider social shifts are directly connected to the types of questions that historians ask, and when the questions change, historians often have to turn to new types of evidence to find answers. This was certainly the case at the end of the nineteenth century. The emergence of democratic and working-class movements, unionism, and the slowdown of industrialization all created economic and social change on a huge scale. Continued economic problems and the persistence of poverty drew historians' attention to the question of longer-term economic and social development, and there were the beginnings of a reaction against the traditional and elitist focus on great men. Historians began to pay more attention to what was happening to 'the masses', and to seek out sources that might tell them more about the history of the non-elite.

As the twentieth century went on, the study of history underwent a series of radical transformations. In the 1920s Marc Bloch and Lucien Febvre founded the Annales School and promoted a sort of 'long-term social history', trying to grasp the structural features of the past and to understand the 'totality' of historical eras.[15] The Annales placed a new emphasis on forces that were *external* to men – the environment and the landscape. Later generations led by Fernand Braudel, Georges Duby, Jacques Le Goff, Emmauel Le Roy Ladurie and Phillippe Ariès continued to draw on the methodologies, conceptual models and ideas of sociology, anthropology, geology, economics and psychology in order to produce their histories – as you can imagine, this extended the types of primary sources that historians were examining enormously.[16] The 1950s and 1960s brought new interpretations of Marx's writings, and as a result the study of population, labour, economics and the family came to the fore. This was the first time that 'history from below' became firmly established as part of professional historical study. E. P. Thompson and his contemporaries did not just seek to put the 'ordinary folk' back into history, they wanted to put them centre stage, to make them the primary focus of historical enquiry.[17] They were also keen to ensure that women would be granted equal attention alongside men.

The Annales School was perhaps the most important influence on this 'new social history', and in turn the new social history inspired scholars of the 1980s to continue to explore fresh terrain. This later movement was to become known as 'the cultural turn'. Applying new approaches, new techniques and new methodologies, scholars such as Carlo Ginzburg, Robert Darnton and Natalie Zemon Davies began to reinterpret key historical moments and events, as well as some of the long-term processes that seemed to underpin historical development.[18] A key aim of these cultural historians was to identify the cultural constraints that shaped ways of thinking and doing in the past. Studying the ideas, beliefs, ceremonies, rituals and practices of communities allowed historians to reconstruct the world view or 'mentality' of people in the past, providing deep contextualization for events and uncovering the meaning people found in their lives.

Historians' interest in 'the masses', in social, economic and cultural change, and in the 'totality' and 'mentality' of historical eras meant that they could not restrict their research to primary resources relating solely to government and 'great men'. As the discipline developed and new fields of enquiry were established, the types of sources that were consulted in the course of historical research expanded enormously. Whilst this is obviously only a crude summary of the development of professional history, it allows us to appreciate the current range and scope of historical investigation, and to begin to understand why it is appropriate for *any* physical remnant of the past to be considered a primary source. The main types of sources that current historians use are summarized in the next section, which explains the focus of the first half of this volume.

Part I: Sources

Part I of this book introduces the reader to seven of the most important types of sources used by early modern researchers. In Chapter 1, Natalie Mears discusses the types of documents that early, political historians often turned to: 'State Papers and related collections'. These are documents relating to the government of early modern England, principally papers of successive Principal Secretaries to the monarch. Mears details the history of the State Paper Office to explain how it developed, thus providing an invaluable guide to any student who wishes to make use of these sorts of primary sources. Mears shows that contemporary historians have gone far beyond their nineteenth-century ancestors, since the papers of government are now used to explore a diverse range of historical topics, not just high political history.

What other sorts of primary sources do early modern historians use? For a start, they might turn to the types of legal and judicial sources discussed by Henry French in Chapter 2. In his chapter, French describes the complicated system of law courts in early modern England, and explains how the legal process worked. These sources can be used to study the history of crime: both patterns of incidence, the social profiles of offenders and victims, and the moral messages conveyed by the existence and functioning of the law. Another key type of source are records generated by the Church, explored by Jonathan Willis in Chapter 3. Willis explains that since religion was absolutely central to the early modern world, ecclesiastical sources can reveal much more about early modern society than just what people believed and how they worshipped. Since religion was so embedded in everyday life, evidence drawn from these sources is much more broadly applicable, and might shed light on such areas as communities, sociability, households, gender relations and individual identity.

In Chapter 4, Ian Green investigates the printed sources referred to earlier in this introduction. Green summarizes the development of the print market in England, exploring the types of materials that were produced, and he considers who the audience was for such material and what sort of influence it might have had on societies of the time. Since printed texts are so various, they can be used to study an immeasurable number of historical themes. Collectively, social mores and expectations are embedded in these materials, thus they can also be used to identify the cultural attitudes and constraints that characterized the early modern mentality. Ceri Sullivan then turns our attention to literary aspects of early modern sources in Chapter 5, explaining how early modern writers and readers thought about texts (both fictional and non-fictional). Sullivan highlights the rhetorical, imitative and didactic dimensions of our sources, reminding us of the need to think about the structuring effects of genre when we analyse and interpret any written texts. This chapter is required reading for anyone seeking to uncover the strategies and techniques at work on the early modern page. Again, analysing texts in this manner can tell us more about prevailing contemporary world views, uncovering meaning and significance in the past.

In Chapter 6, Laura Sangha surveys the two most common types of personal documents – letters and diaries. Though it is tempting to think of such material as much more candid and direct than many other types of sources, we find that social and intellectual conventions are just as likely to dictate the form and content of these sources as of any other types of material. Personal documents are often used to study past cultures, travel, medicine, farming, the household, and social networks of friends and families. They also shed light on inherent social expectations, value systems, as well as ideas relating to the construction and representation of the 'self'. Finally, in Chapter 7 Tara Hamling casts her eye over visual and material sources, establishing the value, limitations and challenges of object-based study for historians. Hamling provides both an introduction to this multidisciplinary field, and a systematic method for object-based analysis through a series of case studies.

Moving beyond government papers to legal sources, ecclesiastical documents, printed matter, personal documents, literary texts, and visual and material evidence has allowed historians to expand their field of enquiry enormously. In various combinations these sources types can be used to investigate both 'elite' and 'popular' politics and culture; the social history of work, gender relations and the family; religious beliefs and practice; the function and significance of the economy; and the role and impact of warfare and early science and the impact of encounters with non-European people and cultures. Exactly how historians write such histories is explored in Part II, 'Histories'.

Part II: Histories

Part II of this book is entitled 'Histories'. While Part I is designed to introduce you to some of the most important types of sources used by early modern historians, the second part aims to do something rather different. First and foremost, the chapters in this section are thematic, rather than based around a particular genre of source. They therefore aim to show how historians can use a whole range of different sources to tell a single history. Furthermore, the themes that these chapters take are not random: they represent some of the most important areas of change in early modern society, and some of the most exciting topics of historical study that are available to you. We begin with gender. The historical study of women and gender has been transformed several times since the first wave of feminism hit academia in the 1970s, and early modern history is no different. However, gender has been an area of particular interest for early modern historians in a number of respects. In Chapter 8, Merry E. Wiesner-Hanks begins by looking at the types of sources that give clues to commonly held ideas about men and women and the differences between them, before moving on to sources that attempted to regulate and enforce gender norms, and finally exploring sources that actually enable us to hear the historical voices of early modern women. From gender we move on to religion. Reformation was one of the defining themes of early modern history, and in Chapter 9 Alec Ryrie considers the official records of various churches, along with music and sermons, polemical and devotional works, religious manuscripts, the visual arts, administrative records, and 'everything else' in his survey of the rich body of source material available for telling its history.

Early modern society was hugely stratified and unequal, and in Chapter 10 Janet Dickinson gives an insight into how to write early modern political histories: from accounts of political thought and the importance of counsel through to studies of patronage, the court, royal image and popular politics. Expanding on this last point, there has been a strong tendency, particularly amongst early modern social, cultural and religious historians, not only to write about elites, but also to tell histories that include and even prioritize the vast majority of the population. Many of these people were poor, they were often illiterate, and therefore we have to think more creatively about the sources we use to uncover information about them; but without them early modern society would have ceased to function, and as Mark Hailwood explains in Chapter 11, 'Popular culture', the sources that can be used to tell their histories are just as valuable and interesting as those that exist for the gentry and aristocracy. We move on from popular culture to economic life. Economic history may conjure up images of dusty old books full of graphs and statistics, but as Brodie Waddell shows in Chapter 12, a new generation of historians are using qualitative sources alongside quantitative data to shed new light on this most fundamental reality of everyday life. Warfare was also an inescapable reality of living in the early modern world, and in Chapter 13 Neil Younger demonstrates some of the ways in which early modern military history has moved beyond counting bullets and mapping battlefields to show the sources that can be used to explore the wider social and cultural dimensions of armed conflict. The early modern period was also one of significant scientific and intellectual change, and in Chapter 14 Helen Cowie provides a fascinating insight into how to discover more about the people, places, contexts and audiences by, in, out of which and before whom early modern science was conducted. Finally, but perhaps most importantly of all, the early modern centuries witnessed the geographical expansion of Europe's horizons, across Africa, Asia and – crucially following their new discovery by Europeans – the Americas. In Chapter 15, Margaret Small shows how historians can conduct research into this wider world, by considering conquest and colonization; the activities of religious missionaries; and the narratives of captives, travellers, traders and chroniclers.

In other words, whatever your interest in early modern history, we hope that there is something here for you. Conducting historical research and writing history is hard work, but it can also be an immensely rewarding, fulfilling and enjoyable process. If this book helps you even a little on the pathway to becoming an early modern historian, then we will be happy that we have achieved our aims. Good luck!

Notes

1 Tim Hitchcock, 'Stuff and Dead People', *Historyonics*, 22 May 2013, http://historyonics.blogspot.co.uk/2013/05/stuff-and-dead-people.html (accessed 27 August 2015).
2 See (for example) David Cressy, *Literacy and the Social Order: Reading and Writing in Tudor and Stuart England* (Cambridge: Cambridge University Press, 1980); Ian Green, *Print and Protestantism in Early Modern England* (Oxford: Oxford University Press, 2000).
3 R. A. Houston, *Literacy in Early Modern Europe* (Harlow: Longman, 2002), Chapter 8. These figures are necessarily imprecise since the evidence is fragmentary.
4 For a broader introduction to the benefits and challenges of using material culture see Karen Harvey (ed.), *History and Material Culture: A Student's Guide to Approaching Alternative Sources* (London and New York: Routledge, 2009). For an example of how these sorts of histories can be written, see Tara Hamling and Catherine Richardson (eds), *Everyday Objects: Medieval and Early Modern Material Culture and Its Meanings* (Farnham: Ashgate, 2010).
5 Medlyn Millner Kahr, *Dutch Painting in the Seventeenth Century* (London: Harper and Row, 1978), pp. 8–10; Svetlana Alpers, *The Art of Describing: Dutch Art in the Seventeenth Century* (London: John Murray, 1983).
6 Unfortunately it has not been possible to include a chapter specifically on music in this volume, but several of the essays (such as those by Alec Ryrie and Mark Hailwood) mention musical sources, such as Psalms and ballads. One of the best recent attempts to write early modern musical history is Christopher Marsh, *Music and Society in Early Modern England* (Cambridge: Cambridge University Press, 2013).
7 See below for a more detailed description of the contents of each chapter.
8 The National Archives, *Palaeography: Reading Old Handwriting 1500–1800. A Practical Online Tutorial*, http://www.nationalarchives.gov.uk/palaeography (accessed 3 January 2016); University of Cambridge, *English Handwriting 1500–1700: An Online Course*, https://www.english.cam.ac.uk/ceres/ehoc/alphabets.html (accessed 3 January 2016); Yale University's list of links to numerous online courses: http://www.library.yale.edu/cataloging/rarebookteam/paleography.htm (accessed 3 January 2016); Hilary Marshall, *Palaeography for Family and Local Historians* (Chichester: Phillimore, 2004).

9 The series also contains Harvey, *History and Material Culture*; Joan Tumblety (ed.), *Memory and History: Understanding Memory as Source and Subject* (London: Routledge, 2013); and Sarah Barber and Corinna Peniston-Bird (eds), *History Beyond the Text: A Student's Guide to Approaching Alternative Sources* (London: Routledge, 2008). For details, see https://www.routledge.com/series/ RGHS (accessed 4 September 2015).

10 Phil Withington, *Society in Early Modern England: The Vernacular Origins of Some Powerful Ideas* (Cambridge: Polity Press, 2010), p. 5.

11 Withington, *Society in Early Modern England*, pp. 45–8; Randolph Starn, 'The Early Modern Muddle', *Journal of Early Modern History*, 6.3 (2002), 296–307 (pp. 297–8). It is worth noting that Withington substantially revises Starn's chronology for the first usage of the term 'early modern' in his book.

12 Euan Cameron, 'Editor's Introduction', in Euan Cameron (ed.), *Early Modern Europe: An Oxford History* (Oxford: Oxford University Press, 2001), pp. xvii–xxxi.

13 Beat Kümin, 'Introduction', in Beat Kümin (ed.), *The European World 1500–1800: An Introduction to Early Modern History,* 2nd edn (Abingdon: Routledge, 2014), pp. 1–9 (p. 3).

14 Merry Wiesner-Hanks, 'Introduction', in Merry Wiesner-Hanks, *Early Modern Europe 1450–1789*, 2nd edn (Cambridge: Cambridge University Press, 2013), pp. 1–16 (p. 4).

15 Marc Bloch, *The Royal Touch: Sacred Monarchy and Scrofula in England and France*, trans. J. E. Anderson (London: Routledge and Kegan Paul, 1973); Lucien Febvre, *The Problem of Unbelief in the Sixteenth Century: The Religion of Rabelais*, trans. Beatrice Gottlieb (Cambridge, MA: Harvard University Press, 1982).

16 Fernand Braudel, *The Mediterranean and the Mediterranean World in the Age of Philip II*, trans. Siân Reynolds, 2 vols (London: Collins, 1972–73); Georges Duby, *Rural Economy and Country Life in the Medieval West*, trans. Cynthia Postan (London: Arnold, 1968); Jacques Le Goff, *The Birth of Purgatory*, trans. Arthur Goldhammer (London: Scolar, 1984); Emmanuel Le Roy Ladurie, *Montaillou: Cathars and Catholics in a French Village, 1294–1324*, trans. Barbara Bray (London: Scolar Press, 1978); Philippe Ariès, *Centuries of Childhood*, trans. Robert Baldick (London: Jonathan Cape, 1962).

17 E.g. Edward Palmer Thompson, *The Making of the English Working Class* (London: Gollancz, 1963).

18 Carloe Ginzburg, *The Cheese and the Worms: The Cosmos of a Sixteenth-Century Miller*, trans. John and Anne Tedeschi (London: Routledge and Kegan Paul, 1980); Robert Darnton, *The Great Cat Massacre: And Other Episodes in French Cultural History* (London: Allen Lane, 1984); Natalie Zemon Davis, *The Return of Martin Guerre* (Cambridge, MA: Harvard University Press, 1983).

Part I

Sources

1   State Papers and related collections

Natalie Mears

There are few collections so vast and varied that manuscript 'placards', vilifying Mary Queen of Scots' involvement in the murder of her husband, Lord Darnley, in 1567, jostle with news reports of hundreds of apprentices attacking a brothel in Worcester a century later, but such is the scale and depth of the State Papers, housed in The National Archives in London.[1] The State Papers are those documents, principally papers of successive Principal Secretaries to the monarch, that were collected together in the State Paper Office from the sixteenth century to the late eighteenth century. They comprise 107 separate classes, divided into Domestic, Scotland, Ireland and Foreign series (the latter divided by country from 1577) stretching over 13,000 volumes, bundles and cases, and totalling millions of documents and many maps.[2] The collection largely covers the period from 1509 to 1780, but contains manuscripts dating as early as 1231 and as late as 1888. A separate set of State Papers – State Papers Colonial, comprising the State Papers themselves, as well as the records of the Privy Council and Board of Trade relating to the American colonies and the West Indies, from 1574 to 1782 – are gathered in a separate collection: the Colonial Office.

As will soon become apparent, however, while the State Papers might seem a comprehensive, coherent, distinct and official collection, that is far from the case. It is, in many ways, a rather haphazard collection built up from what the keepers could obtain from successive Principal Secretaries and could prevent from being 'permanently borrowed' by both politicians and enthusiastic collectors. The collections need to be combined, particularly for those working on political and administrative history, not only with other departments in The National Archives (such as the Privy Council Office) but also, and perhaps more especially, with other collections, such as those in the British Library, private archives, local record offices and libraries abroad. These other archives contain not only whole or partial collections of Principal Secretaries that were not given to the State Paper Office but also the papers of other major and secondary figures.

With the growing availability of databases that include digitized images of documents, such as *State Papers Online* and *The Cecil Papers*, it is increasingly tempting for scholars to conduct their initial research through keyword searches and dip in and out of these electronic archives. This temptation needs to be avoided. Such a methodology presumes that all 'relevant' material will contain words that the researcher can identify at the start; it does not allow for the proper contextualization of search results; it does not allow for the important serendipitous find, and, simply, not all databases are designed to search for variant spellings. It remains essential for scholars to 'know their archives': not just what the collection contains, but how, why and by whom it was created and developed, and how it was organized and reorganized. This enables the researcher to know what they might find, explain why things are absent – and possibly point to where they are – and understand the documents contained therein better. For these reasons, this chapter will address the history of the State Paper Office and some of its allied collections, and it will discuss how these collections were ordered by contemporaries and later archivists. The chapter will then discuss some of the 'finding aids' for key collections – the catalogues and calendars that have been created by successive archivists and historians – including their strengths and pitfalls.

The history of the State Papers

The State Paper Office was founded by the Crown as a working archive that could be consulted during the formulation of policy. *When* the office was founded is not clear. Its establishment is commonly dated to 1578 but the interpretation of the evidence on which this is based – the memoirs of one of the first keepers, Sir Thomas Wilson – is open to question.[3] Rather, it appears that the State Paper Office, and its organization, developed over many decades. By the late sixteenth century, the papers of former Principal Secretaries, and other important figures such as Cardinal Wolsey, were in the custody of the current Principal Secretary, alongside the records of the Signet Office and the Privy Council, and were overseen either by one of the Secretary's own servants or one of the clerks of the Signet.[4] By 1610, an official Keeper(s) was appointed, though they continued to be selected from those who had worked with the Principal Secretary or in the Signet Office.[5]

In maintaining a working archive, the Crown was not interested in preserving all of the papers of its Principal Secretaries, and personal items seem to have been weeded out. This probably explains why there are no personal papers belonging to Sir Francis Walsingham or William Davison in the collection, though many of their political papers are there.[6] As late as 1705, papers 'which are of no use or Curiosity [were] laid aside or burnt'.[7] However, the completeness of the State Paper archives was also affected by several other factors. Some Principal Secretaries, and their families, did not want to give up their papers. Like most officers of the State, some saw their papers as private property. Others did not want their papers to reveal, posthumously, their political and financial corruption, and either retained or burned their archives. Some Keepers, such as William Boswell (Keeper from 1629), were more effective than others, such as Wilson, at acquiring Secretaries' archives; some also received more support from the Crown and the Principal Secretary.

The unevenness of the State Papers between 1509 and the 1780s also needs to be seen in the light of what we might term 'impersonal factors'. The first of these is the simple ebb and flow of government business: the abundance of material for the 1630s is partly because it was a decade of intense government activity. The second is any change in the structure and practice of governance: this could not only generate more documents, but could also place them beyond the reach of individuals who, as we have seen, may have been reluctant to relinquish possession. After the assassination of Lord Admiral Buckingham in 1628, control of the navy devolved to a commission whose members did not see its papers as their own personal property. Consequently, the commission's archive moved seamlessly to the State Paper Office.

It should also be noted that not all The National Archives' 'State Papers' are in the State Paper Office. First, the Colonial State Papers are in the Colonial Office. In the seventeenth century, Principal Secretaries had little involvement in the nascent British empire because most dealings between the Government and its colonies were handled either by committees of the Privy Council or by special commissions, such as the Committee for Foreign Plantations (1634–41), the Council for Trade (from 1660), the Council for Foreign Plantations (from 1660) and the Board of Trade (from 1695). This changed in the course of the eighteenth century, largely because of war, and, in 1768, a third Principal Secretary was appointed to deal with colonial matters. Though this position lapsed after the American War of Independence (and duties passed to the Home Office), it was revived in 1794 and the colonial business that had earlier been assumed by the Home Office was transferred back. Further developments in the nineteenth century meant that the Colonial Office built up its own archive, though one that overlapped with the Department of War, the Home Office and the Commonwealth Office.

Second, there are a number of other classes that contain 'State Papers'. 'Special Collections', for instance, include the Ancient Correspondence (SC1), comprising sixty-two volumes of correspondence, drafts and memoranda from the twelfth century to the early sixteenth century gathered from the Chancery, Exchequer and Privy Seal Office. There are also collections of gifts and deposits (PRO30/1–99 and PRO44) and transcripts (PRO31/1–20), often from foreign archives, such as those made by M. Armand Baschet of correspondence relating to England from the French archives dating from the early sixteenth century to the early eighteenth century (PRO31/3).

Other collections

As the State Papers in The National Archives are, therefore, neither complete nor comprehensive, it is necessary to look elsewhere as well. The other main collections of 'State Papers' are those in the British Library (particularly the Cotton, Harley, Lansdowne and Additional manuscripts); private archives, particularly those calendared by the Historical Manuscripts Commission (HMC); major public archives (such as Lambeth Palace Library); local record offices; and archives and libraries abroad.[8] These are not all 'State Papers' as defined by the State Paper Office's remit: i.e. they are not all the papers of Principal Secretaries. Rather, they include the collections of a whole range of people who were involved, in varying capacities and in varying degrees, in the work of central government. Thus, they are part of what could be termed a 'virtual archive' of 'State Papers'. There is not space to describe all of these collections in full, so this section will focus on the main collections and provide pointers to where other collections can be found.

The British Library's Cotton collection was created by Sir Robert Cotton, an inveterate collector of manuscripts, and contains some of the papers of one of Elizabeth I's favourites and Privy Councillors, Robert Dudley, Earl of Leicester,[9] as well as originals and copies of material that had been in the State Paper Office and that Cotton 'borrowed'. There are also a significant number of scientific manuscripts. The Harley collection, created by Robert Harley, Earl of Oxford and Lord Treasurer to Queen Anne, includes not only Harley's own papers and those of his son (another manuscript collector), but also those of Elizabeth I's Principal Secretary William Davison (who delivered Mary Queen of Scots' execution warrant), and the MP and parliamentary writer, Sir Simonds D'Ewes. The Lansdowne manuscripts, largely the collection of Sir Michael Hickes, one of the secretaries of William Cecil, Lord Burghley (Principal Secretary and Lord Treasurer to Elizabeth I), contain a very large proportion of Burghley's papers. The Additional manuscripts include the very important Yelverton Papers of Robert Beale, one of the clerks of the Elizabethan Privy Council, and into which some of the papers of the MP and City Alderman, Thomas Norton, were absorbed.

There are a number of significant private archives of 'State Papers', most of which were examined by the Royal Commission on Historical Manuscripts (more commonly referred to as the Historical Manuscripts Commission or HMC), established in 1869 to identify, examine and make information available on major private (and some public) archives. The biggest and most significant of these are the Cecil Papers at Hatfield House. These contain the remainder of Burghley's papers as well as most of those of his second son, Robert Cecil, Earl of Salisbury (Principal Secretary to Elizabeth I, and Principal Secretary and Lord Treasurer to James VI and I). In addition, the collection includes papers that Burghley 'borrowed' from the State Paper Office, including some of Thomas Cromwell's. Other important collections calendared by the HMC include the manuscripts of Lord De L'Isle and Dudley (the Sidney family), the Marquess of Ormonde and the Duke of Rutland, as well as the Shrewsbury Papers, which are divided between Lambeth Palace Library and the College of Arms.

Though the HMC's coverage was wide – it is always worth checking the Keeper's reports and the volumes of 'various collections' that calendared smaller archives – it was not comprehensive and some important, smaller collections in public archives were not calendared by them. One example is the large collection of the Fitzwilliam (Milton) Papers at Northamptonshire Record Office, which includes, amongst other things, some of the papers of Sir Walter Mildmay (Chancellor of the Exchequer and Elizabethan Privy Counsellor) and Sir William Fitzwilliam (Lord Deputy of Ireland, 1588–94).

As has already been noted, not all 'State Papers', whether in public or private archives, remain in the United Kingdom. The papers of Lord Ellesmere (Lord Chancellor, 1596–1617) and his descendants, for instance, are now at the Henry E. Huntington Library in California. The Folger Shakespeare Library, in Washington, DC, has a number of family collections including those of the Bacon-Townsend and Shrewsbury-Talbot families, as well as a rich variety of individual items.

Just because these collections – whether they remain in private hands or have moved to public libraries – are those of individuals or families, it does not mean that they are any more complete or comprehensive than the State Papers themselves. There are a number of reasons why an individual's archive may be incomplete or scattered across a number of different libraries, and why some collections, such as the Cotton manuscripts, might appear a hotchpotch of manuscripts. First, political figures, such as Salisbury, stored their papers in several locations. Thus, they could easily be scattered on the owner's death and either be lost or end up in different archives. Second, the longevity of the dynasty: the archive of Burghley and Salisbury has survived very well partly because the family has maintained its social and financial position to this day. By contrast, the archive of their contemporary, Leicester, was quickly scattered because the Earl had no direct, undisputed heir. Third, secretaries, like Hickes, were regularly in possession of large collections of documents belonging to their masters: it was their responsibility to look after them and they needed access to them as part of their work. Fourth, papers were also working documents that counsellors, courtiers or officials might need to consult. Burghley, for instance, was a great 'borrower' of manuscripts, which is why, for instance, some of Cromwell's papers are now at Hatfield House. Fifth, some of these archives or collections – notably the Cotton and Harley manuscripts – were assembled by those who were collectors as well as officials. They either 'permanently borrowed' manuscripts from the State Paper Office or purchased collections commercially. Cotton, for instance, appears to have borrowed large quantities of Wolsey's and Cromwell's papers from the State Paper Office. His collection of Burghley's Scottish Papers may have also been taken from the Office or acquired from the historian William Camden, who had access to Burghley's archives to write his *Annales* (*History of Elizabeth*). Robert Harley and his son, Edward, took advantage of the thriving commercial market in historical manuscripts that had developed in Britain by the early eighteenth century.[10]

Scope and subjects

Both the State Papers and allied collections are of central importance for investigating the high political history of the early modern period, as they abound with correspondence to and from the Crown and between counsellors, and lively, gossipy ambassadorial reports. They also reveal much about how national political issues were understood – or even known about – outside the court, about local politics and about the interaction between the two. News was reported in both private correspondence amongst the nobility and gentry – such as the assassination of Henry III of France revealed in all its gory detail in a letter to Elizabeth Talbot ('Bess of Hardwick') – and, in the seventeenth century, formal newsletters, the precursors of newspapers.[11] Justices of the Peace reported potentially seditious and treasonous cases to the Privy Council, or individual counsellors, to seek their advice as to what to do. SP12 and SP15, for instance, include a number of reports of men and women who had publicly stated that Queen Elizabeth had had an illegitimate child; the Lansdowne collection contains a report on Anne Burnell, who claimed that she was the daughter of Philip II of Spain and had the arms of England on her back.[12] There is also much that might be considered the more mundane aspects of local government – poor roads and crumbling bridges – where local elites sought the Council's authority to put pressure on those responsible to repair them. Far from commonplace, however, these can reveal very important things about how local communities were organized, responsibilities shared and shirked, and local disputes resolved.

However, it would be a mistake to think that these collections are only of use to political historians. They are rich in variety of material and cover a huge range of subjects pertinent to religious, social, cultural and economic historians, as well as to those interested in politics. Aristocratic and gentry collections can tell us much about the family squabbles, legal wranglings, local rivalries and spending habits of the elite. Even their love lives can be scrutinized: Elizabeth, wife of the Third Duke of Norfolk, wrote repeatedly to Cromwell in the 1530s complaining about her estranged husband, alleging that he kept her a virtual prisoner and that both he and his servants beat her. She also had ripe words to say about the Duke's mistress. The papers of Sir Thomas Cawarden, first Master of the Revels, which form part of the Loseley Papers at the Folger Shakespeare Library, can be used to investigate court entertainments. Reports of religious change as a result of the Reformation filtered up into the State Papers, including a dispute in 1545 between the parish priest of Milton, Kent, and most of the parish choir when the latter refused to sing the new English litany and stormed out of the church leaving the priest 'w^t owte eny to anser him, saue ij of the parishe the which do not commonly singe and if thei had not ben, he had songe alone'.[13] One of the most striking documents in the Lansdowne collection is the examination of Agnes Bowker, a maidservant who alleged she had given birth to a cat in 1569. It includes a large drawing of a cat that the Archdeacon of Leicester, Anthony Anderson, had killed, flayed and boiled to

Figure 1.1 Agnes Bowker's cat, MS Lansdowne 101/6.

help prove that the Agnes had not given birth to the cat but had used one to cover up the birth and death of an illegitimate child.[14]

The structure and arrangement of the State Papers

The papers in the State Paper Office were originally gathered in paper books (sometimes indexed) and in bundles (or pacquets). From the sixteenth to the mid nineteenth century, they were housed in various places: initially in the Banqueting House, then in the Holbein Gatehouse at Whitehall and, later, in St John's Chapel at the Tower of London. There was little security or fire-proofing – as we have seen, officials and antiquarians were able to purloin manuscripts – and the Banqueting House was damaged in a fire in 1619.[15] The collection was broadly divided into 'Domestical' and 'Foreign'. From descriptions of the papers of Charles I and Charles II, it appears that foreign papers were usually further divided by country and that domestic ones were organized either chronologically or thematically.[16] Though this seemed orderly, a report issued in 1705 argued that the State Paper Office was overcrowded and chaotic, and Keepers apparently had difficulty in finding even recent manuscripts.

While there were attempts to reorganize the Office in the eighteenth century, real progress was not made until the State Paper Commission was established in 1832. The Commission's aims were to make the collection more coherent and to reorganize it to make it easier to use. Its efforts defined the collection and how historians use it to this day. The Commission's effects were twofold. First, it gathered most, but (as we have seen) by no means all, of the 'State Papers' from disparate parts of the Government's archives. The most notable transfer was of more than 100 volumes of Henrician correspondence (including some of Wolsey's papers, the Lisle Papers and the Wriothesley Papers) from the Treasury of Receipt of the Exchequer in Westminster Abbey's Chapter House to the State Paper Office. And, as if to underline the chaos of the eighteenth-century archives, 118 *sacks* of uncatalogued manuscripts were also moved from the Chapter House to the Office. Second, the Commission began to reorder the various collections and impose a uniform cataloguing system; this included attempting to date undated manuscripts.

The Commission broadly divided the collection into four categories: Domestic, Foreign, Scotland and Ireland. As noted at the start of this chapter, the colonial papers were the responsibility of the separate Colonial Office (see below, p. 26). The Domestic series was largely divided by reign, but there are two main exceptions: the reign of Henry VIII and the Civil War and Interregnum period. The papers covering Henry VIII's reign were divided into seven separate categories or collections: the general series covering incoming (and some outgoing) correspondence to the King's secretaries and other officials, working papers, memoranda, treatises, etc. on domestic and foreign matters (SP1); large documents (SP2); the Lisle papers, formerly belonging to Arthur Plantagenet, Viscount Lisle and Lord Deputy of Calais (SP3); papers dated between September 1545 and January 1547 that had been stamped with the King's signature rather than signed personally by him (SP4); miscellaneous documents from the Exchequer (King's Remembrancer) relating to the dissolution of the monasteries (SP5); theological tracts, mainly from the 1530s (SP6); and the Wriothesley Papers, formerly belonging to Thomas Wriothesley, Clerk of the Signet and Thomas Cromwell's secretary (SP7).

The subdivisions covering the period of the Civil War and the Interregnum are particularly complicated, partly because, between 1642 and 1649, there were two competing governments in England and partly because the parliamentarians created a series of committees to deal with specific issues arising during, and as a result of, the war. SP16 and SP17 (large documents) contain the correspondence of Charles I's Principal Secretaries, as well as material on the navy, taxation, Crown lands, the Court of High Commission, and the trials of Archbishop Laud and Charles I himself. The equivalent classes for the parliamentary side, as well as the Interregnum Government itself, are SP18 and SP25, SP26 and SP27, the last three classes being the papers of the Council of State. The classes relating to specific parliamentary or Interregnum committees are: SP19 for the Committee for the Advance of Money, which dealt with voluntary and compulsory collection of money to pay for the war against the King; SP20 (the Committee for the Sequestration of Delinquents' Estates) and SP23 (the Committee for the Compounding with Delinquents), which both dealt with royalists, Catholics and recusants, including imposing and collecting fines and compositions or the sequestering of property; SP21 for the Committee for Both Kingdoms (or Derby House Committee), an *ad hoc* committee formed to replace the Committee of Safety after the Scots entered England in January 1644; SP22 for the Committee for Plundered Ministers, which organized support for ministers who had been ejected from their parishes by royalists; SP24 for the Committee and Commissioners for Indemnity, dealing with those who had supported the parliamentary cause in the 1640s but were being vexatiously sued; and SP28, the Commonwealth Exchequer papers.

Within the larger class of State Papers Domestic, there are also other discrete or general collections of which the three most important are probably SP15 (Addenda, Edward VI to James I), SP45 (Various, Edward VI to 1862) and SP46 (Supplementary, fourteenth century to George III). There are also separate classes for the Channel Islands (SP47, SP111) and the Isle of Man (SP48).

Papers relating to foreign matters during the reign of Henry VIII were incorporated into the General Series (SP1 and SP2). Those dated between 1549 and 1577 were organized chronologically by reign: Edward VI (SP68), Mary (SP69) and Elizabeth (SP70). Papers dating from 1577 onwards continued to be organized chronologically but were subdivided by country, rather than reign, beginning with the Barbary States (SP71) and culminating in Venice (SP99). There are also several other 'thematic' classes in State Papers Foreign, including News Letters (SP101), Ciphers (SP106) and Treaties (SP108).

State Papers Scotland – in particular the Border papers – is largely an artificially created collection of material drawn from other classes. It is divided into three sections. State Papers Scotland (Series I) is the series of successive Principal Secretaries' correspondence relating to Scottish affairs from 1509 to 1603, organized chronologically by reign, with a further class (SP54) covering the period from 1688 to 1782. This series also includes material relating to Mary Queen of Scots' imprisonment in England (SP53). Series II contains the outgoing correspondence of the Secretary of State principally responsible for Scotland between 1709 and 1746 (Letter Books, SP55); the Secretaries' correspondence with the General Assembly of the Scottish Kirk (Church Books, SP56); the Secretaries' entry book of warrants, docquets and letters relating to Scotland (Warrant Books, SP57); and a collection of transcripts, made in the sixteenth and seventeenth centuries, of Anglo-Scottish material dating from 1065 to 1503 (SP58). The final section of State Papers Scotland is the Border Papers (SP59), containing material relating to the Wardens of the Marches. It is unclear whether this collection was originally a separate one or one artificially created in 1840 when the Commissioners of the Public Records had these papers bound together in volumes. However, it was subsequently partly broken up by the early editors of the Scottish Calendars, and some material was transferred either to the other Scottish series or to the Foreign series.[17]

Like State Papers Scotland, State Papers Ireland is also, to some extent, an artificially created collection. At its core lies the correspondence of successive Lord Deputies, Lord Lieutenants, counsellors, treasurers and higher clergy to the English Government – sometimes accompanied by copies of letters from provincial governors, noblemen, chieftains, mayors and corporations – as well as drafts, memoranda, minutes, treatises and books. But it also contains material culled from Sir Nicholas Throckmorton's collection and some of the Conway papers: from Sir Edward Conway, Baron Conway and Viscount Killultagh, Principal Secretary to James I and Charles I.[18] Primarily organized chronologically in four classes (SP60 Henry VIII; SP61 Edward VI; SP62 Mary; SP63 Elizabeth to George III), it also has separate classes for maps (SP64), large documents (SP65, SP66) and entry books (SP67).

As already noted in the previous section, the Colonial Office had a somewhat chequered history as responsibilities and oversight of the colonies was assumed by different individuals, committees, commissions and departments. The reorganization of the Office's archives also began later than that of the State Paper Office: not until 1910. Broadly, the archive was arranged topographically by dominion, with these classes further subdivided by type of record: primarily correspondence, entry books, sessional papers, acts (ordinances, proclamations and acts of executive and legislative councils) and miscellanea. For instance, there are classes for Barbados (CO28–30, CO33), Bermuda (CO37–41), Canada (CO42–5, CO47), Gibraltar (CO91, CO95), and Jamaica (CO137–42). There are also classes that cover regional groups of dominions – including the East Indies (CO77) and Leeward Islands (CO152) – and classes for countries one might expect to appear in the Foreign series but that were, at some point, British possessions, such as Minorca (CO174).

The exception to this is the collection of papers relating to the Americas and West Indies between 1574 and 1757, where the original order was retained. Thus, manuscripts dating from 1574 to *c.* 1688 are collected in Colonial Papers, General Series (CO1); papers relating to America from *c.* 1688 are in CO5; those relating to the West Indies after *c.* 1688 are in CO318 and in the relevant topographical class.[19] There are also a number of general classes: Original Correspondence (CO323), which includes the Board of Trade's series 'Plantations General', official and semi-official correspondence and some legal reports from 1689; Entry Books (series I, CO324; Series II, CO381) which contain Orders in Council, petition, warrants, commissions and some correspondence; the Board of Trade series, which includes the registers and indexes of correspondence from 1623 (Registers, General, CO326); the Original Correspondence from 1654 (CO388); Entry Books (CO389); Miscellanea (CO390); and minutes of the Board's journals and proceedings from 1675 (CO391).

The structure and arrangement of other collections

The structure and arrangement of 'State Papers' in other public and private archives varies and there is no space in this short chapter to describe them all. The most famous arrangement – and possibly the oddest to novices – is that of the Cotton manuscripts. These were originally kept in fourteen bookcases, each of which was surmounted by a bust of either a Roman emperor (Julius, Augustus, Tiberius, Caligula, Claudius, Nero, Galba, Otho, Vitellius, Vespasian, Titus and Domitian) or an imperial lady (Cleopatra and Faustina). The classification of each volume comprised the name of the bookcase it was in, the shelf (denoted by a letter of the alphabet) and a roman numeral denoting the volume's order on the shelf. This neat and precise ordering contrasts with that found by John Brewer when he went to assess the Cecil papers at Hatfield House in the 1870s. He found that not even the manuscripts that had been bound in one of the 310 volumes in the library were in chronological order.

Some of these collections – such as the Cotton and Harley manuscripts and the Cecil papers – have retained their original classifications. Despite the 'disorder' of the Cecil Papers, Brewer was careful not to alter 'the place or position of the papers in the volumes where they now stand'.[20] Other collections, however, were reordered by later archivists and cataloguers. For instance, the HMC rearranged the papers of Lord De L'Isle and Dudley at Penshurst Place into sections, including Deeds, Accounts, Family Papers, Irish Accounts, and Papers relating to the Council of the Marches of Wales.[21]

Scholars have debated the impact of the reorganization of early modern archives in the State Papers Office and in other libraries, and the imposition, through cataloguing, of what are perceived as nineteenth- and twentieth-century perceptions of politics. Geoffrey Elton, for example, deplored the 'many grave sins' the Public Record Office had committed in reorganizing collections, picking especially (but unsurprisingly) on Cromwell's papers, 'preserved for three centuries in a separate collection, [and] now broken up and redistributed'.[22] It is argued that, though reorganization might make a collection easier to use without the need for complex finding aids, it masks how contemporaries understood politics as reflected in the way they ordered their (working) archives, as well as obscuring 'office practice' (i.e. how contemporaries ordered and stored working records). By reordering collections, we lose an important insight into how individuals and societies engaged with, and understood, politics.

These criticisms are, perhaps, not fair, and we might more sensibly agree with one of the Commission's archivists, John Brewer, who said, when surveying the Henrician State Papers, that retaining the original (or even existing) order of the manuscripts was 'desirable' but 'altogether impossible'.[23] First, it is important to recognize that the Commission did retain some of the original or existing broad categories of the State Papers ('Domestic' and 'Foreign') and maintained the integrity of some specific collections (e.g. the Lisle and Wriothesley papers).

More importantly, as we have seen, though the State Papers were a working archive, it was not always well organized. The Office had also been reorganized many times already so that the original order was not readily apparent. The task facing the Commission was also immensely challenging. Different offices (including the State Paper Office and the Record Office) used different classification systems; many manuscripts were not dated; others were in pieces spread across different archives; some enclosures had been separated from the letters to which they belonged, and, as we have seen, there were sacks of uncatalogued manuscripts. It is, perhaps, unsurprising that Brewer (so keen to retain the order of the Cecil papers) concluded of the State Papers that 'Nothing remained except to bring the different series together, and patiently proceed *de novo* to arrange the whole in uniform chronological order.'[24]

Calendars, catalogues and other finding aids

The State Paper Commission (1832) was just one of the most prominent commissions founded between 1800 and 1837 to organize the State Papers. As well as sorting and cataloguing the manuscripts, these commissions also made the collections available to the public by printing 'calendars': volumes that not only listed the contents of each class of State Papers but also provided summaries or partial or full transcriptions of all the individual manuscripts contained therein. Thus began some of the Commission's most important, influential and long-lasting work. It not only provided finding aids scholars could use to study the State Papers themselves but also influenced the work of the HMC and individual scholars by setting precedents and standards for finding aids for other collections. This section outlines some of the different finding aids for these collections.

The Commission's first calendar was *State Papers during the Reign of Henry the Eighth* (11 volumes, 1825–32). This, however, only included a selection of the Henrician State Papers and so was followed by the comprehensive *Letters and Papers, Foreign and Domestic*, published in twenty-four volumes between 1860 and 1932. *Letters and Papers* not only included the State Papers themselves, but also other Henrician material from other departments in the Public Record Office (notably the Patent Rolls) and from other public and private archives.

It quickly became apparent that *Letters and Papers* was a huge, ambitious and expensive project that could not be sustained for the rest of the collection. Therefore, a new Commission formed in 1840 and, led by Senior Clerk of the State Paper Office, Robert Lemon, instigated a new structure beginning with the Edwardian State Papers (1547–53). First, no attempt was made to combine different classes of papers, as had been the case with *Letters and Papers*. Instead, separate series of calendars were begun for the Domestic, Foreign, Scotland and Ireland classes. Second, material from other sections of the Public Record Office was largely (though not completely[25]) ignored and manuscripts from other archives and libraries were not included. Third,

Lemon chose to summarize each document very briefly: each entry for the
*Calendar of State Papers, Domestic Series, of the Reigns of Edward VI, Mary,
Elizabeth 1547–1580*, for instance, is only two or three lines long.[26]

The calendars for the Domestic, Foreign and Ireland series and the
Colonial Papers are straightforward because there is a relatively uniform
series for each. The *Calendars of State Papers Domestic* were organized by
reign starting with Edward VI, though, as we have just seen, the first volume
covered the reigns of Edward VI and Mary, and the first twenty-three years
of Elizabeth's. The *Calendars of State Papers Foreign* (covering the period
1547–July 1589) also organize the material chronologically, even though
the actual manuscripts dating from 1577 onwards are subdivided by country. The period from August 1589 to 1596 is covered by R. B. Wernham's
seven-volume *List and Analysis of State Papers Foreign, Elizabeth I* (1964–
c. 2000). State Papers Ireland are calendared in the *Calendar of State Papers
Ireland*, but some Henrician manuscripts were selected for inclusion in *State
Papers during the Reign of Henry the Eighth* and all Henrician manuscripts
relating to Ireland are also calendared in *Letters and Papers*. Colonial Papers
relating to America and the West Indies were calendared in the *Calendar of
State Papers Colonial, America and West Indies* (forty-five volumes, including
a supplement to Vol. XIV, with addenda covering the years 1688 to 1696).
The minutes for the Board of Trade are included in this calendar until 1704,
whereafter (at least until 1784) they are printed in full in the *Journals of the
Board of Trade and Plantations* (fourteen volumes, 1920–38). Other colonial
records are indexed in Vol. XXXVI of the List and Index Society.

The calendars for State Papers Scotland are more complicated; there
are a number of overlapping calendars and some material is calendared in
other series. The 'main' calendar is the *Calendar of State Papers, Scotland,
1509–1603*, which covers the sixteenth century, but its entries are very brief.
Some Henrician material is also contained in the fourth and fifth volumes of
State Papers during the Reign of Henry the Eighth, and all Henrician manuscripts relating to Scotland are also calendared in *Letters and Papers*. Longer,
more detailed entries are provided for material dating from 1547 to 1597 in
the *Calendar of State Papers Relating to Scotland and Mary Queen of Scots,
1547–1597*. Scottish material dating from 1558 to June 1577 is calendared in
the *Calendar of State Papers Foreign*. The Border Papers are calendared separately. The revised three-volume *Guide to the Public Record Office*, edited by
M. S. Giuseppi (London, 1963–68), is an invaluable guide to identifying the
correct calendar(s) for each class, not just those relating to Scotland.

In the 150 years over which the calendars were produced, there have been
some changes. Lemon's brief entries allowed him to cover over three decades
in one volume – as opposed to the twenty-one volumes (in thirty-five parts)
required for *Letters and Papers* – but the brevity of entries was unpopular.
Consequently, the Commission adopted the editorial approach practised by
one of the Commission's four external editors, Mary Anne Everett Green.
Green summarized each document fully, ensuring all significant information

was included and that the structure of her summary followed the structure of the original; important phrases were repeated verbatim or clearly quoted. As a result of the unpopularity of the *Calendar of State Papers, Domestic Series, of the Reigns of Edward VI, Mary, Elizabeth*, new calendars of the Edwardian and Marian Papers, with very full summaries, were published in 1992 and 1998, edited by Charles Knighton. A new *Calendar of State Papers Ireland*, covering the period 1571–75, was also produced in conjunction with the Irish Manuscripts Commission in 2000 under the editorship of Mary O'Dowd.

Unfortunately, some classes of State Papers, such as SP28 Commonwealth Exchequer Papers, have not been calendared at all. For other classes, there are only handwritten or typed lists of contents, either available in The National Archives' reading rooms only or through the List and Index Society, founded by Professor Geoffrey Elton to make these lists available publicly. The Society has also published calendars of some classes of State Papers to fill the gaps left by the Commission; these include calendars for State Papers Supplementary (SP46).

Most university libraries and some archives have full sets of the calendars of State Papers, either in their original editions or in reprints. Electronic versions can also be found on the website *British History Online* (hosted by the Institute of Historical Research, London) and through sites such as TannerRitchie's *Medieval and Early Modern Sources Online* (*MEMSO*), where the volumes are available as online searchable facsimiles or facsimile PDFs to download. *State Papers Online* also provides non-facsimile versions of the calendars.[27]

Moving from calendar to document is easy on *State Papers Online* because links are provided between each calendar entry and its corresponding document (providing that the document is in the State Paper Office of The National Archives). Otherwise, readers need to identify the volume and item number of the document from the calendars. This is usually signified in one of two ways. For instance, in the *Calendars for State Papers Domestic*, the content of each manuscript volume is listed in order, with the number of the volume printed as both a subheading and as a running head. Each entry is then numbered, providing the item number of the manuscript. In contrast, for the *Calendars of State Papers Foreign* covering the period after June 1577, each entry is followed by a document reference number comprising the class and volume number, e.g. SP78/10. Some of the referencing in the early calendars is a little opaque, there are some quirks, and some call numbers have changed altogether. Some of these issues are addressed in the essays by Charles Knighton and Amanda Bevan on *State Papers Online*. The National Archives also has excellent information on its website about each class, what finding aids are available and how to use them.

Finding aids for other 'State Papers' in other archives and libraries vary. The British Library collections have only been catalogued, usually with very brief notes of the contents of each document, and not all these catalogues are available online. Nevertheless, it is worth trawling through the paper catalogues to ensure that you identify everything you might possibly need, rather than relying on online keyword searches (where available). The Cotton manuscripts have been refoliated several times, so it is important to use the item numbers from the catalogue – as well as to be consistent in which foliation you will adopt and follow when you study the manuscripts themselves.

Many major collections in private and public archives benefited from the attention of the HMC. There are four series. The main series are the first nine General Keeper's reports, which address many different archives in one volume; these volumes include collections that were subsequently given more extensive treatment in the other series. The second series comprises fourteen later Keepers' or inspectors' reports that tend to calendar smaller collections. The third and fourth series contain individual series of calendars of larger collections (such as the twenty-four-volume series on the Cecil Papers); appendices to the tenth and fifteenth Keepers' report, which calendared individual collections in separate volumes; and the final four Keepers' reports. The HMC broadly adopted the editorial practice of the State Paper Commission (under Green's purview) when producing its calendars. Indeed, some of the same archivists and editors, like John Brewer, worked for both commissions. Thus, there is a summary or a partial/full transcription of the contents of each manuscript, and there were attempts to date undated items, which were placed at the end of the relevant year. Manuscript references are usually given (though, annoyingly, not for the first four volumes of the Cecil Papers). Note that many of these collections are private, and access to them can be restricted for a variety of reasons. The Cecil Papers have long been available on microfilm at the British Library and the Folger Shakespeare Library, but this has now been superseded by the digitized *The Cecil Papers* (available only by purchase or subscription) which simply organizes the collection by volume and item number.

Conclusion: where to start

State Papers, whether in The National Archives or in a public or private archives elsewhere, are daunting collections to start working on, but they can be mastered. As with any other source, collection or archive, it is important to do your homework and understand as much about the collection as possible before visiting the archive. Once there, don't be afraid to ask the archivists for assistance: they know their archives very well and are invariably happy to help readers.

There are many ways in which you can prepare yourself for venturing into State Papers. Though peppered with some rather trenchant criticisms, and a false distinction between 'official' and 'unofficial' manuscripts, Geoffrey Elton's *England, 1200–1640* (London, 1969) is an excellent starting point as it not only discusses the State Papers themselves but also much of the rest of The National Archives (formerly The Public Record Office) and other sources. On its website, The National Archives provides a wealth of helpful detailed guides and information on each class within the State Paper Office (and all the other departments).[28] These explain some of the history of each class, what it comprises, finding aids and any quirks, such as if the class has been re-catalogued and how readers can negotiate between old and new references. Older sources should not be ignored. M. S. Giuseppi's three-volume revised *Guide to the Contents of the Public Record Office* (London, 1963–68) might seem outdated and old-fashioned and, certainly, some of the figures provided on the number of volumes or bundles are now incorrect. But, it provides an excellent introduction to each department within The National Archives, identifies and provides a description of every single class, and lists all the relevant calendars (up to the 1960s). Introductions to the calendars themselves should not be ignored either. Though many of them focus on providing a brief narrative of events to offer some context for the documents, they (particularly the first volumes in the series) can also include important information about the class itself and how it has been calendared. Finally, those who have access to *State Papers Online* should make a beeline for the specially commissioned essays hosted there. Those by Charles Knighton (on the calendars), Amanda Bevan (on the Henrician State Papers), Andrew Thrush (covering 1603–40) and Stephen Roberts (1640–60) are particularly useful starting points.

Starting points for material in other archives are less straightforward. *State Papers Online* includes some useful essays on some of the British Library collections (by Simon Adams) and the Cecil Papers (Stephen Alford), even though the database includes digitized images of only a small selection of the former and none of the latter. The online Cecil Papers includes important essays about the history of the archive and how to use them. Introductions to HMC calendars, websites of archives and scholarly essays on specific collections or individuals (notably those by Simon Adams on the Earl of Leicester) also exist.[29]

Key resources

Adams, Simon, 'The Tudor State Papers in the Yelverton, Cotton and Harleian Manuscript Collections', *State Papers Online, 1509–1714*, http://gale.cengage.co.uk.

Alford, Stephen, 'The Collection of the Cecil Papers, Hatfield House, Hertfordshire', *State Papers Online, 1509–1714*, http://gale.cengage.co.uk.

Bevan, Amanda, 'State Papers of Henry VIII: The Archives and the Documents', *State Papers Online, 1509–1714*, http://gale.cengage.co.uk.

Elton, G. R., *England, 1200–1640* (London, 1969).

Giuseppi, M. S. (ed.), *Guide to the Contents of the Public Record Office*, 3 vols (London: HMSO, 1963–68).

Knighton, C. S., 'The Calendars and Their Editors, 1856–2006', *State Papers Online, 1509–1714*, http://gale.cengage.co.uk.

Marshall, Alan, 'The Secretaries' Office and the Public Records', http://gale.cengage.co.uk.

National Archives, The. See the list of guides in the section on medieval and early modern history in their 'Research Guides', http://www.nationalarchives.gov.uk/help-with-your-research/research-guides/?research-category=medieval-early-modern-history (accessed 4 January 2016).

Perry, Vicky, 'Notes on the Numbering of the Cecil Papers and the Scope of the Digital Collection', *The Cecil Papers* (Cambridge: ProQuest, 2010–15).

Roberts, Stephen K., 'The Government and Its Records, 1640–1660', *State Papers Online, 1509–1714*, http://gale.cengage.co.uk.

Thrush, Andrew, 'The Government and Its Records, 1603–1640', http://gale.cengage.co.uk.

Williams, Robin Harcourt, 'The Cecil Papers: Four Centuries of Custodial History', *The Cecil Papers* (Cambridge: ProQuest, 2010–15).

Notes

1 'The Mermaid and the Hare', [June] 1567, TNA: PRO, SP52/13, fo. 60r; H. Muddiman to George Powell, 14 March 1667, TNA: PRO, SP29/193/113.

2 Though the collection ends with SP110 (State Papers Foreign, Supplementary), classes SP72, SP73 and SP74 have not been used.

3 Wilson never stated the date he was appointed clerk or keeper of the office, only that it had occurred forty-five years previously and before the appointment of his uncle, Dr Thomas Wilson, as one of Elizabeth's principal secretaries. On these grounds, archivists and historians have dated the founding of the State Paper Office to 1578. However, as the archivist and secretary to the Royal Commission on Public Records, Hubert Hall, demonstrated over a century ago, the dating of Wilson's statement (that his appointment had been made forty-five years earlier) to 1623 was 'purely conjectural' (Hubert Hall, *Studies in English Official Historical Documents* (Cambridge: Cambridge University Press, 1908), pp. 32–3, esp. p. 32n2; and see the reference in M. S. Giuseppi (ed.), *Guide to the Contents of the Public Record Office*, 3 vols (London: HMSO, 1963–68), Vol. II, p. 1). Moreover, Dr Wilson was officially sworn in by the Privy Council as Secretary on 12 November 1577 (*Acts of the Privy Council of England*, ed. J Dasent *et al.*, new series, 45 vols (London, 1890–1960), Vol. X, p. 85).

4 Hall, *Studies*, pp. 33–4; A. F. Pollard, 'Wilson, Sir Thomas (*d*. 1629)', rev. Sean Kelsey, *Oxford Dictionary of National Biography* (Oxford: Oxford University Press, 2004), online edn (January 2008), http://www.oxforddnb.com/view/article/29690 (accessed 27 January 2016).

5 It is possible that Wilson's interest was a reversionary one because the patent was cancelled in December 1613 and reissued to Wilson and his son-in-law in July 1614. Hall, *Studies*, pp. 35–6; Pollard, 'Wilson, Sir Thomas'.

6 Simon Adams, 'The Tudor State Papers in the Yelverton, Cotton and Harleian Manuscript Collections', *State Papers Online, 1509–1714*, http://gale.cengage.co.uk (accessed 3 January 2016).

7 Alan Marshall, 'The Secretaries' Office and the Public Records', *State Papers Online*, http://gale.cengage.co.uk/images/Marshall%20The%20Secretaries%20Office%20and%20the%20Public%20records.pdf (accessed 3 January 2016).

8 For an explanation of the term 'calendared', see the section 'Calendars, catalogues and other finding aids', above, p. 28–31.

9 For a full analysis of the location of Leicester's archive, see Simon Adams, 'The Papers of Robert Dudley, Earl of Leicester I: The Browne–Evelyn Collection', *Archives*, 20 (1992), 63–86; Simon Adams, 'The Papers of Robert Dudley, Earl of Leicester II: The Atye–Cotton Collection', *Archives*, 20 (1993), 131–44; Simon Adams, 'The Papers of Robert Dudley, Earl of Leicester III: The Countess of Leicester's Collection', *Archives*, 22 (1996), 1–26.

10 Adams, 'The Tudor State Papers'.

11 Gilbert and Mary Talbot to Elizabeth, Countess of Shrewsbury, [February 1589], Folger Shakespeare Library, Washington, DC, Folger X.d.428 (115).

12 TNA: PRO, SP12/12/51, fo 107r; SP12/13/21.I, fos 56r–57r; SP15/11/86, fos 151r–v; BL, Lansdowne MS 53/79, fos 162r–163r.

13 TNA: PRO, SP1/203, fos 85r–90r.

14 BL, Lansdowne MS 101/6, fos 27r–33r. See also David Cressy, *Agnes Bowker's Cat: Travesties and Transgressions in Tudor and Stuart England. Tales of Discord and Dissension* (Oxford: Oxford University Press, 1999), pp. 9–28.

15 Thankfully, Wilson had removed the State Papers from the Banqueting House before the fire and it was principally the archives of the Privy Council and the Signet Office that were lost or damaged.

16 Marshall, 'The Secretaries' Office'.

17 See *The Border Papers: Calendar of Letters and Papers Relating to the Affairs of the Borders of England and Scotland Preserved in Her Majesty's Public Record Office London*, ed. Joseph Bain, 2 vols (Edinburgh: HM General Register House, 1894–96), Vol. I, pp. vii–x.

18 *Calendar of State Papers Relating to Ireland of the Reigns of Henry VIII, Edward VI, Mary and Elizabeth, 1509–1573*, ed. H. C. Hamilton (London: Longman, Green, Longman and Roberts, 1860), pp. i–iii.

19 Though note that, according to TNA's online catalogue, there is a significant chronological overlap among these classes and it is worth checking all of them to ensure you identify all relevant manuscripts.

20 *Third Report of the Royal Commission on Historical Manuscripts* (London: HMSO, 1872), Appendix, p. 147.

21 *Historical Manuscripts Commission: Report of the Manuscripts of Lord De L'Isle and Dudley Preserved at Penshurst Place*, ed. C.L. Kingsford *et al.*, 4 vols (London: HMSO, 1925–42), Vol. I, pp. v–lx.

22 G. R. Elton, *England, 1200–1640* (London, 1969), p. 72.

23 Amanda Bevan, 'State Papers of Henry VIII: The Archives and the Documents', *State Papers Online, 1509–1714*, http://gale.cengage.co.uk/images/Bevan%20State%20Papers%20the%20archives%20and%20documents%201509-1547.pdf (accessed 3 January 2016).

24 J. S. Brewer, *Preface to Letters and Papers, Foreign and Domestic, of the Reign of Henry VIII, Preserved in the Public Record Office, the British Museum and Elsewhere in England* (London: HMSO, 1861), pp. ix–xi, cited in Bevan, 'State Papers of Henry VIII'.

25 Lemon included some items from SP9 (Grants of Arms) and SP38 (Docquets) in *Calendar of State Papers, Domestic Series, of the Reigns of Edward VI, Mary, Elizabeth 1547–1580, Preserved in the State Paper Department of Her Majesty's Public Record Office*, ed. Robert Lemon (London: Public Record Office, 1856).

26 See ibid.

27 *British History Online*, http://www.british-history.ac.uk (accessed 4 January 2016); *Medieval and Early Modern Sources Online (MEMSO)*, http://www.tannerritchie.com/memso.php (accessed 4 January 2016).

28 The National Archives, http://www.nationalarchives.gov.uk (accessed 4 January 2016).

29 See above, n9.

2 Legal and judicial sources

Henry French

Since the 1990s there have been two contradictory trends in the study of legal and judicial sources in early modern England. On the one hand, historical interest in the study of crime, the courts and the criminal law has declined compared to the buoyancy of research on these subjects between 1970 and 1985. On the other, there has been an explosion in the availability of legal source materials online, led by the extremely impressive effort to digitize the printed proceedings of the Old Bailey Sessions, and encompassing a range of other online resources for criminal and Church court cases.[1] The first generation of social historians and historians of crime, in particular, made extensive use of the records of the Assizes and Quarter Sessions, as well as of the Church courts before 1640.[2] They mapped out the dynamics of offences and changes over time.[3] They were particularly concerned to establish the social profiles of offenders and victims of crime, for a wide variety of offences including theft, violence, murder, witchcraft, sexual offences, poaching, smuggling and vagrancy.[4] They looked at the processes of detection and arrest, the functions of constables and Justices of the Peace (JPs), and tried to establish how often cases ended up in court.[5] They attempted to reconstruct court proceedings, to assess the roles of jurors, defendants, counsel and judges.[6] They reviewed the kinds of punishments inflicted, and the moral messages conveyed by them.[7] More broadly, they sought to answer some big questions about the nature of society and justice in early modern England. They asked whether changes in the dynamics of crime (particularly declining rates of indictments for violent offences) and in the severity of punishments inflicted meant that early modern society was undergoing some kind of 'civilizing' process.[8] They debated whether the justice system really operated in the interests of the propertied elite, under the cover of justice for all.[9] They also examined the gaps within the legal record itself, and the more troubling issue of the unknowable 'dark figure' of unreported crimes.[10]

This last issue came to the fore in the 1980s, at the same time as the 'cultural turn' asked methodological questions about the quantitative approaches routinely employed by social historians of crime. In particular, scholars realized that the sketchy evidence in legal sources did not always explain 'crime' as a cultural phenomenon.[11] However, historians of gender remained very interested in the decisions of the Church courts, particularly in cases of sexual misconduct and slander, to reveal attitudes to female sexuality and the patriarchal assumptions beneath gender norms in the first half of the period.[12] More recently, historians of popular 'political' behaviour and thought have returned to equity court cases, particularly to disputes over customary rights, entitlements, resources and sites.[13] These cases could produce highly detailed statements by witnesses, which indicate ordinary villagers' attitudes to these local 'customs', and their relationship to landlords who contested these rights. They also depict a popular 'legal-mindedness', encompassing the senses of justice and entitlement of those outside the educated elites in early modern England.[14]

Meanwhile, since 2003 the Old Bailey Online project has digitized the printed proceedings of the Old Bailey Sessions between 1674 and 1913, making available almost 200,000 criminal cases. These can be searched by the identity of plaintiff and defendant, by location, by type of offence, by verdict and by sentence. Other freely available digital resources have published existing printed volumes of Quarter Sessions records, particularly for London and Middlesex; notebooks of JPs; records of capital punishments; records of manorial courts; and the Ecclesiastical Court Papers of the Archdiocese of York, to name but a few.[15] At the same time, *Early English Books Online* (*EEBO*) and *Eighteenth-Century Collections Online* (*ECCO*) can be combined with various digital collections of eighteenth-century newspapers and pamphlets, to provide a level of detail unimaginable to the first generation of scholars of crime half a century ago.[16] However, the limitations and hidden features of this material have to be understood, before users get carried away by the initial excitement of seeing the results generated by a context-free word search!

This chapter will begin by exploring the records generated by the criminal process in Common Law, and then move onto the Church courts and the central equity courts. It is based on the author's experience as a practical user and interpreter of these categories of source material, rather than being informed by specialist knowledge of the detailed legal processes of these courts.

The criminal courts

In 1500 many minor offences (particularly breaches of the peace, minor assaults and thefts) were still heard outside the royal justice system in the thousands of manorial courts that existed throughout England and Wales. Manorial courts were accessible to ordinary people, relatively inexpensive and often swift in hearing cases. However, because their procedure was governed by local custom, their processes could also be capricious, and might be used by hard-up manorial lords to extract fines from their tenants. By the mid seventeenth century most manorial courts in the south of England, and the Midlands, had stopped hearing minor criminal cases and dealt only with nuisances against property (such as over-flowing ditches, un-ringed pigs and offensive dung-heaps).[17] A wider variety of cases continued to be heard in some upland manorial courts in northern England, where distances and difficult transport links left manorial courts as the most accessible form of locally recognized justice.[18]

The structure of the legal system in the royal courts is illustrated in simplified form in Figure 2.1. J. S. Cockburn's *History of English Assizes* emphasizes that although this system was relatively simple in theory, in practice many of the neat distinctions between Quarter Sessions and Assizes became very

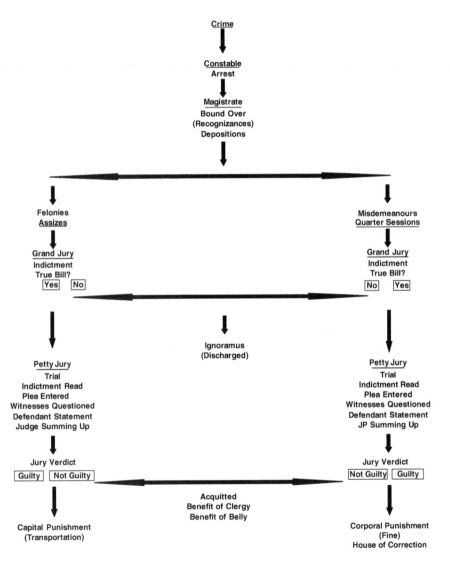

Figure 2.1 Diagram showing the process of cases through the criminal courts.

blurred.[19] The lowest administrative official in the royal legal system was also a manorial official – the constable. These manorial origins meant that constables were selected by a variety of methods, depending on the custom of the manor. Generally, though, they were drawn from those tenants who held some land or property in the manor (occasionally including women, who normally chose a man to deputize).[20] Gradually more prosperous members of the community sought to avoid this potentially onerous and unpopular post by appointing deputies. Constables rarely served for more than one year, unlike some other local officers.[21] Over time, the office of constable tended to migrate into a parish post, with constables chosen by the parish rate-payers each Easter.[22] Consequently, constables' records are often found among parish vestry records, rather than within manorial court rolls.

Constables had two main tasks. They were charged with maintaining the King's (or Queen's) Peace, and also acted as the lowest rung of governmental administration, reporting to JPs and to Quarter Sessions or Assizes about matters such as public highways or bridges, the collection of royal taxes and the implementation of policies such as military musters.[23] If a crime had been committed, the victim or his or her neighbours might apprehend the perpetrator directly, and bring him or her to the constable for further proceedings, or the constable might act directly himself. Constables' activities are recorded in their accounts, where these survive. These record claims for reimbursement, for activities such as journeys to arrest an individual, or to take him or her to a JP, the Quarter Sessions or Assizes. However, such costs only illustrate part of the constable's day-to-day business. Constables often negotiated settlements between neighbours after a fight or in relation to petty thefts or trespasses. If matters went no further, such agreements were often not recorded.

If the case was more serious, or the victim was more aggrieved, the constable's next step was to take the matter before the local JP. Justices of the Peace operated under the 'Commission of the Peace', and were chosen by the Privy Council, from lists provided by county Lords Lieutenant, and were normally relatively wealthy local landowners.[24] The office of JP was unpaid, so its holders needed the time (and money) to undertake it for relatively minimal financial compensation. They did not have to possess legal training, although many gentlemen often spent some time at the Inns of Court in London learning aspects of the law, or read advice manuals, such as Michael Dalton's much reprinted early-seventeenth-century work, *The Country Justice*.[25] The role of the JP expanded considerably through the early modern period, effectively supplanting that of the sheriff in most judicial matters.[26] Like the constable, the JP dealt with both the enforcement of the criminal law, and the implementation of royal government and administration in the localities.[27]

The JP's role was expanded by the passage of an act in 1554–55 that made JPs responsible for bailing defendants, and assembling the evidence to be presented to the Assizes and Quarter Sessions to establish the facts of a criminal case.[28] This meant gathering the correct evidence about the identities, places of residence and occupations of the persons concerned, as well as establishing the facts of the case to be used by the Crown (prosecution).[29] They also had to ensure that those involved presented themselves to court, by binding them to appear (making them enter financial bonds, with neighbours or substantial residents standing surety, and risking the forfeit of their money if the accused absconded). In addition, after the mid fifteenth century JPs gained more powers to hear less important cases either summarily on their own, or with two or three other justices in hearings that became known as 'petty sessions'.[30] Such hearings took place without a jury, and were normally used to commit individuals to the county house of correction for a few days or weeks of confinement for offences such as insubordination by servants or apprentices, or minor assaults. These hearings became much more common by the eighteenth century, and really supplanted earlier manorial systems of justice.[31] This may have meant that most cases in the criminal justice system were tried without a jury, despite the jury-trial being depicted as the corner-stone of the English Common Law system.[32]

Although these summary hearings were the most frequent method of dispensing justice, they are one of the least documented. Justices of the Peace did not have to preserve a formal record of such hearings, and only a few JPs' notebooks survive, the best of which are those of the Wiltshire JP William Hunt, the Northumberland clergyman-JP Edward Tew and the Hackney JP Henry Norris (available through www.britishhistoryonline), all for the period 1730–60.[33] Tew dealt with over 1,000 cases between 1750 and 1764, but only 21 of these came to trial, which illustrates how many offences never entered the formal legal record.[34]

Surviving JPs' notebooks illustrate that active Justices issued warrants and dealt with minor matters on a daily basis. They normally met with their fellow JPs in 'petty sessions' perhaps once every three or four weeks. Sometimes they reported their concerns or answered questions submitted to them in letters to the Privy Council, which survive in the *Calendar of State Papers (Domestic)*, but there are few official traces of much of their judicial activity.[35] The main record produced by JPs comprised the minority of cases that proceeded to a formal legal hearing in the Quarter Sessions, held at Epiphany (December/ January), Easter (April), Midsummer (July) and Michaelmas (October) in each county and each county borough. The latter were borough towns with 'county' status, which had the right to hold their own Quarter Sessions courts, at which the annually elected mayors or 'chief burgesses' acted as JPs, although there was considerable local variation.[36] The only legal professional required in the Quarter Sessions was the clerk of the peace, who arranged the business of the court, and acted as a legal advisor to the JPs who sat as judges on the bench of magistrates.

The role of Quarter Sessions was clarified and limited over time. After reforms in 1590, Quarter Sessions generally confined themselves within the remit of the 'Commission of the Peace', rather than undertaking 'Gaol Delivery' – that is, dealing with breaches of the peace, for which the usual punishments were corporal punishment (whipping), imprisonment or fines, rather than hearing the cases of those remanded on suspicion of felonies.[37] Normally such 'misdemeanours' consisted of low-value thefts; non-lethal assaults and affrays; and a wide variety of legal infractions, regulatory offences and public nuisances.[38]

Quarter Sessions generated a number of different records, which were kept by the *Custos rotulorum* (the leading JP in each county). The Quarter Sessions' rolls constituted the formal record of proceedings. They listed the Hundred, Grand and Petty (trial) jurors, the persons indicted and the indictment details, and brief marginal notes of subsequent decisions.[39] In administrative matters, the Quarter Sessions were supposed to keep books of orders, recording their decisions about disputes over bridge repairs, provision of poor relief and the imposition of fines, among other matters.[40] Justices might also supply the court with depositions, which consisted of their notes on the statements of witnesses recorded before them when they took evidence after the offence had been reported. Sometimes they were rolled up with the Quarter Sessions' rolls, and at other times written up into books, but often they were not kept after the trial. Clerks of the peace might also keep separate records of the names of persons bound over to enter recognizances for their good behaviour, with their sureties, and sometimes kept books of those indicted, separate from the rolls. By the eighteenth century Quarter Sessions' proceedings might also be reported in local newspapers, but not necessarily in exhaustive detail.

The average record of a case in the Quarter Sessions' rolls was usually brief and fairly cryptic. Here is an example from the Essex village of Earls Colne for January 1612: 'indictment Edw Champness of Earls Colne labourer 1.11.1611 feloniously stole and carried away there a sheet worth 6d belonging to Hen Bridge witness: Hen Bridge confesses judgement to be whipped'.[41] In accordance with the Statute of Additions (1414), the indictment listed Champness' place of residence, and his occupation, information that was regarded as essential to establishing the defendant's identity. It also recorded the date of the offence, the value of the item stolen, and the name of the witness in the case: the owner of the stolen item, Henry Bridge. Even so, while this information appears concrete, it was not always totally reliable. Champness was born in Earls Colne, but in other circumstances the defendant might only have lived in this community for a short time. Similarly, although he is described as a labourer, the record of his occupational identity was largely at the discretion of the clerk of the court. In addition, the threshold for felony was for goods worth 1s or more, so the value of the item stolen was critical. The sheet in question may simply have been worth 6d, or the Grand Jury could have reduced its value so as to mitigate Champness' punishment.

The abbreviation of the Sessions' roll omits large parts of the process, illustrated in Figure 2.1. It does not record how Henry Bridge detected the offence, nor who apprehended Champness. In this case, the records of the process book of indictments survives, and here it is stated that Champness 'came from the gaol to the bar and argued that he had not done it'.[42] At some point thereafter in the (brief) trial, he must have changed his story, and his plea, to guilty – but the reasons for this are not recorded. There are no accompanying witness depositions, and no indication of where or whether the sentence was carried out. So, although surviving Quarter Sessions' rolls constitute a formal legal record, they often omit many (perhaps most) of the interesting details of the case.

The same basic processes applied at the twice-yearly Assizes, except that the types of offences tried were more serious, and the stakes were higher, because felonies carried the death penalty. Consequently, by the end of the sixteenth century, the Assizes dealt routinely with the most serious thefts (items worth more than 1s, but increasingly those worth more than 5s – 'grand larcenies'), as well as severe crimes of violence, particularly those resulting in death, plus rapes, arson, witchcraft, riots and sedition. The key difference between the procedures of the Quarter Sessions and those of the Assizes was in the judicial personnel. Assize judges were legal professionals, experienced judges who for the rest of the year dealt with criminal cases in Westminster on the King's or Queen's Bench. These judges rode out across one of the six Assize circuits (the Home, Midland, Norfolk, Oxford, Northern and Western circuits), and over a period of six to eight weeks held Assizes in perhaps half-a-dozen 'Assize' towns and cities on their circuit, each court session lasting perhaps four or five days at the most.[43] One of the judges heard the criminal cases, while the other (often a specialist from the Court of Common Pleas) heard *nisi prius* civil cases, the records of which are patchy post 1660, and non-existent before.[44] Assizes were also an opportunity for judges to transmit messages from the royal Government, enquire into particularly pressing concerns, receive reports from Justices and Grand Juries in the localities, and push for the enforcement of particular regulations. The best description of proceedings in Assizes in this period remains Chapter 6 of Cockburn's *History of English Assizes*, and readers should refer to this.

Once again, the surviving records of the Assizes (held in The National Archives, rather than in county records offices) embodied in the rolls can be very brief and unrevealing. Another case relating to Earls Colne in the summer Assizes of 1608 shows that (if anything) it is even more cryptic than the Quarter Sessions material: 'Thos Hamond alias Dowe of Earls Colne labourer 26.12.1607 there stole eight yards of broadcloth worth 4li belonging to Phil Storye confessed hanged witness Jn Pearson'.[45] In this instance, 'Hamond alias Dowe' was remanded to appear at the Assizes because of the high value of the goods stolen (at £4 this cloth was eighty times the minimum figure for felonious theft). He had been forced to wait six months for his trial, the record of which is particularly scant. All the issues mentioned above in relation to Quarter Sessions' rolls also apply in this case. Hamond alias Dowe is recorded as coming from Earls Colne, yet this is the only record in the village in which his name appears. Presumably, the witness in this case, John Pearson, had been able to identify him as the thief, forcing his confession. We do not know why the court did not attempt to mitigate the extreme sentence imposed, but perhaps the large value of the goods concerned made this more problematic. In short, we are left guessing about the motives that lay behind the actions and the punishment stated so starkly in this record.

The brevity of most Assize materials may be one reason why historians have been so attracted to the much more voluminous records generated by the proceedings of the Old Bailey. The operation of the Old Bailey Sessions is explained fully and comprehensively on the project website, so the following discussion will not attempt to replicate this detail.[46] Although the chaplains of Newgate Prison in London had supplemented their earnings by publishing accounts of the lives, deaths and (usually) repentant last words of felons housed there since the 1620s, it was only in the mid-1670s that printers experimented with summaries of the proceedings of the Old Bailey, picking up on the existing market for the lives of prisoners held at Newgate. Until the late 1720s, the published proceedings generally only contained summaries of trials that extended to one or two paragraphs at most. There was always a steady volume of material, because unlike other serious criminal courts, the Old Bailey Sessions met eight times a year, in order to deal with the much larger volume of serious offences emanating from London, a city of some 500,000 people in 1700. Early editions survive quite comprehensively between 1674 and 1699. Between 1699 and 1714 editions are missing for two-thirds of the sessions. Thereafter, the proceedings were expanded, first to twenty-four pages in 1729, eventually being published at much greater length in several editions (as many as five) across the year by the 1740s. This allowed much fuller reporting of cases, and was accompanied by the development of short-hand reporting of the speeches of witnesses, the cross-examinations, and the responses of defendants. By the 1740s, therefore, the proceedings amount to a fairly complete annual record of the trials for felony in the largest city in Europe.

Early Old Bailey Sessions cases follow the moral template of their progenitors, the clerically authored 'Last Dying Speeches', and the hack-written criminal biographies, whose purpose was to titillate or shock but also to frame the offence within a conventionally providential framework in which the truth would be arrived at and justice would (eventually) always be done, and be seen to be done.[47] Later cases appear less overtly didactic, but contain some hidden editorial decisions. In general much less attention is given by the reporters to the defence account, compared to the witnesses' statements and their cross-examination. This may simply reflect biases against the defendant in court proceedings, where the lack of defence counsel until the 1780s may have made silence the most effective defence. Arguments between prosecution and defence counsel were also often omitted because they turned on obscure points of law.

Large amounts of additional material have also been added to the Old Bailey project site, notably 25,000 'associated records' held in databases linked to a wide variety of libraries and other archives, plus a large number of other London legal records (such as petitions and pardons, calendars of prisoners, and records of transportation). Beyond this, the associated *London Lives* database makes it possible to search for individuals who ended up in the

Old Bailey, through the records of metropolitan parishes, institutions (such as charities and workhouses) and other legal proceedings.[48] The burgeoning collections of eighteenth-century newspapers and pamphlets also enable the identification of further accounts of the trials, executions, last words and wider circumstances of many offenders condemned at the Old Bailey Sessions. This ability to cross-reference between such comprehensive databases should transform our understanding of crime, criminality and the law after 1660, but also risks representing the metropolitan experience as the norm, in a society that was still overwhelmingly rural, and in which serious felonies remained very rare.

Beyond the Assizes and the Old Bailey, there were the King's criminal courts in Westminster, most notably the King's or Queen's Bench, which heard both civil cases on the 'Plea side', and criminal cases on the 'Crown side'. These courts heard serious cases from the localities, and Assize cases could be transferred to them by a writ of *certiorari*, particularly in instances where defendants alleged that local prejudices might prevent them receiving a fair trial.[49] The records of the King's and Queen's Bench remain relatively unstudied, because these materials (held in The National Archives) are fairly inaccessible.[50] Indictments are indexed by name and by session, but it is difficult to locate cases relating to a particular place, county or type of offence. The other higher criminal court was the Court of Star Chamber, which operated between 1520 and 1642 according to civil law principles, and will be dealt with below in the section on the equity courts.

The Church courts

The Church courts dealt, primarily, with offences against the teaching of the Church, and with disputes arising out of the Church's ceremonies for the three vital events of life: baptism, marriage and burial. In particular, the Church's function until 1858 as a probate registry meant that the Church courts remained the site of a great deal of litigation over wills and inheritance. The courts followed the hierarchy of the Church. The lowest level of courts was located at the archdeaconry level dealing with parishes as they were gathered together in these units of jurisdiction. Above them were the dioceses, and the bishops' consistory courts. Above them were the two archdiocesan courts of Canterbury and York. By the later sixteenth century, the highest ecclesiastical jurisdiction was the new Court of High Commission, the clerical equivalent of the Court of Star Chamber (and about as popular with Common lawyers).[51] The Church was also shot through with a large number of 'peculiar' jurisdictions, the largest of which were the 'palatine' jurisdictions of the diocese of Durham and Chester, which had jurisdictions separate from the archdiocesan machinery. Below them diocesan 'peculiars' held their own courts outside the jurisdiction of archdeacons and bishops. Although there was some variation in officials and processes, each followed the general procedures outlined below. Alan Macfarlane's Earls Colne website gives a very useful overview of Church court records, although the nature of the surviving material varies considerably between ecclesiastical jurisdictions.[52]

There were two main categories of trial heard before the Church courts. The first were Plenary or Instance cases, usually matters between two individuals, such as cases of slander, or those relating to the Church's registration processes (about whether or not marriages or testaments had been valid, for example). Their processes were copied by the equity courts in the fifteenth and sixteenth centuries, and will be dealt with below. The second type of Church court proceedings involved low-level moral and behavioural regulation within the parish, which formed the staple business of these courts before and after the Reformation, until their temporary abolition in 1642. Such cases included moral failings (actual or suspected sexual misconduct, drinking during divine service and slander); non-payment of church dues and tithes, non-attendance at church, and improper registration of vital events (primarily marriages solemnized outside church); religious misconduct, primarily liturgical failings by clergy, but also 'sermon-gadding' to other churches, and very occasional instances of doctrinal errors; and failure to maintain or repair church property. Such cases were recorded in Latin, generally very briefly, but historians have used them as an indication of puritan 'moral reform' efforts between 1560 and 1640.[53] Figure 2.2 illustrates the process by which these cases were heard.

A case could be initiated in several ways, but generally churchwardens reported suspected or detected alleged miscreants directly to the archdeaconry courts, or cited them as offenders in their regular (usually monthly) presentments to the court. This 'bill of detection' was considered by the archdeacons. Unlike the Common Law, those 'detected' and cited before the Church courts were required to *disprove* the allegation – that is, they were assumed to be guilty until they proved their innocence. If the allegation proceeded, the archdeacons produced a 'citation', which they gave to a court official called an 'apparitor'. The citation named the day, location and judges, the person cited and his or her offence. It was given to the parish clergyman, because he and his churchwardens were required to ensure that the accused attended.

If the accused failed to appear (as often happened) he or she would be excommunicated – deprived of the right to receive communion. If the accused died whilst excommunicate, he or she could not be buried in consecrated ground. The sentence of excommunication would only be revoked if the accused was reconciled to the Church, either by doing a public penance or by paying a fine.

If the accused appeared, the court administered an oath by virtue of the authority of the court. The accusations took the form of articles to which the accused had to make answer. If he or she admitted guilt, then a penance was ordered. If not, the accused was required to take another oath that asserted his or her innocence, and then back this up by finding witnesses who would also take the oath. These fellow oath-takers were called 'compurgators'. If more than two compurgators swore to the innocence of the accused he or she was usually discharged. If not, the penalty was, again, a penance

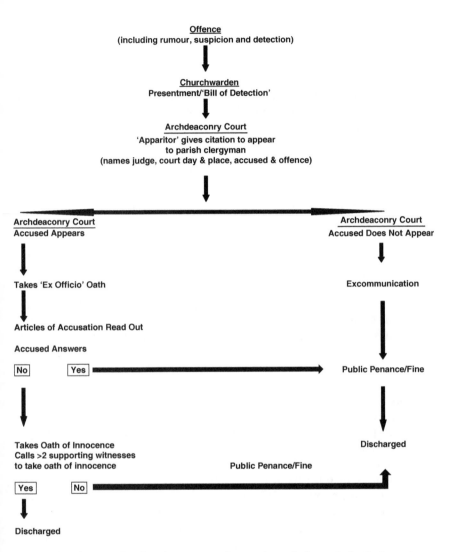

Figure 2.2 Diagram showing the process of cases through the ecclesiastical courts.

or a fine in lieu, under threat of excommunication. These penalties were relatively light, but after the Reformation there is considerable evidence that they were resented by ordinary people, either because excommunication held less fear in an era that disputed the doctrine of purgatory, or because advanced Protestants believed that the whole process was unsanctioned by scripture.[54]

Archdeaconry courts recorded the bills of presentment and the citations of the case, and the archdeacon's 'Act Book' noted down the proceedings and sentence (and whether or not the accused appeared). In more extensive cases depositions might be taken, too. However, most of the surviving evidence is contained in the Act Books, which are often one- or two-line summaries of proceedings. We can cite another example from Earls Colne, from October 1578, translated into English:

> office of the judge against Hen Abbott of Earls Colne detected as in the bill of incontinency with Grace Dirrick of Earls Colne by public fame he appeared personally and denied the articles therefore the judge ordered him to purge himself with five neighbours.[55]

Three weeks later, Abbott produced five neighbours to swear to his good name. Therefore the judge 'pronounced him sufficiently purged and restored him and ordered that testimonial letter should be made 5s6d'.[56] In most instances this would be all the information that was recorded. However, in February 1580 Abbott was accused of the same offence with the wife of a farmer from a neighbouring village. This time he failed to find sufficient compurgators, and his punishment was:

> that upon sunday next at morning prayer in Earls Colne church he shall openly stand in a sheet and there openly confess bareheaded that whereas he hath lived with one *Rootes* offensively he is sorry for it desiring god and the congregation to forgive him.[57]

This gives us a good idea of the normal penance inflicted in such cases. In this instance, though, the sentence clearly had little effect on Abbott, who in the same record 'unreverently abused the judge and the court and openly did revile them presenting him to this court calling them knaves contemptuously'. Abbott's general demeanour both before and after this case indicates how the Church courts were often derided as 'bawdy courts' concerned only with salacious and sometimes malicious gossip.

   The largest single collection of accessible Church court materials is the dig-itized records of the Archdiocese of York's cause papers.[58] The York Cause papers comprise some 13,000 records of cases heard in the York Archdiocese between *c.* 1300 and 1858. As with the Church court records discussed above, they are divided between 'office' and 'instance' cases. The project website gives a clear explanation of the processes involved in instance cases between two parties, which make up many of the cases. These tend to be much more detailed than office cases, because they involve depositions by witnesses to provide evidence in cases of slander, libel, breach of promise, bigamy, adul-tery and so on. However, the digitized records on the website are normally images of the original cause papers, in Latin or English, and have not been transcribed. Therefore, while they provide an excellent training in later medi-eval and early modern palaeography, some practice is required before they can be read easily.

The equity courts

As has been noted already, the equity courts (the courts of the Exchequer, Chancery, Requests, and of the Duchy of Lancaster) and the court of Star Chamber adopted processes derived from the plenary or 'instance' processes of the Church courts. Since the equity courts decided disputes outside Common Law, it is not surprising that they became guided by the principles of civil (or Church) law developed in the two universities since the twelfth and thirteenth centuries. This applied to trial processes as well. When Thomas Wolsey wanted to establish an additional system of justice to settle disputes over illegal enclosures after 1517, he fell back on his considerable expertise as a canon lawyer, to adapt the court of Star Chamber on lines derived from the Church courts, even though it exercised a Common Law jurisdiction (earning the undying hatred of common lawyers until its abolition in 1642).[59]

The different equity courts had various names for officials (judges were called barons in the Exchequer and masters in Chancery) and processes, but their systems were broadly similar. Figure 2.3 presents a (very) simplified illustration of the equity process, and it is worth consulting specialist texts on operations of the courts of Exchequer and Chancery in the early modern period.[60] Although the process appears relatively simple in the figure, in practice each stage was contested by both sides and court officials had vested financial interests in drawing out proceedings as long as possible.[61] Eventually this created the obfuscatory system immortalized by Charles Dickens in *Bleak House* in 1856.[62] In each of these courts the process was begun by a system of bills of 'libel' and 'rejoinder'. If a dispute could not be resolved amicably, the plaintiff would pay a solicitor to draw up a bill of complaint against the person or persons he or she regarded as responsible. The Exchequer court was an offshoot of the Royal Exchequer or Treasury, and cases were supposed to involve some kind of infringement of royal rights. Star Chamber was supposed to deal with cases of riot, and the civil courts of the Duchy Chamber of Lancaster, Chancery of the County Palatine of Lancaster, Chancery of Durham and Exchequer of Chester could only hear cases involving lands within the boundaries of these jurisdictions.[63] Those accused of wrong-doing were then supposed to submit a rejoinder to attempt to clear their names, and resolve the matter. These might be followed by further bills from the plaintiff, and answers from the defendants.

In the sixteenth and early seventeenth centuries these bills, answers, rejoinders and demurrers were engrossed onto single sheets of parchment. By the mid eighteenth century they were usually much larger, with extensive excerpts from other evidence attached to them, such as extracts of accounts, wills, deeds, bonds and so on. These represent an extremely valuable window onto personal and business records that have otherwise usually been lost. These bills are full of legal verbiage designed in part to fill up space (and add cost). This makes them difficult to read, because each sentence runs the entire width of the (metre-wide) parchment, with no punctuation! Access to the bills is

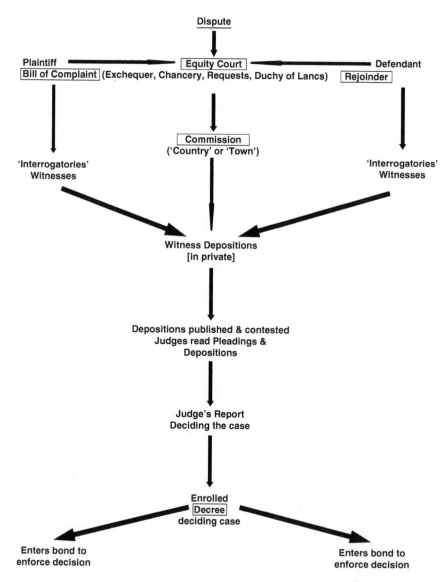

Figure 2.3 Diagram showing the process of cases through the equity courts.

dependent on the extent of cataloguing in The National Archives. Henry Horwitz estimated that there are perhaps 750,000 pieces of evidence surviving for Chancery between 1600 and 1800.[64] Every case was indexed at the time, but only by the names of the plaintiff and defendant in each session, with the session dated by regnal year (so that 1 Jas 1 would be the first year of the reign of James I, or 1603–04). For most of the 'divisions' of Chancery (each division was under the control of a separate clerk and master) these indexes also give brief descriptions of the location of the case and its subject matter (such as 'land in Denbighshire' or 'debts'). The same applies to pleadings in the Exchequer 'country' series (that is, Exchequer cases heard by commissioners in the provinces rather than in London before the barons), and the Duchy of Lancaster. Bills and answers are the most numerous type of surviving evidence from the equity courts because a substantial number of disputes progressed no further. The matter in dispute had to be very important or involve lots of people, or the parties had to be wealthy, to make further expense worthwhile.[65]

After the defendants had answered, the onus was on the plaintiff to continue the case. The judges could investigate further at this stage by delving into the written evidence and asking further questions of both parties.[66] If no settlement could be reached, each party arranged a series of witnesses to confirm their version of events. These statements could be taken in London in the courts themselves, or by commissioners chosen by the court in the provinces, to spare each party the costs of bringing a number of people to London.[67] Country depositions in Chancery and Exchequer are well catalogued, including details of location, and subject matter of the case. Town depositions are catalogued only by plaintiff and defendant's surnames.[68]

The evidence of witnesses was recorded individually and in private, but only in response to a series of questions (or 'interrogatories') drawn up by each side's solicitors. The depositions can be rather seductive documents because they appear to record individual voices, whose other opinions are otherwise lost. They give the name, age, place of residence and occupation of witnesses. Often witnesses stated their relationship to either party in the case. In Church court cases witnesses routinely had to state how much they were worth, 'all their debts being paid', evidence that Alexandra Shepard has recently exploited brilliantly.[69] Their statements provide a great deal of evidence about the lives, routines, memories, assumptions and values of ordinary villagers, neighbours, labourers, farmers, craftsmen and women in the period. Andy Wood's work *The Memory of the People* has investigated these depositions to illustrate the remembered and invented traditions used by ordinary villagers as a guide to practice in the disposition of rights, resources and responsibilities.[70]

Equity pleadings are so fascinating that it is sometimes easy to forget that they were gathered in the midst of highly adversarial court proceedings. Such statements are reported speech, noted down by a clerk and then written up later. They were supposed to be read back to the deponent, who would then attest to their accuracy, but this means that the words recorded are unlikely to represent what was actually said.[71] In addition, witnesses were directed to answer in relation to the questions posed in the (highly partisan) interrogatories. It is important to read the interrogatories as well as the depositions, because witnesses' statements sometimes parroted phrases directly from the questions. Second, witnesses were often much less forthcoming in response to the interrogatories posed by the other side ('and further he cannot depose'), because they did not want to get trapped into making statements that contradicted their original evidence. It is important to read depositions from both sides of the case, because they can often provide radically different versions of the same events, and even radically different descriptions of apparently 'fixed' things, like the landscape of an area under dispute, and of its boundaries or markers. We still do not know enough about the processes of these courts to establish how far solicitors played the system by coaching witnesses into giving evidence that they thought would be received favourably.[72]

The interrogatories and depositions were engrossed on sheets of parchment, and then sealed up, so that they could not be tampered with when they were sent to London, where they were 'published', so that the other side of the case could read and challenge them. Horwitz noted that there are still 391 boxes of sealed (that is, unopened) depositions remaining for the Court of Chancery between the reign of Elizabeth and 1778![73] In cases heard in London, each side might bring in lots of accompanying evidence, particularly records of business debts, deeds, wills or expenses going back over many years, and so on. Normally, these were returned to the parties at the end of the case. However, in Chancery quite large amounts of evidence were retained by the court for reasons that are unclear. These 'Chancery Masters' Exhibits' (classmarks C103–C116 and C171) provide remarkable insights into some of these cases and types of document that do not survive very frequently elsewhere, particularly the ledgers and accounts of early modern businesses.[74] They are catalogued fairly comprehensively by plaintiff, defendant, place, location and case details, and are available via The National Archives' online 'Discovery' catalogue system.[75] After further legal processes, including further investigations, contesting of evidence and statements, the judges would eventually write reports on the cases, which recited the evidence and gave their verdicts.[76] The successful party could then pay to have the verdict enrolled in the records of the equity court, and the court would make both parties enter into penal bonds to abide by the decision that had been reached.

As noted above, these verdicts are a potentially very valuable resource, because they are the only place in which we get evidence about how the emotive, partisan and detailed witness statements were actually interpreted by legal professionals. However, these judges' reports and decrees are difficult to access, because many cases never proceeded to a formal verdict, and because decrees are indexed only by plaintiff and defendant, making it difficult to trace a case through to its conclusion. Such judgements are important in revealing some of the hidden legal games that were being played within this information.[77]

In addition, between 1634 and 1640, the Earl Marshal's Court or the High Court of Chivalry sat to determine cases between supposedly arms-bearing gentlemen and nobles. There are 738 surviving cases, which have been studied by Richard Cust and Andrew Hopper, and organized into a searchable database by the University of Birmingham.[78]

A 1613 Court of Chancery ruling declared that all cases involving the College of Heralds had to be heard before the Earl Marshal's Court, rather than the equity courts. In 1621, one of the leading civil lawyers, Dr Arthur Duck, was appointed as King's advocate in the court, and it was determined that the Earl Marshal had jurisdiction over cases involving chivalric honour, status, names, titles and reputation, whenever there was a vacancy in the office of Lord High Constable. Duck constructed procedure in the court on civil law lines, echoing the equity courts and Star Chamber. Under Charles I 90 per cent of the business of the court pertained to adjudication in matters involving a challenge to the honour of one of the parties, as a means of preventing duelling among the elite.[79]

The cases for the Court of Chivalry are gathered together in a database. This is searchable by the names of plaintiff and defendant and the year of the case between 1634 and 1640. Cust and Hopper published a printed subject index as part of their Harleian Society volume on the Court of Chivalry, and this should be used in conjunction with the online case index to find cases relating to specific themes or controversies.[80]

Conclusion

The abundance of court cases accessible through Old Bailey Online, the plethora of printed trial reports and contemporary pamphlets to be found on *EEBO* and *ECCO* or in newspaper collections, and the powerful word-search facilities on most online databases make innovative research possible without even having to travel to an archive. Yet what we gain in instant accessibility, we sometimes lose in our understanding of the administrative processes that created a particular document, or the archival mechanisms that led to its preservation – because we no longer have to understand these in order to locate the information concerned. In this chapter, I have attempted to explain where and how legal sources were generated by the prosecution processes in criminal, ecclesiastical and civil courts. This knowledge is not crucial only to interpreting the available evidence accurately, because it explains not only what was recorded and preserved, but what was not, and *why*. Historians' understanding of this administrative context lags far behind the volume of material being put online, because we are always (and understandably) more interested in the content of legal evidence than in the processes that produced it. We can gain a working knowledge of such things without needing to become experts in Common Law writs or the business of Chancery clerks, and by doing so we can start to extract the maximum benefit from these unprecedented archival riches, opening up fresh areas for research and innovative ways of analysing these sources.

Key resources

Baker, J. H., *An Introduction to English Legal History*, 4th edn (London: Butterworths, 2002).

Calendar of Wigan Borough Court Leet Rolls, 1626–1724, http://www.wiganworld. co.uk/stuff/leet2.php?opt=leet&subopt=1 (accessed 14 April 2015).

Capital Punishment UK, http://www.capitalpunishmentuk.org/contents.html (accessed 14 April 2015).

Cause Papers in the Diocesan Courts of the Archbishopric of York, 1300–1858, http:// www.hrionline.ac.uk/causepapers/index.jsp (accessed 14 April 2015).

Cockburn, J. S., *A History of English Assizes 1558–1714* (Cambridge: Cambridge University Press, 1972).

Earls Colne, Essex: Records of an English Village 1375–1854, http://linux02.lib.cam. ac.uk/earlscolne/intro/index.htm (accessed 14 April 2015).

Horwitz, H., *Chancery Equity Records and Proceedings 1600–1800* (London: HSMO, 1995).

Horwitz, H., *Exchequer Equity Records and Proceedings, 1649–1841* (London: Public Record Office, 2001).

London Lives 1690 to 1800: Crime, Poverty and Social Policy in the Metropolis, http:// www.londonlives.org (accessed 14 April 2015).

'Middlesex Sessions Rolls: 1603', in *Middlesex County Records*, Vol. II: *1603–25*, ed. John Cordy Jeaffreson (London: Middlesex County Record Society, 1887), pp. 1–5, available at http://www.british-history.ac.uk/middx-county-records/vol2 (accessed 14 April 2015).

Norris, Henry, 'The Justicing Notebook of Henry Norris: 1730–1 (nos 1–34)', in Ruth Paley (ed.), *Justice in Eighteenth-Century Hackney the Justicing Notebook of Henry Norris and the Hackney Petty Sessions Book* (London: London Record Society, 1991), pp. 1–7, available at http://www.british-history.ac.uk/london-record-soc/ vol28/pp1-7 (accessed 14 April 2015).

The Proceedings of the Old Bailey: London's Central Criminal Court, 1674 to 1913, www.oldbaileyonline.org (accessed 4 January 2016).

Notes

1 *The Proceedings of the Old Bailey: London's Central Criminal Court, 1674–1913*, www.oldbaileyonline.org (accessed 4 January 2016).
2 J. S. Cockburn, *A History of English Assizes 1558–1714* (Cambridge: Cambridge University Press, 1972); J. H. Langbein, *Prosecuting Crime in the Renaissance: England, France, Germany* (Cambridge, MA: Harvard University Press, 1974); C. W. Brooks, *Pettyfoggers and Vipers of the Commonwealth: The Lower Branch of the Legal Profession in Early Modern England* (Cambridge: Cambridge University Press, 1986); C. B. Herrup, *The Common Peace: Participation and the Criminal Law in Seventeenth-Century England* (Cambridge: Cambridge University Press, 1987); M. Ingram, *The Church Courts, Sex and Marriage in England, 1570–1640* (Cambridge: Cambridge University Press, 1987); J. S. Cockburn and T. A. Green (eds), *Twelve Good Men and True: The Criminal Jury in England, 1200–1800* (Princeton, NJ: Princeton University Press, 1988).
3 Cockburn, *Assizes*, pp. 23–48; J. M. Beattie, 'The Pattern of Crime in England, 1660–1800', *Past & Present*, 62 (1974), 47–95; James Sharpe, *Crime in Early Modern England 1550–1750* (London: Longman, 1984), pp. 41–72; P. King, *Crime, Justice and Discretion in England, 1740–1820* (Oxford: Oxford University Press, 2000), Chapters 8–10.

4 THEFT – P. Lawson, 'Property Crime and Hard Times in England, 1559–1624', *Law and History Review*, 4 (1986), 95–127; G. Walker, 'Women, Theft and the World of Stolen Goods', in J. I. Kermode and G. Walker (eds), *Women, Crime and the Courts in Early Modern England* (London: University College London, 1994), pp. 81–105. VIOLENCE – A. Macfarlane in collaboration with Sarah Harrison, *The Justice and the Mare's Ale* (Oxford: Basil Blackwell, 1981), pp. 1–27, 171–99; S. D. Amussen, 'Punishment, Discipline and Power: The Social Meanings of Violence in Early Modern England', *Journal of British Studies*, 34 (1995), 1–34. MURDER – L. Stone, 'Interpersonal Violence in English Society, 1300–1980', *Past & Present*, 101 (1983), 22–33; J. A. Sharpe, 'The History of Violence in England: Some Observations', *Past & Present*, 108 (1985), 205–15; L. Stone, 'The History of Violence in England: A Rejoinder', *Past & Present*, 108 (1985), 216–24. WITCHCRAFT – A. Macfarlane, *Witchcraft in Tudor and Stuart England: A Regional and Comparative Study* (London: Routledge and Kegan Paul, 1970); J. A. Sharpe, *Instruments of Darkness: Witchcraft in England 1550–1750* (London: Penguin, 1996). SEXUAL OFFENCES – Ingram, *Church Courts*, pp. 169–321; G. Walker, 'Rereading Rape and Sexual Violence in Early Modern England', *Gender and History*, 10 (1998), 1–25. POACHING – E. P. Thompson, *Whigs and Hunters: The Origins of the Black Act* (London: Allen Lane, 1975); J. Broad, 'Whigs and Deer-Stealers in Other Guises: A Return to the Origins of the Black Act', *Past & Present*, 119 (1988), 56–72. SMUGGLING – W. A. Cole, 'Trends in Eighteenth-Century Smuggling', *Economic History Review*, 2nd series, 10.3 (1957–58), 395–410; H. C. Mui and L. H. Mui, '"Trends in Eighteenth-Century Smuggling" Reconsidered', *Economic History Review*, 2nd series, 28 (1975), 28–43. VAGRANCY – A. L. Beier, *Masterless Men: The Vagrancy Problem in England, 1560–1640* (London: Methuen, 1985); K. D. M. Snell, 'Pauper Settlement and the Right to Poor Relief in England and Wales', *Continuity and Change*, 6 (1991), 375–415.

5 J. Kent, *The English Village Constable, 1580–1642: A Social and Administrative Study* (Oxford: Clarendon Press, 1986); N. Landau, *The Justices of the Peace, 1679–1760* (Berkeley: University of California Press, 1984); A. J. Fletcher, *Reform in the Provinces: The Government of Stuart England* (New Haven and London: Yale University Press, 1986).

6 J. H. Baker, 'Criminal Courts and Procedure at Common Law 1550–1800', in J. S. Cockburn (ed.), *Crime in England 1550–1800* (London: Methuen, 1977), pp. 15–48; chapters by J. S. Cockburn, D. Hay and P. King, in Cockburn and Green, *Twelve Good Men and True*; P. King, 'Decision-Makers and Decision-Making in the English Criminal Law, 1750–1800', *Historical Journal*, 27 (1984), 25–58; J. H. Langbein, *The Origins of Adversary Criminal Trial* (Oxford: Oxford University Press, 2003); F. Dabhoiwala, 'Summary Justice in Early Modern London', *English Historical Review*, 121.492 (2006), 796–822.

7 T. Laqueur, 'Crowds, Carnival and the State in English Executions, 1604–1868', in A. L. Beier, David Cannadine and James M. Rosenheim (eds), *The First Modern Society* (Cambridge: Cambridge University Press, 1989), pp. 305–56; V. A. C. Gatrell, *The Hanging Tree: Execution and the English People 1770–1868* (Oxford: Oxford University Press, 1994); J. A. Sharpe, '"Last Dying Speeches": Religion, Ideology and Public Execution in Seventeenth-Century England', *Past & Present*, 107 (1985), 144–67; P. King, 'Newspaper Reporting, Prosecution Practice and Perceptions of Urban Crime: The Colchester Crime Wave of 1765', *Continuity and Change*, 2 (1987), 423–54.

8 Debates derive from N. Elias, *The Civilizing Process: Sociogenetic and Psychogenetic Investigations*, rev. edn (Oxford: Blackwell, 2000). See T. R. Gurr, 'Historical Trends in Violent Crime: A Critical Review of the Evidence', *Crime and Justice*, 3 (1981), 295–353; R. B. Shoemaker, 'Reforming Male Manners: Public Insult and the Decline of Violence in London, 1660–1740', in T. Hitchcock and M. Cohen (eds),

English Masculinities, 1660–1800 (London: Longman, 1999), pp. 133–50; P. Spierenburg, *A History of Murder: Personal Violence in Europe from the Middle Ages to the Present* (Cambridge: Polity Press, 2008).

9 See E. J. Hobsbawm, 'Social Criminality', *Society for the Study of Labour History: Bulletin*, 25 (1972), 5–6; Thompson, *Whigs and Hunters*; D. Hay, P. Linebaugh and E. P. Thompson (eds), *Albion's Fatal Tree: Crime and Society in Eighteenth-Century England* (London: Allen Lane, 1975); pp. 135–53; B. Sharp, *In Contempt of All Authority: Rural Artisans and Riot in the West of England, 1586–1660* (Berkeley and London: University of California Press, 1980); J. Innes and J. Styles, 'The Crime Wave: Recent Writing on Crime and Criminal Justice in Eighteenth-Century England', in A. Wilson (ed.), *Rethinking Social History: English Society 1570–1920 and Its Interpretation* (Manchester: Manchester University Press, 1991), pp. 201–65.

10 King, *Crime, Justice and Discretion*, Chapter 9; L. A. Knafla, '"Sin of all sorts swarmeth": Criminal Litigation in an English County in the Early Seventeenth Century', in E. W. Ives and A. H. Manchester (eds), *Law, Litigants and the Legal Profession* (London: Royal Historical Society, 1983), pp. 50–67; J. Kent, 'The English Village Constable, 1580–1642: The Nature and Dilemmas of the Office', *Journal of British Studies*, 20 (1981), 26–49; D. Hay, 'Prosecution and Power: Malicious Prosecutions in the English Courts, 1750–1850', in D. Hay and F. Snyder (eds), *Policing and Prosecution in Britain, 1750–1850* (Oxford: Clarendon Press, 1989), pp. 343–96; N. Landau, 'Indictment for Fun and Profit: A Prosecutor's Reward at Eighteenth-Century Quarter Sessions', *Law and History Review*, 17 (1999), 507–36.

11 J. A. Sharpe, (ed.), *Crime and the Law in English Satirical Prints, 1600–1832* (Cambridge: Chadwyck-Healey, 1986); J. C. Oldham, 'Truth-Telling in the Eighteenth-Century English Courtroom', *Law and History Review*, 12 (1994), 95–121; M. Gaskill, *Crime and Mentalities in Early Modern England* (Cambridge: Cambridge University Press, 2000); L. B. Faller, *Turned to Account: The Forms and Functions of Criminal Biography in Late Seventeenth- and Early Eighteenth-Century England* (Cambridge: Cambridge University Press, 1987); H. Gladfelder, *Criminality and Narrative in Eighteenth-Century England: Beyond the Law* (Baltimore: Johns Hopkins University Press, 2001); I. A. Bell, *Literature and Crime in Augustan England* (London: Routledge, 1991); C. McCreery, 'A Moral Panic in Eighteenth-Century London? The "Monster" and the Press', in D. Lemmings and C. Walker (eds), *Moral Panics, the Media and the Law in Early Modern England* (Basingstoke: Palgrave Macmillan, 2008), pp. 195–220.

12 S. D. Amussen, *An Ordered Society: Gender and Class in Early Modern England* (New York: Columbia University Press, 1988), pp. 95–133; L. Gowing, *Domestic Dangers: Women, Words and Sex in Early Modern London* (Oxford: Oxford University Press, 1996), pp. 60–110; A. Shepard, *Meanings of Manhood in Early Modern England* (Oxford: Oxford University Press, 2003), pp. 152–85.

13 R. W. Hoyle, 'Redefining Copyhold in the Sixteenth Century: The Case of Timber Rights', in B. J. P. van Bavel and P. Hoppenbrouwers (eds), *Landholding and Land Transfer in the North Sea Area (Late Middle Ages–Nineteenth Century)* (Turnhout: Brepols, 2004), pp. 250–64; N. M. Whyte, *Inhabiting the Landscape: Place, Custom and Memory, 1500–1800* (Oxford: Windgather, 2009), pp. 91–124; P. Withington, *The Politics of Commonwealth: Citizens and Freemen in Early Modern England* (Cambridge: Cambridge University Press, 2005), pp. 94–115; A. Wood, *The Memory of the People: Custom and Popular Senses of the Past in Early Modern England* (Cambridge: Cambridge University Press, 2013), pp. 43–93.

14 C. W. Brooks, *Law, Politics and Society in Early Modern England* (Cambridge: Cambridge University Press, 2008), pp. 241–77; Wood, *Memory of the People*, pp. 287–340.
15 For example: 'Middlesex Sessions Rolls: 1603', in *Middlesex County Records*, Vol. II: *1603–25*, ed. John Cordy Jeaffreson (London: Middlesex County Record Society, 1887), pp. 1–5, available at http://www.british-history.ac.uk/middx-county-records/vol2 (accessed 14 April 2015); Henry Norris, 'The Justicing Notebook of Henry Norris: 1730–1 (nos 1–34)', in Ruth Paley (ed.), *Justice in Eighteenth-Century Hackney: The Justicing Notebook of Henry Norris and the Hackney Petty Sessions Book* (London: London Record Society, 1991), pp. 1–7, available at http://www.british-history.ac.uk/london-record-soc/vol28/pp1-7 (accessed 14 April 2015); Capital Punishment UK, http://www.capitalpunishmentuk.org/contents.html (accessed 14 April 2015); *Calendar of Wigan Borough Court Leet Rolls, 1626–1724*, http://www.wiganworld.co.uk/stuff/leet2.php?opt=leet&subopt=1 (accessed 14 April 2015); *Cause Papers in the Diocesan Courts of the Archbishopric of York, 1300–1858*, http://www.hrionline.ac.uk/causepapers/index.jsp (accessed 14 April 2015).
16 http://eebo.chadwyck.com/home; http://gale.cengage.co.uk/product.../eighteenth-century-collections-online (both accessed 12 January 2016).
17 C. Harrison, 'Manor Courts and the Governance of Tudor England', in C. W. Brooks and B. Lobban (eds), *Communities and Courts in Britain 1150–1900* (London and Rio Grande: Hambledon Press, 1997), pp. 43–60; M. K. McIntosh, *Controlling Misbehaviour in England, 1370–1600* (Cambridge: Cambridge University Press, 1998), pp. 34–45; B. Waddell, 'Governing England through the Manor Courts 1550–1850', *Historical Journal*, 55.2 (2012), 279–315.
18 P. Holdsworth, 'Manorial Administration in Westmorland 1589–1693', *Transactions of the Cumberland and Westmorland Antiquarian and Archaeological Society*, 3rd series, 5 (2005), 137–65.
19 Cockburn, *Assizes*, pp. 86–134.
20 See Kent, *English Village Constable*, pp. 80–151.
21 Ibid., p. 75.
22 See H. R. French, *The Middle Sort of People in Provincial England 1600–1720* (Oxford: Oxford University Press, 2007), pp. 90–140.
23 Ibid., pp. 25–50.
24 J. H. Gleason, *The Justices of the Peace in England, 1558–1640* (Oxford: Clarendon Press, 1969), p. 85.
25 Michael Dalton, *The countrey iustice conteyning the practise of the iustices of the peace out of their sessions. Gathered for the better helpe of such iustices of peace as haue not beene much conuersant in the studie of the lawes of this realme. By Michael Dalton of Lincolnes Inne, Gent.* (London: printed [by Adam Islip] for the Societie of Stationers, An. Dom. M.DC.XVIII. [1618]), *STC*, 6205.
26 Sheriffs' main responsibilities became organizing and paying for hospitality at the Assizes, and staging parliamentary elections. Cockburn, *Assizes*, pp. 105–7.
27 B. W. Quintrell, 'The Making of Charles I's Book of Orders', *English Historical Review*, 95.376 (1980), 553–72.
28 Herrup, *Common Peace*, p. 90.
29 Cockburn, *Assizes*, pp. 102–3.
30 Sir T. Skyrme, *History of the Justices of the Peace*, Vol. I: *England to 1689* (Chichester: Barry Rose and the Justice of the Peace, 1991), pp. 138–62.
31 Dabhoiwala, 'Summary Justice', p. 797.
32 Summary cases could be appealed to Quarter Sessions after 1670. J. H. Baker, *An Introduction to English Legal History*, 4th edn (London: Butterworths, 2002), p. 511.

33 For Norris, see above, n15; E. Crittall (ed.), *The Justicing Notebook of William Hunt 1744–1749* (Wiltshire: Wiltshire Record Society, 1982); G. Morgan and P. Rushton (eds), *The Justicing Notebook (1750–64) of Edmund Tew, Rector of Boldon*, Publications of the Surtees Society, 205 (Woodbridge: Boydell Press for the Surtees Society, 2000).
34 Morgan and Rushton, *Edmund Tew*, p. 16.
35 For more on State Papers see Chapter 1 of this volume, pp. 15–34.
36 Skyrme, *Justices of the Peace*, Vol. I, pp. 256–66.
37 Cockburn, *Assizes*, pp. 91–7, gives numerous examples of this distinction being breached into the mid seventeenth century.
38 Ibid., pp. 185–6.
39 Ibid., p. 136.
40 Ibid., pp. 186–205.
41 Available via www.alanmacfarlane.com (accessed 14 April 2015). *Earls Colne, Essex: Records of an English Village 1375–1854*, http://linux02.lib.cam.ac.uk/earls-colne/session/20500772.htm, Quarter Sessions Rolls (ERO Q/SR 197/28), 6 January 1612 [20500772] (accessed 14 April 2015). Archival citations may no longer match current Essex Records Office catalogue entries.
42 *Earls Colne: Records*, http://linux02.lib.cam.ac.uk/earlscolne/session/21100005.htm, Quarter Sessions Process Books of Indictments (ERO Q/SPa2/1), January 1612 [21100005] (accessed 14 April 2015).
43 For a full discussion of these circuits see Cockburn, *Assizes*, pp. 23–48.
44 Ibid., p. 136. *Nisi prius* ('unless before') described the terms of the writ used for such business. This specified that the case would be heard at Westminster unless it was tried on the Assize circuit before that date. Such writs were normally dated *after* the next available Assizes, to ensure that they were heard locally. Ibid., p. 17n6.
45 *Earls Colne: Records*, http://linux02.lib.cam.ac.uk/earlscolne/common/14000659.htm, Assize Indictments (PRO ASSI35/51/T), June 1608 [14000659] (accessed 14 April 2015).
46 http://www.oldbaileyonline.org/static/Crime.jsp (accessed 4 January 2016).
47 P. Lake, 'Deeds against Nature: Cheap Print, Protestantism and Murder in Early Seventeenth-Century England', in K. Sharpe and P. Lake (eds), *Culture and Politics in Early Stuart England* (Basingstoke: Macmillan, 1994), pp. 257–83, 361–7.
48 *London Lives 1690 to 1800: Crime, Poverty and Social Policy in the Metropolis*, http://www.londonlives.org/static/Background.jsp, version 1.1 (accessed 14 April 2014).
49 Baker, *English Legal History*, p. 521.
50 D. Hay, *Criminal Cases on the Crown Side of King's Bench: Staffordshire, 1740–1800*, Collections for the History of Staffordshire, 4th series, 24 (Stafford: Staffordshire Record Society, 2010); R. Paley, 'The Kings Bench (Crown Side) in the Long Eighteenth Century' in C. Dyer, A. J. Hopper, E. Lord and N. J. Tringham (eds), *New Directions in Local History since Hoskins* (Hatfield: University of Hertfordshire Press, 2011), pp. 231–46.
51 Baker, *English Legal History*, p. 131. The Court's power to force witnesses to incriminate themselves via the *ex officio* oath was particularly unpopular, and it was abolished with Star Chamber in 1642.
52 http://linux02.lib.cam.ac.uk/earlscolne/reference/church.htm. See also Gowing, *Domestic Dangers*, pp. 30–59.
53 The classic study is K. Wrightson and D. Levine, *Poverty and Piety in an English Village: Terling 1525–1700*, 2nd edn (Oxford: Oxford University Press, 1996), pp. 110–41.
54 Ingram, *Church Courts*, pp. 323–63.

55 *Earls Colne: Records*, http://linux02.lib.cam.ac.uk/earlscolne/office/1002162.htm, Archdeaconry Act Book (ERO D/ACA8), 2 October 1578 [1002162] (accessed 14 April 2015).

56 *Earls Colne: Records*, http://linux02.lib.cam.ac.uk/earlscolne/office/1002171.htm, Archdeaconry Act Book (ERO D/ACA8), 25 October 1578 [1002171] (accessed 14 April 2015).

57 *Earls Colne: Records*, http://linux02.lib.cam.ac.uk/earlscolne/office/1100070.htm, Archdeaconry Act Book (ERO D/ACA8), 8 February 1580 [1100070] (accessed 14 April 2015).

58 *Cause Papers*. For information on how the courts worked see University of York, 'What Are Cause Papers?', http://www.york.ac.uk/borthwick/holdings/guides/research-guides/what-are-causepapers (accessed 4 January 2016).

59 Baker, *English Legal History*, p. 118.

60 H. Horwitz, *Exchequer Equity Records and Proceedings, 1649–1841* (London: Public Record Office, 2001); H. Horwitz, *Chancery Equity Records and Proceedings 1600–1800* (London: HSMO, 1995).

61 For a full transcript of a series of early-eighteenth-century Exchequer cases, see T. Gates (ed.), ' "The Great Trial": A Swaledale Lead Mining Dispute in the Court of Exchequer, 1705–1708', *Yorkshire Archaeological Society Record Series*, 162 (2011–12), introduction, pp. xix–li.

62 Baker, *English Legal History*, pp. 111–13.

63 Ibid., p. 121n21. The Duchy Chamber jurisdiction encompassed the lands of the Duke of Lancaster (across England), the County Palatine of Lancaster the lands within the county of Lancashire.

64 Horwitz, *Chancery*, p. 30.

65 Ibid., pp. 13–17.

66 Ibid., pp. 17–18.

67 Ibid., pp. 18–20.

68 Ibid., pp. 60–2.

69 A. Shepard, *Accounting for Oneself: Worth, Status, and the Social Order in Early Modern England* (Oxford: Oxford University Press, 2015), pp. 35–81.

70 Wood, *Memory of the People*, pp. 156–87.

71 C. Churches, ' "The Most Unconvincing Testimony": The Genesis and Historical Usefulness of the Country Depositions in Chancery', *The Seventeenth Century*, 11 (1996), 209–27.

72 Ibid., pp. 215–16.

73 Horwitz, *Chancery*, p. 62.

74 Horwitz lists 3,430 boxes of surviving Masters' Exhibits! Ibid., pp. 66–7.

75 http://discovery.nationalarchives.gov.uk (accessed 5 January 2016).

76 Horwitz, *Chancery*, pp. 20–2, 64–6.

77 Churches, 'The Most Unconvincing Testimony', p. 217.

78 University of Birmingham, 'The High Court of Chivalry in the Early Seventeenth Century', http://www.birmingham.ac.uk/schools/historycultures/departments/history/research/projects/court-of-chivalry/seventeenth-century/index.aspx (accessed 4 January 2016). R. P. Cust, *Charles I and the Aristocracy, 1625–1642* (Cambridge: Cambridge University Press, 2013), pp. 140–71.

79 R. P. Cust and A. J. Hopper, 'Duelling and the Court of Chivalry in Early Stuart England', in S. Carroll (ed.), *Cultures of Violence: Interpersonal Violence in Historical Perspective* (Basingstoke: Palgrave Macmillan, 2007), pp. 156–74.

80 R. P. Cust and A. J. Hopper (eds), *Cases in the High Court of Chivalry 1634–1640*, Harleian Society, n.s. 18 (London: Harleian Society, 2006).

3 Ecclesiastical sources

Jonathan Willis

Introduction

This chapter deals loosely with early modern ecclesiastical sources: that is, sources relating to or generated by the Church. At first glance this might seem like quite a narrow topic; however, both religion and the Church were intimately involved in almost every aspect of early modern life. Two things may therefore be observed about early modern ecclesiastical sources at the outset. First, the boundaries of the category are artificial and porous. Is an Act of Parliament regarding the Church a religious document, or a political one? Is an individual's last will and testament an ecclesiastical source, a personal document or a legal instrument? Even attempting to categorize sources according to the individual or institution generating them is problematic. When the King is also Supreme Head of the Church, are his instructions for how that Church should be run given by him in a temporal (earthly) or sacred (religious) capacity? Is everything written by a clergyman automatically an 'ecclesiastical' source? This chapter will not attempt to provide neat answers to these questions, but I would like to suggest that they raise some interesting issues for consideration. Second, the breadth of influence of the Church in the political, economic, social and cultural spheres, as well as the religious, means that 'ecclesiastical' sources can reveal a huge amount about early modern life in general, not just the Church itself. A good deal of this chapter will explore the ability of ecclesiastical sources to shed light on early modern religion and religious change, but where appropriate it will also highlight areas where these sources can be used in other interesting and unexpected ways. If this chapter aims to do anything, it is to demonstrate beyond doubt that nobody should be put off by words like 'ecclesiastical', 'Church' or 'religion'. This is a diverse, rich and fascinating seam of historical evidence, and there is something here for everybody.

Shaping the Church

Let us begin our survey of ecclesiastical sources with a discussion of the documents that helped to shape the Church itself. The early modern period was, as much as anything else, the age of Reformation. The unified Latin Christendom that had held sway in Western Europe for over a millennium was irrevocably fractured at the beginning of the sixteenth century, and so the Church as an institution had to be reimagined, reinvented and reformed. I will use England as my case study; its experience may be taken as illustrative, but should not be seen as typical, for every country in Europe experienced Reformation differently. Revisionist historians such as Christopher Haigh, Jack Scarisbrick and (most comprehensively) Eamon Duffy have shown us that England was perhaps one of the least likely candidates in Europe for a fully fledged Protestant Reformation, because of the strength of lay piety in and popular enthusiasm for the late medieval Church.[1] However, Henry VIII's desire to rid himself of his first wife, Catherine of Aragon (who over the course of two decades of marriage had proved herself incapable of bearing him the legitimate son he so desperately craved) unexpectedly aligned with the activities of a small but zealous group of evangelical reformers, and resulted in England breaking away from the Church of Rome. Owing in part to the influence of Thomas Cromwell, the English Reformation was at the outset conducted largely through a series of legislative changes, and it is still possible to study and glean some interesting information from those formative Acts of Parliament, such as the 'Act in Restraint of Appeals' (1533) and the 'Act of Supremacy' (1534). Some of these key texts exist in edited forms, published and online, but the most comprehensive database of such legislation is probably the nine-volume *Statutes of the Realm*, published in the early nineteenth century, and also accessible digitally through the subscription resource HeinOnline.[2] Document calendars (summaries) and references to the enforcement of this type of legislation are also available through the various State Papers resources (*Letters and Papers, State Papers Online, British History Online*, etc.).[3] Such Acts of Parliament are interesting not only for what they say, but also for how they say it: they are rhetorical as much as they are bureaucratic documents. For example, the 1534 Act of Supremacy begins:

> Albeit the Kynges Majestie justely and rightfully is & oweth to be the supreme heed of the Churche of England, and so is recognysed by the Clergy of this Realme in their convocacions; yet neverthelesse, for cor-roboracion & confirmacion thereof, and for increase of vertue in Christis Religion within this Realme of England, and to repress and extirpe all errours, heresies, and other enormyties and abuses heretofore used in the same, Be it enacted, by aucthorite of this present Parliament that the Kyng our soveraign Lorde, his heires and successours Kynges of this Realme shalbe takyn acceptyd & reputed the onely supreme heed in erthe of the Churche of England called *Anglicana Ecclesia*.[4]

The text reveals that England's radical break with the Church of Rome (which is not mentioned once in the Act by name) was presented to contemporaries not as an innovation, as something new, but merely as the formal confirmation of a pre-existing state of affairs. Henry was keen to present his actions not as radical and reckless, but as being in line with the ancient traditions and customs of England, and so his legislation was worded accordingly. This was nonsense – the content of the Act was unprecedented in English history – but through careful rhetorical framing Henry was essentially able to construct his own alternate version of reality.[5]

As well as legislation of the type just discussed, national churches in the early modern period were also shaped by statements of faith, known as 'confessions'. Nothing to do with the process of individual or collective confession to a priest, or the Catholic sacrament of penance, historians often speak of early modern Europe as a 'confessional age', and have even written extensively in favour and against a so-called 'confessionalization thesis'. This thesis posits that, as the number of variants of Christianity proliferated and became increasingly narrowly defined, Church and State worked ever more closely together to regulate the beliefs and behaviours of their citizens.[6] That historiographical debate does not concern us here, but the fact remains that these 'confessions', which took the form of programmatic statements of belief, are an important source for understanding the Reformation churches, and the differences between them. Perhaps the most famous of all such statements was the *Confessio Augustana*, or Augsburg Confession, submitted to the Catholic Holy Roman Emperor Charles V by the Lutheran cities and princes of the empire in 1530. Consisting of a lengthy preface and some twenty-eight articles, the Augsburg Confession outlines the Lutheran faith at this key point in time. To give just one example, Article IV, 'Of Justification', begins: 'men cannot be justified before God by their own strength, merits, or works, but are freely justified for Christ's sake, through faith' – a clear statement of the core Lutheran doctrine of justification by grace through faith alone.[7] Most Lutheran territories within the Holy Roman Empire developed their own confessional church orders, sometimes based upon but often significantly different from one other, and these can also fruitfully be compared and contrasted, both against one another and with previous editions as they were modified over time.[8] Other Protestant confessions include the First and Second Helvetic Confessions (for the Reformed Churches), and the Edwardian Forty-Two Articles and Elizabethan Thirty-Nine Articles (for England).[9] The Catholic Church did not produce a comparable neat list of articles of faith in quite the same way, but the canons and decrees of the Council of Trent are also, in a sense, a confessional document, containing a comprehensive series of judgements on key matters of doctrine and belief.[10]

Teaching, preaching and worship

While legislative frameworks and confessions shaped the overarching beliefs and structures of early modern Churches, a different set of documents give an overview of the day-to-day teaching, preaching and worship that went on in individual parishes. On a fundamental level, one of the most important sources we have for knowing what went on in churches (or at least, what was *supposed* to be going on in them) is liturgical documents. The liturgy of a particular national or regional church was effectively the dramatic script that determined what the minister and congregation should say and do during formal religious services. Liturgical sources therefore contain important information about theological belief, but they also tell us about how the clergy and laity interacted, and the relative priorities of different activities. Liturgical sources could be merely indicative, such as Luther's 'German Mass and Order of Divine Service' (1526), in which he explained:

> Nor is it my meaning that the whole of Germany should have to adopt forthwith our Wittenberg Order. It never was the case that the ministers, convents, and parishes were alike in everything. But it would be a grand thing if, in every several lordship, Divine Service were conducted in one fashion; and the neighbouring little townships and villages joined in the cry with one city. Whether in other lordships they should do the same or something different, should be left free and without penalty.[11]

Other liturgies were prescribed and enforced with much greater unity, however. One of the most famous and enduring early modern liturgies was the English Book of Common Prayer (BCP), or rather its various editions (1549, 1552, 1559, 1662).[12] The BCP contained the liturgies for morning and evening prayer, Holy Communion, baptism, the funeral service, marriages, and much more besides: the texts (both the addresses and prayers composed for the rite, as well as the inclusion of specific passages from the Old and New Testaments) therefore tell us much about attitudes to community, to death, to women, to children, etc. As well as common prayers to be used routinely in churches, the Church of England also regularly produced special liturgies to be used in recognition of particular trials and triumphs, such as the defeat of the Gunpowder Plot in 1605, or in times of plague. Many of these texts are available through *EEBO*, or in Victorian editions, but as of 2013 there is also a very impressive modern critical edition of Special Prayers published under the auspices of the Church of England Record Society.[13] Liturgical texts were just one of many types of books that individual churches might be required to own. In England, for example, it was required by law for churches to own a copy of the Bible (in English). Under Edward VI churches were required to purchase Erasmus' paraphrases of the gospels, and churches might also commonly own a prose psalter; one or more books of Psalms in metre; Foxe's *Acts and Monuments*; Musculus' *Commonplaces*; and a range of other religious, musical or other learned texts.

The business of the Church did not end with the provision of the liturgy: religious education was another vitally important part of its mission. The early modern period was the great age of the catechism: that is, of texts designed to educate 'Children in Yeeres and Children in Understanding' in the fundamental tenets of the faith.[14] Luther wrote two catechisms – the *Kleine Catechismus* (small catechism) for the education of younger children, and a large catechism to aid in the training of clergymen themselves. Some catechisms are very well known indeed – the reformed Heidelberg Catechism, Alexander Nowell's Latin Catechism and its English translation – but there are huge numbers of Lutheran, Reformed, English and Catholic catechisms, of varying lengths, formats and degrees of complexity, which remain understudied.[15] There were, generally speaking, four elements common to all catechisms: expositions of the Ten Commandments, the Creed, the Lord's Prayer and the Sacraments (seven or two, depending on the confession). Catholic catechisms also tended to include additional elements, such as the 'Ave Maria'; 'Commandments of the Church'; lists of sins, virtues, vices; and more. Some very interesting work has been done, and continues to be done, on catechisms.[16] Clearly the emphasis is again on theology and belief, but in catechetical expositions of the Ten Commandments, for example, we also find out a great deal about attitudes to sexual morality ('Thou shalt not commit adultery'), violence ('Thou shalt not kill'), parental authority ('Honour thy father and thy mother'), and honest (and dishonest) economic conduct ('Thou shalt not steal').

It is also possible to learn much about faith, morality, and social and cultural attitudes through the printed texts of sermons. Most sermons, of course, were produced not by the Church as an institution, but by individuals, although in many parts of Europe preachers needed to have a special licence from the Church authorities in order to be able to deliver sermons in church.[17] English clerics, however, also had recourse to two volumes of pre-prepared sermons, or homilies, written by leading Protestant reformers during the reigns of Edward VI and Elizabeth I. These homilies covered topics from 'the reading and knowledge of Holy Scripture', through 'the misery of mankind', 'salvation', 'faith', 'the fear of death', 'gluttony', 'fasting', 'rebellion' and everything in between.[18] Two of the main difficulties in dealing with sermons are: first, that we often don't know where, when or to whom they were delivered; and second, that it is frequently impossible to tell how far the published version accurately represents the sermon as it may have been preached.[19] The Books of Homilies do not completely dispel these problems, but we can safely say that most of the population of England heard these sermons many, many times over the course of their lives, and that the printed texts remained unchanged over decades, even if individual performances of them may have varied.

Running the Church

We also know a lot about the activities of early modern churches because of the lists of instructions that were given to regulate their behaviour, as well as periodic investigations that aimed to monitor and assess their performance. Some of these sources can be grouped under the broad label 'visitation articles and injunctions', which includes several different types of document.

Sets of injunctions (essentially lists of instructions) could be generated at the very highest levels. One of Thomas Cromwell's first acts as Henry VIII's Vicegerent in Spirituals (effectively 'deputy head' of the Church of England), was to issue a set of injunctions in 1536, which demanded of the clergy that:

> To the intent that all superstition and hypocrisy, crept into divers men's hearts, may vanish away, they shall not set forth or extol any images, relics or miracles for any superstition or lucre, nor allure the people by any enticements to the pilgrimage of any saint.[20]

This was followed by a second, more radical set of injunctions in 1538. Edward VI, Mary I and Elizabeth I all issued their own sets of Royal Injunctions, which are an incredibly succinct and telling way to chart the changing religious priorities of the successive Tudor monarchs.[21] Mary's, for example, discussed at considerable length the penalties to be faced by married priests, while Elizabeth's made careful provision for the maintenance of the elaborate forms of church music of which she herself was so fond. Injunctions contain plenty of theology, but they also allow us to get much closer to considering the practical impact of religious reform in the local setting. What was ordered to be taken out of churches, and what was to be put up in its place? How were ministers to conduct themselves? How should the laity behave? As well as Royal Injunctions, issued by the monarch to the entire national Church, individual bishops also had the right to issue injunctions for all of the clergy in their own diocese. Some bishops – such as Hooper of Gloucester – were tireless reformers, while others – e.g. Parkhurst of Norwich – proved to be pretty useless administrators, even when their heart was in the right place. Bishops and archbishops were also entitled to conduct periodic visitations of the churches and cathedrals within their diocese or province, and to assess the performance of the clergy and the learning of the laity. Lists of questions, or interrogatories, were demanded of the clergy or laity (or both), although sadly the answers to these inquisitions generally do not survive.[22] One of the most thorough English visitations, however, was Bishop Hooper's visitation of the Diocese of Gloucester in 1551, in which he discovered that, of 311 members of the clergy examined, 168 did not know the Ten Commandments.[23] In the Lutheran context visitation records and lay responses have been controversially used to demonstrate the failure of official Church teachings to take root in the hearts and minds of the German populace.[24]

Visitations were comparatively rare events in the life of the average parish church. For an insight into the experience of church worship as felt by the majority of ordinary people during the rest of the time we need to turn from centrally generated sources to the parochial document par excellence, the churchwardens' accounts (Figure 3.1). The parish, and the parish church, were at the centre of most people's religious lives. Tradition dictated that while the clergy were responsible for the upkeep of the chancel – the holiest

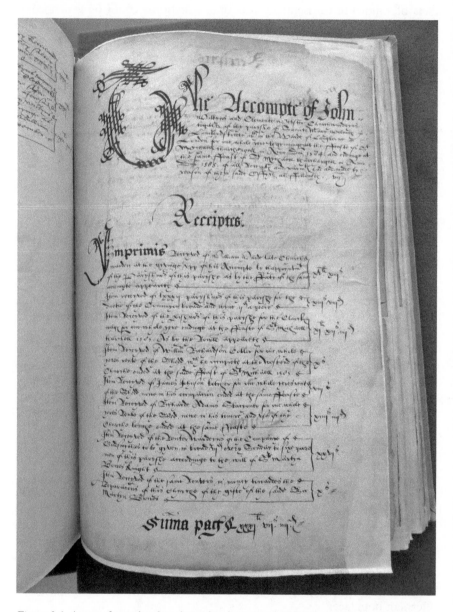

Figure 3.1 A page from the churchwardens' accounts of St Mary Woolnoth, London, London Metropolitan Archives, P69/MRY15B, not paginated (1585).

part of the church, at the east end of the building – the main body of the church (the nave) was the responsibility of the congregation: the parish community as a whole. Over the medieval period, therefore, the office of churchwarden evolved. This was a temporary elected official, drawn from amongst the better sort in the local community, who was responsible for maintaining the finances of the parish church, collecting receipts, and paying for necessary maintenance and improvements.[25] Churchwardens usually served in pairs, and were required to keep detailed accounts of their income and expenditures, which were usually presented to the rest of the parish annually, at which point one or more replacement churchwardens would be elected. Accounts usually begin with the name of the parish/church, the names of the churchwardens and the year of the account. Receipts for things like rents and sales of goods and services come next, followed by the longest part of the account, the list of disbursements (payments), with figures given in roman numerals, in pounds, shillings and pence. The following is a reproduction of the account produced by the wardens of St Michael's Church in Cornhill (London) in 1570:

1570
Thomas Porte, William Hawle and George Dale, Wardens.

RECEIPTES

General Receipts	xxij^{li} xvij^s ij^d
And for the poore	xviij^{li} v^s viij^d
Item in the hands of Mr Aldreman Haws	Cxx^{li}

PAYMENTES

Item paide for ij Pslastere [*sic*] bookes the viijth of Decemb	iij^s viij^d
Item paide for mending of the Communion booke	xvj^d
Item paide for a prayer of thanckes gevinge for the over throwe of the Rebelles in the North	iij^d
Item paide unto Mr Kydd for making of the wrytinges for ye newe ffeffers of ye Churche landes	v^s
Item paide for mending of the greate bell clapper	iij^s iiij^d
Item paide to Mr Atkynson the scryvener for drawinge a draughte of the writinges for the newe howsys	ij^s
Generall Paymentes	xxij^{li} vj^s v^d
And to the Poore	xij^{li} viij^s x^d

This is a short account – they don't come much shorter, and some can go on for many pages – but it gives a good indication of the sorts of routine and extraordinary detail that can be found in churchwardens' accounts.[26] We have here a sense of how parish finances could be augmented through the purchase, ownership, letting and sale of land and property, through references to payments to professionals for drawing up legal documents ('ye newe ffeffers', i.e. feoffees, or trustees). We get an impression of the rhythms of liturgy, through repairs to the BCP, and the purchase of two psalters (probably prose Psalm books; the hymn-like rhyming versions of the Psalms tended to be described as 'Psalm books' or 'in metre'). We get a hint of the social and ritual significance of bells, which loom larger than most other expenditures in English churchwardens' accounts.[27] And we also see the purchase in this year of a special prayer giving thanks to God for the Government's defeat of the Catholic Northern Rising in 1569, a topical event of national significance.

Churchwardens' accounts have some significant limitations. They can tell you *what* was done, but not *why* it was done. When Edwardian churchwardens were ordered to overpaint 'offensive' religious imagery, they dutifully recorded the expense for the whitewash and the labour in their accounts, but we cannot usually tell whether the undertaking was characterized by enthusiastic zeal or grudging compliance. Churchwardens' accounts can also seem seductively comprehensive, whereas we know from some detailed case studies that they rarely captured all of the activities of the parish community.[28] Eamon Duffy's *Voices of Morebath* is a brilliant example of how churchwardens' accounts can be used to tell a complex and moving story of historical change in a small rural village community, but only because of the atypically rich and detailed nature of the accounts (including some personal commentary on events by the priest, Christopher Trychay).[29] Still, precisely because of their often mundane nature, such accounts can tell us about much more than just religious matters. Payments for labour and materials for work done on the church building and grounds can tell us about prices and construction methods, as well as how and by whom such work was usually carried out. As well as the ritual and festive life of the parish, we also gain an insight into named members of the community, and their involvement with the parish church. It is also the case that the expenditures detailed in churchwardens' accounts can tell us a lot about the importance of music, of bells and of investment in material culture within the church.[30] The percentage of churchwardens' accounts that survive today is minuscule in comparison to the *c.* 9,000 parishes that existed in early modern England; however, there is a good range of published material. There is no fully comprehensive or reliable list of printed churchwardens' accounts, but the best finding aid is probably still the list of extant accounts in the appendix to Ronald Hutton's *Rise and Fall of Merry England*.[31]

Parish churches, of course, were not the only ecclesiastical institution in early modern Europe generating valuable source material. Even heavily mobile religious orders, like the Jesuits, generated huge quantities of letters and other documents, which give an insight into their missionary efforts across the globe, from Asia to the New World, an increasing number of which are becoming available in translation, in modern editions.[32] So too did more physically rooted institutions, such as monasteries and cathedrals. Save for a distinctly half-hearted attempt at Marian restoration, England's monasteries shut their doors for good during the reign of Henry VIII, but England was unusual amongst Reformed Churches in maintaining a structure of bishops and cathedrals, and a great many records survive that give an insight into the administration of cathedrals and the lives of their staff, although the amount of material that has been translated (usually from Latin) and published is relatively small. Still, we have easy access to a fairly wide range of materials, such as the statutes of Lincoln Cathedral, a calendar of the manuscripts of Wells Cathedral, the chapter acts of Lincoln, Bishop Redman's visitation of Norwich, extracts from the minute books of Norwich Cathedral and more besides.[33] Chapter acts and similar sources relate solely to the closed world of the cathedral, but they are far from dull. Richard Marwood, a vicar choral at Wells Cathedral, was convicted of sexual incontinence on 17 April 1601, and ordered to do penance as follows:

> uppon the first day of July next following he shall come into the chapter howse between the howers of ix and xi of the fornoon, in his usuall apparel, and that before the chapter and company of the vicars ... then presente, he shall kneel downe on his knees and openly confess his offens, viz that he hath committed the cryme of fornicacion or adultery with Susan Giffard, and that he is hartely sory therfor, and shall desire God to forgeve hym his offence and the company there present for his ill example; and further betwixt this day and the first day of July next, he shall write and prick out services for the quyer of the cathedral church, at the discretion of Mr D Cottington, the chaunter of the said church, or his deputy.[34]

Even (sometimes especially) religious institutions had to cope with the same human weaknesses as the rest of early modern society.

Policing behaviour

The punishment of a fornicating vicar choral in the chapter acts of Wells Cathedral takes us out of the world of the day-to-day running of the Church, and well and truly into the world of punishment and behavioural enforcement. Most people (not living or working in a cathedral precinct) would not have had anything to do with the justice meted out by cathedral chapters, but they would more than likely at some point in their lives have had some contact with the Church courts, as either a claimant, a defendant or a witness. In Chapter 2 of this book, Henry French gives an excellent overview of the structure, organization and business of the Church courts, and I do not intend to replicate that information here. It is worth pointing out, however, that of all ecclesiastical sources, churchwardens' presentments and the records of the business of the Church courts are probably some of the most colourful and versatile. The crimes dealt with by the Church courts encompassed church attendance, and 'religious' offences such as blasphemy or working on the Sabbath, but also a wide range of moral offences, such as those concerning defamation and allegations of sexual misconduct. These sources, therefore, are not only entertaining to work with; they can also shed light on a wide variety of activities. The churchwardens' presentments for Banbury (an ecclesiastical Peculiar jurisdiction administered by the Dean and Chapter of Lincoln), a notable puritan town in the early modern period, reveal community strife between godly puritan parishioners and their conformist co-religionists. The godly minister, William Whately, was presented for administering communion to those who would not kneel (in breach of the rubrics or instructions in the BCP), and in turn a local parish clerk was presented for *not* administering to those who would not kneel.[35] Historians such as Martin Ingram have made brilliant use of Church Court records to study gender relations, the language of sexual insult, and popular views of sexual and criminal morality, and this remains a fertile field of study.[36] Churchwardens' presentments exist in published form for a number of towns, including Banbury and Stratford-upon-Avon, and Henry French also discusses the Cause Papers of the Diocesan Courts of the Archbishopric of York in his chapter; this is a valuable catalogue and manuscript archive, which is available online.[37]

One of the most dramatic forms of ecclesiastical justice in the early modern period was the heresy examination. Religious violence and persecution have been a significant growth area for researchers in recent years, and continue to fascinate, in part perhaps because religious violence is (unfortunately) still a feature of the modern world in which we live. The harshest punishment that could be handed down by the Church courts was excommunication – penance or a fine was much more common – but while heresy examinations generally began under ecclesiastical supervision, those judged guilty were handed over to the secular arm for execution, usually by burning. One man's (or woman's) heretic in early modern Europe was often somebody else's martyr, and individuals like Jean Crespin and Simon Goulart in France, and John Foxe in England, began to record every aspect of the persecution of their religious brethren in voluminous martyrologies. These are problematic documents – biased, selective, polemical – but they often represent the best sources of evidence we have about contemporary persecutions. As well as containing detailed narratives, they also record the speech of the accused (sometimes invented), as well as transcribing letters or examinations, often with a heavy editorial gloss. A recent University of Sheffield/British Academy project produced a brilliant scholarly edition of Foxe's *Acts and Monuments*, combining the 1563, 1570, 1576 and 1583 editions, which is available to view online, without subscription.[38] Other key martyrological texts include John Bale's edition of the examinations of Anne Askew, as well as Crespin's *Livres des martyrs* and Richard Verstegan's *Theatrum crudelitatum haereticorum nostri temporis*, which contains detailed images of the persecution of Catholic martyrs by Protestant authorities. John Foxe's 'book of martyrs' has generated a cottage industry of academic research all of its own, while transformative works on Catholic, Protestant and even Anabaptist martyrs have been written recently by Eamon Duffy, Brad Gregory, Peter Lake and Michael Questier, to name but a few.[39]

Elizabethan England famously pronounced that it did not execute Catholics for religious reasons, but only traitors convicted of treasonous behaviour. That, at least, was the rhetoric of William Cecil's *Execution of Justice in England*; the reality was that the state redrew the definition of what constituted 'treason' significantly enough to catch out anybody consorting with a foreign priest or dealing in Catholic books or holy objects.[40] But while relatively few English Catholics were executed (at least as a proportion of the broader Catholic population), many more were caught up by the increasingly stringent recusancy laws. Recusants were defined as those people who refused to go to church (from the Latin *recusare*, to refuse). Not everybody who refused to go to church in Elizabethan England was a Catholic, and not all Elizabethan Catholics refused to go to church. Still, church attendance was compulsory, and persistent failure to attend was enough to draw the suspicion of the authorities. Until 1581 recusancy was dealt with by the Quarter Sessions and Assize Courts; from 1581 until 1592 it was dealt with by the Exchequer; and from 1592 the Elizabethan Government empowered special commissions to round up and investigate potential Catholic dissidents in a given county, with offenders' names recorded in dedicated Recusancy Rolls. Some of this evidence remains in manuscript form, in The National Archives and in various county record offices, but much has been published, for example in the volumes of the Catholic Record Society.[41] Anthony Petti's transcriptions of recusant examinations taken from the Ellesmere manuscripts provide some fascinating details of how imprisoned Catholic recusants responded to questions about the right of Elizabeth I to rule, and of the Pope to excommunicate her, or sanction an invasion of England, together with information about the age, gender, occupation and social status of the individuals under interrogation.[42]

Books, buildings and goodbyes

This final section discusses three further important 'ecclesiastical' sources, but there is no particular link between them, whatever the half-hearted alliteration of the subheading might suggest. All three overlap with other chapters in this book, and so my comments on each will be relatively brief.

First, early modern society was awash with religious print: books, pamphlets, woodcuts, ballads, treatises, commentaries, expositions and sermons; texts designed to educate, to console, to illuminate complex theological ideas, and to provide practical self-help for the Christian concerned about their prospects of salvation. Some official and semi-official publications we have already mentioned – such as the BCP, and the Books of Homilies – while others – for example the Henrician 'Bishops' Book' and 'King's Book' – we have not.[43] Religious works could be written by anybody, but a vast number were written by clergymen – archbishops, bishops, university theologians, chaplains, as well as humble (and some not so humble) parish priests. If you want to know what early modern society thought about heaven, hell, sin, salvation and just about everything in between, then religious print (accessible through resources such as *EEBO* and *ECCO*, as described by Ian Green in Chapter 4 of this volume) will usually get you at least part of the way there. There are of course some tricky methodological issues involved in using print in this way – it is very difficult to say, for example, who, or even how many people, might have ever read a specific text, and even harder to say what meanings they might have drawn from it. Still, it is worth remembering that authors are people too, and that a book certainly gives us a view of what the person who wrote it thought (or at least, what they wanted to be seen to be thinking) about a given topic at a given time.

Second, churches provide us with an important material cultural resource, which should not be overlooked either. Church buildings themselves have a lot to say about the Reformation, although material evidence must be treated extremely cautiously. Similarly the objects within churches, many of which – pews, pulpits, plate, royal coats of arms, scripture texts and more – date from the early modern period. The main problems with such evidence are twofold. First, dating is a very difficult issue. Some of what we see in parish churches today (not least often the buildings themselves) is medieval in origin, and much dates from the Victorian period, or later. Churches are living buildings, and have evolved significantly over time, in both appearance and function. Many of the iconoclastic survivals within English parish churches (vandalized images, decapitated statues) date not from the Reformation of the early sixteenth century, but from the Civil War of the mid seventeenth, or the carelessness of subsequent centuries.[44] And second, as Tara Hamling discusses in her chapter on visual and material culture (Chapter 7), we cannot assume that we understand the ways in which early modern men and women might have seen, interacted with or understood particular objects in particular spaces. Documentary evidence (such as churchwardens' accounts) can sometimes help us to understand what changes took place, and when, but it is rare that both manuscript and physical evidence survive for the same church. Still, historians such as Eamon Duffy, Robert Whiting, Nicholas Tyacke and Kenneth Fincham have done some interesting work on the physical appearance of the early modern parish church, and this remains a lively field of investigation.[45]

Finally, wills (and inventories). These are fascinating documents, which sit at the intersection of the ecclesiastical, the personal and the legal. They have also been used in a number of different ways by historians. Wills were, first and foremost, a way for individuals to specify the dispersal of their wealth and possessions after death. They therefore give interesting clues about family relationships, about the significance of certain items as gifts, about material affluence, about attitudes to charitable giving, and about the material culture of the early modern household. Wills were usually dictated by an individual some time before death to a trained clerk: we cannot therefore assume that the language of a will represents accurately or word-for-word the speech of the testator, as analyses of wills have suggested that there were often scribal fashions (and idiosyncrasies) in the ways that they were recorded. After death, wills had to go through a process of probate, to establish them as binding legal instruments. Oversight of probate was the responsibility of the Church courts. Diocesan courts proved most wills, but the wills of individuals who died with goods over a certain value were proved either in the Chancery Court of York (for the northern province) or the Prerogative Court of Canterbury (for the southern province – the records of the latter are now held in The National Archives). Executors were also required to send to the court that was proving the will an inventory of the deceased individual's possessions. Wills might include information about money, land, property and debts, but most recently inventories have been used because they often give an itemized description of the material goods contained within the testator's home. Below is an (abbreviated) example of an early modern inventory from Lancashire, made in the first year of the reign of Mary I (1553):[46]

A true inventorie of all the goodes and cattells remeyninge at Myrescoghe and latelie perteyninge to Thurstan Tyldisley esquire made the iiijth of Julie anno Marie Regine primo &c.

In draughte oxen x le peece xxxviij^s xix^{li} – ij bulles xviij^s xxxvj^s ... iiij milke heyfers xvj^s iij^{li} iiij^s ... ij workehorses iij^s iiij^d vj^s viij^d – one rydinge gelding called Worsley liij^s iiij^d ... Beddinge in fetherbeddes x xv^s vj^d vij-li-xvij^s – in matressis vij vj^s xlij^s in bolsterres xjx iij^s lvij^s – in pillows xiiij xv^d xvij^s vj^d – in blanckettes xxxix ij^s iiij^d iiij^{li} xj^s – coverlettes xxxj iij^s iiij^d v^{li} iij^s iiij^d – one counterpointe tapstre work vj^s viij^d ij coverynges reede seye vj^s – one covering greene sey iij^s iiij^d – in the chamber beyond the chapel chamber one seller with a tester painted worke with curtens lynnyn clooth iiij^s – in the same chamber one cuppebord with a coveringe blue clothe ij^d ... Things in the hall hangings for the hall painted work v^s iiij^d – one longe sytteborde one cuppebord and one forme ij^s ... Thinges in the chapel a chalishe with a patente xx^s – one vestement iij^s iiij^d – one albe xx^d – one ames and one stooale iiij^d – one massebooke vj^d ij tapers and ij torchis partlie brent one saincte Johns hedde xvj^d ...

This is less than half of the full inventory – Tyldisley was clearly a very wealthy man, and it does go on a bit! – but these extracts should give an adequate impression of the sorts of details one might expect to find. Other than land and property, livestock was amongst the most valuable possessions an individual could own, and therefore features prominently in the list. Bedding, fabric and decoration also feature heavily; the level of detail is both surprisingly specific and frustratingly vague. For example, we are told what a piece of cloth was made out of, and whether it was red, blue or green: all details that might affect its value. But we are not told anything about the visual subjects depicted by the tapestries and painted boards hanging in the house for decoration – an exasperating omission for students of visual culture. Kitchens, as one would expect, were full of pots and pans, but inventories often leave us without a sense of the personality of the deceased. Most personal items, smaller items or items with a greater sentimental than economic value did not feature in inventories: they usually changed hands unseen and were not recorded in the official documents.

Tyldisley's house contained a chapel, and considering that the inventory of his possessions dates from only the first year of the reign of Mary I, it is notable how well kitted-out it was for Catholic worship, containing liturgical books, plate, vestments, candles and other decoration, all forbidden and removed from parish churches during the reign of Edward VI. The question of religious belief leads us to consider wills in more detail, because as well as evidence of familial and community relationships, and material wealth and goods, wills (or more specifically, will preambles) have also been used by historians as a way of trying to analyse changing patterns of religious belief over time. When William Woodward of Earles Colne, Essex, died in 1524, his will declared 'I bequeath my soul to almighty god to our blessed lady and to all the company of heaven my body to be buried in the churchyard of Earls Colne in the parish of St Andrews.'[47] The references here to the Virgin Mary and the saints in heaven are fairly typical of a pre-Reformation Catholic preamble. Contrast this with the will made by Reginald Heygatt of Feering in 1552, which declared:

> I thank god the father god the son and god the holy ghost doth ordain and make this my present testament and last will in manner and form following first I bequeath my soul unto our lord jesus christ my maker and redeemer and my body to be buried in Feering church aforesaid.[48]

Gone are the allusions to the saints and the Virgin, to be replaced by explicit reference to 'christ my maker and redeemer'. The utility of attempting to chart the replacement of 'traditional' preambles with 'ambiguous' or 'evangelical' forms of wording as an index of changing religious allegiance, however, has been challenged. Will preambles were usually written according to a form of words devised by the scribe, not the person making the will. As public, legal documents, it is also doubtful whether any but the most committed (or rash) testator (or scribe) would employ in them a form of words that could be deemed heretical in the prevailing religious climate of the day.[49] It is clear that whatever they are used for, wills (like any other source) should be used with care, and with sensitivity to the methodological issues involved. However, they can still tell us a huge amount, and over the last twenty years there has been an explosion in the number of published collections of wills and inventories dating from the early modern period, as well as online databases, such as that for the Essex village of Earles Colne.[50]

Conclusion

Whether your interest is in political history, economic history, gender history, social and cultural history, intellectual history, theology, the history of institutions, individuals, families, communities, visual culture, material culture, or religion and religious change itself, ecclesiastical sources have something valuable to offer. As with all sources, there are potential pitfalls to avoid, but there is also much to be gained. In the early modern world, religion, politics, society and culture were all tightly intertwined. Documents generated for, by or about the Church therefore tell us much, not only about the Church itself, but about almost every aspect of early modern life. There are some brilliant headline resources that facilitate access to early modern primary material (*EEBO*, *State Papers Online*, *The Acts and Monuments Online*), but there is also a surprising quantity of (high-quality) transcribed ecclesiastical source material nestling on the forgotten shelves of county record society volumes, or in the publications of Victorian antiquaries, which can easily be revealed by careful searching of library catalogues and bibliographical databases. And, of course, far more besides is resting, untouched perhaps for generations, in manuscript form in county and national archives, ready to disclose its secrets to anybody with the inclination, patience and palaeographical know-how to visit the archive, order the material up to the reading room and take a look.

Key resources

Cause Papers in the Diocesan Courts of the Archbishopric of York, 1300–1858, http:// www.hrionline.ac.uk/causepapers/index.jsp (accessed 14 April 2015).

Churchwardens' accounts: the best finding aid to both published and manuscript records is still the appendix to Ronald Hutton, *The Rise and Fall of Merry England: The Ritual Year 1400–1700* (Oxford: Oxford University Press, 1996).

Country Record and Archaeological Society publications (also Camden and Surtees Society volumes): search the relevant website, your university library catalogue or http://copac.jisc.ac.uk (accessed 6 January 2016) for details.

Documents of the English Reformation, ed. Gerald Bray (Cambridge: James Clarke, 2004).

Early English Books Online, http://eebo.chadwyck.com/home (accessed 6 January 2016).

Foxe, John, *The Unabridged Acts and Monuments Online* (*TAMO*) (Sheffield: HRI Online Publications, 2011), http://www.johnfoxe.org (accessed 5 January 2016).

Letters and Papers, Foreign and Domestic, of the Reign of Henry VIII: Preserved in the Public Record Office, the British Museum, and Elsewhere in England, ed. J. S. Brewer, James Gairdner and R. H. Brodie, 21 vols (London: HMSO, 1862–1932), available at http://www.british-history.ac.uk/search/series/letters-papers-hen8 (accessed 5 January 2016) and http://gale.cengage.co.uk/state-papers-online-15091714.aspx (accessed 5 January 2016).

The 'Parker Society' volumes, consisting of nineteenth-century editions of the published and unpublished writings of the English reformers: for a full list, see http://www. anglicanhistory.org/reformation/ps.

Predominantly nineteenth-century editions of key sources, such as *Formularies of Faith put Forth by Authority during the Reign of Henry VIII*, ed. Charles Lloyd (Oxford: Clarendon Press, 1825), available online via www.archive.org (accessed 5 January 2016).

Visitation Articles and Injunctions of the Early Stuart Church, ed. Kenneth Fincham, 2 vols (Woodbridge: Boydell, 1994–98).

Visitation Articles and Injunctions of the Period of the Reformation, ed. W. H. Frere and W. M. Kennedy, 3 vols, Alcuin Club Collections, 14–16 (London: Longman, 1910).

Notes

1 Christopher Haigh, *English Reformations* (Oxford: Clarendon Press, 1993); Jack Scarisbrick, *The Reformation and the English People* (Oxford: Blackwell, 1984); Eamon Duffy, *The Stripping of the Altars: Traditional Religion in England, c. 1400–c. 1580* (New Haven: Yale University Press, 1992).
2 *Documents of the English Reformation*, ed. Gerald Bray (Cambridge: James Clarke, 2004); see *Statutes of the Realm*, available through 'English Reports', http://www.heinonline.org (accessed 5 January 2016).
3 *Letters and Papers, Foreign and Domestic, of the Reign of Henry VIII: Preserved in the Public Record Office, the British Museum, and Elsewhere in England*, ed. J. S. Brewer, James Gairdner and R. H. Brodie, 21 vols (London: HMSO, 1862–1932), available at http://www.british-history.ac.uk/search/series/letters-papers-hen8 (accessed 5 January 2016) and http://gale.cengage.co.uk/state-papers-online-15091714.aspx (accessed 5 January 2016). See also Natalie Mears on 'State Papers and related collections', Chapter 1 in this volume.
4 26 Hen. VIII c.1, *Statutes of the Realm*, 11 vols (Record Commission, 1810–28), Vol. III, p. 492.
5 On the literary dimension of early modern primary sources, see Ceri Sullivan in this volume, Chapter 5.
6 E.g. Heinz Schilling, 'Confessional Europe', in T. A. Brady, H. O. Oberman and J. D. Tracy (eds), *Handbook of European History 1400–1600*, 2 vols (Leiden: Brill, 1995), Vol. II, pp. 641–70; Wolfgang Reinhard, 'Reformation, Counter-Reformation and the Early Modern State: A Reassessment', *Catholic Historical Review*, 75.3 (1989), 385–403.
7 The Augsburg Confession, Article IV, availabe at http://bookofconcord.org/augsburgconfession.php (accessed 14 April 2015).
8 Emil Sehling, *Die evangelische Kircheonordnung des XVI. Jahrhunderts*, 22 vols (various publishers, 1902–77).
9 These key sources are often available in modern or nineteenth-century critical editions, or online, although in the latter case you should be careful to check that they are reliable copies of the original, and have not been modified. See, for example, the Second Helvetic Confession at http://www.sacred-texts.com/chr/2helvcnf.htm (accessed 5 January 2016); *Documents of the English Reformation*, ed. Bray.
10 *The Canons and Decrees of the Sacred and Oecumenical Council of Trent*, ed. and trans. J. Waterworth (London: Dolman, 1848), available at https://history.hanover.edu/texts/trent.html (accessed 14 April 2015).
11 'The German Mass and Order of Divine Service' (1526), in *Documents Illustrative of the Continental Reformation*, ed. B. J. Kidd (Oxford: Clarendon Press, 1911), pp. 193–202, available at https://history.hanover.edu/texts/luthserv.html (accessed 14 April 2015).
12 Available in various physical and digital editions. One good recent critical edition is *The Book of Common Prayer: The Texts of 1549, 1559, and 1662*, ed. Brian Cummings (Oxford: Oxford University Press, 2013), although it does not contain the 1552 edition in full.
13 E.g. *Liturgies and Occasional Forms of Prayer Set Forth in the Reign of Queen Elizabeth*, ed. William Keatinge Clay (Cambridge: Cambridge University Press, 1847); see *National Prayers: Special Worship since the Reformation*, Vol. I: *Special Prayers, Fasts and Thanksgivings in the British Isles, 1533–1688*, ed. Natalie Mears, Alasdair Raffe, Stephen Taylor, Philip Williamson and Lucy Bates (Woodbridge: Boydell, 2013).
14 See, for example, Ian Green, *The Christian's ABC* (Oxford: Clarendon Press, 1996); Ian Green, '"For Children in Yeeres and Children in Understanding": The

Emergence of the English Catechism under Elizabeth and the Early Stuarts', *Journal of Ecclesiastical History*, 37.3 (1986), 397–425.

15 https://www.ccel.org/creeds/heidelberg-cat.html (accessed 5 January 2016); Alexander Nowell, *Nowell's Catechism*, trans. Thomas Norton, ed. G. E. Corrie (Cambridge: Cambridge University Press, 1853).

16 See, for example, Green, *The Christian's ABC*; Ruth Atherton, 'The Pursuit of Power: Death, Dying and the Quest for Social Control in the Palatinate, 1547–1610', in Elizabeth Tingle and Jonathan Willis (eds), *Dying, Death, Burial and Commemoration in Reformation Europe* (Farnham: Ashgate, 2015), pp. 25–48.

17 Collections of sermons abound, on *EEBO* and in edited collections, such as the Parker Society editions of the sermons of key reformers, including Hugh Latimer and Edwin Sandys. For a full list of Parker Society volumes, see http://anglican-history.org/reformation/ps (accessed 27 January 2016).

18 Church of England, *Sermons, or Homilies, Appointed to Be Read in Churches, in the Time of Queen Elizabeth, of Famous Memory* ... (Dublin: printed for Anne Watson and B. Dugdale, 1821), available at https://archive.org/details/sermonsorhomilie0a0chur (accessed 5 January 2016).

19 There has been some excellent scholarship on sermons recently. See, for example, Peter McCullough, Hugh Adlington and Emma Rhatigan (eds), *The Oxford Handbook of the Early Modern Sermon* (Oxford: Oxford University Press, 2011); Peter McCullough, *Sermons at Court: Politics and Religion in Elizabethan and Jacobean Preaching* (Cambridge: Cambridge University Press, 1998); Mary Morrissey, *Politics and the Paul's Cross Sermons, 1558–1642* (Oxford: Oxford University Press, 2011); Arnold Hunt, *The Art of Hearing: English Preachers and Their Audiences, 1590–1640* (Cambridge: Cambridge University Press, 2010).

20 *Documents of the English Reformation*, ed. Bray, p. 176.

21 See the originals on *EEBO*, or edited versions online or in print, for example in Bray, *Documents of the English Reformation*.

22 *Visitation Articles and Injunctions of the Period of the Reformation*, ed. W. H. Frere and W. M. Kennedy, 3 vols, Alcuin Club Collections, 14–16 (London: Longman, 1910); *Visitation Articles and Injunctions of the Early Stuart Church*, ed. Kenneth Fincham, 2 vols (Woodbridge: Boydell, 1994–98).

23 'Copy of Visitation Book', in *Later Writings of Bishop Hooper, Together with His Letters and Other Pieces*, ed. Charles Nevinson (Cambridge: Cambridge University Press, 1852), pp. 117–56.

24 Gerald Strauss, *Luther's House of Learning: Indoctrination of the Young in the German Reformation* (Baltimore: Johns Hopkins University Press, 1978).

25 For a detailed description of the evolution of the office of churchwarden, see Beat Kümin, *The Shaping of a Community* (Aldershot: Scolar Press, 1996).

26 *The Accounts of the Churchwardens of the Parish of Saint Michael, Cornhill, in the City of London, from 1456 to 1608*, ed. W. H. Overall (London: Alfred James Waterlow [for private circulation only], 1868), pp. 164–5.

27 On bells, see David Garrioch, 'Sounds of the City: The Soundscape of Early Modern European Towns', *Urban History*, 30.1 (2003), 5–25; Christopher Marsh, '"At it ding dong": Recreation and Religion in the English Belfry, 1580–1640', in Natalie Mears and Alec Ryrie (eds), *Worship and the Parish Church in Early Modern Britain* (Farnham: Ashgate, 2013), pp. 151–72; Christopher Marsh, *Music and Society in Early Modern England* (Cambridge: Cambridge University Press, 2013), Chapter 9.

28 There is a lively debate on the relative merits of churchwardens' accounts over several issues of the *English Historical Review*: see Clive Burgess, 'Pre-Reformation Churchwardens' Accounts and Parish Government: Lessons from London and Bristol', *English Historical Review*, 117 (2002), 306–32; Beat Kümin, 'Late

Medieval Churchwardens' Accounts and Parish Government: Looking beyond London and Bristol', *English Historical Review*, 119 (2004), 87–99; Clive Burgess, 'The Broader Church? A Rejoinder to "Looking Beyond"', *English Historical Review*, 119 (2004), 100–16; Ronald Hutton, 'Seasonal Festivity in Late Medieval England: Some Further Reflections', *English Historical Review*, 120 (2005), 66–79.

29 Eamon Duffy, *The Voices of Morebath: Reformation and Rebellion in an English Village* (New Haven and London: Yale University Press, 2001).

30 See, for example, Jonathan Willis, '"A Pottle of Ayle on Whyt Sonday": Everyday Objects and the Musical Culture of the Post-Reformation Parish Church', in Tara Hamling and Catherine Richardson (eds), *Everyday Objects: Medieval and Early Modern Material Culture* (Farnham: Ashgate, 2010), pp. 211–20.

31 Ronald Hutton, *The Rise and Fall of Merry England: The Ritual Year 1400–1700* (Oxford: Oxford University Press, 1996).

32 See, for example, the output of the Institute for Advanced Jesuit Studies at Boston College, http://jesuitsources.bc.edu (accessed 5 January 2016); and for more detailed discussion of such documents see Margaret Small's 'The wider world', Chapter 15 of the present volume.

33 E.g. *Statutes of Lincoln Cathedral Arranged by the Late Henry Bradshaw, with Illustrative Documents*, ed. C. Wordsworth (Cambridge: Cambridge University Press, 1892, 1897); *Calendar of the Manuscripts of the Dean and Chapter of Wells*, 2 vols, ed. William Henry Benbow Bird and William Paley Baildon (London: HMSO, 1907–14); R. E. G. Cole, *The Chapter Acts of the Cathedral Church of Lincoln 1520–1559*, 3 vols (Cambridge: Chadwyck-Healey, 1915); *Diocese of Norwich: Bishop Redman's Visitation, 1597. Presentments in the Archdeaconries of Norwich, Norfolk, and Suffolk*, ed. J. F. Williams (Norwich: Norfolk Record Society, 1946); *Extracts from the Two Earliest Minute Books of the Dean and Chapter of Norwich Cathedral, 1566–1649*, ed. J. F. Williams (Norwich: Norfolk Record Society, 1953).

34 Baildon, *Calendar of the Manuscripts of the Dean and Chapter of Wells*, Vol. II, p. 342.

35 *The Churchwarden's Presentments in the Oxfordshire Peculiars of Dorchester, Thame and Banbury*, Oxfordshire Record Society Series, 10, ed. Sidney Peyton (Oxford: Oxfordshire Record Society, 1928).

36 Martin Ingram, *Church Courts, Sex and Marriage in England, 1570–1640* (Cambridge: Cambridge University Press, 1994).

37 Edwin Robert Courtney Brinkworth, *Shakespeare and the Bawdy Court of Stratford* (Chichester: Phillimore, 1972); http://www.hrionline.ac.uk/causepapers (accessed 5 January 2016).

38 John Foxe, *The Acts and Monuments Online* (*TAMO*) (Sheffield: HRI Online Publications, 2011), http://www.johnfoxe.org (accessed 5 January 2016). There is also an excellent recent resource containing the letters of the Marian exiles available online via the University of Edinburgh: http://www.marianexile.div.ed.ac.uk/index.html (accessed 5 January 2016).

39 Christopher Highley and John King (eds), *John Foxe and His World* (Aldershot and Burlington, BT: Ashgate, 2002); David Loades (ed.), *John Foxe: An Historical Perspective* (Brookfield, VT and Aldershot: Ashgate, 1999); Eamon Duffy, *Fires of Faith: Catholic England under Mary Tudor* (London: Yale University Press, 2009); Brad S. Gregory, *Salvation at Stake: Christian Martyrdom in Early Modern Europe* (London: Harvard University Press, 1999); Peter Lake and Michael Questier, *The Trials of Margaret Clitherow: Persecution, Martyrdom and the Politics of Sanctity in Elizabethan England* (London: Continuum, 2011).

40 William Cecil, Lord Burghley, *The Execution of Iustice in England* (1583), *STC*, 4902. Cf. William Allen, *A true, sincere and modest defence, of English Catholiques that suffer for their faith both at home and abrode against a false,*

seditious and slanderous libel intituled; The execution of iustice in England (Rouen, 1584), *STC*, 373.

41 E.g. *Recusant Roll No. 1, 1592–3: Exchequer, Lord Treasurer's Remembrancer, Pipe Office Series*, ed. M. M. C. Calthrop (London: Catholic Record Society, 1916).

42 *Recusant Documents from the Ellesmere Manuscripts*, ed. Anthony Petti (London: Catholic Record Society, 1968).

43 E.g. *Formularies of Faith Put Forth by Authority during the Reign of Henry VIII*, ed. Charles Lloyd (Oxford: Clarendon Press, 1825), available at https://archive. org/details/formulariesfaith00unknuoft (accessed 5 January 2016). These statements of doctrine represent the rapidly changing definition of orthodoxy during the reign of Henry VIII, alongside brief texts like the Ten Articles of 1536 and Act of Six Articles of 1539; see Bray, *Documents of the English Reformation*.

44 For a conscientious record of Civil-War-era iconoclasm, see *The Journal of William Dowsing: Iconoclasm in East Anglia during the English Civil War*, ed. Trevor Cooper (Woodbridge: Boydell, 2001).

45 Duffy, *The Stripping of the Altars*; Robert Whiting, *The Reformation of the English Parish Church* (Cambridge: Cambridge University Press, 2010); Kenneth Fincham and Nicholas Tyacke, *Altars Restored: The Changing Face of English Religious Worship, 1547–c. 1700* (Oxford: Oxford University Press, 2007).

46 *Lancashire and Cheshire Wills and Inventories from the Ecclesiastical Court of Chester, the First Portion*, ed. George John Piccope (Manchester: Chetham Society, 1857), pp. 111–12.

47 http://linux02.lib.cam.ac.uk/earlscolne/probate/2301802.htm (accessed 16 April 2015).

48 http://linux02.lib.cam.ac.uk/earlscolne/probate/2500350.htm (accessed 16 April 2015).

49 For a good overview of the issues, see Alec Ryrie, 'Counting Sheep, Counting Shepherds: The Problem of Allegiance in the English Reformation', in Peter Marshall and Alec Ryrie (eds), *The Beginnings of English Protestantism* (Cambridge: Cambridge University Press, 2002), esp. pp. 86–7. For uses of wills as an index of religious belief, see Claire Cross, 'The Development of Protestantism in Leeds and Hull, 1520–1640: The Evidence from Wills', *Northern History*, 18 (1982), 230–8; Margaret Spufford, 'Religious Preambles and the Scribes of Villagers' Wills in Cambridgeshire, 1570–1700', in Tom Arkell, Nesta Evans and Nigel Goose (eds), *When Death Do Us Part: Understanding and Interpreting the Probate Records of Early Modern England* (Oxford: Leopard's Head, 2000), pp. 144–57. For a more critical assessment, see J. D. Alsop, 'Religious Preambles in Early Modern English Wills as Formulae', *Journal of Ecclesiastical History*, 40 (1989), 19–27; Christopher Marsh, 'In the Name of God? Will-Making and Faith in Early Modern England', in G. H. Martin and Peter Spufford (eds), *The Records of the Nation* (Woodbridge: Boydell, 1990).

50 Wills from Earles Colne can be found at http://linux02.lib.cam.ac.uk/earlscolne/ probate/index.htm (accessed 16 April 2015). Printed volumes include (but are not limited to): *Surrey Will Abstracts: Archdeaconry Court 1480–1649*, CD-ROM, ed. Cliff Webb (Woking: West Surrey Family History Society, 2013); *Bedfordshire Wills 1543–1547*, ed. Patricia Bell, George Ruscoe *et al.* (Bedford: Bedfordshire Family History Society, 2012); *Wills in the Consistory Court of Lichfield 1650–1700*, ed. Clifford Reginald Webb (London: British Record Society, 2010); *Sussex Clergy Inventories 1600–1750*, ed. Annabelle Hughes (Lewes: Sussex Record Society, 2009); *Wills at Hertford, 1415–1858*, ed. Beryl Crawley (London: British Record Society, 2007); *Derbyshire Wills Proved in the Prerogative Court of Canterbury, 1575–1601*, ed. David G. Edwards (Chesterfield: Derbyshire Record Society, 2003); *Stratford-upon-Avon Inventories, 1538–1699*, ed. Jeanne Jones, 2 vols (Stratford-upon-Avon: Dugdale Society, 2002–03); etc.

4   Print

Ian Green

The advent of printing by movable type in the western world is usually associated with the innovations made by a German goldsmith, Johannes Gutenberg, in the second quarter of the mid fifteenth century. By 1500 similar presses were found in hundreds of European cities, and this expansion continued over the next two centuries, in what is still described in some quarters as the 'Printing Revolution'.[1] In recent decades a number of caveats have been entered against drawing too simple an equation between the adoption of movable type and radical change. On the other hand, increasingly sophisticated assessments of the relationships between authors, publishers and readers are also now being offered, so that the pendulum has to some extent swung back. This chapter begins with a brief account of developments on the European mainland, before turning to focus on the nature and impact of printing in England. It also indicates how much access to early modern printed sources the modern student has through digital databases, and some of the benefits and potential problems of using them.

In 1979 Elizabeth Eisenstein published what proved to be the apogee of the view of print as a progressive, transformative medium. In *The Printing Press as an Agent of Change*, she argued that print had transformed communication and culture: it helped standardize texts, made more copies available, enabled scholars to consult and compare different texts and fix concepts, and facilitated the cumulative development of new modes of thought that would underwrite experimental science and other harbingers of modernity.[2] This view of print came under attack from various quarters. It was pointed out that the use of movable type did not guarantee a uniform, authentic text, since printers were as capable as scribes of introducing and perpetuating errors in a text; and publishers got away with frequent piracies, plagiarism and redactions that could distort an author's voice.[3] Medievalists reminded early modernists that for centuries before printing became widespread, 'stationers' operating under university supervision had produced huge numbers of affordable manuscript copies of the core texts needed by students, and Franciscan and Dominican houses had ensured that large numbers of the model sermons needed by preachers were in circulation.[4] Moreover, many of the first texts printed were very similar in form, content and function to their manuscript predecessors.

Indeed, most of the books published in sixteenth-century Europe were still in Latin, and still targeted at scholars, clergy, lawyers and medics. Other scholars pointed out that there were many ways in which manuscript culture continued to be vibrant for much of the seventeenth century; in England these included the dissemination of news, the submission of petitions, the circulation of new poetry and the posting of scurrilous libels.[5] Moreover, since the majority of the population of early modern Europe was still either illiterate or could not afford books, the impact of the press was often greatest in those contexts in which print was blended with oral and visual media: both in formal surroundings, such as worship in church, and informal, such as singing, dancing and mumming round the village. Indeed, even when functional literacy became the norm, and printed texts in the vernacular became widely affordable, perhaps in the mid or late seventeenth century in England, oral and visual media would continue to coexist and work in increasingly close relationship with the literary cultures of manuscript and print.[6]

Other assumptions that have been criticized were that Protestants made much better use of print than Catholics, and that patterns of publication were much the same across Europe. In many parts of Germany, certainly, Lutherans had much greater access to print than before, but this was through the local reprinting of Lutheran texts on the rapidly proliferating presses that the authorities in the decentralized empire found hard to control. In northern Italy and France there were also numerous printing centres, but the Catholic authorities there had sufficient influence over the trade to ensure that the presses produced orthodox liturgical texts and commentaries, anti-Protestant propaganda, and new scholarship in quantities. This changed in France in the late 1550s and early 1560s with the rapid expansion of the Huguenot movement, but most congregations secured their Bibles, psalters and sermons from Geneva or Lyon rather than locally. By the late sixteenth century both Lutherans and Calvinists were facing a new rival – the Jesuits – who arguably made even better use of print, for both indoctrination and scholarship, right across Europe and overseas.[7]

In early Tudor times England had a mostly rural, illiterate population, and with only a limited market for books, the English print trade made a slow start. A high proportion of the books circulating in England until the mid sixteenth century had been produced abroad, in Venice, Cologne, Basel, Paris and Rouen. Moreover, since the personnel of the print trade (many of them craftsmen or entrepreneurs born abroad) were anxious to stay on the right side of the authorities (who handed out lucrative 'privileges' to publish officially approved works), there was only limited publication of heretical or unauthorized works inside early Tudor England.[8]

Only in the closing decades of the sixteenth century was the English trade sufficiently equipped with machinery, type, woodcuts and engravings, skilled operatives, and capital to be capable of meeting most domestic needs. And even then, there remained specialist areas such as theology, classical texts, science and medicine where texts produced on the Continent were imported: the catalogues of the books sold each year at the international book fairs in Frankfurt circulated in England.[9] Moreover, while the English book trade belatedly took off, production abroad did not stand still. In commercial centres such as Antwerp, engraved prints were being produced in near-industrial conditions and, when imported into England in large numbers or copied into English publications, had a huge impact on styles of masonry, plasterwork, carving, metalwork, painting, tapestry and embroidery.[10]

The rate of expansion in England cannot be measured precisely, but if we use new titles and editions as a criterion, as recorded in the standard short-title catalogues (see below), the pattern is moderately clear. From the 1480s there was uneven growth from a low base of a handful of new editions or titles each year to a hundred or more by the 1560s; from the 1570s production speeded up steadily, reaching up to a few hundred new titles or editions each year by the 1630s; then in the 1640s (for reasons we will come to shortly) there was an explosion of new titles to over a thousand each year, which was followed by higher-than-pre-war levels from the 1650s to the 1690s, and a new peak in the 1680s (see Table 4.1).[11]

This pattern of expansion was probably due in part to increased demand, but also to the greater willingness of English publishers and authors to attempt new genres and target new readerships. This diversification can be described in various ways, but here a threefold division is offered, based on content and function.

One category consisted of texts that were officially authenticated for use throughout the kingdom, and that remained major staples of the print trade to the eighteenth century. The most significant titles comprised the Bible, the Book of Common Prayer, the Homilies, primers, psalmbooks and psalters for use in churches and chapels, and core texts for schools, but also included law books for the law courts, proclamations, ecclesiastical injunctions, visitation articles, and special forms of prayer. A monopoly on publishing these works was given to the royal printer or other leading members of the Stationers' Company, and since most official titles were printed in runs of twice the size normally permitted, millions of copies of works in this category were produced. This ensured that there were always enough copies not only for the relevant officials to buy, but also for individual readers who wanted copies for professional or personal reasons.[12]

The second category consisted of books for scholars and those in the professions; production of these works expanded substantially, but they remained a niche market. This category included many of the staple academic texts used in the senior forms of grammar schools and in the universities and the courts, on grammar, rhetoric, philosophy, science, medicine and law (canon, civil and common), but above all on what contemporaries called 'divinity', which embraced theology, ecclesiastical history and controversy, and a wide range of commentaries and the more advanced aids to Bible study. Since scholars across Europe could read Latin but few read English, many of these works

Table 4.1 Number of new titles/editions printed
in England, 1480–1700.

Decade	Number of new titles/editions
1480s	136
1490s	290
1500s	304
1510s	585
1520s	831
1530s	1,043
1540s	1,470
1550s	1,501
1560s	1,634
1570s	2,117
1580s	2,724
1590s	2,987
1600s	3,935
1610s	4,883
1620s	5,635
1630s	6,394
1640s	18,246
1650s	13,991
1660s	9,624
1670s	12,695
1680s	18,650
1690s	17,520

Adapted from Barnard and McKenzie, *The Cambridge
History of the Book in Britain*, Vol. IV, pp. 779–84.

were initially published in Latin. However, where an audience outside the
Latinate minority was deemed to exist and be worth the effort, they were translated into English, as with Bishop John Jewel's *Apologia Ecclesiae Anglicanae*
and William Camden's *Britannia*. Eventually many scholarly works would be
published first in English, such as Henry Hammond's *Paraphrase and annotations upon all the books of the New Testament* (1653) and William Dugdale's
Antiquities of Warwickshire (1656). Nevertheless, many of the works in this
second category were still printed in relatively short print runs, and in large,
expensive folios that had to be consulted in university or cathedral libraries, or purchased from booksellers in London, Oxford and Cambridge by
the small minority of readers who were able to afford and had the time to
study them.[13]

The third and most innovative category comprised vernacular works targeted primarily at non-specialist, general readers. This was the category that
diversified and expanded most, and sold in increasingly large numbers from
the 1570s to the early eighteenth century. Literary genres included plays,
poetry, romances and novels – all in a variety of styles: some were heavily

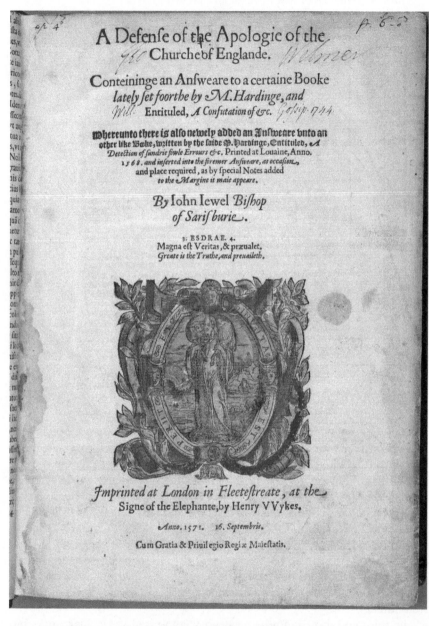

A Defenſe of the Apologie of the Churche of Englande.

Conteininge an Anſweare to a certaine Booke
lately ſet foorthe by M. Hardinge, and
Entituled, A Confutation of &c.

**Whereunto there is alſo newely added an Anſweare vnto an
other like Booke, written by the ſaide M. Hardinge, Entituled, A
Detection of ſundrie fowle Errours &c,** Printed at Louaine, Anno.
1568. and inſerted into the former Anſweare, as occaſion
and place required, as by ſpecial Notes added
to the Margine it maie appeare.

By Iohn Iewel Biſhop
of Sariſburie.

3. ESDRAE. 4.
Magna eſt Veritas, & præualet.
Greate is the Truthe, and preuaileth.

Imprinted at London in Fleeteſtreate, at the
Signe of the Elephante, by Henry VVykes.

Anno. 1571. 16. Septembris.

Cum Gratia & Priuilegio Regiæ Maieſtatis.

Figure 4.1 Title-page of John Jewel, *A defense of the Apologie of the Churche of Englande* (1571). 'This title-page has been carefully set up, using three type-faces, an elaborate printers device, and supplying the date of publication. Here in the printer Henry Wyke's device, there is an image of Christ the Good Shepherd with the lost sheep (Luke 15:4-5) across his shoulders. Possible a dozen printers used variants of this device in over two dozen publications between 1567 and 1635.

indebted to late medieval verse, others influenced by humanist or continental models, and yet others were native inventions. Then there were genres that combined information with improvement or an element of fashion: history, geography, the fine arts, outdoor pursuits, and courtesy and civility. Practical titles included how to learn a foreign language or mathematics, how to be a magistrate, or how to improve one's husbandry, horticulture, cooking and health care. Edifying works – easily the largest group in terms of new titles and repeat editions – provided simpler aids to Bible study, devotional handbooks, improving handbooks, catechisms, sermons, and inspiring biographies and cautionary tales. During the sixteenth century there were also growing numbers of topical works: reports of providential events and strange births, and criminal court proceedings turned into a pamphlet or a ballad; and from the mid seventeenth century there were also far more newsbooks and pamphlets on current political developments.[14] The massive explosion of new titles in the 1640s, following the collapse of censorship during the Civil War and the novel uses to which print was put, resulted in a rapid switch from the larger, more staid works that had provided the core of production for well-established publishers, to the political, polemical and satirical texts that depended for their sales on their immediate appeal, but that normally provided only a day's or a few days' labour for a workshop compared to the months it took to set a large book. Once monarchy and episcopacy – and censorship – returned at the Restoration, the older pattern of production partly reasserted itself, with approved works of 'divinity' well to the fore right through to the early eighteenth century, though shorter political tracts continued to sell well, especially at times of intense parliamentary activity in the later Stuart period.[15]

There were some overlaps but also many variables among the works in these three categories. One was variation in price and quality. At the top end of the scale – usually in folio, with engraved title pages and illustrations, printed on good quality paper with generous margins, and costing several shillings, or more if one included a substantial leather binding – were copies of works in the first two categories: English translations of official and scholarly works, such as larger-format Bibles and Books of Common Prayer and copies of Jewel's *Defense of the Apologie* (see Figure 4.1), and handsome editions of fashionable works in English, such as William Shakespeare's collected *Comedies, Histories and Tragedies*, John Dryden's *Works of Virgil* and Edward Hyde, Earl of Clarendon's *History of the Rebellion*.[16] Next, in a wide intermediate sector, was a wide range of works – smaller Bibles, handbooks, sermons, playbooks and many pamphlets – published in quarto, octavo or duodecimo, on average-quality paper; priced from a few shillings down to about sixpence; and readily affordable by gentry, professionals, merchants and others of middle rank, and by a determined artisan like the London woodturner and diarist Nehemiah Wallington.[17] At the bottom end were almanacs, broadsheets and chapbooks, priced at a penny or two up to threepence or fourpence. These were printed quickly on thin paper, often with crude woodcuts and in the old black-letter typeface, and offered romances, 'merry tales', jokebooks, ballads, tunes, and other works of entertainment and edification.[18] Targeted at 'the people', they proved especially popular with young apprentices and schoolboys, but also with well-educated bibliophiles.[19]

There were other variables. Practical and edifying works were intended to be consulted and studied over a period of time, and there was sufficient demand for repeat editions to be published over several decades, either in the original or in a revised or simplified version, and run off at the upper limit of the permissible print run of 1,250 or 1,500, or double that on petition. This could be exceeded, as in the case of John Rawlet's *Christian Monitor*, which claimed that 95,000 copies had been sold by the time of the nineteenth edition in 1696 (priced at threepence each, or a pound for a hundred if to be given away).[20] By contrast, topical works were produced quickly and cheaply to capture the moment; experience taught that many would not sell well enough to pass through more than one edition, so print runs of speculative items were sometimes only a few hundred copies.[21] There was one major exception: the ubiquitous almanac, which contained an ecclesiastical calendar and lunar cycles, prognostications for the coming year, and astrological and medical information. By the 1660s there were enough in circulation for every third family to acquire one.[22]

The mechanics of disseminating printed works in the three categories also varied widely. Throughout the early modern period, by far the greatest centres of production and bookselling remained in London, and especially in the St Paul's area, so that a reader based in the capital was far more likely to hear about new works of all types and prices than someone living in a provincial town or village. The London shops catered not only for residents but also for the gentry and many other visitors to the capital; and to supplement the written or oral recommendations that passed between readers with similar interests, some booksellers circulated catalogues as means of publicizing the titles they currently held. The London stationer George Thomason was able to collect nearly 15,000 pamphlets and 7,216 newspapers between the early 1640s and the early 1660s.[23] But by the 1640s, apart from the booksellers in Oxford and Cambridge who catered mainly for scholars, there is evidence of regular bookselling (as opposed to occasional or part-time retailing) in relatively few centres, such as York, Norwich, Exeter, Durham, Newcastle and Chester, all but one of these being cathedral towns; and the stock there usually consisted of steady sellers such as prayer books, catechisms and school texts rather than the latest hits from the capital.[24]

The other main outlets were the itinerant ballad-singers, pedlars and petty chapmen who roamed the country with backpack or packhorse carrying a few copies of the lightest, cheapest printed items, such as ballads, chapbooks and almanacs. As literacy rose, standards of living recovered from the population pressure and rampant inflation of the late sixteenth century, and cheaper titles became more available, the numbers of chapmen grew to perhaps 10,000 by the 1690s, by which time they were thought to need regulating by statute.[25] However, in the mid and late seventeenth and early eighteenth centuries the number of booksellers based in provincial towns increased fast; and by the late eighteenth century they would not only be legion, but would also be beginning to acquire presses and print items of local interest, such as sales bills and provincial newspapers.[26] In some corners of sixteenth- and seventeenth-century England, clergy and laity who lacked the funds to buy their own copies had access to books in a school or local town library set up by a benefactor or corporation; and from the 1690s there were scores of parish libraries set up by Thomas Bray and his fellow Trustees for Erecting Parochial Libraries. Circulating libraries, subscription libraries, Sunday school libraries and public lending libraries were becoming widespread in the late eighteenth and early nineteenth centuries, but the modern lending library dates from outside our period.[27]

Assessing the impact of print poses a number of problems. Who had access to all these new books? How thoroughly did they read them? And how far did they understand or agree with or act upon the arguments they contained? Did the expansion of education and the rising literacy of early modern times create a demand for more books, or did the greater availability of books stimulate the education of more children and adults? (If the latter, what do we make of the fact that early modern Scotland developed a more comprehensive educational system than England but had a very limited print capacity?) Unfortunately, below the level of readers who kept a catalogue of their libraries or whose collections were valuable enough to be listed title by title in their probate inventories, we are often unable to link particular works with specific owners. Inventories were rarely drawn up for poorer ranks or for women, and when books were mentioned it was often in very general terms, such as 'books and other lumber' (especially where the value was below a shilling) without a single title being listed. And even when a title was given, such as a Bible, it may simply reflect the gift of a literate relation or pious benefactor rather than a recipient who deliberately sought it out and read it regularly. Bibles were produced in increasingly large numbers and small formats, but in some households were apparently kept for what were seen as their magical qualities rather than as a sacred text to be read daily.[28]

It is unlikely that the redoubling of the numbers of titles registered by the Stationers' Company every three or four decades from the 1530s to the 1680s meant that the numbers or types of readers were expanding at the same rate. Rather it may indicate, at least until the 1640s, that regular book buyers, such as academics and institutional librarians, and a growing number of better-educated gentry, clergy and professionals, were accumulating larger collections than their predecessors had done in the early Tudor period. Not only is there the evidence provided by hundreds of catalogues of institutional and private collections, archival records of purchases, and the copying of passages into commonplace books, but also we know that growing numbers of noble and gentry households contained a separate 'library'. In this room were stored a wide range of texts – practical and fashionable, pious and entertaining – and also (increasingly) globes, coins, instruments, maps and esoteric collections, all designed to fill the owner's spare moments and impress visitors with his wealth and sophistication.[29]

Recent attempts to assess impact have taken various forms. One method still favoured by political theorists and historians of ideas is to trace the geneal-ogy of a concept such as liberty or representation through the pages of the relevant texts of the day, though given the limited numbers of copies printed of many of these texts it is hard to establish how widely their authors' ideas spread.[30] Another moderately straightforward if laborious method is to study individual readers whose annotations and commonplace books throw light on how they read and why. Gabriel Harvey read his (imported) Livy repeat-edly, looking for lessons he could apply, as did Sir William Drake when he reread his copies of Tacitus, Machiavelli and Bacon.[31] More recently, efforts have also been made to assess how pious individuals read the Bible: privately or in family or household groups, a chapter from each Testament each day, or as advised by a more experienced reader, or as the spirit moved them?[32] But the evidence is patchy, and, even allowing for the fact that the reading prac-tices identified so far were varied and idiosyncratic, it is hard to establish how typical these readers were of wider groupings.

Another approach that has gained support in some circles is to use con-structs such as 'interpretive communities' and 'communicative practices' in an attempt to measure how the attitudes of authors, publishers and readers impacted on each other, especially in the case of topical texts such as pam-phlets and newspapers. This approach is sometimes linked to Habermas' the-ory of a growing 'public sphere' in the early modern State, or portrays print as an agent of liberation or democratization, contributing to growing popular participation in contemporary political and religious debates. In *Pamphlets and Pamphleteering in Early Modern Britain*, for example, Joad Raymond argued that 'pamphlets became a foundation of the influential moral and political communities that constitute a "public sphere" of popular, political opinion'.[33] In *Print and Public Politics in the English Revolution*, Jason Peacey has provided much the most subtle contextualization and explanation of the explosion of print in the 1640s and 1650s. His focus is less on the polem-ical discourse embodied in the pamphlets and newspapers of those decades than on what the form and function of such materials can tell us about their impact. The problems all scholars face is that the lower down the social lad-der they probe, among the lower-middling shopkeepers and clerks, and the workers such as labourers and artisans, the less plentiful and the less direct is the evidence for literacy, book ownership and reading practices. Moreover, such material as there is often consists of hostile comments from the edu-cated elite and the 'middling sort', or prosecutions for circulating dangerous ideas. Peacey's solution is twofold. He focuses on the many uses to which print was put in the rapidly changing circumstances of the 1640s. Print was used increasingly to circulate what had hitherto been regarded as privileged information (such as parliamentary speeches and voting lists), to foster understanding of the mechanics of parliamentary proceedings (including the role of committees and of 'parties' or 'factions'), and to facilitate and encourage participation in various forms of political action (such as petitioning and mass meetings), even among those who did not have a vote. Through these means a revolutionary new 'print culture' was born. And he offers another construct – 'ordinary citizens', the 'general public' drawn from all ranks and all parts of the country, whose lives could be transformed when they became avid but critical consumers of print. Such readers soon became aware of the differences between commercial and targeted publication, and, in conjunction with authors and publishers, showed enough tactical awareness to adopt different forms of print for different purposes, sometimes in sequence to ratchet up pressure. This clever use of print and other media led to a broadening and deepening of the political nation and a democratization of 'public' or 'common politics' that left a permanent mark on English parliamentary practices.[34]

There were clearly massive changes in patterns of publication in the 1640s and 1650s, but Peacey's constructs of a rapidly but deliberately modified print culture and an increasingly sophisticated readership rely heavily on developments in London and among the most active supporters and opponents of Parliament. The capital was not only the judicial, political and cultural hub of the kingdom, but was also responsible for 95 per cent of book production and bookselling. It also had the highest rates of literacy in England, with three-quarters of tradesmen and craftsmen being able to read, so it is not surprising that a significant proportion of pamphlets, ballads and almanacs reflected London life. And yet it is hard to track the distribution of pamphlets within London, and even harder to track them outside London, where literacy rates were lower, prices could be dramatically higher, and distribution less organized.[35] The full impact of political tracts on the lower-middling and lower ranks outside London was perhaps not felt permanently until literacy rates were much higher, regional distribution was much more efficient and metal printing presses were introduced – that is in the late eighteenth and nineteenth centuries.

What we can be moderately sure were spread round the country and widely used both before and after the Civil War fell into two categories. One was the Bibles, prayer books, Homilies, psalters, catechisms and schoolbooks that were required by the ecclesiastical authorities.[36] Bishops and archdeacons checked that parish churches possessed copies of the relevant texts, while schoolmasters purchased copies of titles prescribed by the authorities and school statutes. The texts used most frequently in church did not even require much literacy in the congregation: the essential messages were driven home by the sequence of Bible readings and Homilies declaimed each Sunday; the Psalms 'lined out' and sung; the catechisms repeated orally until children and youths had learned them; and the key texts such as the Apostles' Creed, Ten Commandments and Lord's Prayer painted on the walls, sometimes with iconography borrowed from the title page of a Bible. The second category comprised the devotional works, godly-living handbooks and other edifying works that sold steadily for decades and can be traced to the homes of many pious readers.[37] These steady sellers have been dismissed by some scholars, such as Peter Lake[38] and Joad Raymond, as designed to produce a cosy conformity, and lacking the kind of cultural and intellectual dynamism that their study of polemical works has convinced them was the norm for religious belief and practice in the period up to 1640 (Professor Lake apparently has an 800 lb gorilla in his room, reminding him: 'it's the Civil War, stupid'). But as Alec Ryrie has pointed out in his penetrating analysis of the experience of *Being Protestant in Reformation Britain*, 'it is hard to see how any method other than frequency of printing can be used systematically to assess books' popularity'.[39] Moreover, many of the same texts were revived after the Restoration, and supplemented by new ones that again put instruction before polemic, were carefully crafted to meet the needs of different groups, and increasingly found favour with both conformists and nonconformists. Two highly successful cases were Isaac Watts' *A Short View of the Whole Scripture History*, published in small format twenty-six times between 1732 and 1820, and Philip Doddridge's *The Family Expositor*, published in quarto in instalments from 1738 to 1756 (thanks to the subscriptions of hundreds of men and women, laity and clergy, conformists and nonconformists) and as a single work many times thereafter. Watts' *Short View* contained selected historical passages with explanatory notes, for 'persons of younger years and the common ranks of mankind' who had 'fewer conveniences and advantages of knowledge'. Doddridge's *Family Expositor* deployed different typefaces on the same page to provide texts suited to family members with different levels of knowledge and education: the original King James text and a paraphrase (for average readers), 'critical notes' (for the more scholarly) and 'practical improvements' (providing explanation, exhortation and a basis for meditation or extempore prayer for the less confident).[40]

By the mid eighteenth century the supremacy of 'divinity' was being overtaken by the growing popularity of the vernacular genres described above, and new genres such as novels and children's books.[41] But print would still be central to the rise of Methodism and the Tractarian Movement, as well as to the rise of trade unions, Chartists and modern political parties. Is the term 'print revolution' not better applied to the late modern period, when universal education, daily newspapers and cheap paperbacks were widely available?

Today many students have ready access to information about early modern printed works, either direct and for free, or through a good library at which they are a registered reader. The University of St Andrews, backed by the Arts and Humanities Research Council, has pioneered the *Universal Short Title Catalogue* (*USTC*), available free online at http://ustc.ac.uk. So far the *USTC* has identified the books printed in France, Iberia and the Netherlands in the sixteenth century, and it is hoped to extend coverage into the seventeenth century, as well as investigate collections of German and Italian books not yet covered by the bibliographical projects already available online for those areas. The British Library has made available the British equivalent – the *English Short Title Catalogue* (*STC*) – free online at http://estc.bl.uk. This is an amalgamation of three older short title catalogues, all of which were heavily revised in the late twentieth century.[42] Based on the holdings of the British Library and over 2,000 other libraries, the *STC* lists over 460,000 items published between 1473 and 1800, mainly in the British Isles and North America, and mainly in English. If you have a specific author, title or keyword to pursue, *STC* is relatively easy to use: see 'Quick tips' under 'Basic search'. But persistence and use of the 'Advanced search' facility may be needed to reduce the thousands of 'hits' for a term such as 'parliament' to manageable proportions.

Students today also have access to facsimiles of most of the titles printed in the British Isles and North America from 1473 to 1800, in two digital databases. These were commercially sponsored, so use is restricted to readers who are registered at an institution or library that has subscribed to its regular exploitation, or who are prepared to pay their own way. *EEBO (Early English Books Online)* provides reproductions of the original text of over 125,000 titles for the period 1473 to 1700, while *ECCO (Eighteenth Century Collections Online)* includes over 180,000 titles dating from 1701 to 1800.[43]

These databases represent a huge bonus for students but also pose some problems. On the plus side, they provide vastly improved access to original sources that would otherwise have to be consulted in a rare books or special collections room, and also make it much easier to make a copy of significant passages for further study. Both databases also offer a variety of search modes, and at a more advanced level, the student can search for a number of elements simultaneously: subject, author, title, and date and place of publication. Both databases also offer a facility to search the full text for keywords. In the case of *ECCO*, which reproduces texts in the more familiar roman typeface, the student can search all 33,000,000 pages for keywords at the touch of a button. But in the case of *EEBO* the facility exists only for the selection – a not inconsiderable proportion – of pre-1700 texts that have been transcribed into a modern typeface, which is easier to read for those not used to confronting works published in cramped, early modern black-letter type.

There are, however, drawbacks too. Partly because the only surviving originals of some texts were not in good condition, and partly because the recent digitization was based on microfilm copies made some decades ago, the quality of the reproduction of texts in *EEBO* and occasionally in *ECCO* too is not of top quality. The *EEBO* transcripts are also often incomplete or inaccurate, and usually do not include the marginal notes on the original page. The quality of the reproduction of woodcuts and engravings is often poor: students interested in visual imagery should see the better quality images in the new database *British Printed Images to 1700*, which is searchable by five categories: producer, person shown, subject, date and technique.[44]

The databases present other less obvious problems. They reproduce a standardized unit of text that will fill the screen of the device on which it is being viewed, but this conceals the huge variation between contemporary formats – for example, between a large folio that was used for the Bibles and Books of Common Prayer placed on lecterns in church for oral declamation in public, and a duodecimo or smaller format that could be slipped into the pocket for different occasions and needs. The texts selected for reproduction in the original microfilms also appear to have been 'clean' ones, so that there are few signs of use by former owners, such as underlinings and marginal comments, which can tell us much about reader reaction. Moreover, many surviving texts have not yet been uploaded, especially of less fashionable works, so a search for examples of the use of a particular name or term will be extensive but not exhaustive. If you are amassing references to a particular term or phrase, remember that the same rules apply to handling them as to source material in any other format. Try to contextualize the genesis of the whole work as well as the individual paragraphs in which the references occur (*ECCO* offers a series of 'contextual essays' on topics such as enlightenment, reason, religion, political parties in England, romanticism and sensibility). Also consider the different functions of a particular text, in the minds of the author, the publisher and the target readership; and if a particular phrase is crucial to an argument and there are repeat editions, check that the original usage of the term or phrase has not been altered subsequently. Students using such databases on a regular basis in the twenty-first century will not need to be alerted to the irony that the revolutionary potential of the printed page may be about to be overtaken by the digital revolution. Good hunting!

Key resources

Capp, Bernard, *Astrology and the Popular Press: English Almanacs 1500–1800* (London: Faber, 1979).

Early English Books Online, http://eebo.chadwyck.com/home (accessed 12 January 2016).

Eighteenth Century Collections Online, http://gale.cengage.co.uk/product-highlights/history/eighteenth-century-collections-online.aspx (accessed 12 January 2016).

English Short Title Catalogue, http://estc.bl.uk (accessed 12 January 2016).

Green, Ian, *Print and Protestantism in Early Modern England* (Oxford: Oxford University Press, 2000).

Hellinga, Lotte and J. B. Trapp (eds), *The Cambridge History of the Book in Britain*, Vol. III: *1400–1557* (Cambridge: Cambridge University Press, 1999); and Vol. IV: *1557–1695*, ed. John Barnard and D. F. McKenzie (2002).

Peacey, Jason, *Print and Public Politics in the English Revolution* (Cambridge: Cambridge University Press, 2013).

Raymond, Joad (ed.), *The Oxford History of Popular Print Culture*, Vol. I: *Cheap Print in Britain and Ireland to 1660* (Oxford: Oxford University Press, 2011).

Spufford, Margaret, *Small Books and Pleasant Histories: Popular Fiction and Its Readership in Seventeenth-Century England* (Cambridge: Cambridge University Press, 1981).

Watt, Tessa, *Cheap Print and Popular Piety, 1550–1640* (Cambridge: Cambridge University Press, 1991).

Notes

1 See, for example, the *Wikipedia* entries on 'Johannes Gutenberg' and 'Printing Revolution'.
2 Elizabeth L. Eisenstein, *The Printing Press as an Agent of Change: Communications and Cultural Transformations in Early-Modern Europe* (Cambridge: Cambridge University Press, 1979).
3 Adrian Johns, *The Nature of the Book: Print and Knowledge in the Making* (Chicago and London: University of Chicago Press, 1998); David McKitterick, *Print, Manuscript and the Search for Order, 1450–1830* (Cambridge: Cambridge University Press, 2003).
4 David d'Avray, 'Printing, Mass Communication, and Religious Reformation: The Middle Ages and After', in Julia Crick and Alexandra Walsham (eds), *The Uses of Script and Print, 1300–1700* (Cambridge: Cambridge University Press, 2004), pp. 50–70.
5 Harold Love, *Scribal Publication in Seventeenth-Century England* (Oxford: Clarendon Press, 1993); and Harold Love, 'Oral and Scribal Texts in Early Modern England', in John Barnard and D. F. McKenzie (eds), *The Cambridge History of the Book in Britain*, Vol. IV: *1557–1695* (Cambridge: Cambridge University Press, 2002), 97–121. Adam Fox, *Oral and Literate Culture in England 1500–1700* (Oxford: Clarendon Press, 2000), Chapter 6; Jason Peacey, *Print and Public Politics in the English Revolution* (Cambridge: Cambridge University Press, 2013), index s.v. 'scribal culture'.
6 Fox, *Oral and Literate Culture*, pp. 11–19, 393–6 and *passim*.
7 R. W. Scribner, *For the Sake of Simple Folk: Popular Propaganda for the German Reformation* (Cambridge: Cambridge University Press, 1981); Mark U. Edwards, Jr, *Printing, Propaganda and Martin Luther* (Berkeley and London: University of California Press, 1994); Andrew Pettegree and Matthew Hall, 'The Reformation and the Book: A Reconsideration', *Historical Journal*, 47.4 (2004), 785–808; R. Po-Chia Hsia, *The World of Catholic Renewal 1540–1770*, 2nd edn (Cambridge: Cambridge University Press, 2005), pp. 179–86. See also Chapter 15 of this volume.
8 Andrew Pettegree, 'Printing and the Reformation: The English Exception', in Peter Marshall and Alec Ryrie (eds), *The Beginnings of English Protestantism* (Cambridge: Cambridge University Press, 2002), pp. 159–79; Andrew Pettegree, 'Centre and Periphery in the European Book World', *Transactions of the Royal Historical Society*, 6th series, 18 (2008), 101–28; Lotte Hellinga and J. B. Trapp (eds), *The Cambridge History of the Book in Britain*, Vol. III: *1400–1557* (Cambridge: Cambridge University Press, 1999), Chapters 1, 8. Scholars are still adjusting to the findings of Peter Blayney in his monumental two-volume *The Stationers' Company and the Printers of London 1501–1557* (Cambridge: Cambridge University Press, 2013).
9 Ian Green, *Print and Protestantism in Early Modern England* (Oxford: Oxford University Press, 2000), pp. 12–24; Barnard and McKenzie, *The Cambridge History of the Book in Britain*, Vol. IV, Chapter 6; Graham Rees and Maria Wakely, *Publishing, Politics and Culture: The King's Printers in the Reign of James I and VI* (Oxford: Oxford University Press, 2009), Chapter 9 and *passim*.
10 Anthony Wells-Cole, *Art and Decoration in Elizabethan and Jacobean England: The Influence of Continental Prints* (New Haven and London: Yale University Press, 1997); and see Tara Hamling, *Decorating the 'Godly' Household: Religious Art in Post-Reformation Britain* (New Haven and London: Yale University Press, 2010).
11 These estimates are based on Barnard and McKenzie, *The Cambridge History of the Book in Britain*, Vol. IV, pp. 779–84, but must be read in conjunction with Peter W. M. Blayney, 'STC Publication Statistics: Some Caveats', *The Library*, 7th series, 8.4 (December 2007), pp. 387–97, esp. p. 392: 'if used with proper

92   *Ian Green*

awareness of their origins and limitations, [these statistics] provide a valuable (if approximate) guide to the number of printed items surviving from each STC year'.

12 Green, *Print and Protestantism*, pp. 52–6, 176–7, 182–4; Rees and Wakely, *Publishing, Politics and Culture*, Chapter 4; Ian Green, *Humanism and Protestantism in Early Modern English Education* (Farnham: Ashgate, 2009), pp. 33–52; A. W. Pollard and G. R. Redgrave, *A Short-Title Catalogue of Books Printed in England, Scotland, & Ireland and of English Books Printed Abroad 1473–1640*, 2nd edn, rev. and enlarged by W. A. Jackson, F. S. Ferguson and K. F. Pantzer, 3 vols (London: Bibliographical Society, 1976–91) (*RSTC*), Vol. I, pp. 85–131, 346–451, 451–64, and Vol. II, pp. 87–105; and Donald Wing (ed.), *Short-Title Catalogue of Books … 1641–1700*, 2nd edn, rev. and enlarged, 3 vols (New York, 1972–98), Vol. I, pp. 549–60, 842–954.

13 Hellinga and Trapp, *The Cambridge History of the Book in Britain*, Vol. III, Chapters 14–21; and Barnard and McKenzie, *The Cambridge History of the Book in Britain*, Vol. IV, Chapters 6–15.

14 Hellinga and Trapp, *The Cambridge History of the Book in Britain*, Vol. III, Chapters 22–8; and Barnard and McKenzie, *The Cambridge History of the Book in Britain*, Vol. IV, Chapters 16–25, and pp. 788, 791; Joad Raymond (ed.), *The Oxford History of Popular Print Culture*, Vol. I: *Cheap Print in Britain and Ireland to 1660* (Oxford: Oxford University Press, 2011), Part IV; Green, *Print and Protestantism*, Chapters 3–8; *RSTC*, Vol. II, pp. 179–85; Carolyn Nelson and Matthew Seccombe (comps), *British Newspapers and Periodicals 1641–1700* (New York: Modern Language Association of America, 1987).

15 See above, pp. 86–7; Barnard and McKenzie, *The Cambridge History of the Book in Britain*, Vol. IV, p. 788; Peacey, *Print and Public Politics*, pp. 403–13.

16 For bibliographical sources for these works, see above, n12 and p. 89. When a single large sheet of paper was printed on both sides and folded once, it was known as a 'folio', and consisted of two leaves and four pages, each approximately the size of a modern A4 sheet. If the sheet was folded twice and then cut, it was called a 'quarto' (four leaves, eight pages); and if three times, 'octavo' (eight leaves, sixteen pages). The smallest formats in common usage were 'duodecimo' (twelve leaves) and 'sextodecimo' (sixteen leaves).

17 Raymond, *Cheap Print*, pp. 453, 464–5.

18 English black-letter, derived from the form of minuscule script used in manuscripts after the Norman Conquest, was used by the first English printers such as Caxton, but by the late sixteenth century had been largely replaced by the roman type favoured by humanist publishers, surviving for another century only in ballads, chapbooks and other forms of cheap print.

19 Tessa Watt, *Cheap Print and Popular Piety, 1550–1640* (Cambridge: Cambridge University Press, 1991), pp. 11–12; Bernard Capp, *Astrology and the Popular Press: English Almanacs 1500–1800* (London: Faber, 1979), pp. 41, 44; Margaret Spufford, *Small Books and Pleasant Histories: Popular Fiction and Its Readership in Seventeenth-Century England* (Cambridge: Cambridge University Press, 1981), pp. 48, 50–1, 91–8; Jan Fergus, *Provincial Readers in Eighteenth-Century England* (Oxford: Oxford University Press, 2006), Chapters 3–4. If well-educated men like John Selden, Anthony Wood and Samuel Pepys had not collected such cheap works alongside more expensive items, our knowledge of these genres would be much more limited.

20 Green, *Print and Protestantism*, pp. 13–14, 652–3.

21 Ibid., p. 19; Raymond, *Cheap Print*, pp. 458, 482.

22 Capp, *Astrology*, p. 23.

23 *Catalogue of the Pamphlets, Books, Newspapers and Manuscripts ... Collected by George Thomason, 1641–1661*, 2 vols (London: printed by order of the Trustees, 1908).

24 Barnard and McKenzie, *The Cambridge History of the Book in Britain*, Vol. IV, pp. 665, 668.

25 Spufford, *Small Books*, Chapter 5.

26 Michael Suarez and Michael Turner (eds), *The Cambridge History of the Book in Britain*, Vol. V: *1695–1830* (Cambridge: Cambridge University Press, 2009), Chapters 15, 21. For longer-term surveys, see John Feather, *A History of British Publishing*, 2nd edn (Abingdon and New York: Routledge, 2005); and James Raven, *The Business of Books: Booksellers and the English Book Trade, 1450–1850* (New Haven: Yale University Press, 2007).

27 *The Cambridge History of Libraries in Britain and Ireland*, Vol. I: *To 1640*, ed. Elisabeth Leedham-Green and Teresa Webber (Cambridge: Cambridge University Press, 2006); and Vol. II: *1640–1850*, ed. Giles Mandelbrote and K. A. Manley (Cambridge: Cambridge University Press, 2006).

28 David Cressy, *Literacy and the Social Order: Reading and Writing in Tudor and Stuart England* (Cambridge: Cambridge University Press, 1980), pp. 25, 45–53; Spufford, *Small Books*, p. 48.

29 Peacey, *Print and Public Politics*, pp. 43–54; Barnard and McKenzie, *The Cambridge History of the Book in Britain*, Vol. IV, pp. 326–8.

30 See, for example, Quentin Skinner, *Liberty before Liberalism* (Cambridge: Cambridge University Press, 1998); and Markku Peltonen, *Classical Humanism and Republicanism in English Political Thought 1570–1640* (Cambridge: Cambridge University Press, 1995).

31 Lisa Jardine and Anthony Grafton, '"Studied for Action": How Gabriel Harvey Read His Livy', *Past & Present*, 129 (1990), 30–78; Kevin Sharpe, *Reading Revolutions: The Politics of Reading in Early Modern England* (New Haven and London: Yale University Press, 2000).

32 Andrew Cambers and Michelle Wolfe, 'Reading, Family Religion, and Evangelical Identity in Late Stuart England', *Historical Journal*, 47 (2004), 875–96'; Andrew Cambers, *Godly Reading: Print, Manuscript and Puritanism in England, 1580–1720* (Cambridge: Cambridge University Press, 2011); Kate Narveson, *Bible Readers and Lay Writers in Early Modern England* (Farnham: Ashgate, 2012); and Femke Molekamp, *Women and the Bible in Early Modern England* (Oxford: Oxford University Press, 2013).

33 Jürgen Habermas, *The Structural Transformation of the English Public Sphere*, trans. Thomas Burger (Cambridge, MA: MIT Press, 1989); Joad Raymond, *Pamphlets and Pamphleteering in Early Modern Britain* (Cambridge: Cambridge University Press, 2003), p. 26.

34 Peacey, *Print and Public Politics*, pp. 399–402 and *passim*; and Jason Peacey, 'Pamphlets', in Raymond, *Cheap Print*, pp. 453–700.

35 Peacey, *Print and Public Politics*, pp. 294–307, 455–7, 469–70.

36 See Chapter 3 in this volume for more on ecclesiastical sources.

37 Green, *Print and Protestantism*, Chapters 2–9.

38 E.g. Peter Lake, *The Boxmaker's Revenge: 'Orthodoxy', 'Heterodoxy', and the Politics of the Parish in Early Stuart London* (Stanford: Stanford University Press, 2001); Peter Lake and Michael Questier, *The Antichrist's Lewd Hat: Protestants, Papists and Players in Post-Reformation England* (New Haven: Yale University Press, 2002).

39 Raymond, *Cheap Print*, pp. 62–3, 235; A. Ryrie, *Being Protestant in Reformation Britain* (Oxford: Oxford University Press, 2013), p. 10n20, and *passim*.

40 Green, *Print and Protestantism*, pp. 154–5, 124.

41 See above, pp. 80–3; Fergus, *Provincial Readers, passim*.

42 *RSTC*; Wing, *Short-Title Catalogue*; *Eighteenth-Century Short Title Catalogue*.

43 http://eebo.chadwyck.com/home; http://gale.cengage.co.uk/product-highlights/ history/eighteenth-century-collections-online.aspx (both accessed 12 January 2016).

44 http://www.bpi1700.org.uk (accessed 12 January 2016). See also Ruth Samson Luborsky and Elizabeth Morley Ingram, *A Guide to English Illustrated Books 1536–1603*, 2 vols (Tempe, AZ: Medieval and Renaissance Texts and Studies, 1998); Malcolm Jones, *The Print in Early Modern England: An Historical Oversight* (New Haven and London: Yale University Press, 2010); and J. A. Sharpe, *Crime and the Law in English Satirical Prints 1600–1832* (Cambridge: Chadwyck-Healey, 1982) – part of a series on 'The English Satirical Print 1600–1832'.

5   Literary sources

Ceri Sullivan

For a historian to appeal to literary sources in a credible way – at least from the point of view of literary critics – she needs to be aware of three things: first, how the period categorized different sorts of writing as being literature; second, how literary genres frame the thinking about life done in these texts; and third, how, today, she can find literary primary sources, how she can use today's commentary on them, and the elephant traps that exist in selecting and using these sources.

What does the early modern period think literature is and does?

Literature, Terry Eagleton remarks, is a functional, not an ontological term: a category developed by the way in which we treat texts, not an inherent quality in them.[1] Literary studies are greedy about taking into the discipline all manner of non-fictional genres, such as biographies, essays and accounts of travel. Readers make them into literature by looking at the structures in which the content is arranged, and the language in which it is expressed. In doing so, we literary critics gaily admit that we, not the texts, provide their literary quality. And we claim the right to do so for any discursive product; all of them are potentially literary.

The literary theory of the 1970s and 1980s lies behind such swashbuckling: in particular, reception theory and New Historicism. Reception theory claims that the reader cooperates with the writer in producing meaning out of words. Thus, there are multiple and ever-changing 'texts' (not static 'works'). The text is not a thing, but a moment of understanding in time, which the reader creates from the words currently under her eyes. Such creation is done according to context – the developing narrative within the text, of course, but also the context outside the text, the reader's purpose in reading it and her cultural position as she does so (as female, or middle class, or an accountant, or in a rush, or on a bus, or online, or whatever). While she proceeds through the text, the reader forms an interpretative ('hermeneutical') circle, where her understanding of the present moment of the text accords with what she has already read and what she expects to read. Her purpose in reading the text is part of the moment of reception, and she can decide to create a version that is literary. New Historicism (more of a new practice than a new theory) assumes that all texts evidence a political position in their literary shape and methods. All representations of events, by writers and readers then and now, reproduce powerful political and social positions, even when those representations claim to be objective. The critic should be 'suspicious', turning to detailed ('thick') analyses of fictional and non-fictional texts to site them in their own context, as well as her reading in hers. Heady stuff for today's reader, if she is accustomed either to losing herself in a realist narrative, or to contemplating, passively, a canonical work. But it would not seem so surprising to early modern readers, who expected to cooperate with literary texts, in being moved to intervene in situations after reading about them. Fiction in the early modern period is more of a rhetorical than an aesthetic category. This makes it of particular interest to any historian who is interested in how situations become thinkable and doable.

This section will detail the five principal features of how early modern writers and readers thought about what we would now call literary texts (whether fictional or not). They understood them to be rhetorical, imitative and didactic. They were proud of their use of the vernacular, wary about the charges of falsehood in fiction – but reversed most of these attitudes when it came to religious writing.[2]

The first and foremost element of early modern literary theory is rhetoric: the powerful skill of getting the hearer or reader to agree with the speaker's point of view. In rhetoric a word does not assert a thing's essence or existence; it exists as an intellectual structure only, invented for a particular purpose. The rhetorically educated speaker does not endlessly try to push through language to a pre-existent reality beyond. Her view, of both herself and of language, is public, dramatic and argumentative.[3] The period invested heavily in training in language skills. In grammar schools, classical texts, particularly from first-century Rome, were exhaustively studied with an eye to both their speeches and the civic values they expressed – for eight hours a day, six days a week, for up to eight years. Crafting a speech is a satisfyingly schematic action, which is attentive to a particular occasion and audience. Initially the speaker considers the three main elements of the intended speech: the current and desired disposition of the audience, the self-projection of the speaker needed to attract that particular audience, and the topic to be addressed (the pathos, ethos and logos of the speech, respectively). She then turns to the purpose of the speech. Must she awake the judgement of the audience (judicial rhetoric, appealing to reason), or make the audience decide to act (deliberative rhetoric, appealing to the will), or move it to feel good or bad about someone or something (epideictic or demonstrative rhetoric, appealing to the emotions)?

Having settled the context, the speaker can start to compose the speech, which is done in five stages.[4] The first is invention, when she draws material out of commonplaces (that store of information on the topics in hand, that previous speakers have found useful), and by formal strategies (that previous speakers have found useful). In the case of the latter, for judicial rhetoric she interrogates her topic in terms that are conjectural (the question of fact), legal (how to interpret this fact) and juridical (whether is it right and equitable to do so). In the case of deliberative rhetoric, she asks if her audience could do something (either with might or with craft) and whether it should do it (whether it is right or praiseworthy). For demonstrative rhetoric, there are lists of suggestions about what to praise or dispraise (in the case of people, for instance, try external circumstances such as wealth or titles, physical attributes, and qualities of character). Having gathered together this mound of material, the speaker now moves to the second stage (disposition), where she selects the most telling points, and then arranges the content. Typically, a speech would require an introduction, a statement of facts, a division of reasons for or against her position, proofs, a conclusion, and a peroration, to send the audience away to act on the speech. The third stage of invention is elocution, where she 'clothes' in moving words the selected and arranged material. In particular, the speaker looks to use tropes (or turnings of meaning, such as metaphor) and schemes (or arrangements of sound, such as rhyme) to give richness and passion to her work. The fourth stage, memorizing the speech, is less important in Renaissance literature, but the advice on the fifth and final stage, delivery, is key to public and stage speaking in the period. The speaker is advised about her voice (volume, pitch and intonation) and body (clothing, stance, countenance and gestures).

Nothing here is left to chance. The speaker is programmed to persuade anyone to her point of view. But, equally, her audience is similarly armed, so it can assess her technical performance and counterbalance its effect. Given that rhetoric is so powerful, the early modern period debated the ethics of its use, developing earlier arguments against it (in Plato) and for it (in Aristotle, Cicero, Quintilian and Augustine). True, it is an art of lies – but then, human speakers can never be entirely accurate. True, reason should determine decisions – but then, the emotions were given us by God, so may legitimately be appealed to. True, rhetoric gives power to the clever, not the right – but then, use is not abuse. Any historian reading literary sources needs both to keep in mind the mechanics of how rhetoric works to structure texts, and also take into account the awe and suspicion aroused at the time by a confident use of these techniques.

The second major issue in early modern literary theory is the pleasure (rather than anxiety) of influence from other writers. The Romantic idea about authorship is that originality is the keynote of creativity. The artist is a loner, who breaks free from conventional ideas and stale language. The early modern idea of creativity is directly opposite. Originality means building on others' work and so moving a whole body of shared knowledge forward: everyone quotes everyone else, on purpose, and with the expectation that the quotations will be recognized and applauded. Literature is a communal activity, the present writer bringing together past writers and present readers. The usual tag for this process is that writers are dwarfs on the shoulders of giants. Schooling is focused on developing literary crafts-manship, boys taking passages from the great classical authors, parsing them, analysing their style, translating them into English, writing their own examples in imitation of them, then translating them back into Latin (and, more rarely, Greek).[5] Such exercises in writing were held to produce wit, not to extinguish it. The historian needs to recognize commonplace pas-sages in literary texts as the operatic arias they are, in which reader or audience is gratified to see, once again, 'found' arguments or expressions from elsewhere.

Third, writers expected literature to teach the reader what is right, to delight them as it does so, and thus to move them to act on their new insight. Literature is neither ornamental, nor expressive of an author's inner being, nor realist; it is a power tool to change events in the real world. Writers regu-larly reached back to the first-century treatise by Horace on the art of poetry. Horace was acutely aware that to get his reader to act well, he needed to make her clear about what the right thing is, and make her want to act on it – hence, the need for delight.[6] Writing in about 1581, Philip Sidney puts poetry above philosophy and history for that reason. Philosophy allows the reader to understand the truth, but goes nowhere towards moving her to act on it, since its discourse is abstract and rational. History has the opposite problem, showing her lots of examples of the rise and fall of men that are delightful because they are such vivid, concrete instances, but entirely failing to point her towards what should be, rather than what is. Literature, however, com-bines the best of both disciplines, changing the reader, who will then go on to change the world.[7] So a historian needs to ask about each passage in a text, each speech of a character in a play, how it is trying to change the situation, what it is doing, not what it is expressing.

Fourth, historians have to keep in mind the period's exuberant self-consciousness about the capabilities of the vernacular.[8] Early modern writers take immense pride in the fact that English is finally a language able to prod-uce a variety of genres, from the humble and ephemeral pasquil to the most revered form, the mighty and eternal epic. Finally, we are a match for contin-ental nations (whose artistic and literary Renaissance had preceded ours by a century or more). The development of English is partly as the natural result of increasing regularity over the sixteenth century in the areas of spelling and syntax. A mutually reinforcing growth in literacy and in printed books leads the way on this. There is, moreover, a deliberate attempt to enrich the language, with words from the past (archaisms); words from other dialects or languages, especially Latin (loan words); and some ingenuity in making up new words (neologisms). The ability to pour forth these riches, without visible effort (that is, with *sprezzatura*), is valued. The writer must not 'smell of the lamp' (that is, of too much study for the words), or show signs of dipping too often into the 'inkhorn'. Today's historian must develop a nose for the lan-guage of the period, for when the unusual register of word or passage nudges her towards an implied attitude about what is being said, or, alternatively, when a passage asks not to be taken literally, given its inebriated pleasure in words.

Fifth come debates over the legitimacy of staging fictions, all of which sound rather like our own worries about massive online multiplayer war games. At the very least, watching a play wastes time that should be devoted to godly activities within a vocation. More darkly, though, detractors of the playhouse argue that theatre is a form of falsehood, of living in a virtual reality. Visual representations are particularly able to encourage viewers to change their ways of behaving, by imitating those on stage (a problem, given the amount of sex and violence that is the stuff of early modern drama). Even the circumstances of performance are suspicious: large groups of youth together on wasteland (the 'liberties' of London), drinking and gazing at inflammatory material.[9] The defence by playgoers is usually that use is not abuse. If theatre has the power it is credited with by those who decry it, then it can also be a powerful tool for good, especially given drama's possibilities as a thought experiment.[10] A historian citing a play in evidence needs to understand that an early modern audience is interested, provoked, upset or encouraged by having its social and political problems and opportunities relived in front of it (and hence, the historian will appreciate how sensitive authorities are about these performances). Historians need to track down the available evidence of how the play was performed and what reception it had, on specific occasions.

In dealing with religious literature, a different understanding of language applies to that used in reading secular texts. All early modern writers and readers become highly trained textual analysts specifically as a result of the Protestant reliance on the Word of God.[11] If salvation depends on faith, and faith stems from hearing and understanding God's word, then independent practical criticism of the Bible is key. The Bible is where all literary activity is first and most pressingly and extensively practised. Children learn to read using the Lord's Prayer on a hornbook, and progress to picking their way through biblical verses. They learn to listen in sermons that analyse the Word of God in minute detail. They read Bibles that are the product of extremely sophisticated scholarly editing, which drew on the development of stemma (the relationship between the original manuscript and subsequent copies of it) the collation of editions across multiple languages, and the provision of both textual and substantive footnotes. Even lay readers examined these Bibles further by using such aids as historical and philological commentaries, theological treatises, concordances and illustrations. Tough textual questions faced by a lay reader included when to take a sentence metaphorically and when literally, how to interpret and apply parables, whether to take certain words as having godly presence in themselves (in effect, as speech acts), and how to discern the working Word of God in the heart. Historians should understand that the peculiar texture of religious literature does not necessarily (or even primarily) operate through the understanding and will of the reader. Doctrinal and devotional issues are fought out inside the language, not by looking through to the content.

Why should a historian know about early modern literary genres?

Historians feel confident about a linguistic turn, but more wary about a literary one: they may approach literary texts without a sufficient sense of the genre in which they exist. Genre is a slippery term, since it is a classification that can be either written into a text by the author or assigned by the reader. Yet its structuring effects – particularly in a non-realist aesthetic – produce meaning, so must be recognized if literary sources are to be appealed to as evidence.

There are four major features to any genre: its function (what that sort of passage usually sets out to do to the reader), its thematic structure (what that sort of passage usually deals with; what sort of conventional topoi are used; what sort of conventional, albeit schematic, world it projects), its speaking position (what that sort of passage usually uses, in terms of an actual as opposed to an implied reader, and an actual writer as opposed to an authorial persona), and, finally, a set of formal linguistic features (what sort of typeface, font and page layout are usually used for that sort of passage; what is the usual organization of sounds; what sorts of syntax and vocabulary are used).[12]

English early modern genres were recognized as having discrete social functions. By the end of the sixteenth century a number of texts discuss major genres, like history and epic. The most accessible of the vernacular discussions is George Puttenham's *Arte of English Poesie* (1589), which provides a family history of genres, and details the intentions and the formal features of relation.[13] Starting with hymns (there to praise the gods), he moves on through satire (reproving vice in humans, bitterly but covertly), comedy (dealing with the middling sorts, and tending to amend their lives) and tragedy (there to improve the greatest of men by exemplifying the fall of those who act badly), pastoral (competitive and political, not mere entertainment), histories, epics and heroic panegyrics (tracing the course of great men's lives, to encourage others to live well), epigrams, epitaphs and posies (similar in intention, but about the lower ranks, so on a smaller scale), sonnets, odes, elegies, ballads and other ditties (uttering the inconstant passion of love), encomia and epithalamia (for happy times, like marriages), and elegies (for the unhappy times).

Given that genre is an effect of reading as much as of writing, neither Puttenham nor anyone else can ever list all the genres. However, *not all* does not mean *none*. To develop a sensitivity toward genre, the historian can (in order of speed), first consult a dictionary of literary terms (issued by all major presses, usually giving a paragraph and further reading on each term). More detail can be found in the New Critical Idiom series, with a volume devoted to each major genre, and in stand-alone monographs on genres, some keyed to individual authors, some not. If the historian wants to go behind the English literary theorists, then keep in mind that Puttenham and his colleagues were drawing on treatises on poetics by Horace, Aristotle and Boccaccio, and on sixteenth-century Italian critics Julius Caesar Scaliger and Antonio Minturno.

How can a historian find and use early modern literary sources?

Having got the right mindset for interpreting early modern literary sources, how can the historian find and use them? This section advises on selecting the relevant editions, collections and databases, on the need for historians to consult today's literary criticism, and on taking stage productions as a form of literary criticism.[14]

If you require completeness in bibliographical matters about texts in English start with the *Revised Short Title Catalogue* (*RSTC*), which gives a full list of extant editions, impressions, issues, and states of books published in the British Isles, and abroad in the English language, to 1640. It gives the location of up to five copies, and indicates where other copies are known about, so you can chase up further originals if studying variants and marginalia. Volume III gives indexes of printers and publishers, places of publication other than London, London imprints, and dates of publication.[15] If researching the publication history of a particular source (in particular, who owned the text, and whether it was licensed or censored), then use the records of the Company of Stationers, which have been transcribed and calendared.[16] Be aware that texts were registered as a claim to ownership, and not necessarily printed afterwards, nor always with the title given in the register.

The widest set of primary texts, which includes literary material, is in *EEBO*. This contains the page images of over 125,000 titles listed in Pollard and Redgrave's *Short Title Catalogue* (*1475–1640*) (*RSTC*) and Wing's *Short Title Catalogue* (*1641–1700*). The full text of about 25,000 of these can now be searched, as a result of the *EEBO* Text Creation Partnership (and this number will increase over time). While one can search by title keyword and assigned topics from the metadata (in the MARC record), there is no possibility of comprehensive searching by literary genre. Try using the advanced-search 'record keyword' option, to elicit some suggestions. *JISC Historic Books*, which aims to be the successor to *EEBO*, and uses its database of texts and metadata, has two principal advantages: its interface allows the viewer to read original and keyed text side by side, and it is integrated with *Eighteenth Century Collections Online* (*EECO*), allowing searches over the period division between the two databases.[17] *Early European Books* (Collections 1 to 4) digitizes the holdings of non-anglophone books from before 1700 in the Royal Library of Copenhagen, the National Central Library of Florence, the National Library of the Netherlands and the London Wellcome Library.[18]

EEBO is comprehensive and relatively easy to use, but there are hidden dangers. It does not give the full range of copies, includes incomplete copies, supplements some incomplete copies with pages from other copies, does not necessarily give the most authoritative version of the text, may have metadata that does not match the original and (for those texts that are not fully searchable) relies on someone else's classification by subject. Thus, both the metadata and any keyed version on which you rely should always be checked against the original images in *EEBO* (and vice versa).

Having started with these databases – in order to select which early modern literary texts to use – it is sensible to revert to a standard scholarly edition, if one exists. This is partly because the editors will have established a stable and authoritative text out of the different editions and states (which they record in the textual footnotes, known as 'lemma'), and partly because editors can give some sense of how words are interpreted, then and now (in their substantive footnotes). It is impossible to be specific about which standard edition to use. Some sense of this is best gained from browsing the footnotes of recent literary criticism about the author. The following list, therefore, is to be treated with caution. For drama, the usually cited series are the Arden (currently published by Bloomsbury, and including the Third Series of Arden Shakespeare), the New Mermaids (Bloomsbury) and the Revels (Manchester University Press). For Renaissance Latin texts, the University of Toronto Press, the Medieval and Renaissance Texts and Studies series, and the publications sponsored by the Renaissance Society of America are trusted. English canonical authors tend to fall under the province of Oxford and Cambridge University Presses. If reliance is to be placed on very detailed textual readings, it is important to look at as many states of the text as possible, being guided by the lemma, or, if no scholarly edition exists, by the different states of the texts (relying on *EEBO* if necessary, but preferably consulting the originals in their home libraries).

Since the quality of literariness depends on how a text is read, then historians must make up their minds to approach today's literary criticism about early modern texts. Literary critics (languid text-fondlers that we are) snigger at historians who assume that a certain text is definitively literary or non-literary, and who do not flex it through a range of possible meanings. The two outstanding annotated bibliographies are *The Year's Work in English Studies* (*YWES*) and the *Modern Language Association International Bibliography* (*MLA*). The former comprehensively, independently and succinctly reviews all editions, books and articles published in the year.[19] It contains discrete chapters on Shakespeare, other dramatists, and on poetry and prose from the sixteenth and seventeenth centuries. Surfing *YWES* (say for a five-year period) gives a rapid overview of what the latest opinions are about the period or about a particular author. It will also give a sense of what authors are regarded as canonical, currently. Though full-text searches are possible, *YWES* is not primarily set up as a topic-based resource. For this, turn to the *MLA*, which indexes articles published in over 4,400 humanities journals from 1926 to the present, and makes complex combined keyword searches easy.[20] Equally as comprehensive as *YWES*, the *MLA*'s entries on articles and books are summaries of content rather than qualitative reviews.

Other useful collections include *Literature Online*, which provides access to the full text of more than 350,000 British and American original works (as well as links to reputable background material).[21] It can be used for stylistic comparison, for word-finding, as an online concordance and simply for reading texts. The premier international bibliography of scholarship on the Renaissance, which covers all disciplines including literature, is the *Bibliographie internationale de l'humanisme et de la Renaissance.*[22] The historian should approach literary criticism crisply: some of it may be expressed in numinous terms, which at best may veil a substantive argument, or, at worse, hide a vacuum. When pressing early modern literary passages to produce meaning, literary scholars make use of the new *Oxford English Dictionary*, not merely for its definitions, but also for the etymologies it gives, hints for parallel primary texts in the quotations it cites and its timelines of how frequently a word appears in its quotation banks (the rough biography of a word).[23] Concordances, which list all the times a particular word appears in an author's works, and are keyed to a standard scholarly edition, are useful in widening the range of a search. The *Oxford Dictionary of National Biography* provides possible leads for primary sources for the biography of literary authors.[24]

'Literary' manuscripts are a subset not covered by the resources above. There is a descriptive *Index of English Literary Manuscripts* for a selection of canonical authors (the first volume covering 124 British and Irish authors to 1700), which lists literary but not biographical manuscripts from the authors concerned (including copies by scribes).[25] Again, the historian is advised to search out standard scholarly editions where they exist, and, where they do not, to try keyword searches in the relevant national archives.[26] There are stand-alone digitized collections of manuscripts, such as the Folger Library's, and the Perdita collection of early modern women's manuscripts, which are ever-increasing. The website *Luminarium* is usually alert to these collections.[27] The above approach is suitable for historians who are comprehensively searching for texts relating to specific topics, authors or years, and can employ searches in indexes or by keywords. Historians who are trying to find out what are generally considered to be the important primary texts in a particular genre or on a particular topic need to orientate themselves in different way. Two series, the Cambridge Companions to Literature and the Blackwell Companions to Literature and Culture, both available in print and online, are helpful in this, and well regarded by library critics as starter packs. Each includes bibliographies of primary reading. Both the individual volumes, and the range covered by the two series, are regularly updated to include the authors and topics currently firing literary criticism. The standard scholarly literary histories for the period also point up the major primary texts. In particular, historians should look at the relevant volumes in the (recently completed) twentieth-century series, the Oxford History of English Literature, which is now in the process of being superseded by a new series, the Oxford Literary History.

A historian dealing with dramatic texts would be expected (by literary critics) to have considered how performance changes the meaning of a dramatic text, then and now. The *World Shakespeare Bibliography* is the most comprehensive international list of works that are of relevance to the Renaissance drama generally, as well as to Shakespeare.[28] It covers books, articles, dissertations, productions, films and digital media. Gerald Eades Bentley's *The Jacobean and Caroline Stage* gives information on primary sources by theatre company, theatre, actor, dramatist, play and reception.[29] Performance-based studies turn to the *Records of Early English Drama*, an ongoing and multi-volume series of historical documents containing comprehensive evidence of drama, secular music, and other communal entertainments and ceremonies to 1642. The series is divided by place and date.[30] Recordings of current and past performances are held in the archives and on the websites of theatres that regularly perform early modern drama, and in some cases these have been released commercially. There is currently no comprehensive database of recordings of performances of early modern drama. However, *Shakespeare Survey* gives a single individual's review of productions in Britain each year, and *Shakespeare Quarterly* an *ad hoc* range of performances from across the world. Standard scholarly editions usually give details of the reception history and major productions of that play. Recordings of the London Globe's two stages, indoor (private) and outdoor (public) give a sense of what it is like to act and watch an early modern play.[31]

In conclusion, this chapter has urged the historian to accept that, for the literary critic, literature is what she makes of a text, so there can be no list of literary sources set apart from historical sources. The historian has to develop a sensibility to the form and function of a text, bearing in mind debates both then and now about the possibilities for making meaning.

Key resources

Early English Books Online, http://eebo.chadwyck.com/home (requires subscription).
Literature Online, http://literature.proquest.com/marketing/index.jsp (requires subscription).
Modern Language Association International Bibliography, https://www.mla.org/bibliography.
Pollard, A. W. and G. Redgrave, *A Short-Title Catalogue of Books Printed in England, Scotland, & Ireland and of English Books Printed Abroad, 1475–1640*, rev. and enlarged W. A. Jackson, F. S. Ferguson and K. F. Pantzer, 3 vols (London: Bibliographical Society, 1976–91).
Records of Early English Drama, http://reed.utoronto.ca.
Vickers, B. (ed.), *English Renaissance Literary Criticism* (Oxford: Oxford University Press, 2003).
The Year's Work in English Studies, http://ywes.oxfordjournals.org (requires subscription).

Notes

1 T. Eagleton, *Literary Theory: An Introduction* (Oxford: Blackwell, 1983), Chapter 1. Eagleton wittily opens out the opportunities for interpretation given by modern literary theory. Peter Barry, *Beginning Theory: An Introduction to Literary and Cultural Theory* (Manchester: Manchester University Press, 1995) yomps through the ideas in a way that novices will find reassuring and of practical use. An incisive example of a historian's sceptical response to literary theory is D. Aers, 'A Whisper in the Ear of Early Modernists; or, Reflections on Literary Critics Writing the "History of the Subject"', in D. Aers (ed.), *Culture and History 1350–1600* (New York: Harvester Wheatsheaf, 1990), pp. 177–202.

2 The early modern literary theory texts can be found in their original editions in *EEBO*, http://eebo.chadwyck.com/home (accessed 12 January 2016). The three principal modern collections are: B. Vickers, *English Renaissance Literary Criticism* (Oxford: Oxford University Press, 1999); G. G. Smith (ed.), *Elizabethan Critical Essays*, 2 vols (Oxford: Clarendon Press, 1904); J. E. Spingarn (ed.), *Critical Essays of the Seventeenth Century*, 3 vols (Oxford: Clarendon Press, 1908–09); Vol. I covers 1605–50. The issues sketched here can be followed up in G. P. Norton (ed.), *The Cambridge History of Literary Criticism*, Vol III: *The Renaissance* (Cambridge: Cambridge University Press, 1999).

3 R. Lanham, *The Motives of Eloquence: Literary Rhetoric in the Renaissance* (New Haven: Yale University Press, 1976), Chapter 1.

4 Vickers provides a brisk summary of the process: B. Vickers, *In Defence of Rhetoric* (Oxford: Clarendon Press, 1987), Chapters 1, 5; J. Richards, *Rhetoric*, New Critical Idiom (London: Routledge, 2008), Chapters 1, 2; P. Mack, *A History of Renaissance Rhetoric* (Oxford: Oxford University Press, 2011). The most approachable Roman rhetoric, parts of which were used in early modern grammar schooling, is the pseudo-Ciceronian *Rhetorica ad Herennium*, trans. and ed. H. Caplan, Loeb Classical Library (Cambridge, MA: Harvard University Press, 1954).

5 R. Ascham, *The Scholemaster* (1570), in Smith, *Elizabethan Critical Essays*, Vol. I, pp. 1–45; S. Daniel, *A Defence of Rhyme* (*c.* 1603), in Smith, *Elizabethan Critical Essays*, Vol. II, pp. 366–7. For a modern study of the uses of imitation in the period, see D. Quint, *Origin and Originality in Renaissance Literature: Versions of the Source* (New Haven: Yale University Press, 1983); Rebecca Herissone and Alan Howard (eds), *Concepts of Creativity in Seventeenth-Century England* (Woodbridge: Boydell, 2013).

6 Jonson translated Horace, excerpted in Vickers, *Criticism*, Chapter 23.

7 Philip Sidney, *An Apology for Poetry; or, The Defence of Poetry* (1595), ed. G. Shepherd, rev. R. W. Maslen (Manchester: Manchester University Press, 2002); Vickers, *Criticism*, Chapter 15.

8 For instance, R. Carew, 'Epistle on the Excellency of the English Tongue' (*c.* 1596), in Smith, *Elizabethan Critical Essays*, Vol. II, pp. 285–94; J. Hope, *Shakespeare and Language: Reason, Eloquence, and Artifice in the Renaissance* (London: Arden, 2010).

9 S. Gosson, *School of Abuse* (1579); J. A. Barrish, *The Antitheatrical Prejudice* (Berkeley: University of California Press, 1981); A. Gurr, *Playgoing in Shakespeare's England*, rev. edn (Cambridge: Cambridge University Press, 2004), Chapters 4, 5.

10 J. Knapp, *Shakespeare's Tribe: Church, Nation, and Theater in Renaissance England* (Chicago: University of Chicago Press, 2002).

11 D. Shuger, *Habits of Thought in the English Renaissance: Religion, Politics, and the Dominant Culture* (Berkeley: University of California Press, 1990); *The Renaissance Bible: Scholarship, Sacrifice, and Subjectivity* (Berkeley: University of California Press, 1994); C. Sullivan, *The Rhetoric of the Conscience in Donne, Herbert, and Vaughan* (Oxford: Oxford University Press, 2008).

12 J. Frow, *The New Critical Idiom: Genre* (London: Routledge, 2006), esp. pp. 6–12, 51–5, 72–7.

13 G. Puttenham, *The Arte of English Poesie*, in Smith, *Elizabethan Critical Essays*, Vol. II, Chapters 11–30.

14 For other early modern datasets, see J. L. Harner, 'Renaissance Literature (1500–1660)', in *Literary Research Guide: An Annotated Listing of Reference Sources in English Literary Studies* (New York: Modern Language Association, 2008), pp. 246–75.

15 A. W. Pollard and G. R. Redgrave, *A Short-Title Catalogue of Books Printed in England, Scotland, & Ireland and of English Books Printed Abroad, 1475–1640*, 2nd edn, rev. and enlarged by W. A. Jackson, F. S. Ferguson and K. F. Pantzer, 3 vols

(London: Bibliographical Society, 1976–91). See also the online *STC*, http://estc. bl.uk (accessed 12 January 2016).

16 E. Arber (ed.), *A Transcript of the Registers of the Company of Stationers of London, 1554–1640*, 5 vols (London: privately printed, 1875–94); W. W. Greg, *A Companion to Arber: Being a Calendar of Documents in Edward Arber's 'Transcript of the Registers of the Company of Stationers of London, 1554–1640', with Text and Calendar of Supplementary Documents* (Oxford: Clarendon Press, 1967); W. W. Greg and E. Boswell, *Records of the Court of the Stationers Company, 1576 to 1602, from Register B* (London: Bibliographical Society, 1930); W. A. Jackson, *Records of the Court of the Stationers' Company, 1602 to 1640* (London: Bibliographical Society, 1957).

17 http://www.jisc-collections.ac.uk/jiscecollections/jischistoricbooks (accessed 12 January 2016).

18 http://eeb.chadwyck.com/home.do (accessed 12 January 2016).

19 http://ywes.oxfordjournals.org (accessed 12 January 2016).

20 http://www.mla.org/bibliography (accessed 12 January 2016).

21 http://literature.proquest.com (accessed 12 January 2016).

22 http://www.droz.org/eur/en/13-bihr (accessed 12 January 2016).

23 http://www.oed.com (accessed 12 January 2016).

24 http://www.oxforddnb.com (accessed 12 January 2016).

25 P. Beal, *Index of English Literary Manuscripts 1450–1700*, 2 vols (London: Mansell, 1980–93).

26 The British archives are on http://discovery.nationalarchives.gov.uk (accessed 12 January 2016). A useful manual for reading the different hands used in primary documents, which includes annotated transcriptions and illustrations of the alphabet in each hand, is H. Jenkinson, *The Later Court Hands in England from the Fifteenth to the Seventeenth Century: Illustrated from the Common Paper of the Scriveners' Company of London, the English Writing Masters, and the Public Records*, 2 vols (Cambridge: Cambridge University Press, 1927).

27 The Folger digital images are at http://luna.folger.edu; the Perdita collection is at http://www.amdigital.co.uk/m-collections/collection/perdita-manuscripts-1500-1700; *Luminarium* is at http://www.luminarium.org (all accessed 12 January 2016).

28 http://www.worldshakesbib.org (accessed 12 January 2016).

29 G. E. Bentley, *The Jacobean and Caroline Stage* (Oxford: Clarendon Press, 1941–68).

30 http://reed.utoronto.ca (accessed 12 January 2016).

31 http://www.shakespearesglobe.com (accessed 12 January 2016).

6   Personal documents

Laura Sangha

In the early modern period a growing number of people put pen to paper (or parchment) to write something down. The motives for picking up a pen were extraordinarily various – writing might be necessary to conduct the business of the State (Chapter 1); to record the proceedings of the judicial system (Chapter 2); to enact or encourage religious reforms (Chapter 3); to entertain, argue, educate, enlighten or make a profit (Chapter 4); or simply as a creative act of the imagination (Chapter 5). In this chapter I am not concerned with any of these institutional, professional or corporate acts of writing, but with what might be thought of as more 'ordinary' or 'everyday' forms of writing and the personal documents that such writing produced. These personal documents came in all shapes and forms, but they shared some common characteristics: they were seemingly undertaken by an individual, were often related to a person's life, were not solely written in a professional capacity, or had a particular significance or importance to a particular person, but most importantly they captured the subjective side of a person's experience. In practice it is of course hard to distinguish between institutional documents (which often contained personal information) and personal ones (which are not always as subjective as they appear). However, by way of example in this chapter I will focus on the two most common types of 'personal' material: correspondence and diaries.

The chapter will begin by defining in more detail the material that falls into the category of personal documents, before offering some suggestions on how to locate original and transcribed versions. Existing scholarship demonstrates the appeal of these documents as primary sources and their status as materials that seem to offer the promise of candour; directness; and an expression of inner desires, beliefs and expectations. Thus the strength of personal documents as historical sources might seem obvious – in contrast with other records they have the potential to reveal what an individual actually thought and felt about the times that they lived through; it seems they have the capacity to reveal the motives and mentality of people in the past. However, the chapter will also address the fact that these sources do not give us unmediated access to the private thoughts of contemporaries, despite their look and feel. Just as with any other source, to analyse such documents properly we need to consider the social and intellectual conventions that shaped the documents, and the historical context within which they were produced. We must ask who was writing, and what the function of their document was. We should also consider whom these authors were writing for, and the ways in which the needs, desires and expectations of the receiver or audience influenced the subject and style of the finished product. We must be sensitive to the genre of these materials, and consider the extent to which contemporary conventions and social mores have dictated the form and tone of the content. Finally, it is worth considering why these documents survived, despite their lack of 'official' public significance. The discussion is based on the assumption that these documents should not be treated unthinkingly as direct, personal accounts, but as 'calculated performances', shaped by many different influences. Though a document might be 'personal' that does not mean that it is one-dimensional or any less complicated than other, more obviously mediated materials.

Definitions

The letters that I consider within this chapter are written communications, usually from a first-person perspective, addressed to another party and often sent by post or messenger. Some of the earliest surviving personal correspondence is that between a fourteenth-century merchant and his wife over the course of eighteen years, offering a unique chronicle of a medieval marriage.[1] Not all letters survive in their original form however, since people had a tendency to copy them out, or perhaps even to publish collections subsequently. Thus other 'letter texts' also survive: drafts, copies, printed letters and letter-books (books in which the senders or receivers of letters copied out their correspondence so that they had a record of what had been written).[2] Since such letter texts might deal with an infinite range of subjects and functions, they have a generic fluidity that makes them and their contents hard to categorize. Studies in early modern letter-writing have flourished over the last decade, providing a rich picture of the contemporary culture of 'epistolarity'. In 2005 and 2006, James Daybell wrote two invaluable bibliographic essays that survey and summarize this scholarship, and that provide lists of printed editions of modern correspondence, and of transcriptions and calendars.[3]

Diaries are perhaps harder to define than letters, but their core characteristic is that they are a record of events or occurrences drawn from the experience of the author. It is important not to think of an early modern diary as a narrative of the significant events of the day, each day, as it happened, since most do not fit this model. It might be objected that the diary of the most famous early modern diarist, Samuel Pepys, is an example of such a record – the entries are arranged by day, Pepys is astonishingly candid about all aspects of his public and private activities, and in reading his diary we feel that we are given a complete insight into the charismatic man's life.[4] Yet we now know that Pepys' entries were 'written up' every few days from a scribbled draft, and collated with other private papers or printed sources that he had to hand. Thus his diary is quite carefully planned and crafted, despite its appearance – and this is true of many other examples of the genre, such as the diary of Pepys' contemporary John Evelyn, whose record was compiled much later from notes, with the result that some of his descriptions are anachronistic. Both diaries are the result of a particular process of record keeping, and could be considered 'fictive texts'.

Thus, whilst there is a consensus that the genre of the diary has its roots in the early modern period, it was not well defined at the time, but rather was a form that was slowly emerging out of other regular writing habits and that blurred with them. These other habits of writing also fall within the classification of personal documents; they were forms of recording information that underpinned diary-writing and that informed the shape that diaries eventually took.[5] In many ways Pepys' diary is actually rather exceptional, bearing little relation to the majority of writings about the self. Some authors kept records of a particular aspect of their lives that served as a sort of diary. For example the gentleman-farmer Robert Bulkeley wrote a record between 1630 and 1636 that contained detailed short notes on his farming work and affairs, whilst Jacob Bee mainly used his diary to note the births, deaths, marriages and accidents in Durham *c.* 1681–1707.[6] Those on a journey were also particularly prone to making a personal record of events – the travel memoirs of Celia Fiennes and Daniel Defoe are perhaps the most famous examples. There are many similar records, such as Robert Burgrave's account of his travels in the service of the Levant Company in 1646 and 1653 or Robert Coverte's formal diary of his journey through Portugal, India, Persia and Turkey from 1607 to 1611, which included notes on his official business, as well as on local peoples, customs, and flora and fauna.[7] Many of the diaries listed in William Matthews' 1950 bibliography recorded aspects of the authors' public lives, describing events tied to their occupation. The botanist James Petiver kept a medical journal in which he recorded details about his work as an apothecary to the Charterhouse, whilst the secretary-at-war in 1697, William Blathwayt, wrote about military movements and King William's activities during his travels in the Low Countries in 1697.[8] Other diarists wrote about their legal practices, their activities as MPs, or other business and State affairs. It is also apparent that great events and dangerous times prompted many people to record aspects of their lives on paper. This is often cited as Samuel Pepys' main motivation (though not all agree) but certainly military and naval diaries are over-represented in Matthews' catalogue, particularly for the period 1640–60 and after the 1688 'Glorious Revolution'.

Other writers noted down their personal concerns in notebooks, almanacs, commonplace books or receipt books. Through the use of such tools, people were able to reflect on their lives in a way that was significant to themselves. These records can be very messy documents that contain snatches and fragments of texts, sometimes ordered and arranged thematically, but on occasions incoherent and incomplete. Commonplacing (the noting of aphorisms gathered from reading or conversation, and listed under a series of thematic headings and then deployed in spoken or written discourse) was a crucial skill for the educated classes, but the resulting texts contain many different genres of writing, and their non-linear, non-narrative composition invites multiple readings and interpretations.[9] You can view examples of these manuscripts at *Scriptorium*: a digital archive of miscellanies and commonplace books from 1450 to 1720.[10] Another form of writing that appears to have contributed to the development of diaries are account books. Whilst noting down the day-to-day financial affairs of the household some people were inspired also to make a record of family or public events that occurred around the same time. The sixteenth-century priest of Morebath Christopher Trychay kept meticulous churchwarden accounts to which he added such a rich level of detail that Eamon Duffy was able to use them to reconstruct the fortunes of the parish through the turbulence of the Tudor reformations.[11]

Perhaps the classic type of autobiographical writing were the works of spiritual self-examination that proliferated following the Reformation. The most well-known examples are those of the puritan artisan Nehemiah Wallington (1598–1658) and the vicar of Earls Colne Ralph Josselin (1617–83), but many other examples survive.[12] In the 1630s the Essex clergyman John Beadle seems to have been the first to advocate writing a spiritual journal, but the practice itself predates this, its roots in the experimental Calvinism that emerged during the Elizabethan period.[13] Though they vary widely in format, these diaries could be thought of more generally as spiritual accounts books that recorded pious exercises and providences, offset by lists of occasions of sin and temptation.[14]

Early modern writing about the self could therefore be defined very broadly to include all these re-creations of details of personal experience in written form: from spiritual and secular 'day-to-day' writing, to commonplace books, recipe books, miscellanies, travel journals, weather and farming diaries, to manuscripts that more closely conform with our expectations of what diaries are that might be described as autobiographies and memoirs.[15] Personal documents can be, and have been, used by historians to write histories about a staggering range of topics, but there are some more common themes that can be detected in this work. For example, the study of personal documents lends itself to the study of religious cultures (letters and spiritual diaries), travel and cultural life (letters and travel journals), farming and rural life (letters and agricultural diaries), medicine (letters and recipe books) or the household and everyday life (letters and commonplace books). They can be used to study the social networks of friends and families that created 'imagined communities', where collections survive. They illuminate the ways in which people gathered information about, interpreted and processed the events of their lives. Beyond these subjects, personal documents also give us special insight into the construction of the self, into self-representation, self-fashioning, self-perception, self-presentation, self-awareness and self-consciousness. They might reveal to

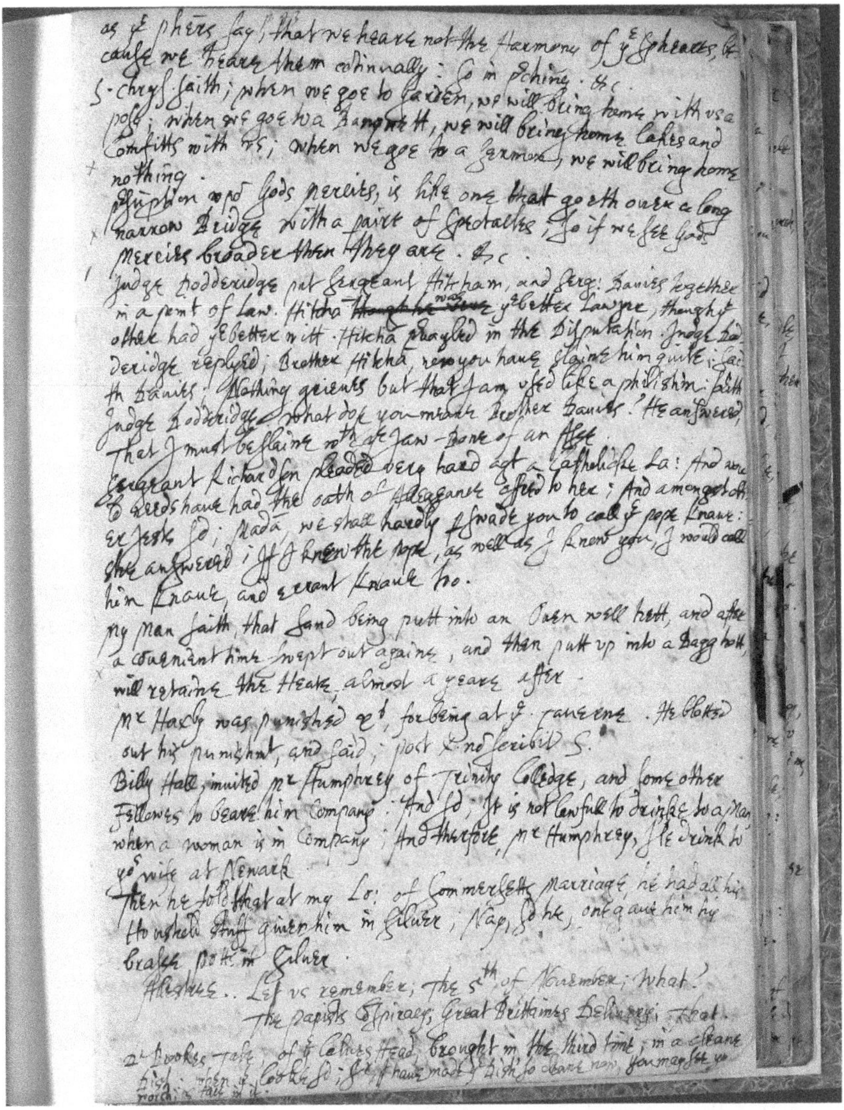

Figure 6.1 William Rawley's miscellany, Lambeth Palace Library, MS 2086, fo. 8r. This page from the notebook of Church of England clergyman William Rawley (*c.* 1588–1667) contains religious material; legal anecdotes; notes on an experiment into heat; and jovial anecdotes on dining, drinking and marriage; as well as verses on the Gunpowder Plot. Rawley kept and added to this book over two decades (1620s–1640s); its 46 pages contain over 900 entries. Diary-writing seems to have emerged from these sorts of regular writing habits that re-created personal experience in written form.

us inherent social expectations, value systems, communal morality, and give us an insight into early modern mentalities.

Locating personal documents

By the sixteenth century, letter-writing had been around for hundreds of years, but a wider range of letters, as well as more collections of letters, survive for the early modern period than the medieval, as letter-writing ability spread to a wider section of the population. Letters survive in three main types of repository: in State Papers, in legal and institutional archives, and among family collections. A wide variety of printed collections of correspondence is available – Daybell includes selective lists of editions in his two bibliographic essays mentioned above. A variety of text publication societies have produced or continue to produce editions of correspondence and diaries that can be searched for in library catalogues: regional record societies (for example the Surtees Society, the London Record Society or county record societies), the Camden Society (merged with the Royal Historical Society they publish the Camden Series), the Parker Society (works of early English Protestant writers), the Catholic Record Society, the Church of England Record Society, the Hakluyt Society (records of voyages, travels), the Selden Society (law). There are also some excellent online databases of particular collections: examples are listed at the end of this chapter.

For correspondence and diaries in the archives, there are numerous finding aids, catalogues and calendars. The National Archives' catalogue 'Discovery',[16] until recently known as 'Access to Archives', is an excellent place to start your search – the catalogue brings together listings of resources from numerous archives in England and Wales. However, it is *not* comprehensive, since not all repositories have signed up to the service, and even for those that have, not all of their collections are listed, and the quality and details of individual records on 'Discovery' can also vary enormously. *Early Modern Letters Online* is a growing union catalogue of sixteenth-, seventeenth- and eighteenth-century correspondence with basic descriptions and a powerful search capability.[17] Libraries and record offices have printed and sometimes electronic catalogues available. Usually correspondence appears as a separate category in archival listings, though these are likely to include only collections of letters – miscellaneous letters are often scattered through borough, parish, estate and personal papers. Susan Whyman's monograph *The Pen and the People* includes a useful appendix listing family archives and letter-writers *c*.1660–1800.[18]

For life-writing, William Matthews' 1950 *Bibliography* of British diaries is an excellent starting place.[19] It is an extensive list of extant diaries, including information on where the originals are located, dates covered, printed editions and brief notes on content. However, the list is now rather dated – Elaine McKay noted in 2005 that a further sixty-six diaries had been deposited in public record offices since Matthews' bibliography was published.[20]

Matthews' list can be supplemented by online catalogues such as the *Diary Search Website*,[21] or Paul K. Lyons' *The Diary Junction*, which brings together information on 500 diarists and provides links to online editions, where they exist.[22] 'Discovery', local library and record office catalogues, calendars, and other finding aids could also be used to locate manuscript diaries, journals, commonplace books and notebooks, and text publication societies also publish editions of these and similar texts.

Analysing personal documents

Whilst it is tempting to think of personal documents as more sincere or frank than other primary materials, they too were the products of social and cultural ideas and practices, and they had their own set of rules, methods and conventions of production. Both a letter and a diary should be considered a 'calculated performance', an exercise in the construction and projection of the self. As such, to understand these documents properly we must analyse them with reference to their origin, production, dissemination and survival.

Authors

It is important to bear in mind the types of people who were most likely to produce personal documents in the early modern period, since they undoubtedly came from a small section of the population that may not be more broadly representative. In the early sixteenth century a growing number of people were able to read and write, but literacy was still confined to a small minority at the top of the social hierarchy, and incorporated many more men than women. Letters and diaries were therefore most likely to be written by male social elites with the education and resources to write analytical accounts of their lives, yet some women and lower sorts can also be found amongst their ranks. As time progressed, letter-writing skills disseminated more widely throughout society, and Susan Whyman has argued that after 1660 the culture of letters embraced lower and middling sorts of writers who engaged in a popular and flexible epistolary tradition.[23] Similarly, Elaine McKay's survey of the 372 extant diaries written between 1500 and 1700 reveals that the occupation most frequently represented amongst English diarists was that of clergymen (40), followed by government officials (39), sailors (22), Members of Parliament (22) and scholars (20). Middling sorts of people such as tradesmen and merchants (13) and yeomen (9) were more likely to write diaries than those below them in the social hierarchy, but are not as well represented as the educated elites. Some of the more plebeian diarists are discussed in Mark Hailwood's 'Popular Culture' chapter in this volume. For the sixteenth century McKay found 37 diaries by men and 2 by women; for the seventeenth century 312 were written by men and 20 by women.[24] Numbers of surviving female-authored letters also increase over the course of the period: more than 3,500 Elizabethan letters written by over 750 women are extant, and more than 10,000 survive for the period to 1642 – in this they are the most ubiquitous female form of early modern writing.[25] Female letter-writers also became more socially diverse over time to incorporate women of landed and mercantile status. Female-authored personal documents may be in the minority, but they are crucial if we wish to appreciate the experiences of women in the past, particularly since they belong to the one genre from which female voices were not excluded. Female letters and diaries shed important light on female education, on family, gender and other social relations, and provide invaluable information on the breadth of female activities.

It is also worth considering who actually wrote early modern documents. Although diaries were almost without exception written by their authors, letters were not. By examining existing examples historians have discovered that a significant proportion of letters were written by an amanuensis – that is to say they were not written down by the author themselves but instead were penned by a scribe.[26] This has a number of implications for analysing a letter, since it is usually not possible to reconstruct the level of input or creative control that the author had over their correspondence in such instances. We cannot know if the 'author' dictated a letter to a scribe word for word, or if they merely provided an outline or notes that were then written up and polished by the amanuensis. Even if we can be sure that something was repeated verbatim to the scribe, the participation of another person in the production of a letter has an impact on the tone and content of what is written. It may mean that the author was forced to be less frank or that they would avoid matters of a sensitive nature. Thus the author's voice may have been self-censored, and 'mediated' by another person – and since scribes and secretaries were almost always men that mediation is most likely to have been male.

Functions

The next aspect to consider is why a personal document was written at all. Letters were a way to conduct business, to exchange news, to request a favour or services, and to stay in touch with friends and family. It would be impossible to describe all of their functions here, but many letters performed particular purposes that were likely to dictate the form they took. For example, if the purpose of a letter was to request services or to petition for a particular action, you would expect it to be formal, deferential and polite, whereas a letter sending news to a sister might be more intimate or candid. In such cases it would be worth considering how authentic the personality projected in the letter is. For example, the gentlewomen Anne Newdigate employed a deft mixture of apologetic and piety when she wrote a letter to the magistrate of a law case she was involved in:

> I desire your favour to me & my sonn as your owne wise iudiciall harte tells you it iustly deserveth ... But God hath hitherto often delivered me

[from] their mischiefous plots & I make no [doubt] but so he ever will especially now I fall into the hands of so gracious A iudge as your Noble selfe.[27]

Newdigate was evidently a skilled practitioner, able to use letter-writing to oil the wheels of friendship and patronage, but we should be chary of accepting her projection of herself without interrogation.

Therefore it should not be assumed that letter-writers were any less likely than other writers to employ rhetorical strategies or literary tropes in their texts. Johanna Harris has explored how the parliamentarian Lady Brilliana Harley was able to defend her family home against a royalist siege in the 1640s by her deliberate and strategic rhetorical use of letter-writing, a form of 'warfare with the pen'. By conducting all of her negotiations with her besiegers on paper, Harley kept her enemies at bay with the conventions, formalities and imperatives of the epistolary genre.[28] Letters reflected social relationships; they were linked to gift-giving, mutual service, reciprocal obligations and social exchange; and the way that letters were constructed reflected this. Lindsay O'Neill has noted the way that the exchange of news, easily inserted into a letter, functioned as a social commodity – good correspondents passed on news as a matter of routine, and readers thirsted after intelligence.[29] For others, letter-writing was an aid to negotiating life, either professionally or personally. Members of the intellectual elite were able to exchange ideas and to discuss new developments in natural and mechanical philosophy, theology and politics in their correspondence, creating networks of correspondents that functioned as 'imagined communities'. Close-knit extended families also kept in touch by letter, offering consolation, advice and assistance. Letters were capable of maintaining mental intimacy across time and space, and networks of epistolary exchange could provide spaces of creative thought, facilitating self-education and self-fashioning. This is the case for the 'Grey Circle', a group of three women who exchanged ideas and discussed their reading in the 1740s.[30] These and similar networks were established and maintained through correspondence. Evidently the most skilled letter-writers could write in very different ways depending on the occasion and the function of their epistle. They could be contrived and artificial, sociable and candid, friendly or distant. In many cases the recipient was therefore also critical to the end form of the letter, as I will go on to discuss in the next section.

With regard to life-writing, when an author focused on only one feature of life in their diary it might be assumed that their motivation was to keep a record of that particular aspect of life. An example would be the parliamentarian iconoclast William Dowsing, who kept a diary where he simply noted what church furniture he had found (and in many cases destroyed) in the series of East Anglian churches and chapels that he visited in the 1640s: 'Allhallows [All Saints, 1643], Jan. 9. We brake about 20 superstitious pictures; and took up 30 brazen superstitious inscriptions, *Ora pro nobis*, and *Pray for the soul* etc.'[31] On other occasions diarists would explain their reasons for writing. The Church of England minister Isaac Archer included a preamble to his diary, stating that it was 'A faithfull account, and register of God's dealings both to bodye and soule, to his glory, and my own peace', whilst the gentleman William Coe simply began with the words 'My accomptall'.[32] However, many diaries begin abruptly with no explanation. The puritan lawyer Robert Woodford began his diary on 20 August 1637 with the words 'I prayed alone and my deare wife prayed in private this morninge', whilst the Lancashire shopkeeper Roger Lowe opened his on 1 January 1663 with: '1.-Friday. Ann Barrow sent for me this morneinge. I went and stayd all day.'[33]

It is therefore not always so easy to discern the function of diaries and notebooks. This is particularly the case when it comes to commonplace or receipt books, those 'messy' texts that are deliberately fragmentary in nature, but other more coherent examples can be equally hard to place. Numerous reasons have been suggested to explain Samuel Pepys' diary – some argue that Pepys wrote as a means to self-discipline, for posterity or perhaps just because diary-writing was fashionable at the time. Some have detected a religious impulse behind his writing, whilst others suggest the preservation of erotic thrills was the true motivation (explaining also why Pepys wrote in code). Most recently, Mark Dawson has suggested that internal evidence, and the structure, tone and content of the diary, point to a different conclusion – that this was 'a narrative of social accounting by a middling man on the make'.[34] Thus diary-writing might be a tool, a means of self-fashioning, of creating and maintaining an identity. Many spiritual journals seem to fulfil this function. The antiquarian and diarist Ralph Thoresby pasted a letter from his father into his memoir, in which we are given a full account of the purpose of Thoresby's life-writing:

> I would have you in a little booke which you may either buy [or] make of 2 or 3 shreads of paper, take a little journall of any thing remarkable every day principally [as] to your self, as suppose Aug: 20 I was at such a place (or) such a one preached from such a text and my heart was touched, (or) I was a negligent hearer, (or) otherwise, etc I have thought this a good method for one to keep a good tolerable decorum in actions because he is to be accountable to himself as well as to god which we are too apt to forgett.[35]

The diary that Ralph Thoresby subsequently kept between 1677 and 1724 is a classic example of a 'hotter sort of Protestant' diary. For a spiritual diarist of Thoreby's ilk, keeping a diary was a religious duty as well as a spiritual labour, since it was in his writing that Thoresby was able to organize and process his spiritual development. His diary was a record of his progress, but since Thoresby also reread, meditated on and annotated the text, it was an instrument of the process as well. The same may be true for other examples of the genre.

It is also the case that many enthusiastic early modern writers kept not one, but many notebooks, each of which served specific functions. The wool-comber Joseph Bufton had twenty-two almanacs, each housing different material – including accounts, things copied out of other books or his own letters, notes on sermons, lists of burials and marriages, poetry, trade, and one that he kept on his board and wrote in daily.[36] The wood-turner Nehemiah Wallington distributed his writing across *fifty* notebooks, only seven of which survive. The material in them includes chronicles of the era, autobiograph-ical writing about his secular and religious life, personal letters, biography, prayers, and sermon notes and so on. If only one of these notebooks had sur-vived in isolation, this could skew the historian's judgement of Wallington's priorities, personality and world view. For example, notebook three, described by Wallington as 'my miserable and sad condition of my corrupt nater with some of the many Marcys of God to my soule and body to the yeere 1630' describes the horrible spiritual temptations that Wallington suffered, and the many times that he attempted to take his own life as a result. It gives a sense of Wallington as a terribly tortured, sinful and emotionally unstable man, entirely prey to his spiritual insecurity. Yet the other notebooks contradict this construction of the man, projecting an affectionate individual and good friend, who was admired for his godliness, honesty and plain dealing.[37] When dealing with life-writing it is therefore important to consider the extent to which the function of a piece of life-writing might be relational – that is to say it might only be one part of a bigger puzzle. In such a case, one notebook offers an insight into only one aspect of person's character or life, the aspect that they themselves have, *in this instance*, chosen to focus on and record. Diaries are rarely complete pictures offering comprehensive coverage.

Being sensitive to the internal or implicit features of life-writing is usually key to understanding why it was written. Some diaries might serve as a site of recollection, preserving the memory of deceased parents or friends. Others were a reminder of past behaviour, a calendar of significant events, or a record of sinful behaviour and the need for repentance – a sort of moral accounting and record keeping. Many appear to be written as a means to hand down advice to the next generation – several writers explicitly stated this in fact. Nehemiah Wallington added a note at the beginning of one of his books that 'the beginning of November 1647 my sonne John Horthan and I did begine to read in this Booke every morning by ourselves alone and by Gods marcy we have read over this Booke January the XXXI 1647'.[38] Similarly, one of the purposes of Ralph Thoresby's diary was that it should function as a source of advice for his children, that they might benefit from his own experiences; he noted: 'these things are noted for caution not Imitation, that my children may set a double guard upon their affections under the like circumstances'.[39] Other diaries might serve as a means of recording educational and intellectual pro-gress, becoming an instrument of improvement. In many cases, life-writing performs not one function, but many.

Audiences

Whilst it is tempting to see personal documents as more 'private' than printed sources, a form where people were likely to reveal their more intimate and honest thoughts, the author's willingness to lay bare their soul is dependent both on the function and intended readership of a document. All authors exercise a form of self-censorship, bearing in mind to whom they are writing – authors adapt their style and subject matter accordingly. The artifice behind letters and diaries means that they are shaped by the consciousness of the receiver as well as the self.

Most obviously, letters were meant to be read by the person they were addressed and sent to. It is crucial to consider the author's relationship with the addressee when analysing letters. A letter-writer might be formal when addressing a superior, someone they were less familiar with, or who they were writing to on business. With family and friends they might be more intimate and free with their emotions. In a letter you can choose to present yourself in a certain light, subtly devising different versions of yourself to suit the occasion – Anne Newdigate's pious representation of herself, discussed above, is a good example of this. Another would be the Church of England clergyman George Plaxton, who was well known for his humorous style and his tendency to apply nicknames to his acquaintances. In 1709, after his friend Ralph Thoresby had not visited him for some time, he penned a letter that began:

> I am now satisfy'd that Ralph Thoresby is dead, for had he been alive he would have seen mee this Frost, but he is certainly gone to the other world to converse with Selden, Cambden, Goltzius, St Simon d' Ewes and other Antiquaries. I hope he will meet with [Jacobethan traveller and writer] Tom Coryat, and other Learned Foot-pads in his Travells, and compare notes and compare shoes with them.[40]

The letter continues in this frivolous vein, imagining Thoresby sharing a drink with other celebrities of the afterlife, before passing through purgatory and reaching his 'journey's end'. We cannot decipher the meaning of the letter at all unless we know of Plaxton's propensity for playfulness. In light of such examples, Patricia Meyer Spacks' cautions against seeking authentic personality in private correspondence are fitting, since letters are only carefully crafted projections of the self, intended for other eyes.[41]

The author's relationship with the individual that they addressed would determine the appropriate, socially acceptable, way to write to them. The identity of the recipient also dictated the layout, style and language used by a letter-writer. There were elaborate protocols that governed both the valedictions and subscriptions used, as well as the visual organization of a letter – the use of space on the page, and the selection, folding and seal of the writing paper were a means to express deference and indicate constant attention to rank and social status.[42] Codes of deference and social courtesy were therefore intricately utilized when communicating with other individuals, and the historian needs to be sensitive to the ways in which these shape letter-writing. This also alerts us to the status of letters as one side of a conversation between the author and their addressee. Where the evidence allows, letters should not be considered in isolation, but as one part of a longer, cumulative exchange, marked by the memory of previous interactions. Collections of correspondence offer the opportunity to consider individual letters within this broader context.

The intended recipient of a letter was not the only person that might read it, however, since the epistolary medium was inherently insecure. The trustworthiness of the person who carried a letter to its destination was paramount, since before Charles I's postal reforms in 1635, when the Royal Mail was opened up to the public, letters were delivered in a makeshift manner.[43] They might be entrusted to bearers (servants, merchants, carriers or perhaps just an associate heading in the right direction) who could function as 'corporeal extensions of the letter', but who might also read it. Humorous George Plaxton often used nicknames on the outside of his letters – Ralph Thoresby was variously addressed as 'Ralpho', 'Mercury', 'Sydrophil', 'the Great Antiquary', 'a Mystical Conjuror' and 'the Wizzard' – a practice that deliberately invited the bearer into the joke as well.[44] In the sixteenth century letters were not necessarily thought of as private – they were frequently sent unsealed, they were passed around among family members, read aloud to assembled company, and perhaps copied and circulated (a practice known as scribal or manuscript publishing). Mary Evelyn's letters to her friend and intellectual confidant Ralph Bohun were habitually read out to a group of University of Oxford academics where Bohun worked – they appreciated her polished style and critiques of contemporary cultural production.[45] However, it does seem that throughout the period there was a developing sense of the letter as a private form. James Daybell has chronicled a growing tendency for writers to forgo the use of an amanuensis, and for the deployment of measures to safeguard the contents of letters. Writers became more likely to seal their letters; they implored recipients to burn them; and bearers would carry them sewn into collars and sleeves or hidden in trunks, bottles and barrels. Cipher systems were developed to encode secret messages in letters, and books of secrets provided recipes for making invisible ink, a method widely used by Catholics seeking to evade the Protestant authorities' watchful eye.[46]

Neither was diary-writing a 'private' activity. This is particularly true of the most common type of life-writing – the spiritual diary – since the most vital audience for these pious works was God, and writing was an act of devotion.[47] As well as rereading and meditating on their own spiritual diaries, earnest Protestants also circulated hand-copied versions of their own writings amongst their family and friends, another example of scribal publication. As already mentioned, many diaries were conceived of as storehouses of practical advice for later generations, and were written with this audience in mind.[48] Thus the intended audience might be reasonably limited; Kate

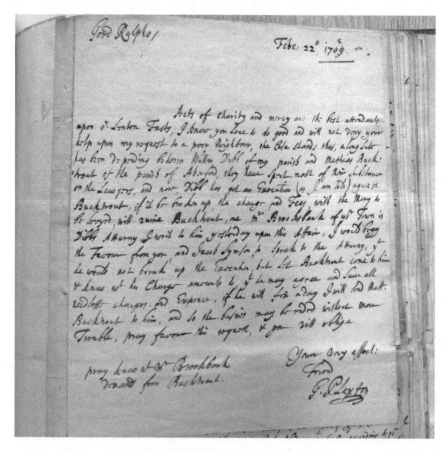

Figure 6.2 Letter from George Plaxton to Ralph Thoresby, 22 February 1709, University of Leeds, Brotherton Library Special Collections, YAS MS15. Plaxton's playful personality and close friendship with Ralph Thoresby is reflected in the way he addresses his letter to 'Good Ralpho'. Plaxton had a rambunctious writing style and used a wide range of nicknames for his associates. Other letters to Thoresby were addressed to 'Mercury', 'Sydrophil', 'the Great Antiquary', 'a Mystical Conjuror' and 'the Wizzard'.

Narveson uses the term 'household publication' to describe the preparation of text for family use.[49] In other cases the eventual readership might be much broader, since diaries were shared for edification. Ralph Thoresby was part of a circle of dissenting individuals who regularly circulated diaries and personal spiritual accounts (often via messengers) amongst themselves, whilst the diary written by the godly lawyer Robert Woodford between 1637 and 1641 was annotated by later generations of the family.[50] This both sustained nonconformist religious cultures and helped to establish life-writing as a prescribed spiritual task with specific individual and communal aims. The implications for analysis are again significant – the circulation and publication of diaries meant that in many cases they may have been written with a specific audience in mind, increasing the likelihood that the content might have been self-censored. These circulating diaries also provided exemplary models for life-writing and conventions that may have conditioned people to conceive of diaries in similar ways, creating generic conventions that shaped and restrained what people put down on the page.

It is therefore not always appropriate to think of a diary as written by the self, for the self. The question of who a diarist wrote for is of course intimately tied up with a document's function; many diaries therefore repay close attention to their themes and focus, and the internal features of the writing. When considering a diarist, it is worth asking whether a writer seemed to be particularly concerned with one aspect of their life – their individual spiritual development, local events, national politics, the weather, their progress up the social ladder – each might offer a clue as to the perceived audience for these texts. On the other hand, occasionally diaries do bear signs that they were intended to be private, for the eyes of the author only. Diarists such as Nehemiah Wallington and Samuel Rogers wrote in simple numerical codes; others wrote in Latin and Greek; whilst a few, such as Simonds D'Ewes and John Janeway, wrote in full blown ciphers. Each was presumably intended to keep the contents a secret. Samuel Pepys wrote in shorthand, making it much harder for the casual reader to understand his diary. On occasions he also resorted to his own private code, based on words in Spanish, French and Italian, especially when writing about his illicit sexual activities:

> December 20, 1664. After dinner I found occasion of sending him abroad; and then alone avec elle je tentoy a faire ce que je voudrais, et contre sa force je la faisoy, bien que pas a mon contentment [then alone with her I tried to do what I wanted to, and against her will I did it, although not to my satisfaction].[51]

The doubly coded nature of these and the content of similar entries suggest that this material was originally intended for Pepys' eyes only.

Genre

As mentioned in the previous section, there were strict rules governing correspondence, dictating the ideal form, tone and appearance of letters. Early modern diaries were also shaped by generic conventions that should also be taken into account when dealing with such primary sources.

Printed letter-writing manuals and manuscript formularies provided models that could be copied or adapted by authors, and the use of such 'how-to' books was widespread before 1500. These manuals were written for different audiences and purposes, outlining prescriptions for business, commercial and social situations.[52] An example would be Angel Day's 1586 *The English Secretorie*, which provided advice on the tone, style, language and format of letters. Day began by advising his readers to pay close attention to the 'aptnes of words & sentences' chosen, 'breuity of speach' and 'comeliness in deliuerance' when composing a letter.[53] He then moved on to recommend a 'simple plaine' style of writing, to explain the conventions around salutations and subscriptions, superscriptions and divisions. Day and other manual authors also provided models of different types of letters: of business, advice, recommendation, command, exhortation, congratulation, remonstrance, counsel, complaint, excuse, thanks, consolation and even merriment.

There is no doubt that the rhetorical conventions found in manuals shaped addresses and salutations and dictated formal occasions of letter-writing, especially when writing to social superiors. The historian should be alert to these 'social signs', embedded in the text. Yet various scholars have questioned the extent to which everyday letter-writers conformed to letter-writing etiquette beyond this. James Daybell has suggested that 'despite the prevalence of letter-writing theory ... in actual practice very little seems to have transferred from manuals to the early modern manuscript page', and Roger Chartier has argued that nineteenth-century French manuals 'had nothing to do with any immediately practical function'.[54] In practice there was a great variation in the way that people wrote letters, from formal, regularized and 'correct' versions to irregular and impromptu letters that defied conventions. It seems likely that in reality people came to know epistolary conventions through contact with the form, rather than through slavish copying of published manuals.

Diaries were less bound by prescriptive models, but as has already been discussed, there were some examples and traditions of writing that could influence the ways that people wrote about themselves. Whilst some diaries were contemporaneous, written closely following the events that they described, others were a retrospective written sometime later. For the former, historians are generally agreed that spiritual diaries were being written some time before godly ministers began promoting the practice; in the later sixteenth century it is unlikely that people would have encountered examples. Perhaps surprisingly, very few early spiritual diaries seem to have drawn on the most obvious existing model for a spiritual diary – Augustine's *Confessions* (though the first English translation was not published until 1620).[55] However, by the mid-to-late seventeenth century ministers were advocating the practice publicly, and individuals such as Ralph Thoresby were sharing and copying the diaries of friends and relatives – a process that no doubt helped to shape expectations about what such personal writing should look like and contain, and that may also have inspired more 'secular' records as well.[56]

During the early modern period there was no clear line between diary and autobiography; indeed, 'autobiography' was first conceptualized as a genre only towards the end of the eighteenth century. Yet the publication of printed lives provided models for life-writers to draw on. Martyrologies contained models for life stories, from Jacob de Voragine's *Golden Legend* to John Foxe's *Actes and Monuments*. Renaissance 'lives' were also exemplary narratives of political figures who embodied self-restraint and civic virtue. Religious histories and biographies supplied further models, and diaries were turned into moralized biographies, fulfilling both pastoral and polemical ends.[57] Yet whilst these models of life-writing did exist, the fact remains that the genre was only slowly coalescing, and as we have seen, incorporated much variety. In part, this is because life-writing is an action as well as a record. Letters and diaries, and personal documents more generally, should also be considered in their capacity as 'technologies of the self'. They might be considered to be mechanisms 'for turning the ephemerality of action and speech into an artefact', a material site for the creation of the self.[58] Whilst they might therefore exhibit generic elements, and though they issued from the culture of a period as well as from the author, they can still reveal the struggle to claim individual difference and the process of fashioning the self.

Survival

A series of choices, decisions and events has determined the preservation of documents in the past, and this process of selection has profoundly shaped the kinds of personal documents that have survived down to the present. In the case of correspondence, surviving letters in institutional and State archives are predominantly elite, formal, business-related, legal or subversive, kept and filed away according to their perceived significance to the preserver. Yet it is also possible to find other kinds of letters, since families and individuals also thought their history worth preserving. Other personal letters might be found in legal and administrative archives that contain petitioners' or litigants' letters. Family and private letters were often kept in muniments rooms of stately homes, preserved by virtue of continued residence in one place. Collections of family papers, though they also privilege landed elites, might contain letters from those lower down the social scale, including women, children and servants.

But family papers must be approached with caution, since the papers, passed down from generation to generation, may have been altered and edited in order to manage and control the family's image and reputation. The fact that personal documents are personal, perhaps containing intimate and private information, may actually make them more vulnerable as historical artefacts. Later generations might destroy documents that preserved unsavoury ideas and behaviour, or that recorded information that clashed with, or perhaps seemed irrelevant to, the family's subsequent understanding of itself. Alec Ryrie speculates that given spiritual diaries were often 'searingly honest records of sin' there is every reason to believe that their survival rate was rather low.[59] Embarrassingly honest diaries or difficult letters might have been deliberately destroyed either by the author themselves or by subsequent generations. The survival of a single volume of Robert Woodford's diary seems to have been accidental – the diary descended through his family until 1970, when one volume was donated to New College, Oxford, but the other volumes appear to have been deliberately burnt with many other family papers during the custodianship of Samuel Woodforde (1695–1771).[60] In other cases, such personal records may merely have been seen as insignificant or even worthless in subsequent eras. Sir Gyles Isham, despite being an antiquarian and founder of the Northamptonshire Record Society, deemed Elizabeth Isham's diary too peripheral to his family history to be worth keeping, and he sold the manuscript off in the 1940s.[61]

Family papers may also have been dispersed across several record offices and libraries, creating further obstacles to interpretation. The organization of these materials in turn influences the ways in which we locate, read, interpret and understand personal material. Archivists may catalogue material thematically (for example into 'personal' and 'official' sections), imposing artificial boundaries that may not be well suited to the material itself. In all cases it is therefore worth considering why a personal document has survived down to this day, and if possible to reconstruct how it was transmitted. Asking such questions alerts us to the extent to which personal documents may have been subsequently edited, rearranged or censored.

Summary

Personal documents must be handled with care. Each should be treated not as a direct, personal account, but as a 'calculated performance', shaped by many different influences both before, during and after its creation. These documents do not offer a straightforward window into people's most intimate thoughts, but instead represent a mixture of art and artifice; they are partly private, but also public. This does not mean that they are any less authentic or useful; it just reminds us that they must be researched and analysed with the same care as any other primary source.

Key resources

Archilet: Reti epistolari. Archivio delle corrispondenze letterarie di età moderna, http://www.archilet.it.
Bess of Hardwick's Letters, http://www.bessofhardwick.org. Letters to and from the Elizabethan dynast and indomitable matriarch Bess of Hardwick, *c.*1521/2–1608.
Centre for Editing Lives and Letters, http://www.livesandletters.ac.uk. Useful resources and links.
Correspondance de Pierre Bayle, http://bayle-correspondance.univ-st-etienne.fr/?lang=fr.
Diary Search Website, http://diarysearch.co.uk/index.html. Contains the bibliography published by Christopher Handley (ed.), *An Annotated Bibliography of Diaries Printed in English*, 3rd edn (Aldeburgh: Hanover Press, 2002). The website provides a list of diaries that are available in printed editions.
'Discovery', http://discovery.nationalarchives.gov.uk. The National Archives catalogue for British resources.

Early Modern Letters Online, http://emlo.bodleian.ox.ac.uk/home. Catalogue of international learned letters created by the Cultures of Knowledge Project, whose links page lists many other online resources relating to letters.

Havlice, Patricia P., *And So to Bed: A Bibliography of Diaries Published in English* (Metachen, NJ: Scarecrow Press, 1987).

Matthews, William, *British Diaries: An Annotated Bibliography of British Diaries Written between 1492 and 1942* (Berkeley: University of California Press, 1950).

The Newton Project, http://www.newtonproject.sussex.ac.uk/prism.php?id=1.

The Paston Letters, available at British Library, 'Digitised Manuscripts', http://www.bl.uk/manuscripts/Default.aspx. Search for Add. MS 43488, Add. MS 43489, Add. MS 43490, Add. MS 43491, Add. MS 33597.

Scriptorium: Medieval and Early Modern Manuscripts Online, http://scriptorium.english.cam.ac.uk. For miscellanies and commonplace books.

Sir Hans Sloane's Correspondence Online, https://drc.usask.ca/projects/sloaneletters/doku.php.

Notes

1 *Le lettere di Francesco Datini alla moglie Margherita: 1385–1410*, ed. Elena Cecchi (Prato: Società Pratese di Storia Patria, 1990).

2 Gary Schneider, *Culture of Epistolarity: Vernacular Letters and Letter Writing in Early Modern England, 1500–1700* (Newark: University of Delaware Press, 2005): Chapters 5 and 6 address the publication of letter collections in print. Examples of editions of letter-books: *The Letter Book of Robert Joseph, Monk-Scholar of Evesham and Gloucester College, Oxford, 1530–3*, ed. Hugh Aveling and W. A. Pantin (Oxford: Clarendon Press, 1967); *The Letter Book of John Parkhurst, Bishop of Norwich Compiled during the Years 1571–1575*, ed. Ralph A. Houlbrooke (Norwich: Norfolk Record Society, 1974, 1975); *Sir Henry Whithed's Letter Book*, Vol. I: *1601–1614*, ed. Hampshire Record Office ([Winchester]: Hampshire County Council, 1976); *Journal and Letter Book of Nicholas Buckeridge, 1651–4*, ed. John R. Jenson (Minneapolis: University of Minnesota Press,1973).

3 James Daybell, 'Recent Studies in Sixteenth-Century Letters', *English Literary Renaissance*, 35.2 (March 2005), 135–70; James Daybell, 'Recent Studies in Seventeenth-Century Letters', *English Literary Renaissance*, 36.1 (December 2006), 331–62. Important works published subsequently include Philip Beale, *England's Mail: Two Millennia of Letter-Writing* (Stroud: Tempus, 2005); Susan E. Whyman, *The Pen and the People: English Letter Writers 1660–1800* (Oxford: Oxford University Press, 2009); James Daybell, *The Material Letter in Early Modern England: Manuscript Letters and the Culture and Practices of Letter-Writing, 1512–1635* (Basingstoke: Palgrave Macmillan, 2012).

4 Phil Gyford, http://www.pepysdiary.com (accessed 13 January 2016) provides a searchable edition of the diary with detailed glosses.

5 R. A. Fothergill identifies four classes of writing that coalesced into the diary proper in *Private Chronicles: A Study of English Diaries* (London: Oxford University Press, 1974); pp. 14–22. Adam Smyth discusses almanacs, financial accounts, commonplace books and parish registers in *Autobiography in Early Modern England* (Cambridge: Cambridge University Press, 2010).

6 Robert Bulkeley, Diary, *Anglesey Antiquarian Society's Transactions* (1937) 26–168; Jacob Bee, Diary, *North Country Diaries*, 2 vols, Vol. I, Publications of the Surtees Society, 98 (Durham: Surtees Society, 1910), pp. 43–63, and Vol. II, Publications of the Surtees Society, 124 (Durham: Surtees Society, 1914), pp. 54–174.

7 Celia Fiennes, *The Illustrated Journeys of Celia Fiennes, 1685–c. 1712*, ed. Christopher Morris (Stroud: Alan Sutton, 1995). Fiennes worked her notes into a travel memoir for family reading in 1702; extracts were first published in 1812. Daniel Defoe's *A Tour through the Whole Island of Great Britain* was published in three volumes, 1724–27. Robert Burgrave's diary: MS Bodleian Library; Robert Coverte's diary was subsequently published as *A True and Almost Incredible Report* (London, 1612).

8 William Matthews, *British Diaries: An Annotated Bibliography of British Diaries Written between 1492 and 1942* (Berkeley: University of California Press, 1950). James Petiver, Journal, BL; Sloane MS, Add. MSS 5267, 5291, 433, 968–9. William Blathwayt, Journal, BL, Add. MS 22031.

9 For more on commonplacing see Victoria E. Burke, 'Recent Studies in Commonplace Books', *English Literary Renaissance*, 43.1 (March 2013), 153–77; Smyth, *Autobiography*, Chapter 3.

10 *Scriptorium: Medieval and Early Modern Manuscripts Online*, http://scriptorium. english.cam.ac.uk (accessed 13 January 2016).

11 Eamon Duffy, *The Voices of Morebath: Reformation and Rebellion in an English Village* (London: Yale University Press, 2001).

12 Many are listed in Matthews' *British Diaries*. Published examples include the diaries of Isaac Archer; Margaret Hoby; Oliver Heywood; Elizabeth Isham; Roger Lowe; Elizabeth, Viscountess Mordaunt; John Rastrick; May Rich, Countess of Warwick; Richard Rogers; Ralph Thoresby; Samuel Ward; and Michael Wigglesworth.

13 John Beadle advocated the practice in a sermon that became the basis for his manual *Journal or Diary of a Thankful Christian* (London, 1656).

14 An excellent introduction is Tom Webster, 'Writing to Redundancy: Approaches to Spiritual Journals and Early Modern Spirituality', *Historical Journal*, 39.1 (1996), 33–56.

15 There is a vast literature on the topic; a good recent overview is Michael Hunter, 'Review Article: Life-Writing in Early Modern England', *Historical Journal*, 56.2 (2013), 583–92.

16 The National Archives, 'Discovery', http://discovery.nationalarchives.gov.uk (accessed 5 January 2016).

17 *Early Modern Letters Online*, http://emlo.bodleian.ox.ac.uk (accessed 13 January 2016).

18 Whyman, *The Pen and the People*, Appendixes 1–4.

19 Matthews, *British Diaries*.

20 Elaine McKay, 'English Diarists: Gender, Geography and Occupation, 1500–1750', *History*, 90.298 (April 2005), 191–212.

21 *Diary Search Website*, http://diarysearch.co.uk/index.html (accessed 14 January 2016). It contains the bibliography of printed editions of diaries first published by Christopher Handley as *An Annotated Bibliography of Diaries Printed in English*, 3rd edn (Aldeburgh: Hanover Press, 2002).

22 *The Diary Junction*, http://www.pikle.co.uk/diaryjunction.html (accessed 14 January 2016).

23 Whyman, *The Pen and the People, passim.*

24 McKay, 'English Diarists', 191–212.

25 James Daybell, 'Letters', in Laura Knoppers (ed.), *The Cambridge Companion to Early Modern Women's Writing* (Cambridge: Cambridge University Press, 2009), pp. 181–93 (p. 182).

26 A letter written by the signatory themselves is referred to as an 'autograph' letter. A 'holograph' strictly refers to letters where the signature and main body of the text are in the same hand, though confusingly this is often used interchangeably with autograph in archival catalogues and calendars. For a full discussion of scribal

practices see James Daybell, 'Women's Letters and Letter Writing in England, 1540–1603: An Introduction to the Issues of Authorship and Construction', *Shakespeare Studies*, 27 (1999), 161–86.

27 Warwick County Record Office, CR136, B313, quoted in Vivienne Larminie, 'Fighting for Family in a Patronage Society: The Epistolary Armoury of Anne Newdigate (1574–1618)', in James Daybell (ed.), *Early Modern Women's Letter Writing, 1450–1700* (Basingstoke: Palgrave, 2001), pp. 94–108 (p. 102).

28 Johanna Harris, '"Scruples and Ceremonies": Lady Brilliana Harley's Epistolary Combat', *Parergon*, 29.2 (2012), 93–112.

29 Lindsay O'Neill, 'Dealing with Newsmongers: News, Trust and Letters in the British World, *c.* 1670–1730', *Huntington Library Quarterly*, 76.2 (Summer 2013), 215–33.

30 Leonie Hannan, 'Making Space: English Women, Letter-Writing, and the Life of the Mind *c.* 1650–1750', *Women's History Review*, 21.4 (2012), 589–604.

31 *The Journal of William Dowsing: Iconoclasm in East Anglia during the English Civil War*, ed. T. Cooper (Woodbridge: Boydell, 2001).

32 *Two East Anglian Diaries, 1641–1729*, ed. Matthew Storey (Woodbridge: Boydell, 1994), pp. 43, 203. 'My Accomptall' is written twice in two different hands, so perhaps was not actually Coe's own description.

33 *The Diary of Robert Woodford, 1637–1641*, ed. John Fielding (Cambridge: Cambridge University Press, 2012), p. 95; *The Diary of Roger Lowe*, ed. William L. Sachse (London: Longmans, Green, 1938), p. 13.

34 Mark S. Dawson, 'Histories and Texts: Refiguring the Diary of Samuel Pepys', *Historical Journal*, 43.2 (2000), 407–31 (p. 422).

35 University of Leeds, Brotherton Library Special Collections, YAS MS26.

36 Bufton is discussed in Henry French, *The Middle Sort of People in Provincial England, 1600–1750* (Oxford: Oxford University Press, 2007).

37 *Notebooks of Nehemiah Wallington 1618–1654: A Selection*, ed. D. Booy (Aldershot: Ashgate, 2007).

38 Ibid., p. 29.

39 University of Leeds, Brotherton Library Special Collections, YAS MS26, p. 29.

40 George Plaxton to Ralph Thoresby, 21 December 1709, University of Leeds, Brotherton Library Special Collections, YAS MS15.

41 Patricia Meyer Spacks, 'Personal Letters', in John Richetti (ed.), *The Cambridge History of English Literature, 1660–1780* (Cambridge: Cambridge University Press, 2005), pp. 623–48.

42 Sue Walker, 'The Manners of the Page: Prescription and Practice in the Visual Organisation of Correspondence', *Huntington Library Quarterly*, 66.3–4 (2003), 307–29.

43 For an introduction to the development of the postal system see Whyman, *The Pen and the People*, Chapter 2.

44 University of Leeds, Brotherton Library Special Collections, YAS MS15.

45 Hannan, 'Making Space', p. 594.

46 James Daybell, 'Secret Letters in Elizabethan England', in James Daybell and Peter Hinds (eds), *Material Readings of Early Modern Culture: Texts and Social Practices, 1580–1730* (Basingstoke: Palgrave Macmillan, 2010), pp. 47–64.

47 Alec Ryrie, *Being Protestant in Reformation Britain* (Oxford: Oxford University Press, 2013), pp. 312–14.

48 Isaac Stephens considers Elizabeth Isham's diary to be a good example of this; Isaac Stephens, '"My cheefest work": The Making of the Spiritual Biography of Elizabeth Isham', *Midland History*, 34.2 (Autumn 2009), 181–203.

49 Kate Narveson, *Bible Readers and Lay Writers in Early Modern England* (Farnham: Ashgate, 2012), p. 70.

50 These annotations are not reproduced in the most recent edition, *The Diary of Robert Woodford, 1637–1641*, ed. John Fielding (Cambridge: Cambridge University Press, 2012).
51 Samuel Pepys, *Pepys' Diary*, extracts selected and ed. Robert Latham (London: Guild Publishing, 1981), p. 92.
52 For a list of later manuals see Walker, 'The Manners of the Page', pp. 329–448.
53 Angel Day, *The English Secretorie* (London, 1586), p. 4.
54 Daybell, *The Material Letter*, p. 26; Roger Chartier, Alain Boureau and Cécile Dauphin, *Correspondence: Models of Letter-Writing from the Middle Ages to the Nineteenth Century*, trans. Christopher Woodall (Princeton, NJ: Princeton University Press, 1997), p. 5.
55 Ryrie, *Being Protestant*, p. 301.
56 Webster, 'Approaches to Spiritual Journals', pp. 38–40.
57 For further discussion see Kevin Sharpe and Steven N. Zwicker (eds), *Writing Lives: Biography and Textuality, Identity and Representation in Early Modern England* (Oxford: Oxford University Press, 2012).
58 Webster, 'Writing to Redundancy', p. 40.
59 Ryrie, *Being Protestant*, p. 299.
60 Fielding, *The Diary of Robert Woodford*, p. 91.
61 The MS eventually ended up in the library of Princeton University. Stephens, 'My cheefest work', pp. 202–3.

7 Visual and material sources

Tara Hamling

What can this humble wooden bowl (Figure 7.1) tell us about early modern history? At first glance the object seems mundane and unremarkable, a plain and practical solution to the quotidian and timeless practice of eating. How can a simple bowl offer evidence worthy of the serious attention of historians? This chapter asks that you never take an object's apparent worth or significance at face value and encourages you to think in a rounded way about the potential of visual and material sources to inform the writing of history. Even on a surface level it is possible to draw some analysis from the material qualities of the bowl; what is the value of a wooden item like this? Further investigation reveals that wooden items of tableware (called 'treen') were the most common in Tudor England. William Harrison's *The Description of England* of 1577 identified a shift from treen to metal wares as indicative of a revolution in the living standards of relatively ordinary people over the course of a generation; he describes:

> the exchange of vessel, as of treen platters into pewter, and wooden spoons into silver or tin. For so common were all sorts of treen stuff in old time that a man should hardly find four pieces of pewter (of which one was peradventure a salt) in a good farmer's house

whereas in Harrison's time even 'inferior artificers and many farmers ... have, for the most part, learned also to garnish their cupboards with plate' with a 'fair garnish of pewter on his cupboard, with so much more in odd vessel going about the house ... a silver salt, a bowl for wine (if not a whole nest), and a dozen of spoons to furnish up the suit'.[1] So, an understanding of period and social context allows us to situate this bowl within an emerging hierarchy of tablewares, which in turn suggests its economic worth to contemporaries.

Investigating the provenance of the bowl (by provenance I mean the record of ownership, custody or location of a historical object) allows some con-textualization of the item; as one of sixty wooden bowls recovered from the *Mary Rose* warship, which sank in 1545, it is part of a body of artefacts that provides exceptional, tangible detail about the nature and quality of life on board (a microcosm of Tudor society).[2] This treen bowl reflects the

Figure 7.1 Wooden bowl, beech, *c.* 1500–45, 20 cm diameter, The Mary Rose Trust (82A1712).

communal conditions and status of the crew of sailors while other items in pewter found on board distinguish the status and dining practices of the officers. But it would be a mistake to stop analysis at this relatively surface observation about social status and differentiation. A closer look at the object reveals a series of markings that turn this apparently common, ordinary item into a highly singular, meaningful one.

Inside the bowl are some crudely incised marks. More than half of the bowls recovered from the *Mary Rose* have been marked with unique symbols to identify ownership by a specific individual.[3] This suggests a proprietary investment in a particular, recognizable piece that moves beyond mere utility. This particular bowl also contains inverted and overlapping 'V' marks that have been identified as Marian symbols invoking protection from harm, so these markings reveal a sense of trepidation in the face of very real onboard threats from food poisoning and, of course, drowning, and represent the

MR 82 A 1712

Figure 7.2 View of interior of wooden bowl, showing personal markings, The Mary
   Rose Trust (82A1712).

practical steps people took to try to protect themselves by appealing to supernatural forces.[4] Analysis of this one object, therefore, can inform studies of
various aspects of early modern history; domestic goods and everyday practices, social status and identity, military history, popular belief and superstition. Our initially uninspiring bowl suddenly seems far more rich and
significant as a source of evidence.

In what follows I set out the range of visual and material sources that can be used to study early modern history, with particular focus on England (my own area of expertise).[5] The chapter points towards recent developments in 'visual culture' and 'material culture' as interdisciplinary areas of study or fields of enquiry with a range of approaches, before setting out some basic practical guidelines for close attention to visual and material sources at first hand. Finally, these steps in the study of visual and material sources are demonstrated through discussion of three case studies. While these three case studies ostensibly share the same subject matter (or 'iconography' – here defined narrowly as the content and composition of an image), sustained attention on, and analysis of, their visual characteristics and physical form highlights quite different contexts for display, use and response. A case is made for the particular value of visual and material sources in the study of otherwise neglected or marginalized areas of early modern history, such as 'low' or popular culture, everyday experience, lived religion and domestic life.

The status of visual and material sources

Traditionally, if historians bothered with images or objects at all it was purely for illustrative purposes rather than as evidence on its own terms. Examples of such uncritical use is the illustration of portraits within biographies of individuals and paintings or woodcuts to illustrate spaces or practices; often any accompanying reference or caption contained insufficient information even to locate the source of the image. As Leora Auslander observes, 'historians are, by profession, suspicious of things', and while there are examples of historians pushing the evidentiary boundaries beyond words – and she mentions scholars of the ancient, medieval and early modern worlds in particular – in general 'most historians view words as the most trustworthy as well as the most informative sources; everything else is merely illustrative or supplementary'.[6]

Over the past three decades or so, however, there has been a pronounced 'turn' to visual – and especially material – sources in humanities disciplines, which has invigorated the study of early modern history. It is not exaggerating things to state that the field of Reformation studies, for example, has been transformed by attention to the role of images and objects in persuading people to the ideology and practice of reformed and resurgent systems of faith.[7] At the same time a growing literature on the 'material renaissance' from the fifteenth century onwards has pushed further back in time the emergence of consumerism and a commodity culture, previously associated with developments of the eighteenth century.[8] Attention to visual and material sources has been invaluable to the study of court culture and State propaganda.[9] Studies of visual and material culture have been central to a wider interest in selfhood and social and cultural identity, as well as early modern modes of memorialization and commemoration.[10] This is only to touch on some of the big themes of the early modern period, but it is the case that current historical research pays considerably more attention to visual and material sources than ever before.

Much of this new interest in the visual and material cultures of the early modern period was led initially by art historians influenced by social and cultural history, but the field has developed as a truly interdisciplinary one with recent publications representing collaborative projects by researchers in various disciplines.[11] A body of scholarship exists to support the claim that there is now such a field as 'early modern material culture studies'.[12] There is also a growing literature dedicated to material and other sources for the study of history that extends 'beyond the text'.[13]

What do we mean by visual and material sources?

'Visual and material sources' can be defined in simple terms to encompass any image, object or material remnant that was crafted, to a greater or lesser extent, by human hands. This includes the kind of things that probably spring to mind as familiar from museum displays and heritage sites – paintings, portraits, sculpture, buildings, print, clothing, furniture, jewels, coins and so on – but also includes various natural objects or landscape features that have been utilized or adapted by people for some function: shells, bones, fresh water springs, roadways.

The nature of visual and material wares created and used within a given society is culturally, geographically and period-specific to a considerable extent. In their book *Visual culture: An Introduction*, published in 1997, John Walker and Sarah Chaplin provided a diagrammatic 'field of visual culture' 'as it exists at the end of the twentieth century', which identified four core categories of content: fine arts, crafts/design, performing arts and the arts of spectacle, mass and electronic media.[14] Even since 1997 the rise and proliferation of digital media and its extension to smartphones might merit a separate category again. For the early modern period, the field of visual culture would comprise rather different elements. I've created a diagram similar to that provided by Walker and Chaplin to reflect the visual culture of early modern England (Figure 7.3), following their stated principle that visual culture may 'serve aesthetic, symbolic, ritualistic or ideological-political ends, and/or practical functions, but which *addresses the sense of sight to a significant extent*'.[15]

I have adopted a fairly inclusive definition of 'visual' culture to include material display and ephemeral events such as performance, though in no way is this diagram meant to be comprehensive. In practice these various groupings are not mutually exclusive, existing in separate boxes, but reference each other – the iconography found in prints, for example, was copied to inform paintings, clothing, monuments and interior decoration; and while heraldry often took a painted form it was also commonly integrated within the decoration of buildings, clothing, manuscripts, shop signs, etc.[16]

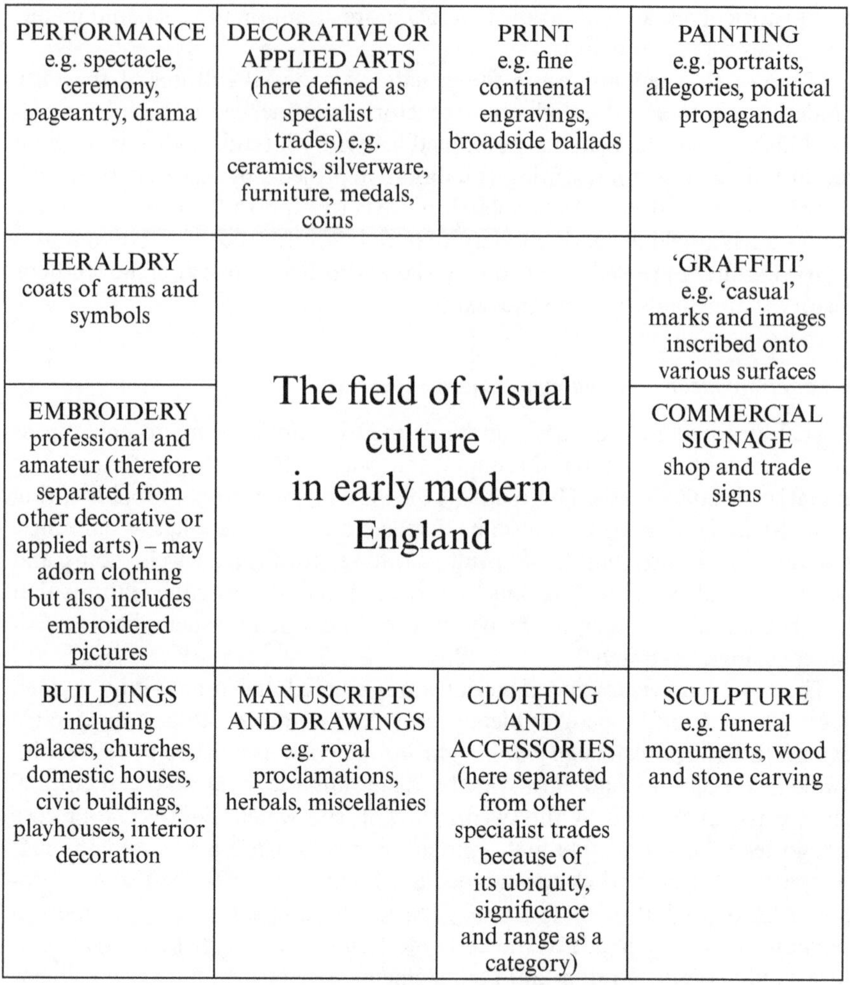

PERFORMANCE e.g. spectacle, ceremony, pageantry, drama	DECORATIVE OR APPLIED ARTS (here defined as specialist trades) e.g. ceramics, silverware, furniture, medals, coins	PRINT e.g. fine continental engravings, broadside ballads	PAINTING e.g. portraits, allegories, political propaganda
HERALDRY coats of arms and symbols			'GRAFFITI' e.g. 'casual' marks and images inscribed onto various surfaces
EMBROIDERY professional and amateur (therefore separated from other decorative or applied arts) – may adorn clothing but also includes embroidered pictures	The field of visual culture in early modern England		COMMERCIAL SIGNAGE shop and trade signs
BUILDINGS including palaces, churches, domestic houses, civic buildings, playhouses, interior decoration	MANUSCRIPTS AND DRAWINGS e.g. royal proclamations, herbals, miscellanies	CLOTHING AND ACCESSORIES (here separated from other specialist trades because of its ubiquity, significance and range as a category)	SCULPTURE e.g. funeral monuments, wood and stone carving

Figure 7.3 The field of visual culture in early modern England.

A comparable diagram for the field of material culture, no longer con-strained by the requirement of addressing the sense of sight to a significant extent, would be more expansive again, incorporating the range of crafted wares indicated in the diagram but also including other categories such as foodstuffs, textiles, books, waste, the manipulated landscape, musical instru-ments, trade tools – even substances such as perfumes, alcohol and other intoxicants through the containers and receptacles used to hold or dispense them.[17] Indeed, you might want to have a go at creating your own diagram-matic 'field of material culture' for your given area! In defining the body of sources available for study, the distinction between visual and material culture is essentially one of sensory emphasis, so from now on references to 'object' are intended to include visual as well as material sources; this is because an image always has a material form and quality and so can be defined as an object even where its visual characteristics are especially distinctive.

So far we have established categories and examples of things that fall within the study of visual and material culture. But as historians we are not interested simply in the things themselves but in their role within people's lives and imaginations. This is why the definitions and applications of the terms 'visual culture' and 'material culture' are much broader than might be assumed. Students of 'visual culture' emphasize the practices of looking that condition response to visual media, while interest in material culture focuses on the interactions between people and things – that is, the practices that put things into operation. As Karen Harvey has observed:

> material culture is not simply objects that people make, use and throw away; it is an integral part of – and indeed shapes – human experience. For historians, there are at least two important and related implications of these definitions of and approaches to material culture: first, material culture is a source type that demands new research practices and skills of the historian; second, objects are active and autonomous, not simply reflective.[18]

The next section of this chapter addresses this question of the type of research practices and skills required to study visual and material sources, while the third part explores some case studies of specific items in order to emphasize the active role of images and objects in creating and shaping, rather than simply reflecting, behaviours.

Steps in the study of visual and material sources

Ways of studying the visual and the material

The interdisciplinary field of material culture studies has placed considerable emphasis on the bodily, sensory and ephemeral aspects of human interactions with their environment, following the anthropologist Daniel Miller's interest in the large compass of 'materiality' (a broader term than material culture), which encompasses not only artefacts but 'the ephemeral, the imaginary, the biological, and the theoretical'.[19] This wider interest situates the visual and the material within a larger conceptualization of culture, which is the main focus of investigation. Interest in the role of the material environment in human experience means that scholars interested in visual and material culture do not always work with images and objects as the centre of analysis. Many studies in the field of material culture studies are concerned with how objects are described, evoked or imagined in other sources, such as letters and diaries, probate materials, account books, and literary texts. In these studies any consideration of objects is usually secondary to the primary concern with analysis of textual sources. There are three broad models for the direction of source analysis in the interdisciplinary field of material culture studies: (1) object-based, extending to texts; (2) text-based, extending to objects; (3) culture-based, concerned with representations of images and objects. There is no single, universal method for the study of visual and material culture according to this broader definition of interest in the materiality of human experience within social and cultural historical approaches – indeed the field benefits from a range of disciplinary perspectives and approaches.

In an address aimed specifically at students of history, Giorgio Riello identified three ways in which historians relate to material culture: 'history from things' (objects as primary sources), 'history of things' (historical analysis of the relationship among objects, people and their representations) and 'history and things' (positioning things outside history altogether in order to unlock more creative and freer ways of conveying ideas about the past).[20] In this chapter I am concerned with the practicalities and skills involved in doing 'history from things', that is, object-based study involving close visual – and wherever possible physical – engagement with the material evidence. Such object-based analysis usually opens out to consider how such items are documented and described in contemporary sources, but this approach starts with the physical characteristics of the object and foregrounds these visual and material qualities. While Riello is right that in the subject of history the material finding does not in itself constitute research and that the emphasis in historical analysis is on the relationship among objects, people and their representations, it is the case that an ability to treat objects as raw materials for the discipline of history is essential in order to maximize the possibilities and opportunities of visual and material sources in the interpretation of the past. In other words, a 'history of things' is best approached through a 'history from things'.

There are, however, methodological implications involved in the use of extant visual and material wares as primary sources. While object-based disciplines such as art history and archaeology embed methods for the close study of visual and material sources at first hand as a fundamental part of academic training, there is a danger that historians may be put off by a lack of the requisite skills or confidence. What follows is designed to offer reassurance that object-study is not only relatively straightforward, once broken down into steps, but an especially rewarding and enjoyable way of doing history.

Finding visual and material sources

The great news is that it has never been easier to find visual and material evidence. It used to be the case that researchers had very limited general access to information about museum holdings and records, with only 'showcase' items featured in displays and in published catalogues, which skewed scholarly attention towards a handful of items that were considered exceptional in some way (usually in terms of quality or rarity and in relation to a famous maker or patron) while the vast bulk of collections remained neglected and inaccessible in museum storerooms. With the development of digital resources most of the major museums and many provincial museums have made available a substantial part of their collections online, including items not on display. The quality of the supporting information varies considerably; the Victoria and Albert Museum's 'Search the Collections' website provides particularly rich supporting information wherever available, for example, whereas the Museum of London's online collections have relatively basic information.[21] Funded projects have created specialist resources such as the *English Broadside Ballad Archive* (*EBBA*) website – which is extraordinarily rich in providing facsimiles, text transcriptions and recordings of thousands of printed ballads, as well as interpretative feature essays – and the *Portable Antiquities Scheme* website for the voluntary recording of archaeological objects found by members of the public in England and Wales, thus making available more modest and undocumented materials beyond museum holdings.[22] The digital revolution means it is now possible to locate relevant but understudied visual and material sources in a few clicks with some carefully chosen search terms. Once identified, a downloadable image is usually free of charge for educational purposes.

Accessing visual and material sources

A few clicks and a downloaded image is not job done, however, but only the start. The bald information about an image or object provided within online resources is rarely sufficient for the purposes of analysis. Wherever possible, it is important to engage with the source material at first hand in order to understand how its physical features relate to its uses and meanings. A comparison can be made with more conventional historical documents, which we often access in the form of transcribed edited publications. The edited version has been mediated through the judgements of the scholar responsible, so we cannot rely on the accuracy of the recording or interpretation. Small marks, marginalia, doodles or other interventions (such as evidence of cutting) not included within the neat, ordered product of conventional editing practices can provide important information about writing and reading practices.[23] In the same way, information about objects provided by museums has been filtered through the lens of curatorial decisions and practices, most notably museum classification by typology and maker, which can limit the range of possible responses and interpretations.

It is also the case that the physical context in which we encounter objects acts in a powerful way to shape interpretation. There are a range of institutional and historic sites and spaces where you can view and access visual and material sources, the two main contexts being museum exhibitions and storerooms; but you may also need to access source materials in galleries, private collections, stately homes and churches, as well as archives, which often contain a range of material artefacts as well as documents. Formal methods of display in a glass case or behind a barrier not only place obvious limitations on the process of analysing the physical features of an object, these contexts also impart an atmosphere of rarity, value or privilege. In designed exhibitions objects are deployed as representational signifiers to highlight specific meanings according to the background and aims of the display context.[24] Wherever possible try to strip away the layers of information that package and present the object within particular narratives and concentrate attention on the visual and material characteristics of the thing itself. The context of presentation/ display should be analysed and considered separately (see Table 7.1).

Table 7.1 Example 'checklist' for object-based analysis.

Stage 1: close object study to inform description

What is it?	Say what you see. What does the form of the object suggest about its ostensible function? This is a ... [plate, painting, tennis ball, bed, portrait of Charles I ...].
What is it made from? (materials)	Usually evident from first-hand analysis but the particular technique, type or combination of materials may require investigation under 'Additional information' below.
Who made it?	May contain a signature or maker's mark. Maker is often unknown but may be attributed – see under 'Additional information' below.
Where was it made?	Country, region, workshop, factory – may contain marks for such information or may be attributed under 'Additional information' below.
When was it made?	May contain a date. Date is often unknown but may be attributed – see under 'Additional information' below.
Dimensions?	If possible measure the item. Dimensions are often provided under 'Additional information' below, but you may want to measure particular aspects of the item.
Weight?	If it is possible to handle the item, gain a sense of its weight. What does this indicate about its quality? Sometimes weight is provided under 'Additional information' below, especially for metal items.
Surface decoration?	Is there any applied ornamentation? Patterns or imagery?
Colours?	Is the item painted or treated to give it particular colours? If it is left untreated, this is worth recording too.
Iconography?	If the item includes imagery what is the iconography? Is it conventional or unusual?
Surface quality/ features?	Is the surface raised or in relief? Does the treatment of the surface create any particular effects?
Inscriptions?	Does the object contain any text or inscription? (This is in addition to identification of maker/date already recorded above.)
Damage, wear and tear?	Evidence of damage or repair may be obvious here and/or may be recorded under 'Additional information' below.
Workmanship?	How do you judge the quality of the item? Does it seem finely or crudely made? NB remember to consider the impact of wear and tear on this.

Table 7.1 (cont.)

Stage 1: close object study to inform description

Sensory qualities?	Does the item invite touch or does it appeal primarily to the eye? Does it make a sound or have a distinctive smell?
Proximity?	What do the size, shape and decoration of the item suggest about the natural or ideal position and distance for engaging with the item?[a]
General assessment	Record your own general impression of the object. Does it seem fragile? Does it have any striking features that distinguish it from other comparable objects?

Stage 2: recording additional information held with object

Location	Is the item in its original location or has it been moved? If still *in situ*, what is the natural or ideal viewing distance from the item? Is it possible to determine its original location? (This is linked to provenance below.)
Provenance	The history of ownership of an item. Museums usually include this information within their catalogue records.
Supporting documentation	This might include information on provenance but could also include letters or other pieces of documentation about the object.
Attributions	Curatorial judgements about the likely maker/workshop, date, origin, etc. of the piece, based on comparison with similar examples. (NB not necessarily correct; museums often revisit these attributions in the light of new discoveries.)
Repair and interventions	Records of historical and more recent modifications including, for example, repairs, cleaning, reframing and conservation treatments.

Stage 3: contextual research and interpretation

Consulting other relevant primary and secondary materials to help place object(s) in a wider socio-cultural context. This may include critical theory.

---

[a] See Adrienne Hood's discussion of concepts of proxemics and the four distance zones (intimate, personal, social, public) in which Westerners operate, applied to material culture study, in 'Material Culture: The Object', in Barber and Peniston-Bird, *History beyond the Text*, pp. 176–98 (pp.183–4).

Engaging with visual and material sources

A rounded piece of object-based analysis combines description with interpretation. There are three basic stages of research and writing: (1) description, (2) contextualization, (3) interpretation. While these stages may be sequential, it is more likely that contextualization and interpretation are embedded within and throughout the describing process.

Description is not as easy or straightforward as it might seem. Creating a description requires sustained attention and focused engagement with the object in the flesh and in the round (wherever possible) in order to derive essential information and details about its physical form and characteristics. This is not something we are used to doing with the things that we own and use, and is not usually considered an essential part of a historian's analysis of conventional textual sources (though it can be beneficial, especially in recent approaches to 'material texts'). Because images and objects are unfamiliar and often enigmatic sources to interrogate, it is important to follow or devise a working model, or checklist, of things to consider when studying objects at first hand. This will help structure in a systematic way the process of engaging with the various physical characteristics and recording salient information to inform your analysis. Having such a practical template or list of things to consider encourages a thorough, methodical and consistent approach, which can be helpful in directing attention to specific aspects of the object and in breaking down existing categorizations, hierarchies and assumptions, thus allowing new insights beyond the established wisdom about the object. There is no single or correct system – indeed any such model could be restrictive and reductive if too rigid in form and application – but all practitioners agree that some working model to guide the process of engaging with visual and material sources is necessary.[25]

Table 7.1 is intended to provide an example of the sort of 'checklist' of characteristics to consider when studying an object at first hand. A third, empty, column could be used to record notes in the field. It is likely that not all this information will be relevant in your final piece of written analysis, but it is important to be thorough and gather as much information as possible while the item is in front of you as it may not become clear what information is relevant to interpretation until later on in the process of analysis. There is no ideal order in which to address these various areas/questions either – there is likely to be a considerable degree of movement across and between these various sections, as is evident in the comments within each box (although there is an order for presenting descriptive details within captions; on this see the paragraph on 'Referencing visual and material sources' to follow below (p. 141)).

According to the model proposed above, the first stage of work involves engaging with the various physical characteristics of the object in a concentrated and sustained way. This is followed by a process of studying and recording other relevant information or documentation held with the object. This second stage probably involves a level of contextualization, but is generally confined to the particular, immediate physical and historical circumstances of the object. Documents shedding light on a particular item may not be held with it in the same collection (an example is a building – any related family papers and probate documents are usually held at the local record office rather than at the property), so this stage moves on to further research utilizing a wider range of source materials including secondary readings and (potentially) critical theory. Finally, the object information, additional information and further research allow you to construct your analysis, balancing description, contextualization and interpretation – that is, understanding the item's form, function and meaning in its physical and historical contexts (including modes of reception – the nature and circumstances for interactions between people and things).

Referencing visual and material sources

Some of the basic information ascertained through stage 1, above, is used to inform references to your source. You will need to provide basic descriptive information about your source in your main discussion and then support this with details in a footnote or caption. It is vital to include the current location and unique identifying reference for your source (museum or ID number) so that the item can be traced by others. Wherever possible try to include an image of your source as this serves to support and verify your analysis and reduces the amount of description required. Examples of the format to use for captions for different kinds of image and object are included within this chapter (the same format can be used for these details when contained in footnotes, but if you have not supplied a supporting illustration then it is advisable to include a link to an online resource where an image of the object in question can be viewed).

Case studies

This final section provides some examples of how the sort of practical method outlined above for the systematic study of visual and material sources might inform a piece of writing. This is intended as an indicative, rather than prescriptive, demonstration of how object-based research – a history from things – informs and produces historical analysis. I have included some commentary on the process and development of analysis as italicized text in square brackets, so you can see how the advice above translates into practice.

The first object to be discussed here is another piece of tableware. It is a large ceramic dish painted with a scene of the Temptation of Adam and Eve and dated 1635, now in the Victoria and Albert Museum. [*NB In this one sentence I have introduced several pieces of essential detail: object type, date, decoration/iconography and present location. A footnote would allow further supporting information if no illustration is provided, though here this supporting information is included in the image caption.*] The dish is an early dated example of English Delftware: tin-glazed earthenware, painted in oxide colours. Polychrome tin-glazed earthenware pottery was produced in England from the 1620s as a result of specialist craft knowledge and skills being brought to England from the Continent, especially the Netherlands. These wares were relatively cheap to make and were aimed at the prosperous middling sort in the capital.[26] [*This contextual information relies on additional knowledge informed by museum information and/or specialist publications.*]

[*Having established this introductory information, my text moves to description.*] In the main, central area of the dish is a representation of the biblical

Figure 7.4 Dish with the Temptation of Adam and Eve. Tin-glazed earthenware, painted in oxide colours, London (probably Pickleherring Pottery), dated 1635, Victoria and Albert Museum, C.26-1931.

story of Adam and Eve's Temptation in the Garden of Eden (Genesis 3). The couple stand either side of the Tree of Knowledge, Adam on the left and Eve on the right. Coiled around the trunk and in the branches of the Tree is the Serpent of Evil. Eve reaches up to the branches with one arm to pluck one of the many apples growing there, and with her other arm she passes another apple to Adam, so that their hands meet around the apple at the centre of the composition; this is the crux of the composition as well as the moral of the story – the act of disobedience that introduced sin into the world [*description of the composition here leads naturally to interpretation of the meaning of the imagery*]. The scene is set within a simple, stylized landscape, with a colour scheme of blues, greens and yellows. To the right-hand side of the figure of Eve is an inscription – the initials 'TTM' in a triangular arrangement – and underneath in smaller lettering is the date '1635'. The scene is set within a bordering frame around the rim of the dish, which is filled with a repeating pattern of flowers, possibly stylized Tudor roses, in blue with green leaves.

[*The following two paragraphs combine contextual research with interpretation, first considering the meaning and significance of the imagery, then considering the possible function of the object.*] The potters working in London did not invent their own imagery but utilized engravings from the Low Countries as a source for their painted decoration, although they did adapt and combine printed sources to create more individual designs. This representation of Adam and Eve's Temptation seems to be copied from an undated print by Crispen van de Passe, as indicated by the position of Eve's arm.[27] This particular moment from the Adam and Eve story was ubiquitous in the arts of early modern England, depicted across the range of categories of visual culture included in Figure 7.3. It had tremendous moral, doctrinal and soteriological significance as one of the great defining moments of Christian history, the moment when man fell from grace through disobedience, resulting in the expulsion from Eden and the hardships of a life alienated from God. But this calamitous moment also held the promise of redemption, brought about through the sacrifice of Christ on the cross.

The presence of figurative painted decoration and this particular biblical scene indicates that this dish was made primarily to be seen, rather than used. This is also supported by its large size, with a diameter of 48.3 cm. The inclusion of initials and a date also marks out the object as special, distinguishing it from the rest of the tablewares in a given household. It is generally accepted that the initials refer to a particular couple and the date records their marriage. These dishes have therefore been interpreted as marriage gifts, thereafter serving a commemorative and inheritance purpose. This special role in the foundation and memory of a family would account for the high survival rate of this type of ceramic relative to more utilitarian wares. Tablewares had inherent significance as goods essential to the founding and operation of a household – as symbols of hospitality and sociability, belonging and community. Wares associated with dining were therefore especially appropriate gifts to mark and commemorate the founding of a household through the institution of marriage. The depiction of Adam and Eve seems particularly appropriate in this context, as the first marriage ordained by God, which may explain why this particular subject remained especially popular for dishes produced in factories in London, and later in Bristol, for at least a century.[28]

My second case study is another image of the Temptation of Adam and Eve, though this time in a very different material and interpretative context. It is a printed image, incorporated within *The genealogies recorded in the Sacred Scriptures* published under licence to John Speed from 1611 as an insert to the Authorized King James Bible.[29] This publication is a thirty-four-page sequence of genealogical charts recording, as explained in the title: 'every familie and tribe with the line of our saviour Jesus Christ, observed from Adam to the Blessed Virgin Marie'.

The depiction of Adam and Eve occupies the large middle area of the first chart, opposite the introductory address 'To the Christian Reader'. This large pictorial woodcut, roughly 10 cm × 7 cm on a total page size of 15 cm × 10 cm, divides the diagrammatic family tree that descends on either side. At the top of the page is a symbolic representation of 'GOD' at the centre of a blazing light, with a sun and moon at the left and right corners to represent the Creation, when Adam and Eve were brought into being; they are represented by their names and scriptural references in decorative cartouches, the frames of which connect in the centre as linked hands (representing marriage). Beneath these cartouches are simple circular shapes bearing the names of their children and lines of family descent working down the page.

The traditional representation of Adam and Eve either side of the Tree of Knowledge is augmented with texts citing scripture, including inscriptions on scrolls held by the couple, and the additional imagery of a recumbent skeleton on a slab at their feet; an inscription underneath reads: 'O death I will be thy death, Hose. 13.14.' A large inscription occupying a panel between the figures of Adam and Eve refers to Romans 5.19:

> As by one mans disobedience many were made sinners, so by the obedience of one, shall many also be made righteous. That as sin had reigned unto deth so might grace also reigne by righteousness unto eternal life through Jesus Christ our Lord.

The elaborated iconography therefore makes plain the doctrinal connection between sin and salvation – the disobedience of Adam contrasted with the saving obedience of Christ – which encapsulates the teleological thrust of the publication in proceeding inexorably to the birth of Christ. The inclusion of the skeleton – a *memento mori* symbol – equates sin with death, while the inscription offers hope that death is defeated through Christ. The image therefore communicates, in relatively simple terms, key aspects of Christian theology as a supplementary and complementary part of an official publication project concerned to consolidate and advance the Protestant faith in Britain. The meaning of the imagery, however, depends on the accompanying texts, and so assumes a literate readership. The detail of the imagery rewards the kind of close looking associated with reading practices and in this sense the context for reception is quite different from that of the tin-glazed dish above.

Figure 7.5 Page from John Speed, *The genealogies recorded in the Sacred Scriptures according to every family and tribe with the line of Our Savior Jesus Christ observed from Adam to the Blessed Virgin Mary* (London, 1616), sig. A2. University of Glasgow Library, Sp. Coll. Eadie 33.

John Speed's *Geneaologies* can be understood in the context of both traditional religious iconography and new and emerging visual forms. [*This paragraph moves from close description of the imagery in the immediate context of its publication to the wider religious and social context that influenced the nature and form of the publication.*] The lineage of Christ had traditionally been represented by the Tree of Jesse, commonly found in medieval art but gradually abandoned in public contexts after the Reformation. The visual structure and form of the charts reflect contemporary interest in diagrammatic modes of communication as well as heraldic representation and dynastic genealogies.[30] There was a particular vogue in the sixteenth and seventeenth centuries for similar diagrammatic family trees recording the ancestry of elite individuals and families, some claiming their descent from ancient times.[31]

The representation of Adam and Eve is not the only biblical imagery contained within the *Geneaologies*; also depicted on further pages are Noah's Ark on the Mountain of Ararat (Genesis 6), the Tower of Babel (Genesis 12), a scene of Lot and his daughters after their escape from the destruction of Sodom and Gomorrah (Genesis 19), and Jacob on his deathbed surrounded by his sons (Genesis 49). A copy of the *Geneaologies* bound together with the Holy Bible of 1614 and the *Whole Book of Psalms* of 1615 in the Victoria and Albert Museum is contained in a tapestry cover of *c.* 1615 decorated with two biblical scenes: Moses and the burning bush on the front (Exodus 3), and Jonah emerging from the whale on the back (Jonah 2).[32] This makes plain that the Protestant emphasis on the Word, encapsulated by the production of the new Authorized translation of the Bible in English, was not incompatible with religious imagery. Attention to visual sources informs a revisionist view of the impact of the Reformation: Protestant culture was not inherently 'iconophobic', but utilized imagery where it had scriptural authority and could serve moral and spiritual ends.[33]

The final case study is also a depiction of Adam and Eve's Temptation, this time as a painting on the wall surface of a domestic room in a seventeenth-century house in Meadle, Buckinghamshire. [*This case study is an example of a lost (or at least inaccessible) visual source, recorded and photographed during the process of listing historic buildings in Meadle, Buckinghamshire. It has subsequently gone unrecorded, which suggests it has been covered up and is no longer accessible to study. Its presence in a private, lived-in home also limits opportunities for object-based study. In this instance, therefore, the student must depend on a photograph and the associated records available in order to reconstruct the form and material characteristics of the artwork as well as the physical location and context for viewing.*]

The wall painting, in a private home, is recorded in a black and white photograph held in the Historic England Archive's Red Box Collection.[34] It shows a very basic, rather schematic depiction of the figures of Adam and Eve standing either side of a stylized tree. An inscription is contained within a rectangular-shaped, framed area between them, which also includes some stylized flowers at the base. Some sense of the scale of the painting can be

Figure 7.6 Wall painting of the Temptation of Adam and Eve, first-floor chamber of farmhouse 'The Spring' in Meadle, Buckinghamshire, *c.* 1627, undated photograph, Historic England Red Box Collection BB89/7707.

determined by its much larger proportion compared to the framed picture hanging above the door on one side and in relation to the top corner of a large wooden wardrobe at the bottom left of the photograph. The supporting information is very limited, comprising a description of the building in the 1912 *Inventory of the Historical Monuments in Buckinghamshire*, which suggests that the building dates to around 1627 (although this is deduced from a fireplace beam inscribed with this date and the name 'John Trip', no doubt an intervention to an existing structure). This listing informed subsequent published sources.[35] Antiquarian sources have their own limitations and biases; a brief account of this wall painting in an article by Francis Reader of 1932 is highly critical of the style and execution of the work, which, he states, 'for crudity of drawing is possibly unsurpassed in the country ... It is difficult to suppose that this is the work of a "Painter-Stainer", and [it] is more probably the production of some local tyro.'[36] [*This kind of prejudicial language of aesthetic judgement, associated with art discourse of the eighteenth and nineteenth centuries, can be hard to shrug off, and the sense that such work is aesthetically unworthy has no doubt restricted the amount of scholarship dedicated to it.*] Reader misinterpreted the scrolls held by Adam and Eve as the misplaced serpent embracing his unfortunate victims, but correctly assumed the derivation of the subject from printed sources, referencing traditional fifteenth-century woodblocks. In fact, while the imagery is relatively crudely executed and much simplified by comparison, the inscription included within the painting reveals a connection to the printed version contained in John Speed's *Genealogies*. It seems that this printed biblical insert was utilized as a source for the painting.

The listed-building information tells us that the painting was in the upper storey of the house, on the sloping ceiling – a position that is also evident in the photograph. We can assume, therefore, based on similar buildings, that this first-floor room functioned as a bed chamber. The popular prescriptive texts of the period placed a great deal of emphasis on devotional duties first thing in the morning, instructing people to meditate and pray from first waking until the start of work. Adam and Eve serves as an appropriate subject for a domestic bed chamber in its depiction of the first marriage and as a warning against sin. It is also an appropriate backdrop to the activities of dressing and undressing, which were also supposed to be accompanied by specific prayers. Richard Daye's *Booke of Christian Prayers* of 1569 and 1578 attempts to deflect any pride and vanity in the act of dressing by providing a set prayer to be said 'at the putting on of our Clothes', which refers, appropriately enough, to the introduction of clothing as a consequence of Adam and Eve's transgression:

> I beseech thee, to strip me out of the old corrupt Adam, which being soked in sin, transfformeth himself into all incumberances, and diseases of the minde, that may lead away from thee. Rid me also quite and cleane of that his tempter the deceitfull Eve, which turneth us away from the obedience of thy Father. Clothe me with thy self O my redeemer and sanctifier, clothe me with thy self, which art the second man, and hast yealded thy selfe obedient in all things to God thy father.[37]

There are other examples of Adam and Eve iconography depicted in large-scale, fixed-surface decoration in upper chambers, which suggests that it was understood as appropriate to the atmosphere and activities of this particular domestic space.[38]

These case studies show how the meaning of an image depends on its material form and the physical and interpretative context for its reception. While these three examples share the same subject of Adam and Eve's Temptation, the three representations all have slightly different emphases and connotations, resulting from their different material forms, contexts and functions. The interpretation emerging from close and sustained study of these artefacts can develop in different directions, illuminating familial, religious and domestic aspects of everyday life as well as behaviours associated with major rites of passage and quotidian devotional habits. What these examples reveal is the practical interconnections among images, objects and spaces – the circulation, transmission, replication and renegotiation of familiar imagery across what we might otherwise see as distinct spheres and modes of experience. In this way such case studies contribute towards a sense of what subjects were common within 'popular culture' and what material forms prompted visual attention and reflection within and across the domestic spaces and possessions of relatively ordinary people. Attention to visual and material sources provides an insight into the practices and preoccupations of a larger proportion of society than more conventional historical documents – or at least those used to construct the grand narratives of history – allow. For all these reasons, visual and material sources should be rescued from their traditionally marginal, illustrative or supplementary role in the writing of history, and it is hoped that this chapter will serve as a practical guide to inform sustained attention to this abundant evidence not just as additional or 'alternative' sources to text, but as a core part of the main business of historical research.

Key resources

BBC, *Your Paintings*, http://www.bbc.co.uk/arts/yourpaintings. Records the UK national collection of oil paintings and where to see them for real. It is made up of paintings from thousands of museums and other public institutions around the country.

Bridgeman Education, https://www.bridgemaneducation.com/en. Searchable access to over 800,000 copyright-cleared images from every medium covering every civilization and period from prehistory to the present.

The British Museum Collection Online, http://www.britishmuseum.org/research/collection_online/search.aspx. Comprises over 8 million objects spanning the history of the world's cultures, from the stone tools of early man to twentieth-century prints.

English Broadside Ballad Archive, http://ebba.english.ucsb.edu. Makes broadside ballads of the seventeenth century fully accessible as texts, art, music and cultural records.

Historic England Archive, http://archive.historicengland.org.uk. Over 1 million catalogue entries describing photographs, plans and drawings of England's buildings and historic sites. Includes links to other searchable sites, such as *Images of England*, with over 300,000 images of England's built heritage from lamp posts to lavatories, phone boxes to toll booths, milestones to gravestones, as well as thousands of bridges, historic houses and churches.

Museum of London collections online, http://collections.museumoflondon.org.uk/online. Approximately 1 million items in the museum's core collections, plus 6 million 'finds', discovered during archaeological excavations.

National Gallery, The, http://www.nationalgallery.org.uk/paintings. One of the largest collections of paintings in the world. Explore or search the paintings.

National Portrait Gallery, http://www.npg.org.uk/collections.php. Explore or search 200,000 portraits from the sixteenth century to the present day.

Portable Antiquities Scheme, https://finds.org.uk. Website for the voluntary recording of archaeological objects found by members of the public in England and Wales.

Victoria and Albert Museum 'Search the Collections' website, http://collections.vam.ac.uk. Collections of historic and contemporary art and design.

Notes

1 William Harrison, *The Description of England: The Classic Contemporary Account of Tudor Social Life*, ed. Georges Edelen (Washington, DC: Folger Shakespeare Library; New York: Dover Publications, 1994), extracts from pp. 200–2.

2 Neil Younger also discusses the Mary Rose in Chapter 13 of this volume, in the context of writing about early modern military history.

3 Julie Gardiner with Michael J. Allen (eds), *Before the Mast: Life and Death aboard the 'Mary Rose'* (Portsmouth: Mary Rose Trust, 2005), p. 481.

4 C. J. Binding and L. J. Wilson, 'Ritual Protection Marks in Goatchurch Cavern, Burrington Combe, North Somerset, with an Appendix on the Use of Conjoined Vs to Protect a Dwelling by T. Easton', *Proceedings of the University of Bristol Spelaeological Society*, 23.2 (2004), 119–33.

5 It is clear, however, that a focus on 'national' contexts cannot ignore the movement of ideas and wares within and beyond the regional confines of Western Europe. See Paula Findlen (ed.), *Early Modern Things: Objects and Their Histories, 1500–1800* (Abingdon: Routledge, 2013); and my discussion of case studies above, pp. 141–9.

6 Leora Auslander, 'Beyond Words', *AHR* (October 2005), 1015–37.

7 R. W. Scribner, *For the Sake of Simple Folk: Popular Propaganda for the German Reformation* (Cambridge: Cambridge University Press, 1981); David Gaimster and Roberta Gilchrist (eds), *The Archaeology of Reformation 1480–1580* (London: Maney Publishing, 2003); Joseph Koerner, *The Reformation of the Image* (London: Reaktion, 2004); Tara Hamling, *Decorating the Godly Household: Religious Art in Post-Reformation Britain* (New Haven and London: Yale University Press, 2010).

8 Richard A. Goldthwaite, *Wealth and the Demand for Art in Italy: 1300–1600* (Baltimore and London: Johns Hopkins University Press, 1993); Lisa Jardine, *Worldly Goods: A New History of the Renaissance* (New York: Doubleday, 1996); Michelle O'Malley and Evelyn Welch (eds), *The Material Renaissance* (Manchester: Manchester University Press, 2007); Evelyn Welch, *Shopping in the Renaissance: Consumer Cultures in Italy 1400–1600* (New Haven and London: Yale University Press, 2005); Linda Levy Peck, *Consuming Splendor: Society and Culture in Seventeenth-Century England* (Cambridge: Cambridge University Press, 2005).

9 Roy Strong, *The Tudor and Stuart Monarchy: Pageantry, Painting, Iconography*, 3 vols (Woodbridge: Boydell, 1997); Margaret Aston, *The King's Bedpost: Reformation and Iconography in a Tudor Group Portrait* (Cambridge, 1995); Maria Hayward, *Dress at the Court of Henry VIII* (London: Maney Publishing, 2007).

10 Simon Schama, *The Embarrassment of Riches: An Interpretation of Dutch Culture in the Golden Age* (New York: Alfred A. Knopf, 1987); Ulinka Rublack, *Dressing Up: Cultural Identity in Renaissance Europe* (Oxford: Oxford University Press, 2010); Nigel Llewellyn, *The Art of Death: Visual Culture in the English Death Ritual, c. 1500–c. 1800* (London: Reaktion, 1991); Michael Peaman (ed.), *Monuments and Monumentality across Medieval and Early Modern Europe* (Donington: Shaun Tyas, 2011).

11 Tara Hamling and Catherine Richardson (eds), *Everyday Objects: Medieval and Early Modern Material Culture and Its Meanings* (Farnham: Ashgate, 2010); and Findlen, *Early Modern Things*.

12 Catherine Richardson, Tara Hamling and David Gaimster in their introduction to *The Ashgate Research Companion to Material Culture in Early Modern Europe* (Farnham: Ashgate, forthcoming 2016). Anne Gerritsen and Giorgio Riello (eds), *Writing Material Culture History* (Bloomsbury: London, 2015).

13 Karen Harvey (ed.), *History and Material Culture: A Student's Guide to Approaching Alternative Sources* (Abingdon: Routledge, 2009); Sarah Barber and Corinna M. Peniston-Bird (eds), *History beyond the Text: A Student's Guide to Approaching Alternative Sources* (Abingdon: Routledge, 2009); Ludmilla Jordanova, *The Look of the Past: Visual and Material Evidence in Historical Practice* (Cambridge: Cambridge University Press, 2012).

14 John A. Walker and Sarah Chaplin, *Visual Culture: An Introduction* (Manchester: Manchester University Press, 1997), p. 33.

15 Ibid., p. 2 (my italics).

16 Anthony Wells-Cole, *Art and Decoration in Elizabethan and Jacobean England: The Influence of Continental Prints, 1558–1625* (New Haven and London: Yale

University Press, 1997); Nigel Ramsay (ed.), *Heralds and Heraldry in Shakespeare's England* (Donington: Shaun Tyas, 2014).

17 E.g. Evelyn Welch, 'Scented Gloves and Perfumed Buttons: Smelling Things in Renaissance Italy', in Bella Mirabella (ed.), *Ornamentalism: The Art of Renaissance Accessories* (Ann Arbor: University of Michigan Press, 2011), pp. 13–39. See the material culture strand of the 'Intoxicants and Early Modernity, England, 1580–1740' project, http://www.intoxicantsproject.org/research-strands/material-culture (accessed 18 October 2015).

18 Harvey, *History and Material Culture*, introduction, p. 3.

19 Daniel Miller, *Materiality* (Durham, NC and London: Duke University Press, 2005), p. 4.

20 Giorgio Riello, 'Things that Shape History: Material Culture and Historical Narratives', in Harvey, *History and Material Culture*, pp. 24–46.

21 http://collections.vam.ac.uk; http://collections.museumoflondon.org.uk/online (both accessed 17 January 2016).

22 http://ebba.english.ucsb.edu; https://finds.org.uk (both accessed 17 January 2016).

23 On cultural practices of cutting up texts see Adam Smyth, 'Cutting and Authorship in Early Modern England', *Authorship*, 1.4 (Summer 2013), http://www.authorship.ugent.be (accessed 20 October 2015).

24 On how museological practices create meaning see Stephen Kelly, 'In the Sight of an Old Pair of Shoes', in Hamling and Richardson, *Everyday Objects*, pp. 57–70.

25 See, for example, the three-step model – (1) description, (2) historical context, (3) socio-cultural context – outlined by Karen Harvey in her introduction to *History and Material Culture*, p.151; and Adrienne Hood's discussion of preliminary exercises and questions while engaging with the physicality of the object in 'Material Culture: The Object', in Barber and Peniston-Bird, *History beyond the Text*, pp. 176–98 (pp. 180–1).

26 Aileen Dawson, *English and Irish Delftware 1570–1840* (London: British Museum Press, 2010).

27 Michael Archer, *Delftware: The Tin-Glazed Earthenware of the British Isles* (London: Stationery Office Books, 1997), p. 81.

28 Anthony Ray, *English Delftware in the Ashmolean Museum* (Oxford: Ashmolean Museum, 2000), p. 12.

29 *Calendar of State Papers*, Domestic Series, James I, Vol. LVII: *1603–1610*, p. 639; 'License to John Speed to print genealogies of the Holy Scriptures, together with the maps of Canaan, for ten years', The National Archives, Kew.

30 See William Dyrness, *Reformed Theology and Visual Culture* (Cambridge: Cambridge University Press, 2004); and Raphael Hallet, 'Pictures of Print: Pierre Ramus, William Perkins and the Reformed Imagination', in Tara Hamling and Richard L. Williams (eds), *Art Re-formed: Re-assessing the Impact of the Reformation on the Visual Arts* (Newcastle: Cambridge Scholars Press, 2007), pp. 201–14.

31 See Sir John Baker, 'Tudor Pedigree Rolls and Their Uses' in Ramsay, *Heralds and Heraldry*, pp.125–65. Lord Lumley's fascination with richly illuminated genealogical trees and pedigrees going back so far as to seem ridiculous prompted King James I to quip 'I didna ken Adam's ither name was Lumley'; see Mark Evans (ed.), *The Lumley Inventory: Art Collecting and Lineage in the Elizabethan Age* (London: Roxburghe Club, 2010).

32 Victoria and Albert Museum, T.45-1954; http://collections.vam.ac.uk/item/O78862/book-cover-sheldon-tapestry-workshops (accessed 4 September 2015).

33 Referring to Patrick Collinson's influential article 'From Iconoclasm to Iconophobia: The Cultural Impact of the Second English Reformation', Stenton Lecture 1985 (Reading: University of Reading, 1986).

34 The England's Places Collection reflects the holdings of the National Buildings Record's Architectural Red Box Collection – photographic records of historic

buildings and structures collected by the Courtauld Institute of Art and the National Buildings Record. Previously physically accessible at the Historic England Archive in Swindon, the collection has been digitized to make online access possible and the physical materials are now held in archival storage: https://www.historicengland.org.uk/images-books/archive/archive-collections/ englands-places (accessed 16 January 2016).

35 'Monks Risborough', in *An Inventory of the Historical Monuments in Buckinghamshire*, 2 vols, Vol. I: *South* (London: HMSO, 1912), pp. 257–63, available at http://www. british-history.ac.uk/rchme/bucks/vol1/pp257-263 (accessed 4 October 2015).

36 Francis W. Reader, 'Tudor Mural Paintings in the Lesser Houses in Bucks', *Archaeological Journal*, 89 (1932), 116–73 (p. 170).

37 Richard Daye, *A Booke of Christian Prayers* (London, 1578), sig. B.iiiv.

38 As discussed in Tara Hamling and Catherine Richardson, *A Day at Home in Early Modern England: The Materiality of Domestic Life* (forthcoming with Yale University Press, 2016).

Part II
Histories

8   Gender

Merry E. Wiesner-Hanks

The vast majority of historical sources in early modern Europe, including every category of source that you read about in the first half of this book, were created by men, and many of them for a largely male audience of fellow scholars, officials and bureaucrats. Thus they are gendered. This fact might seem self-evident to us in the early twenty-first century, when gender is a commonplace category, but it was not when the field of early modern history was being created during the 1950s and 1960s.[1] Most studies focused on men's experiences, but paid little attention to the fact that their subjects were male and instead described them as, say, 'Renaissance thinkers' or 'puritans' or 'nobles' or 'Londoners', thus universalizing their findings, often unconsciously. The feminist movement that began in the 1970s changed this, as it changed so much else. Advocates of women's rights in the present began to investigate the lives of women in the past, which led to a rethinking of the way that history was organized and structured. Widely accepted generalizations about the Renaissance, puritans, nobles or Londoners did not necessarily apply once the focus included women; for the early modern period as well as for other eras, women's history disrupted categories such as historical period, religion, social class and geographic location.[2]

Viewing the male experience as universal had not only hidden women's history, but had also prevented analysing men's experiences as those of men. The very words used to describe individuals – 'artist' and 'woman artist', for example, or 'writer' and 'woman writer' – made maleness what scholars have termed an 'unmarked category', just as 'composer' and 'black composer' or other such terms make whiteness an unmarked category. These terms allowed scholars to avoid considering how being male shaped the lives of Michelangelo or Shakespeare, for example, while forcing them to think about how being female affected Artemisia Gentileschi or Mary Sidney. The global fame of Michelangelo and Shakespeare was (and is) rarely attributed to the fact that they were men, while explanations for the relative obscurity of Artemisia Gentileschi or Mary Sidney always included the fact that they were women. No scholar who studied Queen Elizabeth I neglected to comment on how being a woman shaped her life and the course of history, but practically no one mentioned how being a man shaped Oliver Cromwell's and the history he made.

This situation began to change in the 1980s, and scholars familiar with studying women increasingly began to discuss the ways in which systems of sexual differentiation affected both women and men, and to use the word 'gender' to describe these systems. They differentiated primarily between 'sex', by which they meant physical, morphological and anatomical differences (what are often called 'biological differences'), and 'gender', by which they meant a culturally constructed, historically changing and often unstable system of differences. Historians interested in this new perspective asserted that gender was an appropriate category of analysis when looking at *all* historical developments, not simply those involving women or the family or sexuality (which was also becoming a more common topic of historical enquiry, in part because of the gay rights movement). *Every* political, intellectual, religious, economic, social and even military change had an impact on the actions and roles of men and women, and, conversely, a culture's gender structures influenced every other structure or development.[3] People's notions of gender shaped the way they thought not only about men and women, but about their society in general. As the historian Joan Scott put it: 'Gender is a constitutive element of social relationships based on perceived differences between the sexes, and gender is a primary way of signifying relationships of power.'[4] Gender is therefore a lens through which all of history can be examined, as well as a topic of enquiry.

The word 'gender' spread from academia into more general use, and today it is everywhere. The idea that gender is socially constructed seemed radical when it was first introduced, but now seems patently obvious, with the global diversity of gender ideals and norms evident in all media, gender-bending performers popular on television and YouTube channels, and transsexual and transgender individuals asserting their rights. Transsexual surgery and a well-defined transgender identity were not available options in early modern Europe, of course, but then as well as now gender was to some degree 'performative': that is, a role that could be taken on or changed as individuals conformed to or challenged societal expectations.

Individuals who challenged conventions are often more interesting than those who conformed, and they generally leave more sources. Even more common, however, are sources that created the gender frameworks within which people operated and laid out basic ideas about women and men, and the laws, rules and regulations that built on these. Thus this chapter will begin with sources about ideas, move to prescriptive sources such as laws and regulations and the judicial and financial records that resulted from these, and end with a brief discussion of types of sources in which women's voices can be heard.[5]

Sources for ideas about women and men

The ideas of educated men are the easiest thing to investigate for any time and place that has left written records. This includes their ideas about gender, and particularly about women, for educated men have been thinking and writing about women since the beginning of recorded history, trying to determine what makes them different from men and creating ideals for female behaviour and appearance. Their ideas emerge in works of all types – religious literature, scientific treatises, plays, poetry, philosophical discussions – that have been preserved and read by subsequent generations.[6] This not only makes them accessible sources, but also means that these ideas influenced all later periods. The works that contain them, especially religious, scientific and philosophical writings, came to be considered authoritative and unquestionable, so that the ideas of educated men spread to the vast majority of women and men who could not record their own ideas, and served as the basis for law codes that sought to regulate behaviour. In fact, these ideas and opinions were often no longer recognized as such, but were regarded as religious truth or scientific fact.

The early modern period is often viewed as a time in which key notions changed radically and traditions were overthrown, but in terms of gender there was more continuity than change. Christianity remained the most important source of ideas about women and men, and most books and pamphlets published in Europe before 1650 were religious. The Protestant reformers put an enormous emphasis on the Bible, which served as a spur to basic education in Protestant areas. Individuals who could not read, especially Anabaptists and other radicals, sometimes memorized large portions of the Bible, and its stories were depicted in paintings, stained-glass windows, furniture panels and other visual forms, so were familiar to everyone. The Bible contains accounts of heroic and virtuous women, but those of deceitful ones, beginning with Eve, were repeated more often in all types of works by clerical and lay authors, who used these as justification for their ideas about marriage, parenting, the social order and many other things.[7] Biblical injunctions to women's silence in church were used against the few women who preached or wrote religious works, although these works are also increasingly available in modern translations and editions; in fact, they are often much more easily available now than they were at the time they were written.[8] Religious works by women and non-elite men became more prevalent during the seventeenth and eighteenth centuries, especially among groups such as the Quakers and Moravians that emphasized personal conversion and direct communication with God as sources of authority. In such groups, women and men – and in the Atlantic colonies women and men who were of African or Native American background – served as preachers and missionaries, and their newly discovered writings are fascinating sources about the ways ideas interacted and blended in the multiethnic Atlantic world.[9]

Protestant reformers broke with official Catholic teachings on the relative merits of marriage and celibacy, and wrote large numbers of tracts championing marriage or advising spouses (particularly husbands) how best to run their households and families. Protestant marriage manuals and household guides, available in their original form through such services as *EEBO* or in more recent published versions, provide good information about the ideas of the reformers about gender, which emerge less directly in many of their other writings as well.[10] These make clear that Luther, Zwingli, Calvin and the leaders of the English Reformation regarded women as created by God and saved through faith, but in every other respect as inferior to men. Men were provided with advice about how to enforce their authority within marriage, women with advice about how to be cheerful rather than grudging in their obedience to their husbands. Though the opinions of women who read such works were not often recorded and almost never published, letters reveal that women knew they were expected to be obedient and silent, but they also indicate that women thought competence and companionship were important qualities for a wife as well.[11]

The opinions of Protestant leaders about marriage and women were not contained simply in written works and letters, but were communicated to their congregations orally through marriage sermons and homilies, some of which were collected into printed volumes and thus survive as sources; because people in many parts of Europe were required to attend church, there was no way they could escape hearing them.[12] The opinions of reformers were also reflected in woodcuts and engravings that illustrated religious pamphlets, an important tool in the spread of Protestant ideas. The ideal woman appears frequently in both sermons and illustrations – sitting with her children, listening to a sermon or reading the Bible, dressed soberly and with her hair modestly covered – as does the ideal man – also soberly dressed, and with the tools of a trade.

In response to the Protestant elevation of marriage, Catholic reformers reaffirmed traditional doctrine and agreed that the most worthy type of Christian life was one both celibate and chaste; clerical chastity was defended in formal treatises and enforced though decisions made by bishops, both of which survive as types of sources that provide insight into the ideas about gender of male educated Catholic clergy. Catholic authors also realized that despite exhortations to celibacy, most people in Europe would marry, and so wrote marriage manuals and sermons to counteract those written by Protestants, although their ideals for spousal relations were not very different. As with Protestants, most sources from Catholics come from male authors, but many abbesses and other female religious wrote extensively, and their works are also beginning to see modern editions and translations, which have deepened our understanding of their perspective on celibacy and other aspects of convent life.[13]

Along with religious works and sermons, ideas about gender were also conveyed in secular genres. From the end of the fourteenth century through the eighteenth, men – and a few women – engaged in discussions about women's character and nature that are simply called the debate about women, or sometimes, using the French, the *querelle des femmes*. In Italy, France, England, Germany and Spain, pro-woman authors provided long lists of illustrious women exemplary for their loyalty, bravery, morality and piety, while misogynist authors countered with catalogues of women's vices – pride, obstinacy, talkativeness, jealousy, infidelity, extravagance. Some of these were lengthy learned books in Latin, but most were short works in vernacular languages, and the attacks used satire and humour especially.[14] Songs, stories and jestbooks sold by street vendors and read aloud in taverns – some of which survive – also contained satirical attacks on women and their weaknesses, and a few poked fun at men.

The debate about women also found visual expression, particularly in single-sheet prints that were hung in taverns or people's homes. Prints that juxtaposed female virtues and vices were very popular, with the virtuous women depicted as those of the classical or biblical past, and the vice-ridden dressed in contemporary clothes. The favourite metaphor for the virtuous wife was either the snail or the tortoise, both animals that never leave their 'houses' and are totally silent, although such images were never as widespread as those depicting wives neglecting their housework, beating their husbands or hiding their lovers from them. Prints and material objects such as cups, plates and drinking goblets with such scenes can be found today in the decorative arts sections of many museums, and sometimes in their online exhibitions.[15]

Beginning in the sixteenth century, the debate about women also became one about female rulers, sparked primarily by dynastic accidents in many countries, which led to women serving as advisors to child kings or ruling in their own right – Isabella in Castile, Mary and Elizabeth Tudor in England, Mary Stuart in Scotland, Catherine de Medici and Anne of Austria in France. The questions vigorously and at times viciously disputed directly concerned what we would term the social construction of gender: could a woman's being born into a royal family and educated to rule allow her to overcome the limitations of her sex? Should it? Or, stated another way, which was (or should be) the stronger determinant of character and social role: gender or rank?

The most extreme opponents of female rule were Protestants who went into exile on the Continent during the reign of Mary Tudor, most prominently the Scottish reformer John Knox, whose treatise *The First Blast of the Trumpet against the Monstrous Regiment of Women* (1558), directed against the Catholic Queen of Scotland, Mary Stuart, as well as Mary Tudor, argued that female rule was unnatural, unlawful, contrary to scripture and 'monstrous'. Knox had the misfortune to publish his work in the very year that Mary Tudor died and Elizabeth I assumed the throne, making his position as both a Protestant and opponent of female rule rather tricky. A number of courtiers realized that defences of female rule would be likely to help them win favour in Elizabeth's eyes, and wrote these, although they are less fun to read than *The First Blast*, as attacks on anything are always livelier than defences.[16] The ways that Elizabeth herself astutely used both feminine and masculine gender stereotypes to her own advantage in her speeches, writings, portraits and self-presentation have led to many studies, and sources are readily available for further analysis.[17]

Figure 8.1 Urs Graf, *Christ and the Apostles and the Holy Women*, National Gallery of Art, Washington, DC.

Considerations of the links between gender and power were not limited to places and times with female monarchs; in seventeenth-century England, for example, male monarchs, parliamentarians and political theorists of all persuasions discussed the connections among monarchy, fatherhood and the rights of 'free-born Englishmen', a universalizing category that did not include women. Their ideas can be found in records of political debates, written treatises, periodicals and letters – that is, in very traditional sources for political history; these yield new insights when viewed through a gender lens.

Explicit discussions of women can be found in hundreds if not thousands of early modern texts, but there was less discussion of men as men because male authors were less willing to make generalizations about their own sex. Men defined what it meant to be a man – the phrase often used by scholars today is that they 'constructed masculinity' – not only in relation to women but also in relation to other groups of men. Nobles promoted a masculinity centred on honour and glory, reformers and their middle-class followers a masculinity centred on family and order, journeymen a masculinity centred on camaraderie and transience. Within the last decade scholars have used a huge variety of printed, manuscript and visual sources to study these early modern masculinities, focusing on everything from beards to phalluses.[18] Much of this scholarship argues that masculinity was 'in crisis' or 'fragile', and that men were anxious about their masculinity, worried about contradictions that seem to have emerged in codes of manhood, and concerned because various processes of change led them to doubt the permanent nature of a gender hierarchy in which they were superior.[19]

Once you begin to look for them, ideas about gender can be found in many other types of sources as well. Central works in the Scientific Revolution focused on anatomy and physiology, and debated the role of egg and sperm and the contributions of each parent to the development of the foetus. Learned and popular medical works discussed the role of the bodily humours – four fluids thought to exist in the body – in causing illness and maintaining health, and saw these as gender-related, with women more susceptible to certain illnesses and men to others because of which humour was dominant.[20] Ideas about gender shaped visual sources, including paintings with human subjects, maps in which human figures appear in the margins or on the maps themselves, costume books and tapestries. They also shaped the early modern soundscape – recoverable to us sometimes only in songbooks, ballads, musical scores, or illustrations of musicians and musical performances – as men and women sang different songs while they worked, or as people listened from outside the walls of a convent to the voices of enclosed nuns, or as castrati became preferred to women for the high parts of certain genres of music.[21]

Laws, regulations and judicial records

Many of the most important sources for understanding ideas about gender in the early modern period are prescriptive, including the Bible, religious and didactic treatises, marriage manuals and other types of advice literature, and sermons. Ideas about men and women, or about 'man' and 'woman' in the abstract, also directly influenced the laws, guild statutes, monastic rules, civic codes and other regulations that form another type of prescriptive source, as well as the judicial and other systems developed to enforce these, and the ways these systems actually operated.

Law itself changed significantly in the early modern period. Beginning in the thirteenth century in Italy and most of southern Europe, and in the sixteenth century in Germany and most of northern Europe (though not England), legal scholars encouraged governments to change their law codes to bring them into conformity with Roman law, which was viewed as systematic and comprehensive, and to get rid of the highly localized and often contradictory and conflicting law codes that had grown up in medieval Europe. In most areas of Europe that became Protestant, secular rulers took over the control of matters like marriage and morals from Catholic Church courts, thus further expanding and centralizing their legal systems. However, such moves did not end the bewildering variety of legal and regulatory systems in which people lived, ranging from local market regulations through city law codes to regional and national statutes, and which in Catholic areas included canon law and other Church rules enforced by bishops' courts, and in some times and places by the Inquisition. Both Catholic and Protestant religious authorities sometimes held special investigations called visitations to assess the state of religion and morals in the territories under their control, and their records are wonderful – and sometimes funny, lurid or grim – accounts of behaviour and belief.

Laws made distinctions between men and women on many issues, including property rights and inheritance, and these changed over time. Traditional medieval law codes in Europe had accorded women a secondary legal status, based in theory on their inability to perform feudal military service, and required women to have legal guardians who would also engage in trials by ordeal or combat for them. This gender-based guardianship gradually died out in the later Middle Ages as court proceedings replaced physical trials, and unmarried women and widows generally gained the right to hold land on their own, appear in court on their own behalf, make wills, and serve as witnesses in civil and criminal cases. Thus wills and court proceedings, which are excellent sources for understanding the aims and actions of men from a range of social classes, occasionally provide information about women as well. When using these it is important to remember that all testimony was recorded by educated (and male) clerks, secretaries and notaries, so you are seeing things from their point of view.

Marriage provided another reason for restricting women's legal role, and this continued throughout the early modern period. In both the Roman law that came to prevail on the Continent and the Common Law of England and the English colonies, marriage was described as coverture, a permanent relationship in which the husband's authority was absolute and the wife was not a legal person. She could not sue, make contracts or go to court for any reason without his approval, and often could not be sued or charged with any civil crime on her own. In many parts of Europe, all goods or property that a wife brought into a marriage and all wages she earned during the marriage were considered the property of her husband, a situation that did not change legally until the nineteenth century or, on some issues, until the twentieth century.

These blanket prohibitions grew increasingly out of step with the economic needs and social realities of the commercializing economy, however, and various ways were devised to get around them. (Given widely held notions of the proper gender hierarchy, simply ending coverture outright was far too threatening.) Written marriage contracts – common in families that owned any property at all – sometimes gave wives legal ownership of the dowries they brought into the marriage. In England, two special courts, the Court of Chancery and the Court of Requests, were established specifically to make decisions case by case based, on principles of equity, rather than a strict interpretation of Common Law. These courts heard all types of cases, but became particularly popular with married women, for they allowed them to bring cases independently, even against their husbands.[22] City law codes came to allow married women who carried out business on their own, or alongside their husbands, to declare themselves unmarried (*feme* [*sic*] *sole*) for legal purposes so they could borrow and loan money and make contracts on their own, and also be jailed for debt or for violating civil laws. Wives were also gradually allowed to retain control over some family property if they could prove that their husbands were squandering everything through drink, gambling or bad investments; such laws were described as protection for women and children, but they were also motivated by lawmakers' concerns to keep such families from needing public charity. All of these situations have left legal records, including documents drawn up by notaries, contracts, tax and ownership records, and court proceedings that allow us to discover how the law actually played out in the lives of men and women.[23]

Judicial records also show that women often actively managed their dowry property and carried out legal transactions without getting special approval. Judges and officials were often willing to let women act against the letter of the law if the alternative would be financial problems for the family, or if they thought the law itself was harmful. The financial records of guilds, religious confraternities, hospitals, estates and other institutions thus provide evidence about the economic activities of both men and women, and inventories taken at the time of death provide details about the material objects people had in their homes.

The proliferation of exceptions and the fact that women were often able to slip through the cracks of urban law codes began to bother jurists in many parts of Europe who were becoming educated in Roman law with its goals of comprehensiveness and uniformity. Roman law also gave them additional grounds for women's secondary legal status, for it based this not on feudal obligations or a wife's duty to obey her husband but on women's alleged physical and mental weaknesses, their 'fragility, imbecility, irresponsibility, and ignorance'.[24] These ideas led jurists in many parts of Europe to recommend, and in some cases implement, the reintroduction of gender-based guardianship; unmarried adult women and widows were again given male guardians, and prohibited from making any financial decisions, even donations to religious institutions, without their approval.[25] In many parts of Europe, women lost the right of guardianship over their own children if they remarried, or were only granted guardianship in the first place if they renounced remarriage at the death of the children's father. Governments generally became less willing to make exceptions in the case of women, as they felt any laxness might disrupt public order, and fewer and fewer women appeared on their own behalf. Sources for tracing these changes, as well as other aspects of marriage and family life, include treatises by law professors and legal scholars, statutes, records of churches and convents, marriage contracts, court proceedings, and private or family records such as account books and letters.

In law codes and in practice civil law was deeply gendered, while criminal laws were a bit less so. Law codes and court records reveal that women throughout Europe were responsible for their own criminal actions and could be tortured and executed just like men. Some mildness was recommended in the case of pregnant women, though generally this meant simply waiting until after delivery to proceed with torture. Women were often executed in a manner different from men, buried alive or drowned instead of being beheaded, largely because city executioners thought women would faint at the sight of the sword or axe and make their job more difficult. A few executioners and judges have left memoirs of their actions and decisions, which can serve as fascinating sources into their views of the world.[26] In most parts of Europe, women of all classes were allowed to bring defamation suits to court for insults to their honour, and it is clear from court records that they did this frequently; such records also indicate that the worst thing a man could be called was 'thief', or 'coward', while for women it was 'whore'.

Records of criminal trials are often preserved in great detail, and the more spectacular cases involving prominent or notorious individuals became the subject of ballads, illustrated broadsheets, pamphlets and sometimes even plays, which are also fascinating sources.[27] The actual court proceedings and the presentation of cases in popular literature were shaped by notions of gender; individuals crafted their cases to fit with ideas about the ways men and women were supposed to behave in order to obtain the outcome from the court that they hoped for, while the authors of ballads and pamphlets did the opposite, enhancing the sexual allure, feminine helplessness, male violence and other factors to make the story more interesting (and increase sales).[28]

Certain criminal actions were more likely to be engaged in by men or women, and the sources related to these reveal a great deal about early modern society. Acts of violence against adults, arson, and the theft of large animals or large amounts of money generally involved men, while infanticide and in most parts of Europe witchcraft were more likely to involve women, as alleged perpetrators and as witnesses. Historians of witchcraft have a huge range of sources at their disposal, and have made use of all of them, including climate and price data (large-scale witch hunts often occurred during cold and rainy periods, when harvests were bad and food prices rose); demonological works; illustrated pamphlets; laws; medical treatises; and thousands of records of actual trials, some of these numbering hundreds of pages.[29] Accusations, trials and punishments involving sexual behaviour judged aberrant – all of which have left judicial records–were also gender-related: almost all of the people accused of and tried for homosexual sodomy or bestiality in early modern Europe were men, while almost all of those hauled into court and punished for premarital intercourse (termed 'fornication'), unseemly conduct or out-of-wedlock pregnancy were women.[30]

Hearing women's voices in the sources

All types of sources provide information about the actions of men, and many about the actions of women, but trying to discern women's ideas, feelings or emotions – or those of the majority of men, who could not read or write – is more difficult. Throughout the period, publications by women represent a tiny share of the total amount of printed material; women's works comprise only 1.2 per cent of the publications in England from 1640 to 1700, for example, though even this figure represents a doubling of their pre-Civil War rate.[31] It is more difficult to make statistical comparisons for other countries, but publications by women probably accounted for less than 1 per cent of the total, though their share elsewhere also increased slightly during the early modern period. The last forty years of women's history and social history have led to the discovery of previously unknown sources written by women in archives, libraries, churches, institutions, and sometimes the attics or closets of private homes, however. Some of these had been published in the early modern period and then forgotten, and others were unpublished works such as letters, diaries, memoirs, and personal collections of quotes and reflections.[32]

Until recently scholars generally made a distinction between unpublished personal documents, such as diaries or letters, and published works, but the Web has blurred this line: is a blog, for example, published or unpublished, public or private? What about a comment on someone else's blog? In some ways this represents a return to the early modern situation, in which letters often contained political news as well as personal matters, and their writers knew that they would be circulated among a group of people, and perhaps even copied and sent on, the early modern version of re-tweeting. Women in particular realized that letters might be the best or only place they could demonstrate their learning and creativity with language, and so used letters to develop a personal literary style. Their addressees recognized this, and saved them; for Madame de Sévigné (1626–96), for example, often described as the greatest letter-writer in French literature, more than 1,300 letters survive. Letters thus form the largest body of extant early modern women's writing.[33] Many historians of literature view the letter as one of the ancestors of the novel, a literary form that was also developed to a great extent by women in the later seventeenth and eighteenth centuries. Many early novels were, in fact, written in epistolary form: that is, as an exchange of letters, including Aphra Behn's three-volume *Love-Letters Between a Nobleman and his Sister* (1684, 1685, 1687).

Handwritten journals, diaries and collections of quotes were also often written to be handed down to future generations, with the writer careful about how she portrayed herself and intent on teaching a lesson to others through her writings. Women also circulated fiction, poetry, commentary and other types of writing in manuscript long after the printed book became the standard form of publication, or presented such pieces to patrons. All of these can provide insight into women's inner lives, and scholars have recently begun studying similar manuscript books produced and circulated by men as well.

No matter how many new sources are discovered or recovered, however, written and published works by men will continue to form the bulk of available evidence from the early modern period, and our understanding of gender and every other aspect of life will have to rely on a careful utilization of these. Musical and artistic sources are even more imbalanced, as the number of female composers, musicians, painters and sculptors whose names we know is minuscule. Women made up songs, played instruments and sang, and produced needlework or miniatures that experimented with perspective, paid attention to proportion and shadowing, and took their subjects from antiquity just as did large frescoes or oil paintings, but they were not understood to be musicians or artists (or at best were labelled 'lady musicians'). Gender shaped both women's access to culture and the evaluation of their creative activities, and we now recognize that it did the same with men. For a long time this was invisible, but it is no longer.

Key resources

Chojnacka, Monica and Merry E. Wiesner-Hanks (eds), *Ages of Woman, Ages of Man: Sources in European Social History, 1400–1750* (Harlow: Pearson, 2002).

Gibson, Marion (ed.), *Witchcraft and Society in England and America, 1550–1750* (Ithaca, NY: Cornell University Press, 2003).

Henderson, Katherine and Barbara F. McManus (eds), *Half Humankind: Contexts and Texts of the Controversy about Women in England, 1540–1640* (Urbana: University of Illinois Press, 1985).

Klein, Joan Larsen (ed.), *Daughters, Wives and Widows: Writings by Men about Women and Marriage in England, 1500–1640* (Urbana: University of Chicago Press, 1992).

Luther on Women: A Sourcebook, ed. and trans. Susan C. Karant-Nunn and Merry E. Wiesner-Hanks (Cambridge: Cambridge University Press, 2003).

Otten, Chartlotte (ed.), *English Women's Voices: 1540–1700* (Miami: Florida International University, 1992).

Travitsky, Betty and Anne Lake Prescott (eds), *Female and Male Voices in Early Modern England: An Anthology of Renaissance Writings* (New York: Columbia University Press, 2000).

Wiesner-Hanks, Merry E., *Women and Gender in Early Modern Europe*, 3rd edn (Cambridge: Cambridge University Press, 2008). The companion website (www. cambridge.org/womenandgender) has many original sources, and links to websites with more, available free-of-charge.

Wiltenburg, Joy (ed. and trans.), *Women in Early Modern Germany: An Anthology of Popular Texts* (Tempe: Arizona Center for Medieval and Renaissance Studies, 2002).

Women in World History, http://chnm.gmu.edu/wwh/index.html. Source materials on women in many eras, including the early modern; run by the Center for History and the New Media at George Mason University, and open access.

The Women Writers Project at Northeastern University, http://www.wwp.northeastern. edu. More than 350 fully searchable texts written by women in English between 1526 and 1850, along with introductions and commentary.

Notes

1 For a history of the term 'early modern', see Randolph Starn, 'The Early Modern Muddle', *Journal of Early Modern History*, 6 (2002), 296–307. For its application to women's and gender history, see Merry E. Wiesner-Hanks, 'Do Women Need the Renaissance?', *Gender and History*, 20.3 (2008), 539–57.

2 Hilda Smith, *All Men and Both Sexes: Gender, Politics, and the False Universal in England, 1640–1832* (State College: Penn State University Press, 2002) provides an insightful examination of deceptive universals in early modern England.

3 John A. Lynn II, *Women, Armies and Warfare in Early Modern Europe* (Cambridge: Cambridge University Press, 2008).

4 Joan Scott, 'Gender: A Useful Category of Historical Analysis', *AHR*, 91.5 (1986), 1053–75. This article remains essential reading, as evidenced by the *AHR* Forum 'Revisiting "Gender: A Useful Category of Historical Analysis"', *AHR*, 113.5 (2008), 1344–1430, which has articles by six historians about gender history around the world and a response by Scott.

5 The companion website for my book, Merry E. Wiesner-Hanks, *Women and Gender in Early Modern Europe*, 3rd edn (Cambridge: Cambridge University Press, 2008 [1993]), has many original sources, as well as links to some of the many other websites with sources that have been created by museums, libraries, archives, university departments and individuals: www.cambridge.org/womenandgender (accessed 18 January 2016).

6 Joan Larsen Klein (ed.), *Daughters, Wives and Widows: Writings by Men about Women and Marriage in England, 1500–1640* (Urbana: University of Chicago Press, 1992).

7 An excellent study of religious writings is John Lee Thompson, *John Calvin and the Daughters of Sarah: Women in Regular and Exceptional Roles in the Exegesis of Calvin, His Predecessors and His Contemporaries* (Geneva: Droz, 1992).

8 Many of these, as well as secular works by women, have been published in the series *The Other Voice in Early Modern Europe*, first published by the University of Chicago, and now by Iter Academic Press in Toronto and the Arizona Center for Medieval and Renaissance Studies; together these have more than 100 volumes, with many more on the way: http://www.othervoiceineme.com/index.html (accessed 18 January 2016).

9 Jon Sensbach, *Rebecca's Revival: Creating Black Christianity in the Atlantic World* (Cambridge, MA: Harvard University Press, 2006).

10 *Luther on Women: A Sourcebook* ed. and trans. Susan C. Karant-Nunn and Merry E. Wiesner-Hanks (Cambridge: Cambridge University Press, 2003) contains translations and analysis of Luther's main writings on women, the family and sexuality. The website *Christian Classics Ethereal Library* has searchable versions of many works of both Protestant and Catholic reformers: http://www.ccel.org (accessed 18 January 2016).

11 See, for example, *Letters to Francesco Datini by Margherita Datini*, trans. Carolyn James and Antonio Pagliaro (Toronto: Iter, 2012).

12 Published wedding sermons were most common in Germany, and the vast majority of these have not been translated or republished in modern editions; the original editions are available in research libraries with early modern collections, especially the Duke August Library in Wolfenbüttel, Germany. For a study based on these, see Susan Karant-Nunn, '"Fragrant Wedding Roses": Lutheran Wedding Sermons and Gender Definition in Early Modern Germany', *German History*, 17.1 (1999), 25–40. Karant-Nunn and Wiesner-Hanks, *Luther on Women* contains translations of several of Luther's wedding sermons.

13 For translations of writings about convent life by nuns, see Merry Wiesner-Hanks and Joan Skocir (eds and trans), *Convents Confront the Reformation: Catholic and Protestant Nuns in Germany* (Milwaukee: Marquette University Press, 1996); Maria de San José, *Book of Recreations*, ed. and trans. Amanda Powell and Alison Weber (Chicago: University of Chicago Press, 2002).

14 Many of the English texts that were part of this debate can be found in Katherine Henderson and Barbara F. McManus (eds), *Half Humankind: Contexts and Texts of the Controversy about Women in England, 1540–1640* (Urbana: University of Illinois Press, 1985). Essays evaluating the debate are included in Cristina Malcolmson and Mihoko Suzuki (eds), *Debating Gender in Early Modern England, 1500–1700* (New York: Palgrave, 2002). For translations of German works on women, see Joy Wiltenburg (ed. and trans.), *Women in Early Modern Germany: An Anthology of Popular Texts* (Tempe: Arizona Center for Medieval and Renaissance Studies, 2002).

15 Sara F. Matthews Grieco, *"Querelle des femmes" or "Guerre des sexes"? Visual Representations of Women in Renaissance Europe* (Florence: European University Institute, 1989); Cindy McCreery, *The Satirical Gaze: Prints of Women in Late Eighteenth-Century England* (New York: Oxford University Press, 2004).

16 Amanda Shephard, *Gender and Authority in Sixteenth-Century England: The Knox Debate* (Keele: Keele University Press, 1994).

17 *Elizabeth I: Collected Works*, ed. Leah S. Marcus, Janel Mueller and Mary Beth Rose (Chicago: University of Chicago Press, 2000) includes nearly all of Elizabeth's writings. Carol Levin, *The Heart and Stomach of a King: Elizabeth I and the Politics of Sex and Power* (Philadelphia: University of Pennsylvania Press, 1994) provides an analysis that makes creative use of many different types of sources.

18 Mark Albert Johnston, *Beard Fetish in Early Modern England: Sex, Gender, and Registers of Value* (Aldershot: Ashgate, 2011); Thomas A. King, *The Gendering of Men, 1600–1750: The English Phallus* (Madison: University of Wisconsin Press, 2004).

19 Katherine Long (ed.), *High Anxiety: Masculinity in Crisis in Early Modern France* (Kirksville, MO: Sixteenth Century Journal Publishers, 2002); Alexandra Shepard, *Meanings of Manhood in Early Modern England* (Oxford: Oxford University Press, 2003).

20 Londa Schiebinger, *Nature's Body: Gender in the Making of Modern Science*, 2nd edn (New Brunswick, NJ: Rutgers University Press, 2004).

21 Thomasin LaMay (ed.), *Musical Voices of Early Modern Women: Many Headed Melodies* (Burlington, VT: Ashgate, 2005).

22 Tim Stretton, *Women Waging Law in Elizabethan England* (Cambridge: Cambridge University Press, 1998).
23 Legal records from many parts of Europe on families, the life cycle, work and other topics can be found in Monica Chojnacka and Merry E. Wiesner-Hanks (eds), *Ages of Woman, Ages of Man: Sources in European Social History, 1400–1750* (Harlow: Pearson, 2002).
24 As described by the Justinian Legal Code. See Wiesner-Hanks, *Women and Gender*, p. 38.
25 Julie Hardwick, *The Practice of Patriarchy: Gender and the Politics of Household Authority in Early Modern France* (University Park: Penn State University Press, 1998).
26 Joel Harrington, *The Faithful Executioner: Life and Death, Honor and Shame in the Turbulent Sixteenth Century* (London: Picador, 2013); Natalie Zemon Davis, *The Return of Martin Guerre* (Cambridge, MA: Harvard University Press, 1984).
27 Garthine Walker, *Crime, Gender, and Social Order in Early Modern England* (New York: Cambridge University Press, 2003) examines women's criminal actions and their consequences.
28 Laura Gowing, *Domestic Dangers: Women, Words and Sex in Early Modern London* (Oxford: Clarendon Press, 1996) pays particular attention to the way women and men portray themselves or are portrayed in cases involving sex and gender relations.
29 An excellent collection of sources is Marion Gibson (ed.), *Witchcraft and Society in England and America, 1550–1750* (Ithaca, NY: Cornell University Press, 2003).
30 Helmut Puff, *Sodomy in Reformation Germany and Switzerland, 1400–1600* (Chicago: University of Chicago Press, 2003); Ulinka Rublack, *The Crimes of Women in Early Modern Germany* (New York: Oxford University Press, 1999).
31 *Early English Books Online* (*EEBO*) contains digital facsimiles of most books printed in English before 1700. The Women Writers Project, now at Northeastern University (http://www.wwp.northeastern.edu), has more than 350 fully searchable texts written by women between 1526 and 1850, along with introductions and commentary, and the Emory Women Writers Resource Project (http://womenwriters.library.emory.edu/earlymodern) has others (both accessed 18 January 2016). Hilda L. Smith and Susan Cardinale, *Women and the Literature of the Seventeenth Century* (New York: Greenwood, 1990), a 300-page annotated bibliography of all the books by, for and about women published in English throughout the world between 1641 and 1700, is an invaluable resource.
32 For an example of memoirs, see *Mother and Child Were Saved: The Memoirs (1693–1740) of the Frisian Midwife Catherina Schrader*, trans. and annot. Hilary Marland (Amsterdam: Rodopi, 1984). For a diary, see Joanna Moody (ed.), *The Private Life of an Elizabethan Lady: The Diary of Lady Margaret Hoby 1599–1605* (London: Sutton, 1998). For women's writings on a variety of topics, see Charlotte Otten (ed.), *English Women's Voices: 1540–1700* (Miami: Florida International University, 1992). For a study of the circulation of women's unpublished writings, see Margaret Ezell, *The Patriarch's Wife: Literary Evidence and the History of the Family* (Chapel Hill: University of North Carolina Press, 1987). See also Chapter 6 of this volume: 'Personal documents' (pp. 107–8).
33 For analyses of women's letters, see James Daybell (ed.), *Early Modern Women's Letter Writing, 1450–1700* (New York: Palgrave, 2001); James Daybell, *Women Letter Writers in Tudor England* (Oxford: Oxford University Press, 2006); and Jane Couchman and Ann Crabb (eds), *Women's Letters across Europe, 1400–1700: Form and Persuasion* (Burlington, VT: Ashgate, 2005).

9   Religion and religious change

Alec Ryrie

Researching the history of religion in the early modern period is like catching fireflies. Our subject is manifestly everywhere, but it dances out of reach. When we see patterns, it is hard to make out what is real and what a trick of the light. And if we succeed in grasping it, what we find in our hands bears little relation to the living experience. Altogether it is a frustrating, tantalizing and fascinating business.

The questions historians of religion would truly like to ask are inherently unanswerable. What did early modern people actually believe? In what ways did they believe? How and to what extent did their religion motivate them, govern their actions or dictate their patterns of thinking? What was the balance between sincerity and hypocrisy in their religion, and to what extent did they fuse into self-deception? What meaning did they find in religious practices and rites? Why did early modern people convert from one religion to another, or move between earnest commitment, nominal observance and (occasionally) frank unbelief? How was religion woven into the many fabrics of early modern society, economics, culture, politics and scholarship? We cannot truly answer such questions even for ourselves, let alone for others, and still less for others who are several centuries dead.

Of course, we can and do find plenty of clues and indirect answers to these questions, which in a rough empirical way often seem good enough. But while historians' instinct is to turn swiftly and gratefully from methodological nihilism to immerse ourselves in some real sources, we need always to be aware of the distortions that the vast silences in the evidence create. Like the proverbial drunk looking for dropped keys in a dark street, historians search not where the answers are, but where the light is. We can almost never overhear early modern people's prayers or follow their religious journeys. When we can, even if we believe our sources, we can be sure we are dealing with very unusual people. Even then, the most potent religious experiences are often left unspoken, not least because they are inexpressible. We are reading gardeners' account books in order to recover the sensation of smelling a rose.[1]

This chapter will survey the sorts of clues that historians of early modern religion have used to piece together our provisional and indirect answers to these questions. Since religion professed to touch every area of early modern life, and sometimes did so, the range of sources that we can use is very eclectic. What follows begins from the well-lit terrain closest to the lamp-post and works outwards into the murkier and potentially more interesting realms beyond. Most examples are drawn from my own field of expertise, early modern Britain, but the source-types can be paralleled across Europe and beyond.

Statutes, formulae and confessions of faith

The official records of the various churches of the Reformation era are generally well known and widely available, and obvious starting points for research. The Lutheran Book of Concord, the decrees of the Council of Trent, the legislation of England's Reformation Parliament: documents such as these form legal frameworks that at least aimed to contain the religion of millions of people.[2] It may seem obvious both that they should be consulted, and how they should be interpreted.

In fact, students and scholars are often surprisingly slow to consult them. Sometimes we assume that we already know more or less what they say, and that they have been so well studied that there will be nothing more to find. These texts, however, were usually intensively drafted, with every word weighed, and they repay equally close attention from historians. Nor is their meaning as plain as it may appear. If we compare the final texts to any surviving drafts, or to previous statutes, catechisms or formulae on which they were modelled, they can look very different. The 1539 English anti-heresy law known as the Act of Six Articles was known in its own time and has been remembered since as a general broadside against Protestant doctrines. However, Rory McEntegart has proved that its formulae emerged from the failed diplomatic negotiations between England and the Lutheran Schmalkaldic League, which casts it in a dramatically different light.[3]

Interpreting them is another matter again. Decrees, statutes or proclamations may assert authoritative norms, but did anyone obey them? Did their creators even expect obedience? This is in part a matter of context: some knowledge of a particular jurisdiction's legal culture is needed to understand the status a particular law might have. Laws are rhetorical as well as administrative devices, and we should not assume that they were meant to be enforced or even very long remembered. It is worth paying particular attention to promulgation: how were these decrees circulated, to whom and in what format? Even diligent circulation can change a law's meaning. The Act of Six Articles, despite its origins in a particular diplomatic incident, became a symbol of more general opposition to evangelical doctrines partly thanks to the provision that it be read aloud in each parish church quarterly.[4]

Sometimes the texts themselves provide clues. Repeated condemnations of the same offence can look suspiciously ineffectual, although a law that is not fully enforced is not therefore a mere dead letter. Some decrees are plainly more practical than others. Certain schemes were too elaborate to be credible, such as the Scottish statute of 1552 that imposed an elaborate scale of fines for swearing profane oaths, culminating in (for a fourth offence) banishment or a year's imprisonment: the law reeks of Heath Robinsonish impracticality.[5] Others lacked any teeth at all. The Council of Trent was not the first council to declare that bishops ought to be resident in their dioceses, simply the first to come up with a workable means of enforcing such decrees, by depriving non-resident bishops of their incomes.

Confessions of faith and official catechisms pose slightly different challenges. Again, it is important to be clear exactly what their status is. Were all clergy, all holders of civic office or even the population at large required to adhere to them? Was knowledge of them a prerequisite for admission to communion? Were there perceived ambiguities in them – of the kind that led, for example, to the Scots Confession of 1560 being supplemented by the so-called Negative Confession of 1581, drafted specifically to exclude Roman Catholics? Again, how did their actual texts fit with the symbolic status they often had? The 1530 Augsburg Confession, for example, came to have a genuinely iconic status for Lutherans, as well as a pivotal legal role in the Holy Roman Empire after the 1555 Peace of Augsburg.[6]

In general, we should be wary of assuming that these questions have plain answers, and be suspicious of those who assert that a complex and muddy legal situation was in fact clear-cut. Even in Tudor England, perhaps early modern Europe's most centralized and bureaucratic state, recent research has demonstrated that the supposedly straightforward oaths imposed on the population in the 1530s dissolve into a tangle of chaos and inconsistency on close examination.[7] Early modern bureaucracies lacked the means to enforce or even to communicate their wills consistently. A law, decree or catechism was simply an opening gambit in a process of negotiation, and sometimes the process went no further.

Liturgies, music and sermons

Many of the same caveats apply to these texts, for naturally, we should not simply assume that what was said in a book was what a minister or a congregation did. However, we can assume that liturgies were usually widely circulated, and suppose that they did guide practice fairly closely. Again, texts whose meanings we may think we know often repay close analysis. These were the words that most early modern people heard more often than any others: whether they loved or loathed liturgy, they swam in it. There are excellent modern editions of many liturgies, but the original texts, which survive in large numbers, are an underexploited resource, especially after the medieval period.[8] As with all working books, liturgies often bear revealing marks of their use.

But a printed liturgy is a mere playbook, and rarely reveals much of how the play was staged – especially when daring clerical directors took liberties with it. Even less does it answer the more crucial question of how liturgy was experienced by lay people, who may not have been able to hear its words. For these questions, we must depend on the clues in the texts, in contemporary descriptions that tell us how they were used (usually grinding axes all the while), in the buildings (when they survive) and in the rare contemporary visual depictions of worship (idealized as they are).[9] The growing scholarship on sacred space, and on religion and the body, emphasizes the extent to which liturgy was a visual and lived experience.[10] Alongside this is the longstanding, less fashionable but still essential field of the history of ecclesiastical architecture.

The place of music in worship is an enormous field in its own right, and daunting to non-specialists. Nevertheless it is sufficiently central to the experience of worship that it needs to be engaged with. Of necessity, we read texts that were in fact sung (congregationally or chorally), and must remember how that shaped their meaning (e.g. Figure 9.1). Music overlays texts with its own moods, a process about which early modern theorists had very advanced ideas. It also carries associations: if a new song is sung to an old tune, as was frequently the case in Reformed Protestant psalmody, the old words and meanings still cling to it. And as recent research has made clear, simply establishing which texts were sung to which tune is a question of daunting complexity.[11] Music was sometimes printed with texts, but equally often a text simply referred to a well-known tune.

Sermons are amongst the richest and most plentiful sources for early modern religious history: they survive in vast numbers, in print and in manuscript, and do allow us to come close to eavesdropping on public worship. Any catalogue of early printed books is likely to include a generous helping of self-described sermons, as well as other texts that do not declare their pulpit origins quite so plainly. Likewise, any miscellaneous manuscript collection from the period is likely to include sermons, whether preachers' own fair or working copies, or notes or transcriptions made by pious lay people. However, the relationship between the words of a printed or manuscript sermon and the words that a preacher actually uttered in a pulpit is vexing. The extensive scholarship on early modern sermons does give us some grounds for cautious optimism. Where it is possible to compare preachers' or hearers' notes with printed sermons, there is often a tolerably close relationship between the two.[12] One obvious warning sign is excessive length: early modern congregations often expected hour-long sermons and might tolerate double that, but preachers who felt that they were still warming up after two hours could give fuller vent to their views on the page. By contrast, an elaborate structure and the ostentatious use of ancient languages or theological jargon are perfectly credible features of the sermon as preached. Structures were deliberately used to assist hearers in note-taking or memorization, and there is good evidence that congregations valued and took pride in learned preachers even (or especially) when they could not actually understand all that was said.[13]

Published sermons are, however, more than a source for what the original preacher said. They were frequently published as models, and used by preachers with fewer aspirations to originality. Not many went so far as John Trusler, the eighteenth-century English entrepreneur who printed sermons using a

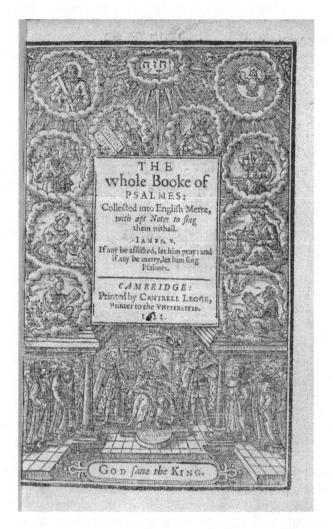

Figure 9.1 Title page of *The whole booke of psalmes: Collected into English metre, with apt notes to sing them withal* (Cambridge, 1623).

typeface resembling handwriting so that preachers might pass them off as their own work.[14] But these were not the only sermons published specifically to be preached by others: the most famous are the English Church's official Homilies, one of the most underused sources for English religious history.[15]

Polemical and devotional works

The spread of printing in the early modern period; online databases such as the *Universal Short Title Catalogue* (www.ustc.ac.uk); scanned facsimile collections such as *EEBO*, *E-Rara*, *Gallica* and those created by major libraries like the Bayerische Staatsbibliothek – all of these factors have ensured that early printed works are the richest, most diverse and most easily accessible set of primary sources for all aspects of early modern studies, especially for those lacking easy access to major archives.[16]

They are also amongst the least complex sources to handle, at least in the sense that they were usually aimed at a fairly broad readership, and so modern historians are not entirely unlike their intended audience. Their apparent accessibility can be deceptive. It is worth being aware of the legal context within which they were created – some books were subject to formal censorship of various kinds, others were not but still tried to avoid provoking trouble, others still were openly illegal and therefore faced formidable problems in production and distribution. Especially when dealing with digital facsimiles, it is easy to forget that early printed books were not disembodied texts, but physical objects created by a complex and heavily capitalized industrial process.[17] To use them effectively it is important to have some understanding of that process, its limitations and peculiarities, and at the very least to remember that a book's printer and publisher can be as important as its author.

We have a wealth of printed texts, but much less useful information about their readers. In the absence of sales figures, it is common to use frequency of reprinting as a proxy for a book's popularity, but since print runs varied dramatically in size, this can make an unexpected success (with a small initial printing) look much more impressive than a book with a guaranteed large market. As a measure, it also favours perennial steady-sellers over topical works that might quickly go out of date. Nor is there a particularly good rate of survival for some printed works, especially cheap ephemera. There is, however, no other systematic means of assessing books' popularity.[18] We are driven on to more haphazard measures such as occasional readers' comments on or responses to books, or imitation or plagiarism of them. If a book is banned – especially repeatedly – that tells us something. It is also worth scouring surviving copies for readers' notes or underlinings, although these are notoriously difficult to date accurately. Only rarely do we have solid information about the provenance of a particular copy.

The genres of printed religious polemic and devotional writing are both blurred and hugely varied.[19] Some, such as biblical commentaries and heavy-weight doctrinal treatises, are evidently written primarily for scholars and ministers. Openly polemical works, which attracted considerable attention at the time and have continued to do so, are more slippery. A book such as Martin Luther's *Address to the Christian Nobility of the German Nation* may claim to be written for one set of readers, while in fact aiming at another. Polemical denunciations were more usually read by friends than foes: they served to shore up support and to win over waverers, rather than to persuade the enemy. Some polemicists were aware of this; some seem not to have been.

Devotional works – books of prayers, guides to meditation, exhortations to moral living and so forth – have had much less scholarly attention than polemics, partly because they are undeniably duller. With some exceptions, they remain a largely untapped resource, despite their perennial popularity with early modern readers. The most obvious exception is literary. The religious poetry of the early modern era has never wanted for scholarly attention, although it is often historians' duty to be more interested in bad than in good poetry: geniuses are by definition unusual. Even so, historians are sometimes too cautious about making use of these sources. Literary scholars read the same texts, but with different questions: their interest is chiefly in the texts themselves, whereas historians' concern is with the people who wrote and read them. And different questions can produce fresh answers.

In practice, of course, polemical and devotional works blur into one another. One genre that is particularly amphibious in this respect is history written to edify: martyrologies and other works of pious story-telling, which have long been quarried as sourcebooks in their own right. Although they invite scepticism, martyr-accounts of the Reformation era are often surprisingly accurate in their details. There were too many living witnesses who could (and did) publicly contradict and discredit martyrologists who massaged their facts or who simply got them wrong. The historians' bias, as ever, tended to be less in distortion than in selection.[20] Martyrologists chose those facts that served the purposes (both devotional and polemical) for which they wrote, and then reproduced them fairly faithfully: leaving us, their historical successors, to listen for the elisions and the silences.

And printed works that have no explicitly religious content at all can provide the most valuable testimony. All manner of popular printed works can open unexpected windows into religious assumptions, practices and prejudices: crime pamphlets, ballads, guides to household management or to letter-writing, even joke books (which can be excruciating to modern readers).[21] It is, unfortunately, all but impossible to rule out the sudden appearance of material of religious interest in almost any kind of text. Religion was supposed to reach into every sphere of life, and sometimes it did. The consolation is the prospect of serendipitous discoveries almost anywhere.

Religious manuscripts

This category is even more miscellaneous than that of printed works, and blurs into it, since plenty of pious early modern people created handwritten books either in imitation of printed works, or in the hope of achieving publication. These vary from beautifully executed fair copies to scarcely legible scraps. Their contents extend to everything that you might find in contemporary printed works, and often include substantial transcriptions from them, undertaken either as a pious exercise or simply as a way of preserving an important text in the pre-photocopier age. But they can also be far more individual and intimate. Personal letters are perhaps the best-known genre of such documents, and also amongst the easiest to use, since we normally know the author, the addressee and perhaps even the date. Many significant letter collections have been published.[22] Other manuscript works are trickier. We should not assume that manuscript works were private: they might be widely circulated within a family or a circle of friends, especially when print publication was not readily available or when (as was often the case) it was seen as unappealingly plebeian. Some, however, were indeed private, either simply notes or drafts for the author's own use, or indeed material sufficiently intimate that the author might actively try to conceal them. Such works are sometimes written in codes or ciphers, some of which can now be broken, some not. We know that a large number of such works were destroyed by their authors or their heirs.

Some of these works can be gathered under the broad heading of 'self-writing' or 'ego-documents': awkward modern categories that include diaries and journals, autobiographies, collections of reflective prayers and many other similar texts. The early modern period is marked by the emergence of extended works of self-examination (many but not all religious in intent), a fact that has again drawn considerable attention from literary scholars. The number of manuscripts is small but their genre is immensely varied, drawing on models as diverse as Augustine of Hippo's *Confessions*, classic martyrology, the medieval chronicle tradition and accountancy. The chief problem with these texts is their siren allure. The chance of an almost unmediated glimpse of an individual's religious life is immensely appealing, and some superb scholarship has been based on such sources. But they are few, wholly unrepresentative, often stylized and rhetorically complex. This is strong meat: it needs careful handling.[23]

Blending into that heavily examined set of materials is another, surprisingly underexploited group: commonplace books, the miscellaneous notebooks and scrapbooks kept by many literate early modern people. Commonplace books offer the same opportunities and frustrations as rummaging through someone's desk drawers: disorganized jumbles of material blending letters, prayers, recipes, sermon notes, medical notes, accounts, poetry, quotations on any subject, snippets of news, music, pornography, doodles, jokes and whatever else you might wish for. Libraries are full of them, and most of them are unloved. Their extremely miscellaneous nature makes them frustrating sources to use, for even when a remarkable scrap leaps out, what does it mean in that context? Even so, there is value in the reminder that early modern lives, like our own, blended the profound with the trivial. They remain a genre still to be quarried by historians of religion.[24]

The visual arts

Historians are often nervous about venturing beyond written texts – and rightly so, because they can be formidably difficult to interpret. Yet as some bold pioneers have demonstrated, there are important insights to be had. There are established specialisms to turn to for assistance, but historians of art and architecture have their own distinct, disciplinary concerns, and even the traditional mutual suspicion between historians and archaeologists reflects genuine disciplinary differences as well as mere prejudice.

As with music, a central problem – and value – of the visual arts as a historical source is their ambiguity: their meanings are inherently more ambiguous and malleable than those of written texts. Teaching ourselves to read complex images can feel like learning to break a code, but we should remember that they were not always even intended to have a single meaning, and that many contemporaries may have found them as opaque as we do. There is a grave risk of over-interpreting visual sources, or of mistaking a plausible conjecture for an established fact.

Visual images were of course themselves a primary site of contention in the Reformation disputes. The medieval truism was that images were 'books for laymen', a vital means of teaching the illiterate.[25] Images from wall paintings to printed woodcuts do offer us the tantalizing possibility of contact with the illiterate majority, but we should not assume that this was their purpose: complex images, often depending on accompanying textual comment, could be at least as hard to read as a written text.[26] As with printed sources, only more so, making any deductions about the reception of visual images is fraught with difficulty, except where there is direct evidence. Even acts of iconoclastic destruction can have many meanings.

As with literary scholarship, art history has tended to focus on the highest-quality works, but historians' interests are likely to be different. Courtly painting and architectural detail can be invaluable clues to the rarefied milieux that produced them, but were beyond the reach of most people. In recent years a number of scholars of early modern religion have turned instead to look at areas such as domestic space, interior decoration and household objects. This has taught us, for example, that Reformed Protestants' supposed 'iconophobia' has been badly overstated.[27] Our attention, so long focused on churches, is moving to the site where most believers, especially women and children, lived most of their religion: the home.[28]

Administrative records

Churches, however, do have some irresistible attractions, not least that their bureaucracies produce rich seams of records whose value for the religious history of the early modern period has long been obvious. In what follows it is possible only to sketch some of the most important categories of such records and what they can teach us.

Churchwardens' accounts or similar financial records survive for many parishes: intractable texts that conceal a wealth of invaluable information. Especially for the earlier part of the period, a good many have been edited and published, often by local record societies.[29] They can be used to track changes in a church's decoration, musical provision and personnel; changes in its pattern of worship, as new books or goods are purchased; the wealth or poverty of a church and a parish; compliance with or resistance to the dictates of bishops, synods or magistrates. Local ecclesiastical power struggles will usually leave their mark in such documents. In combination, multiple sets of accounts can be used as proxies for national and regional change and variations.[30] Occasional sets of accounts can provide much richer material, almost akin to a chronicle or diary.[31] Some jurisdictions also required records to be kept of baptisms, marriages and funerals, which where they exist are invaluable datasets. Beyond the obvious demographic and prosopographical uses, these records can be used to track, for example, some changes in religious affiliation (weighing the saints' names favoured by Catholics against the Old Testament names favoured by some Protestants) or conformity to ecclesiastical strictures on sexual activity (how many children are born nine months after Lent?).[32]

Records of ecclesiastical discipline, whether at the level of the parish, deanery, presbytery or diocese, have long been recognized as a rich source for both official and unofficial religion. Again some have been published, but a great many remain in manuscript.[33] They can reveal the ambitions, capabilities and priorities of different ecclesiastical establishments: it is indispensable, for example, to know when tribunals stop prosecuting non-attendance at church, or begin pursuing Sabbath-breakers with renewed energy. Where ecclesiastical tribunals are responsible for prosecuting heresy, that fact in itself tells us something about power structures in a society, and the details of the proceedings tell us what inquisitors consider the nature of the heresy problem to be at that time and place. The consistorial discipline of Reformed Protestantism can be particularly revealing, whether it is seen as a tool of social control or as a more benign and paternalistic means of preserving order, and these minutes have been studied intensively by historians of France, Scotland, Geneva and elsewhere.[34]

At least as importantly, these records testify to social realities as well as to official policy. Court documents deal with the behaviour of more or less ordinary men and women, and often purport to record their words verbatim. These transcripts need to be treated with some care: they are not audio recordings, but are at the least tidied up by scribes; they are often radically edited – not least because scribes would often only record a witness's answers to questions, not the questions themselves, which can be very distorting; and we cannot rule out the possibility that a witness has been materially misrepresented. And of course, even if the words are accurately recorded, lies and half-truths are told in courtrooms every day.

With all those caveats, church courts can often provide the most vivid glimpses we have of the rougher fringes of everyday religious life. This is especially the case when lay people used those courts to sue one another for religious or religious-related offences – which could be anything from the moral offence of defamation (few things are more revealing than insults), through arguments over seating in church buildings, to disputes over tithes and wills.[35]

The danger in interpreting this rich vein of material is a mirror image of the trouble with early printed sources. It is rawer and perhaps more authentic, but no more representative. If printed texts present an overly tidy and pious image of early modern society, courts show us its raucous underside: most people avoided the law most of the time. The persistent problem of early modern religious life remains: accessing the now-silent majority of those who neither wrote religious treatises nor suffered prosecution for blasphemy – a mass of people whom we struggle to place between nominal conformity and earnest, unshowy piety.

One administrative source that has been extensively mined in an attempt to reveal these people's religion is wills.[36] Most early modern people did not make wills, but a surprisingly large minority did, especially in some juris-dictions and in towns. Some wills include explicit or implicit statements of religious identity, usually associated with a 'bequest' of the testator's soul to God: stereotypically, Catholics would invoke the Virgin Mary and other saints, while Protestants might declare their hope to be justified through faith alone. Historians of the English Reformation, in particular, have attempted to use the shifts in these statements to track religious change statistically, but the methodological problems with this are formidable. Quite aside from the demographic distortions (testators were richer, more male and, by definition, older than average), such statements were often formulaic phrases inserted by scribes or other legal advisors. More reliance can be placed on actual bequests, which we can assume represent testators' own views. It is harder to build statistical models from these, but where we find testators leaving endow-ments for masses to be said for their souls, or for sermons to be preached in their memory; where we find gifts to a church in token of tithes forgotten, or towards a new pulpit lectern; where we find relatives being bequeathed named books, rosaries or paintings, or gifts to the poor in the expectation of their prayers – in these cases, we find early modern religion putting its money where its mouth was.[37]

Above the parish level, the most consistently useful records are those of appointments to ecclesiastical office, and of visitation. These tend to lurk in manuscript records of administration, which can be impenetrable to the nov-ice user and heavy going for anyone, but the material's value for prosopo-graphical and local history has meant that a surprising amount of it has been published. In particular, a good many English bishops' registers are avail-able.[38] A particularly important model of how these records can be made fully available to researchers is the Clergy of the Church of England Database (http://theclergydatabase.org.uk), a freely available online database that, when complete, will collate the principal records of clerical careers from over fifty English and Welsh archives.[39]

Much of this material may seem to be of mostly prosopographical inter-est, sometimes being little more than lists of names and places, but there are riches to be had. What are the patterns of change: are there times and places where the turnover of clergy is particularly rapid? What were the educational or regional backgrounds of new clergy? Who were their patrons? Why did their predecessors leave office, and for how long had the posts been vacant? How and how sustainably were their posts financed? How did all of these factors change over time, and how did they correlate with what other records have to tell us? These records may not often produce compelling personal narratives for us, but they can tell us an enormous amount about the practical condition of churches and their personnel.

Visitations are much more uneven, but their value is that Church authorities were very often asking exactly the sorts of questions in which we are still interested: how was religious change being implemented or resisted on the local level? How conscientiously did the mass of the people observe their religion, and what was done to ensure that they did? In many cases, all that we have are the questions that diocesan or synodal authorities wanted to ask of local churches, but even these can be very revealing of the hopes, fears and priorities of administrations who were charged with turning abstract ideals into practical reality.[40] Where we have answers, we should not assume them to be unvarnished truth, nor anyone's honest perception: local communities tend either to close ranks against nosey officials, or to use them to pursue local grievances. Visitors, of course, knew this, and we should credit them with being able to tease the truth out of their informants at least as well as we are able to do the same with the surviving records.[41]

Everything else

These are the most obviously fruitful sources for researching early modern religion and religious change, but the subject's pervasive nature means that it can leave its fingerprints everywhere. The political and administrative records of early modern states are full of clues about religious life. Tax records tell us about the wealth or poverty of the clergy, the extent to which states were squeezing or discriminating between religious groups, the social shape of religious groups and the extent to which religious minorities were struggling or prospering. Military records can testify to the role of churches in supporting, opposing or collaborating with war; the extent, if any, to which religious principles shaped military conduct, including deliberate targeting and destruction of the persons and property of opposing religious groups; and can allow us to trace individuals both risking their lives for their religion, and betraying it. The many uses of political papers of all kinds hardly need to be mentioned, in an era when religion was a vital political interest and when political actors of all kinds either were or professed to be guided by genuine religious conviction. Guild and trade records can reveal unexpected secrets about religious observance (did the fishing industry genuinely prosper in territories where the Lenten fast was supposedly enforced?) or about the social status of the clergy (who might be employed as guild chaplains). The records of universities, of professional corporations of lawyers or medical practitioners, or of the printing industry may have particular relevance, since in the early modern era each of these was a site of high intellectual ferments and low rivalries that impinged on religious matters.[42] Likewise the fragmentary and often intractable materials that show us how those worlds touched the lives of ordinary people. School textbooks, statutes and accounts can offer a rare glimpse into the workings of a world where many boys and even some girls learned much of their formal religion. The secular law courts can at times be almost as rich a hunting-ground for religious practice and prejudice as their ecclesiastical counterparts. Public health and informal medical practice are generally very poorly documented, but the few materials that survive can be enlightening: from the urban bills of mortality, which testify to the demography and pathology within which popular religion was formed, to the casebooks of unlicenced medics, which can tell a tale of orthodoxy, heterodoxy and unbelief blended together and spiced with desperation.[43]

The truly undiscovered country for historians of early modern religion remains archaeology. Institutional structures and disciplinary cultures are formidable barriers; more so, the fundamentally different questions that historians and archaeologists are trained to ask and that their material equips them to answer. There have been some serious attempts to engage archaeologically with the issues of concern to early modern historians of religion, though not yet consistently or sustainably.[44] Nevertheless, it is invaluable for even the most ideas- and texts-bound historians to engage with the gritty materiality of the past, which brings us forcibly up against the embodied reality of our forebears as both similar to and alien from us. Quite aside from the specific research insights it has to yield, it is also both spur and bridle to that most vital and most wayward of historical tools, the imagination: a vivid reminder that our sources are merely that – sources – the flotsam and footprints of people as real as ourselves.

Key resources

Certain Sermons or Homilies Appointed to be Read in Churches in the Time of the Late Queen Elizabeth ... to Which Are Added the Constitutions and Canons Ecclesiastical Set Forth in the Year MDCIII (Oxford: Oxford University Press, 1844).

Clergy of the Church of England Database: http://theclergydatabase.org.uk.

Kingdon, Robert M., Thomas A. Lambert, Isabella M. Watt and Jeffrey R. Watt (eds), *Registres du Consistoire de Genève au temps de Calvin* (Geneva: Droz, 1996–).

Liturgies of the Western Church, ed. Bard Thompson (Philadelphia: Augsburg Fortress, 1959).

The Notebooks of Nehemiah Wallington, 1618–1654: A Selection, ed. David Booy (Aldershot: Ashgate, 2007).

Robinson, Hastings (ed.), *The Zurich Letters, Comprising the Correspondence of Several English Bishops and Others with Some of the Helvetian Reformers during the Early Part of the Reign of Queen Elizabeth* (Cambridge: Parker Society, 1842, 1845).

Smith, David M., *Guide to Bishops' Registers of England and Wales: A Survey from the Middle Ages to the Abolition of Episcopacy in 1646* (London: Royal Historical Society, 1981).

Smith, David M., *Supplement to the Guide to Bishops' Registers of England and Wales* (York: Canterbury and York Society, 2004).
State Papers Online, http://gale.cengage.co.uk/state-papers-online-15091714.aspx.
Universal Short Title Catalogue, http://www.ustc.ac.uk.
Visitation Articles and Injunctions of the Period of the Reformation, ed. Walter Frere and William Kennedy, 3 vols, Alcuin Club Collections, 14–16 (London: Longmans, Green, 1910).

Notes

1 Alec Ryrie, *Being Protestant in Reformation Britain* (Oxford: Oxford University Press, 2013), p. 10.
2 *The Book of Concord: The Confessions of the Evangelical Lutheran Church*, ed. Robert Kolb and Timothy J. Wengert (Minneapolis: Augsburg Fortress Press, 2000); *The Canons and Decrees of the Sacred and Oecumenical Council of Trent*, ed. J. Waterworth (London: Dolman, 1848); *Statutes of the Realm, Printed by Command of His Majesty King George III*, Vol. III (London: Eyre and Strahan, 1817).
3 Rory McEntegart, *Henry VIII, the League of Schmalkalden and the English Reformation* (Woodbridge: Boydell and Brewer, 2002), pp. 108–27, 150–63.
4 31 Hen. VIII c. 14 art. XVIII, *Statutes of the Realm*, Vol. III, p. 743.
5 *The Acts of the Parliaments of Scotland*, Vol. II: *1424–1567* (London: Eyre, 1814), p. 485.
6 Robert Kolb, 'Luther, Augsburg, and the Concept of Authority in the Late Reformation: Ursinus vs. the Lutherans', in Derk Visser (ed.), *Controversy and Conciliation: The Reformation and the Palatinate, 1559–1583* (Allison Park, PA: Pickwick Publications, 1986), pp. 33–49.
7 Jonathan Gray, *Oaths and the English Reformation* (Cambridge: Cambridge University Press, 2013).
8 Notably *Liturgies of the Western Church*, ed. Bard Thompson (Philadelphia: Augsburg Fortress, 1959); and *Prayers of the Eucharist: Early and Reformed*, ed. R. C. D. Cuming and G. J. Jasper, 3rd edn (Collegeville, MN: Liturgical Press, 1975).
9 See the essays in Natalie Mears and Alec Ryrie (eds), *Worship and the Parish Church in Early Modern Britain* (Farnham: Ashgate, 2013).
10 See, for example, Christopher Marsh, 'Sacred Space in England 1560–1640: The View from the Pew', *Journal of Ecclesiastical History*, 53 (2002), 286–311; Andrew Spicer and Sarah Hamilton (eds), *Defining the Holy: Sacred Space in Medieval and Early Modern Europe* (Aldershot: Ashgate, 2005); Will Coster and Andrew Spicer (eds), *Sacred Space in Early Modern Europe* (Cambridge: Cambridge University Press, 2005); John Craig, 'Bodies at Prayer in Early Modern England', in Mears and Ryrie, *Worship and the Parish Church*, pp. 173–96.
11 Timothy Duguid, *Metrical Psalmody in Print and Practice: English 'Singing Psalms' and Scottish 'Psalm Buiks', c. 1547–1640* (Farnham: Ashgate, 2014). Beth Quitslund, *The Reformation in Rhyme: Sternhold, Hopkins and the English Metrical Psalter, 1547–1603* (Aldershot: Ashgate, 2008) contains a series of useful appendices with details about the best-selling music book in early modern England, 'Sternhold and Hopkins', *The Whole Booke of Psalms*, published by John Day. Jonathan Willis, *Church Music and Protestantism in Post-Reformation England: Discourses, Sites and Identities* (Farnham: Ashgate, 2010) also contains a list of extant English godly ballads. On ballads more generally, see Angela McShane, *Political Broadside Ballads in Seventeenth-Century England: A Critical Bibliography* (London: Pickering and Chatto, 2011); and also the online *English*

Broadside Ballad Archive (EBBA), http://ebba.english.ucsb.edu (accessed 25 August 2015).

12 Now dominated by Arnold Hunt, *The Art of Hearing: English Preachers and Their Audiences, 1590–1640* (Cambridge: Cambridge University Press, 2010). A good example of what a careful modern editor can do with a printed collection of early modern sermons is Roger Edgeworth, *Sermons Very Fruitfull, Godly and Learned: Preaching in the Reformation c. 1535–c. 1553*, ed. Janet Wilson (Cambridge: D. S. Brewer, 1993).

13 For a recent collection of essays on sermons, see Peter McCullough, Hugh Adlington and Emma Rhatigan (eds), *The Oxford Handbook of the Early Modern Sermon* (Oxford: Oxford University Press, 2011). Sermons can be located on *EEBO*, as well as in some later published editions, such as Hugh Latimer, *Sermons by Hugh Latimer, Sometime Bishop of Worcester*, ed. George Corrie (Cambridge: Cambridge University Press, 1844).

14 W. Gibson, 'John Trusler and the Culture of Sermons in Late Eighteenth Century England', *Journal of Ecclesiastical History*, 66.2 (2015), 302–19.

15 Published in a great many early modern editions, but also accessible in *Certain Sermons or Homilies Appointed to be Read in Churches in the Time of the Late Queen Elizabeth … to Which Are Added the Constitutions and Canons Ecclesiastical Set Forth in the Year MDCIII* (Oxford: Oxford University Press, 1844).

16 *Universal Short Title Catalogue*, http://www.ustc.ac.uk; *E-Rara*, http://www.e-rara.ch; *Gallica*, http://gallica.bnf.fr (all accessed 20 January 2016).

17 Andrew Pettegree, *The Book in the Renaissance* (New Haven and London: Yale University Press, 2010).

18 For a much fuller discussion of this problem and approaches to it, see Ian Green, *Print and Protestantism in Early Modern England* (Oxford: Oxford University Press, 2000); as well as Ian Green's chapter in the present volume, 'Print' (pp. 78–94).

19 For more on genre, see Chapter 5 of this volume (pp. 95–106).

20 Patrick Collinson, 'Truth and Legend: The Veracity of John Foxe's *Book of Martyrs*', in his *Elizabethan Essays* (London: Hambledon Press, 1994); David Loades (ed.), *John Foxe and the English Reformation* (Aldershot: Ashgate, 1997).

21 The English prototype is *A. C. mery talys*, *RSTC*, 23664 (London: John Rastell for P. Treveris, 1526).

22 One of the best-known self-contained collections remains Hastings Robinson (ed.), *The Zurich Letters, Comprising the Correspondence of Several English Bishops and Others with Some of the Helvetian Reformers during the Early Part of the Reign of Queen Elizabeth* (Cambridge: Parker Society, 1842, 1845).

23 Andrew Cambers, 'Reading, the Godly, and Self-Writing in England, *circa* 1580–1720', *Journal of British Studies*, 46.4 (2007); James S. Amelang, *The Flight of Icarus: Artisan Autobiography in Early Modern Europe* (Stanford, CA: Stanford University Press, 1998); Sara Heller Mendelson, 'Stuart Women's Diaries and Occasional Memoirs', in Mary Prior (ed.), *Women in English Society 1500–1800* (London and New York: Methuen, 1985), pp. 181–210; Catherine A. Brekus, 'Writing as a Protestant Practice: Devotional Diaries in Early New England', in Laurie P. Maffly-Kipp, Leigh Eric Schmidt and Mark R. Valeri (eds), *Practicing Protestants: Histories of Christian Life in America* (Baltimore: Johns Hopkins University Press, 2006); Ryrie, *Being Protestant*, Chapter 12. See also the chapter on 'Personal documents' in this volume, pp. 107–28.

24 A survey of their uses, mostly by literary scholars, can be found in Victoria E. Burke, 'Recent Studies in Commonplace Books', *English Literary Renaissance*, 43.1 (2013), 153–77. A useful example of the genre, displaying its value and its

limitations, is *The Diary of John Manningham of the Middle Temple, 1602–1603*, ed. Robert Parker Sorlien (Hanover, NH: University Press of New England, 1976).

25 Ann Eljenholm Nichols, 'Books-for-Laymen: The Demise of a Commonplace', *Church History*, 56 (1987), 457–73.

26 Andrew Pettegree, *Reformation and the Culture of Persuasion* (Cambridge: Cambridge University Press, 2005), pp. 102–27.

27 Tara Hamling, *Decorating the 'Godly' Household: Religious Art in Post-Reformation Britain* (New Haven and London: Yale University Press, 2010); Tara Hamling and Catherine Richardson (eds), *Everyday Objects: Medieval and Early Modern Material Culture and Its Meanings* (Aldershot: Ashgate, 2010).

28 Jessica Martin and Alec Ryrie (eds), *Private and Domestic Devotion in Early Modern Britain* (Farnham: Ashgate, 2012).

29 See also the discussion of churchwardens' accounts in Chapter 3, 'Ecclesiastical sources' (pp. 64–6).

30 Ronald Hutton, 'The Local Impact of the Tudor Reformations', in Christopher Haigh (ed.), *The English Reformation Revised* (Cambridge: Cambridge University Press, 1987), pp. 114–38; Beat Kümin, *The Shaping of a Community: The Rise and Reformation of the English Parish c. 1400–1560* (Aldershot: Scolar Press, 1996); John Craig, *Reformation, Politics and Polemics: the Growth of Protestantism in East Anglian Market Towns, 1500–1610* (Aldershot: Ashgate, 2001).

31 As used most famously in Eamon Duffy, *The Voices of Morebath: Reformation and Rebellion in an English village* (New Haven and London: Yale University Press, 2001).

32 Patrick Collinson, 'What's in a Name? Dudley Fenner and the Peculiarities of Puritan Nomenclature', in Kenneth Fincham and Peter Lake (eds), *Religious Politics in Post-Reformation England: Essays in Honour of Nicholas Tyacke* (Woodbridge: Boydell Press, 2006), pp. 113–27.

33 See also Chapters 2 and 3 of this volume (pp. 35–57 and 58–77 respectively). The best-known collection is Robert M. Kingdon, Thomas A. Lambert, Isabella M. Watt and Jeffrey R. Watt (eds), *Registres du Consistoire de Genève au temps de Calvin* (Geneva: Droz, 1996–); at time of writing there are eight volumes in print, covering 1542–54.

34 See, for example, Margo Todd, *The Culture of Protestantism in Early Modern Scotland* (New Haven and London: Yale University Press, 2002); Michael F. Graham, *The Uses of Reform: 'Godly Discipline' and Popular Behaviour in Scotland and Beyond, 1560–1610* (Leiden: Brill, 1996); William G. Naphy, *Calvin and the Consolidation of the Genevan Reformation* (Manchester: Manchester University Press, 1994); Philip Benedict, *Rouen during the Wars of Religion* (Cambridge: Cambridge University Press, 1981); Graeme Murdock, 'Dressed to Repress? Protestant Clergy Dress and the Regulation of Morality in Early Modern Europe', *Fashion Theory: The Journal of Dress, Body and Culture*, 2 (2000), 179–99.

35 Christopher Haigh, *The Plain Man's Pathways to Heaven: Kinds of Christianity in Post-Reformation England, 1570–1640* (Oxford: Oxford University Press, 2007) uses such sources to draw a rounded picture of an entire country.

36 See also the brief discussion of wills in Chapter 3, pp. 70–2.

37 Amongst the extensive scholarship on wills, see J. D. Alsop, 'Religious Preambles in Early Modern English Wills as Formulae', *Journal of Ecclesiastical History*, 40 (1989), 19–27; Christopher Marsh, 'In the Name of God? Will-Making and Faith in Early Modern England', in G. H. Martin and Peter Spufford (eds), *The Records of the Nation* (Woodbridge: Boydell, 1990); Clive Burgess, 'Late Medieval Wills and Pious Convention: Testamentary Evidence Reconsidered', in Michael Hicks (ed.), *Profit, Piety and the Professions in Later Medieval England* (Gloucester: Sutton, 1990), pp. 14–33; David Hickman, 'From Catholic

to Protestant: The Changing Meaning of Testamentary Religious Provision in Elizabethan London', in Nicholas Tyacke (ed.), *England's Long Reformation 1500–1800* (London: UCL Press, 1998). Cf. Ann W. Ramsey, *Liturgy, Politics and Salvation: The Catholic League of Paris and the Nature of Catholic Reform 1540–1630* (Rochester, NY: University of Rochester Press, 1999); Margaret H. B. Sanderson, *A Kindly Place? Living in Sixteenth-Century Scotland* (East Linton: Tuckwell Press, 2002), pp. 155–73.

38 The invaluable publications of the Canterbury and York Society are central here, but for a comprehensive overview see David M. Smith, *Guide to Bishops' Registers of England and Wales: A Survey from the Middle Ages to the Abolition of Episcopacy in 1646* (London: Royal Historical Society, 1981); and his *Supplement to the Guide to Bishops' Registers of England and Wales* (York: Canterbury and York Society, 2004).

39 http://theclergydatabase.org.uk (accessed 20 January 2016).

40 See, for example, Walter Frere and William Kennedy (eds), *Visitation Articles and Injunctions of the Period of the Reformation*, 3 vols, Alcuin Club Collections, 14–16 (London: Longmans, Green, 1910).

41 See, for example, David Newcombe, 'John Hooper's Visitation and Examination of the Clergy in the Diocese of Gloucester, 1551', in Beat A. Kümin (ed.), *Reformations Old and New: Essays on the Socio-Economic Impact of Religious Change, c. 1470–1630* (Aldershot: Ashgate, 1996), pp. 57–70.

42 Many of the English examples have been edited. See, amongst others, the two volumes of the *Records of the Court of the Stationers' Company*, covering 1576–1640 (London: Bibliographical Society, 1930, 1957); William Munk, *The Roll of the Royal College of Physicians of London*, Vols I and II, covering 1518–1800 (London: Royal College of Physicians, 1861); or the four volumes of the *Grace Book … Containing the Proctors' Accounts and Other Records of the University of Cambridge*, covering the period 1454–1589 (Cambridge: Cambridge Antiquarian Society, 1897–1910).

43 See, for example, the digitized casebooks of the London astrologers and medics Simon Forman and Richard Napier, http://www.magicandmedicine.hps.cam.ac.uk (accessed 19 January 2016).

44 The most important work is still David Gaimster and Roberta Gilchrist (eds), *The Archaeology of Reformation 1480–1580: Papers Given at the Archaeology of Reformation Conference, February 2001* (Leeds: Maney Publishing, 2003).

10 Political culture(s)

Janet Dickinson

The study of political culture(s) can appear, at first glance, to be virtually infinite in the range of subjects it can be applied to and in the range of sources that can be used. Fundamentally, 'political culture' is about the worlds – the contexts – in which politics took place, understood in both mental and physical terms. But immediately it becomes more complicated. No singular definition is possible; political cultures need to be studied with a recognition that they were at all times plural, overlapping and subject to change.

Concepts of 'political culture' have not attracted the same kind of scholarly attention as 'popular culture', which has been the focus of a great deal of thought about methodology and sources in recent years.[1] Instead, the idea of political culture has been left rather loosely defined, a useful catch-all term rather than a standalone subject of study.[2] This leaves students seeking to study political culture in something of a methodological vacuum. The work of scholars such as Peter Burke, Natalie Zemon Davies and Keith Thomas on cultural history and on the history of 'mentalities' is useful, reminding us that cultural history needs to be studied as an integral part of political, religious, social and economic history, not as a decorative addition made at the end once the fundamentals have been established. They also remind us that adapting the methods applied by anthropologists to the study of historical peoples is both possible and extremely useful.[3] In this light, students of political culture should feel encouraged to think broadly in terms of their identification of their sources as well as to think very carefully about what they are trying to reconstruct, paying close attention to the people they are studying and their everyday practices, as well as ritual and ceremonial behaviour. We need to think about participation in politics as being expressed as much through policy and patronage as through dress, behaviour, gesture and deference, architecture and buildings, the visual arts, literature, drama, and political theory, to list just a few of the possible areas for study.

A great deal of fruitful work has already been done. There has been a shift away from writing the history of political institutions such as Parliament and the Privy Council and a much greater willingness to think more broadly, both in terms of the questions we can and should ask of the functioning of politics, and in terms of source material. New forms of political history have been written in which the mental worlds of the people involved are treated as part of their actions and their involvement in the practical acts of government.[4] The boundaries among social, political and cultural history were never opaque, and they have dissolved as historians have increasingly sought to understand the mental worlds of the individuals and groups that they are studying. We are now starting to see a much more meaningful reconstruction of the political cultures of the early modern world through the study of processes of state formation, the functioning of government in the early modern period and the growth of popular politics.[5] The concept of 'interdisciplinarity' has become fashionable beyond the point of retaining any claim to novelty or freshness of approach, but when it comes to understanding political culture there is no question that sources must be drawn from a far wider range of disciplines than the traditional historical hunting ground of archival and textual materials. This is something that historians have increasingly come to embrace and that can be neatly encapsulated under the banner of the study of political culture.

This chapter will not attempt the impossible and try to offer a comprehensive introduction to the subject of political culture. It will instead identify a number of key subject areas that might provide useful starting points for students wishing to develop their own study of political cultures of whatever kind. It is the argument of this chapter that it is possible – important – to do this with a conscious awareness that there were overlapping mental frameworks that shaped political behaviour and attitudes. These frameworks, or contexts, should be brought to studies carried out under the name of political cultures – necessarily plural as it would be impossible to separate out any one set of assumptions without simultaneously recognizing that ideas do not exist in a vacuum and cannot be hermetically sealed off from one another. Any of the different forms of political culture discussed in this chapter should be seen as having been subject to change (sometimes sudden, at other times gradual). It is also important to recognize that individuals occasionally coped with conflicting ideas and with contradictions within their own ideas about the world they inhabited and what they were doing in it.

Political thought

One way into understanding political culture in the early modern period is to look at what contemporaries thought they were doing.[6] Works of political theory and manuals of advice for princes and courtiers set out the basic assumptions that shaped the functioning of society and government: that it was hierarchical; concerned with degree, place and identity; and above all with the maintenance of order and stability, understood to form the basis of the security and stability of the common good, or common weal. The body politic was often compared to the human body, with the health of each part dependent on the well-being of the whole.[7] In his *Tree of Commonwealth*, written in 1509–10, the royal administrator Edmund

Dudley varied the metaphor, conceptualizing society as a tree, whose healthy existence depended on all parts of society working together for the good of all members of the common weal. For Dudley, the roots of his political culture were Christianity, justice, truth, concord and peace, all connected together by service to the monarch, who was himself bound to protect and take care of society.[8] Following in the medieval tradition of the 'Mirror for Princes', Dudley's formulation was in no sense original. Similar accounts can be found in many other works on the operation of politics and society, notably Sir John Fortescue's fifteenth-century definition of political order, but it does illustrate the kinds of insights into shared assumptions and beliefs that can be gained from reading works of political theory.[9]

Setting out such ideas is one thing, but it is also important to understand their reception – did people really believe in obedience and duty, and do these ideas provide us with an insight into wider political culture? These audiences can be addressed in a number of ways – by identifying individual case studies or broader processes, and indeed by using the former to illuminate the latter. Studies of popular responses to the reformations of the sixteenth century have shown that the overwhelming response was one of passive conformity. This can in part be attributed to the conviction that to resist and protest would cause far greater ructions in the body politic, suggesting the extent to which people both believed in and actively bought into ideas of the common weal and their role in upholding its good health. Geoffrey Elton's study of the policing of Henry VIII's break with Rome gives us this kind of insight into the functioning of local government, using the letters sent to Thomas Cromwell at the Court in London and surviving in the State Papers. In 1536 an accusation of 'heinous words' said by Lawrence Holland, a gentleman, and Richard Tumber, a fuller, made its way up the social hierarchy from the original accuser, Edward Ryland; who reported them to Robert Neyll and John Branshe; who in turn informed Sir Thomas Neville, the local magistrate; who finally referred the whole matter to Thomas Cromwell.[10] Further details of this case do not appear to survive, but in the other accusations sent in to Cromwell concern was repeatedly expressed about the dangers of 'treasonous words' and suspicious behaviour that might cross over into sedition. This study and other more recent work on the subject have cast considerable light on the workings of passive conformity, showing us Henrician politics in action in a society alive to the threat posed by treason and criticism of the king's policies.[11] It is a useful reminder that ideas and beliefs could be as strong in motivating inaction as in stimulating change.

Counsel

The importance of giving and receiving counsel was something that everyone agreed was a central part of the functioning of politics in the early modern period. Without counsel, rulers might lapse into tyranny; without the right to give counsel, courtiers and politicians questioned what their social position really signified. The political culture surrounding the concept of counsel can be accessed in a number of ways. Some individuals wrote tracts setting out the ideal ruler and the behaviour they should adopt, writing for the benefit largely of aspirational young courtiers but also to assert their own knowledge of such matters, an implicit qualification for holding office themselves. These 'courtesy manuals' were amongst the most popular publications of the period. Baldassare Castliglione's *Book of the Courtier*, written in fifteenth-century Italy, was translated into virtually every major European language and spawned a range of imitations such as the Tudor diplomat Sir Thomas Elyot's *The Boke of the Governour*. Elyot wrote that 'in every thinge concerning a publike weale no good counsailour [should] be omitted or passed over' and advised that rulers should listen to as wide a range of opinions as possible, for 'where there is a great numbre of counsaylours, they all beinge herde, nedes must the counsaile be the more perfecte'.[12]

Humanist scholars such as Elyot saw themselves as having an important role to play, partly in educating the next generation of politicians but also as active participants themselves.[13] The rise of an educated class of bureaucrat administrators to enact the expanding tasks of the State reflects the importance of their ideas and beliefs to political culture. Once again, courtesy manuals are useful sources here, as well as the other texts written by humanists and those in receipt of a humanist education. Thomas More's decision to serve in Henry VIII's council gives one example of an individual who believed himself duty-bound to provide counsel and practical service to the King. Written early on in his career, More's partly satirical, partly serious account of an ideal society, *Utopia*, set out the humanist belief in the importance of good counsel in politics and at the Court:

> If you can't completely eradicate wrong ideas, or deal with inveterate vices as effectively as you could wish, that's no reason for turning your back on public life altogether. You wouldn't abandon ship in a storm just because you couldn't control the winds … You must handle everything as tactfully as you can, and what you can't put right you must try to make as little wrong as possible.[14]

Civic humanism

Counsel overlapped with other elements of political culture. John Guy's important study of the concept has revealed its complexity and scope; as he writes, 'Ideas of counsel might be couched in "humanist-classical" and "feudal-baronial" vocabulary.'[15] Pursuing these languages and their meanings can provide further insights for students of political culture. Concepts of civic humanism became extremely fashionable during the early modern period – people from across society saw themselves as being effectively the descendants of classical governors with a duty to serve and rule.[16] Studying the same classical texts that inspired these ideas can help us to understand the values that early modern people aspired to live up to in their own behaviour.[17] It is of vital importance to recognize that individuals sought to involve themselves in politics not simply for reasons of personal ambition or the desire for power but because they genuinely believed themselves to have a duty to do so; the functioning of politics at all levels, but particularly in the localities, where the offices of local government were increasingly onerous and only modestly remunerated, depended upon this belief.

Phil Withington's study of urban politics highlights the expansion of towns and also their increasing desire for a degree of autonomy: for the right to run their own Government.[18] Incorporation, the practice wherein towns were granted the right to select their own officials and to enjoy a degree of autonomy, is shown to have been an 'intensely political process resting on the agency of people in both locality and metropolis'.[19] This new political independence resulted in shifts in identity and self-perception on the part of urban communities. Towns became mini-commonwealths, concerned with ensuring the public good, expressed through social behaviour; local government; moral regulation; and also architecture, both civic and private. Professional pride and the wealth that came from a successful business were also ways in which the political culture of the urban commonwealth displayed its health and vitality, and can be tracked through financial records, notably tax returns where individuals were grouped according to their wealth and consequent social status: 'the labels "gentleman", "labourer" and "yeomen" were all used on the tax list'.[20] The importance of these social identities reveals yet another underlying assumption of political culture.

Historical perspectives

It would be a mistake to see all of this as having been something entirely new. The idea of a 'Renaissance' obscures the reality that medieval society had also been based on notions and structures arising out of the classical period, as well as reflecting basic realities about a political system based on government by a single monarch. Exploring continuities with the medieval past and how people had thought about their role in government can offer a more balanced sense of what was going on in early modern politics as well as what people thought about it. This was a society that looked backwards for its guide to the present and future; as Daniel Woolf has shown, individuals shaped their own identities by looking to their past, and this stimulated a great enthusiasm for antiquarian and genealogical study on the part of members of political elites.[21]

Once again this can be accessed via a great variety of means. The heraldic stained glass installed at Baddesley Clinton in Warwickshire in the early seventeenth century by Henry Ferrers can be used to shed light on his deep interest in his family's history, an integral part of his identity as a gentleman and member of the local elite (Figure 10.1). Pedigrees and genealogies can also be used to understand this aspect of elite political culture; William Cecil, on rising to become Baron Burghley, became an enthusiastic student of genealogy. At his country home, Theobalds, one wall was painted with an extraordinary representation of the Elizabethan political world:

> In this Green Gallery were painted the coats of arms of all the landed families of the kingdom. The arms were shown to hang on fifty-two trees; between these trees were England's towns, boroughs and rivers ... Here ... was the realm. All at once the visitor saw something of the geography of England and its noble and gentry families.[22]

History also provided warning examples of what could go wrong – would go wrong – if the correct functioning of politics was disturbed. Writers and dramatists could use the defence that they were merely writing about history to disguise their discussion of some quite radical ideas about contemporary political culture. Shakespeare's history plays entertained his Elizabethan and Jacobean audiences by playing out their worst fears of what might happen at the accession and by debating the consequences of bad counsel, such as in *Richard II*, where it is shown to have led to the deposition of the monarch, although the deposition scene itself was often missed out from contemporary performances. Nicholas Rowe's *The Tragedy of the Lady*

Figure 10.1 Stained glass at Baddesley Clinton, Warwickshire.

Jane Grey revived mid-Tudor history for an early Hanoverian audience, the piously Protestant Jane providing a shiver-inducing reminder of why England had turned down Catholic monarchs and offered their allegiance to George instead.[23]

The Court and Parliament

To find sources for political culture we also need to think about where politics took place. The most obvious locale was the royal Court. At the heart of early modern politics stood the monarch, to whom everybody sought to get as close as they could manage. It is possible to argue that every single action that took place within or was related to the Court served as an act of politics, given the importance of the person of the monarch and their command of power, policy and Government, making this an environment that was saturated with political culture.

The Court also overlapped with other important loci for politics, notably Parliament; some MPs were also courtiers, and key figures at the Court built up connections and followings in Parliament. Throughout the reigns of the Tudors, Parliament essentially functioned as an extra-advisory body to the Crown. It met when called by the monarch and discussed what it was told to discuss. The question of when and how this situation changed has been much debated, but by the end of the seventeenth century Parliament had taken on greater powers and authority and established itself as the leading political authority in the country; it is therefore important to consider the shifts in the political culture of Parliament and its members in order to answer key questions about the history of this period.

The starting point for any discussion of the political culture of the Court and Parliament are the State Papers and related collections, as discussed in Natalie Mears' chapter in Part I of this volume. These contain a rich diversity of materials related to the life of the Court and of Parliament, and to the functioning of politics in these worlds. They can provide rich rewards for the study of political culture, giving insights into the personal views of individuals, through their correspondence with colleagues, friends, family members and sometimes the monarch themselves. Memoranda and notes shed light on the concerns of the day and the subjects on which counsel was sought and provided in meetings between members of the Government and with the monarch. Robert Beale's 'Treatise on the Office of a Councillor and Secretary to Her Majesty', written in 1592, set out that a secretary should carry with them 'a memorial or docket of those which he minded to propound and have dispatched at every sitting'.[24] This was certainly a practice followed by William Cecil, who kept copious lists, notes and memoranda that survive in both his own papers and the State Papers. After a meeting on the question of what to do about Mary Queen of Scots' marriage to Lord Darnley, Cecil drew up a list of the pros and cons of the marriage and the possible courses of action to be taken by the English Government, closing with the prompt '[t]hat it may please her Majesty to choose which of these advices she likes, and to put them in execution in deeds'. As an insight into what Cecil, Elizabeth and the Privy Council in England thought about the marriage, this can hardly be bettered, though it should be noted that the decisions taken are not recorded in this particular document.[25]

Records of parliamentary speeches and diaries kept by MPs are also key sources and increase in number as the power of Parliament grew over the course of the seventeenth century.[26] Diaries, probably more than any other source, enable us to glimpse the inner lives of their authors – to know what they thought about their world and what they were interested in and concerned about. Over the course of the seventeenth century the practice of diary-keeping became popular, resulting in a series of valuable accounts of life in and around the Court and Parliament. The diary of Samuel Pepys is a treasure trove of information about and reactions to the events that he was part of during his career as a naval administrator and MP, ranging from his personal health and the entertainments he enjoyed in London to Court gossip and the official duties of his post with the navy, frequently relating to the scarcity of funding.[27]

Patronage

The complicated networks of patronage that connected individuals together and linked them back, ultimately, to the monarch and to the centre of political power, contain the people and interactions that we need to study in order to understand their mental frameworks. In an era of personal monarchy, patronage was the basis of the political system and has long been recognized as having been of crucial importance, giving rise to a series of important studies of how patronage functioned.[28] The first and most obvious point of entry is again through the State Papers and related collections containing the surviving correspondence that passed among members of these patronage networks.[29] The formulaic language used in these letters reflects some of the main shared assumptions of this aspect of political culture, notably that the dispensing and receipt of patronage bound individuals into networks of mutual obligation (both political and social) expressed in the first instance through personal relationships that were sometimes familial and sometimes based on friendship or professional cooperation. In May 1599 Sir Robert Sidney was happy to return to his duties as Governor of Flushing, secure in a new friendship that he had struck up with the Queen's Secretary, Sir Robert Cecil: 'I shall go with the better affection very much, from the assurance it pleaseth you to bid me to have, that you will bee (for the word you are content to give) my frend.'[30]

These networks did not just operate at a high political level but played a vital role in connecting the Crown and the centralized State to the localities, and to those engaged in the operation of local government. These can be studied from both local and central perspectives. Parliamentary elections are one possible focus for study, accessed via the State Papers and local archives; attitudes towards the process can be reconstructed though references to election and office in plays and literature.[31] Some courtiers sought to build up their own followings in the counties as a way of enhancing their power and their ability to turn wider opinion to their advantage. Robert Dudley, Earl of Leicester worked hard to build a powerbase in north Wales and Warwickshire from which to consolidate his favour with Elizabeth I. This was an important part of his sense of the political culture in which he was operating, in terms of both identity and function.[32]

Given the importance of patronage to politics, it is not surprising to find that contemporaries were very concerned with how to make it work well. Courtesy manuals gave advice on how to approach a potential patron, emphasizing the reciprocal nature of the exchange.[33] One way that patronage could be recognized was through the exchange of hospitality. When monarchs went on progress and stayed at the houses of their leading nobles it provided one way of signifying royal favour, as well as the subject in question's willingness to acknowledge it by hosting an expensive royal visit, another example of the reciprocity of patronage.[34]

Connected practices such as gift-giving also provide insights into the playing out of patronage relations and the nature of the connections among people.[35] The anonymous author of a one-sheet publication in 1611, *The Counsell of a Father to his Sonne, in ten severall Precepts*, widely rumoured to have been William Cecil, was mindful of the importance of not overdoing things: 'Be sure thou always keepe some great man to thy friend, but trouble him not for trifles, complement him often, present him with many, yet small gifts and of little charge.'[36]

Gift giving at New Year provided an occasion for established relationships to be confirmed, extended or mended by the exchange of gifts, as well as for new connections to be sought. At the Court gifts were carefully recorded in a register, many of which survive in the State Papers. The importance of the occasion can be seen in John Husee's account of the process at Henry VIII's Court in 1538. As Deputy of Calais, Arthur, Lord Lisle, was absent from the Court and presumably anxious to know how his fortune was prospering in his absence. Husee, Lisle's agent at Court, wrote that on presenting his gift:

> his Grace received it of me smiling and giving more words to me than to any other that came, saying 'I thank my Lord. How doth my Lord and my Lady? Are they merry?' The King stood leaning against the cupboard, receiving all things, and Mr. Tywke at the end of the same cupboard penning ail [*sic*] things that were presented, and behind his Grace stood Mr. Kyngston and Sir John Russell, and besides his Grace stood the earl of Harforde and my lord Privy Seal [Thomas Cromwell].[37]

Such a closely monitored process reminds us of the importance of this ritual as a political statement of favour.

Place

The Court was an environment where material sources provide a great deal of information about political culture. The most important thing of all was access to the monarch – everyone sought it and those who achieved it won influence, power and reward. As the Court increased in size over the early modern period, it became increasingly difficult to gain that access. Historians have turned to study the politics of space in the Court, studying surviving buildings, floorplans and architectural designs as a way of understanding how individuals moved within this space, related to each other and won access to the monarch.[38]

England never quite got as far as developing the highly formalized, complicated set of rules and ceremonies that governed the operation of the Court in France, but it was increasingly necessary (for practical reasons alone) to limit the numbers of people who could circulate within the space of the Court and therefore to limit those who could gain access to the monarch within this environment. In Charles I's reign the King's taste for greater privacy and a much reduced company created a distinctive form of political culture that resulted in a narrowing of the sphere of royal politics and a sense of concern that the King was not making himself available to counsel, which in turn contributed to great upheavals in political culture with the breakdown of the relationship between the King and his subjects, and the outbreak of civil war.[39] John Finet, Charles' Master of Ceremonies from 1627, kept a detailed account of his role in managing Court protocol, relating where and how ambassadors were received, how rooms were decorated and who else was present, even who were assigned to travel together in the carriages taking them to and from the Court.[40]

The royal Court is not, of course, the only example of where to look for the physical dimension of political culture. One might as readily look at civic buildings of all kinds, private houses and taverns: anywhere where people met and engaged in political discussion.[41] Simply understanding the possibilities of these kinds of interactions is hugely revealing: who met and where did they meet to engage in and discuss politics?[42] Public buildings could also be used to make political statements. Thomas Tresham, a recusant landowner in Northamptonshire who was blocked from holding public office, contributed to local government by providing local officials with a meeting house in Market Rothwell, decorated with the arms of local families – a neat way of asserting Tresham's right to involvement in local politics.

Ceremonies and entertainments

The Court was also a space for the construction, display and reaffirmation of monarchical power and for the negotiation of the relationship between monarchs and their elite subjects.[43] Royal image-making has been paid a great deal of scholarly attention, notably by Kevin Sharpe, one of the driving forces behind the bringing together of political, social and cultural history. His trilogy of books on royal representations through the early modern period provides an agenda for further research in the scope of its sources and the questions that Sharpe asks of them.[44] Royal speeches, literature, sermons, architecture, portraits, tapestries, sculpture, instruments of government such as proclamations with the royal seal attached, printed images, coinage and commemorative medals all displayed the royal image both to Court audiences and to the localities, binding people into ideas of loyalty and service to a monarch that they may never have seen in person.[45] Monarchs could also spread notions of how they wanted political culture to take shape, moulding their subjects' perception of authority and the personality of the individual monarch. After the Restoration Charles II's revival of the ceremony of the Royal Touch allowed him to rebuild notions of sacred authority and status; by the end of his reign 'the king was touching on an unprecedented scale' (Figure 10.2).[46]

Beyond the Court, monarchs came into contact with their subjects during civic entries and festivals. Although Government and the monarch were largely based in London, the Court still moved around the country, particularly during the summer, when practical as well as political reasons sent the Court on progress. Interesting sources revealing the interaction among important political figures can be identified by following the Court on its travels. The interruptions to routine and the novelty of location sometimes provided fresh opportunities for individuals and groups to offer advice and counsel to a monarch and for the monarch to respond.

Records of civic entries and other contacts between towns and the monarch survive in chronicles, town histories and records.[47] In his description of the celebrations and events surrounding Elizabeth I's accession and the first Parliament of her reign, the London chronicler John Stow provides an excellent example of how the form and shape of public appearances of this kind and the interaction between the Queen and her Parliament reveal the underlying rules and assumptions of political culture. After they had processed in social order, the Queen agreed to Parliament's petition that she should grant them the right to 'have accesse unto hir graces presence: to declare unto hir matter of great importance, concerning the state of this hir graces realme'. Thus the right of Elizabeth's subjects to offer counsel and her willingness to listen to it were established, notwithstanding the fact that she proceeded to ignore their petition for her to marry.[48]

Popular politics

Popular culture will be discussed in the next chapter of this volume but it is important to note here the recent trend for historians to focus on the 'public sphere' and the opening up of commentary on and involvement in politics to a far wider social range of people, particularly during and following the period of the English Civil War. It is no longer sufficient to write the history of

Figure 10.2 Charles II touching a patient for the 'King's evil' (scrofula) surrounded by courtiers, clergy and general public. Engraving by R. White.

politics as simply relating to high politics and the history of institutions and the Court, but vital to recognize the involvement of individuals and groups from across society: to think broadly about how to define 'politics' and who it relates to. Some of the most important recent work on political culture has opened up this wider political world and provides us with important guides as to what kinds of areas and sources can be studied.[49]

Print culture and the circulation of news and information form one key area of study.[50] Newsbooks and pamphlet literature produced during the period of the English Civil War suggest that people beyond the Court were concerned about and felt themselves entitled to comment upon politics. Ballads, songs and libels were other dynamic media through which new groups became part of political culture. Thomas Cogswell's study of underground verse in the early Stuart period demonstrates how the circulation of libels gathered pace and created a dynamic new force in political culture that members of the Government, notably Archbishop Laud, had no idea how to respond to, and that ultimately contributed to the destruction of his reputation and then his life.[51] This was politics played in a way that Laud simply did not understand, and it highlights the importance of recognizing that political culture could change and take new forms that not all contemporaries recognized or could readily cope with.

These kinds of sources bring us to the heart of the so-called 'public sphere', the wider arena in which politics was discussed and shaped. They also demonstrate why politicians were increasingly aware of the power that could be derived from appealing to these audiences and the dangers of ignoring what they had to say. There is an extent to which this should not be exaggerated – it was not the case that earlier on people at the lower end of the social scale had been completely ignored and irrelevant to the conduct of politics.[52] It would be a foolish medieval ruler who thought that they could continue without the support of their subjects. But the accessibility of print means that many more resources survive to reveal this dimension of political culture to historians, and something much more familiar to the conduct of modern politics emerged at this time.

Change

A final point to make is that political culture could and did change; it would be a mistake to see any set of assumptions or ideas as static or unchanging, even though there may have been – are almost always certain to have been – continuities alongside the shifts. The assumptions that shaped behaviour could alter with the arrival of a new figure in the politics of a particular time and place, and sometimes even with an event or occurrence. This could be the result of a particular set of circumstances, such as during the succession crisis that rumbled on during Elizabeth I's reign. Stephen Alford has described a 'politics of emergency' as having come about as a direct result of the succession issue, as the minds of William Cecil and others concentrated on the reality of what the succession of a Catholic monarch would mean for them and the carefully crafted stability of the Protestant religious settlement. Historians of the period have disagreed over when the precise crisis point was but there is a general agreement that there were meaningful alterations in attitudes towards key political questions about the succession, authority and the nature of hereditary right, each of which played out in a variety of ways.[53] The sources for these subjects are varied, ranging from the kinds of memoranda and occasional notes from figures such as William Cecil that survive in State Papers and related collections, to sermons, political tracts and also Government propaganda. The materials produced and disseminated by the Government in the wake of the 1569 rising are of particular importance to any study of political culture in this period, bearing profound consequences for the position held by Catholics in a dominantly Protestant political culture in which they struggled to find a place.[54]

Broader shifts can also be studied. John Guy has argued that the rhetoric of counsel as employed during the Tudor and early Stuart periods became 'redundant' after the Civil War and Interregnum, with 'a shift in the language of political thought whereby a lexicon of rights and interests was recognized as more relevant to the discussion of liberty and authority than the traditional vocabulary of "counsel"'.[55] Mark Knights has shed considerable light on 'an evolving political culture' in the later Stuart period through studying changes in the use and meaning of political language; changes to political structures; and the emergence of national forms of political identities, disseminated via print.[56] The significance of the Court declined as parliamentary politics took over, and the public sphere took on even greater significance as the electorate expanded. Defining political culture as 'the intersection between politics, society, ideas, and modes of communication', Knights' approach involves paying very close attention to language and its meanings, to texts and their reception, and to politics played out in the public sphere: an approach that is ideally suited to his subject.[57] The challenge for all students of political culture is to identify their subject and the appropriate method with equal clarity and precision.

Conclusion

The study of political culture(s) is diverse; impossible to pin down to a single definition or topic; and open to criticism for its lack of specificity and increasing ubiquity as a way of loosely summarizing the behaviours, attitudes and practices surrounding political life. But without studying the world in which men and women lived and operated, and without understanding the beliefs and motivations that drove and guided their involvement and engagement with politics, we would leave ourselves without vital insights into the mental world of early modern politics and how it operated at all levels, from the Court to the localities. By carefully identifying one's subject and thinking broadly in terms of sources, it is possible to open up insights into the mental worlds of individuals and groups, and thereby to deepen and enrich our understanding of political cultures and how people lived and operated within the early modern world.

Key resources

British History Online, http://www.british-history.ac.uk.

Colvin, H. M. (ed.), *The History of the King's Works*, 6 vols (London: HMSO, 1963–82).

D'Ewes, Simonds (ed.), *The Journals of All the Parliaments during the Reign of Queen Elizabeth* (1682), available at http://www.british-history.ac.uk/no-series/jrnl-parliament-eliz1.

Early English Books Online, http://eebo.chadwyck.com/home.

Goldring, Elizabeth, Faith Eales, Elizabeth Clark and Jayne Elisabeth Archer (eds), *John Nichols's The Progresses and Public Processions of Queen Elizabeth I: A New Edition of the Early Modern Sources*, 5 vols (Oxford: Oxford University Press, 2014).

Historic England, database of listed buildings, http://historicengland.org.uk/listing/the-list.

History of Parliament, http://www.historyofparliamentonline.org.

Letters and Papers, Foreign and Domestic, of the Reign of Henry VIII, ed. J. S. Brewer, J. Gairdner and R. H. Brodie, 21 vols (London: HMSO, 1862–1932).

Loomie, Albert J. (ed.), *Ceremonies of Charles I: The Note Books of John Finet 1628–1641* (New York: Fordham University Press, 1987).

National Trust Collections: http://www.nationaltrustcollections.org.uk.

Pepys, Samuel, *The Diary of Samuel Pepys: A New and Complete Transcription*, ed. Robert Latham and William Matthews, 11 vols (London: Bell and Hyman, 1970–83).

State Papers Online, 1509–1714, http://gale.cengage.co.uk/state-papers-online-15091714.aspx.

State Papers Online: Eighteenth Century, 1714–1782, http://gale.cengage.co.uk/state-papers-online-15091714/state-papers-online-1714–1782.aspx.

Notes

1 See Mark Hailwood's chapter on 'Popular culture' in this volume for further discussion of this work (pp. 206–23).

2 There are a few notable exceptions to this general rule: Kevin Sharpe, *Reading Revolutions: The Politics of Reading in Early Modern England* (London: Yale University Press, 2000), Chapter 1; Mark Knights, *Representation and Misrepresentation in Later Stuart Britain: Partisanship and Political Culture* (Oxford: Oxford University Press, 2005), esp. Chapter 1; Kevin Sharpe, *Selling the Tudor Monarchy: Authority and Image in Sixteenth-Century England* (London: Yale University Press, 2009), Chapter 1. See also Patrick Collinson's important call for a 'new political history' in his '*De republica Anglorum*; or, History with the Politics Put Back', in Patrick Collinson, *Elizabethan Essays* (London: Hambledon Press, 1994), pp. 1–29; and John Guy's development of the agenda: 'Introduction', in John Guy (ed.), *The Tudor Monarchy* (London: Arnold, 1997), pp. 13–15.

3 Peter Burke, *What Is Cultural History?* (Cambridge: Polity Press, 2004); Natalie Zemon Davis, *Society and Culture in Early Modern France* (Stanford: Stanford

University Press, 1965); Keith Thomas, 'History and Anthropology', *Past & Present*, 24 (1963), 3–24; Keith Thomas, *Religion and the Decline of Magic* (London: Weidenfeld and Nicholson, 1971).

4 See, for example, Mervyn James, *Society, Politics and Culture: Studies in Early Modern England* (Cambridge: Cambridge University Press, 1986); Kevin Sharpe and Peter Lake, *Culture and Politics in Early Stuart England* (Basingstoke: Macmillan, 1994); Dale Hoak (ed.), *Tudor Political Culture* (Cambridge: Cambridge University Press, 1995); Linda Levy Peck (ed.), *The Mental World of the Jacobean Court* (Cambridge: Cambridge University Press, 1991); James Epstein, 'Introduction: New Directions in Political History', *Journal of British Studies*, 41 (2002), 255–8.

5 For discussion, see Beat Kümin, 'Introduction', in Beat Kümin (ed.), *Political Space in Pre-Industrial Europe* (Farnham: Ashgate, 2009), pp. 5–15 (pp. 5–6); Stephen Alford, *The Early Elizabethan Polity* (Cambridge: Cambridge University Press, 1998); Michael Braddick, 'State Formation and the Historiography of Early Modern England', *History Compass*, 2 (2004), 1–17.

6 J. G. A. Pocock (ed.), *The Varieties of British Political Thought, 1500–1800* (Cambridge: Cambridge University Press, 1993); A. N. McLaren, *Political Culture in the Reign of Elizabeth I: Queen and Commonwealth 1558–1585* (Cambridge: Cambridge University Press, 1999).

7 Paul Archambault, 'The Analogy of the "Body" in Renaissance Political Literature', *Bibliothèque d'humanisme et renaissance*, 29 (1967), 21–53. Manuals of advice and contemporary works of political theory can be found via *EEBO*.

8 Edmund Dudley, *The Tree of Commonwealth*, ed. D. M. Brodie (Cambridge: Cambridge University Press, 1948).

9 J. Fortescue, *De laudibus legum Anglie*, ed. and trans. S. B. Chrimes (Cambridge: Cambridge University Press, 1942).

10 SP 1/105, fo. 109, in J. S. Brewer, J. Gairdner and R. H. Brodie (eds), *Letters and Papers, Foreign and Domestic, of the Reign of Henry VIII*, 21 vols (London: HMSO, 1862–1932), Vol. XI, p. 140. Cited in Geoffrey Elton, *Policy and Police: The Enforcement of the Reformation in the Age of Thomas Cromwell* (Cambridge: Cambridge University Press, 1972), p. 332.

11 See, for example, Ethan Shagan, *Popular Politics and the English Reformation* (Cambridge: Cambridge University Press, 2003).

12 Thomas Elyot, *The Boke Named the Governour*, ed. and intro. Foster Watson (London: J. M. Dent, 1907), Book III, Chapter 28: 'Of Consultation and Counsayle, and in what forme they ought to be used', pp. 293–4.

13 See, for example, ibid.; Roger Ascham, *The Scholemaster* (1570), available via *EEBO*.

14 Thomas More, *Utopia*, trans. Paul Turner (Harmondsworth: Penguin, 1965), Book I, pp. 64–5.

15 John Guy, 'The Rhetoric of Counsel in Early Modern England', in Hoak, *Tudor Political Culture*, pp. 292–310 (p. 293).

16 Markku Peltonen, *Classical Humanism and Republicanism in English Political Thought 1570–1640* (Cambridge: Cambridge University Press, 1995); Quentin Skinner, *Reason and Rhetoric in the Philosophy of Hobbes* (Cambridge: Cambridge University Press, 1996), Chapter 2.

17 See, in particular, the works of Cicero, *De officiis*; and Aristotle, *Politics* and *Ethics*.

18 Phil Withington, *The Politics of Commonwealth: Citizens and Freemen in Early Modern England* (Cambridge: Cambridge University Press, 2005).

19 Ibid., p. 9.

20 Ibid., p. 105. These categories are also set out and discussed in works of political theory such as Thomas Smith's *De republica Anglorum* (1583), available via *EEBO*. See also Brodie Waddell's chapter in this volume (pp. 224–39).

21 Daniel Woolf, *The Social Circulation of the Past: English Historical Culture 1500–1730* (Oxford: Oxford University Press, 2003). See also F. J. Levy, *Tudor Historical Thought* (San Marino: Huntington Library, 1967); Paulina Kewes (ed.), *The Uses of History in Early Modern England* (San Marino: Huntington Library, 2006).
22 Stephen Alford, *Burghley: William Cecil at the Court of Elizabeth I* (London: Yale University Press, 2008), p. 210. For examples of the genealogies commissioned and collected by Cecil, see the family's archive, in the first instance calendared in HMC, *A Calendar of the Manuscripts of the Most Hon. The Marquis of Salisbury, K.G., & c, Preserved at Hatfield House, Hertfordshire*, 24 vols (London, 1883–1976). The collection is available on microfilm and in digitized form; see *The Cecil Papers*, http://cecilpapers.chadwyck.com (accessed 11 February 2016). For further discussion of how to access this kind of record, see Natalie Mears' chapter on 'State Papers and related collections' in Part I of this volume (pp. 15–34).
23 As discussed by Paulina Kewes, 'History and Its Uses', in Kewes, *The Uses of History*, pp. 1–30 (p. 21).
24 Beale's treatise survives amongst his papers in the Yelverton manuscripts in the British Museum. It was printed in Conyers Read, *Mr. Secretary Walsingham and the Policy of Queen Elizabeth*, 3 vols (Oxford: Clarendon Press, 1925), Vol. I, pp. 421–43.
25 4 June 1565, Conference by the Privy Council on the Marriage of Queen Mary, 'Elizabeth: June 1565, 1–15', in *Calendar of State Papers Foreign, Elizabeth*, Vol. II: *1564–1565*, ed. Joseph Stevenson (London: Public Record Office, 1870), pp. 378–94, https://www.british-history.ac.uk/cal-state-papers/foreign/vol7/pp378-394 (accessed 5 October 2015). For further discussion of how this document was drawn up, along with other relevant material, see Alford, *Early Elizabethan Polity*, pp. 19–20.
26 A great deal of primary source material of this kind can be found at http://www.british-history.ac.uk. See also http://www.historyofparliamentonline.org (accessed 25 January 2016).
27 Samuel Pepys, *The Diary of Samuel Pepys: A New and Complete Transcription*, ed. Robert Latham and William Matthews, 11 vols (London: Bell and Hyman, 1970–83). His contemporary Roger Morrice produced an equally detailed account, now available in a modern edition: Mark Goldie, John Spurr, Tim Harris, Stephen Taylor, Mark Knights and Jason McElligott (eds), *The Entring Book of Roger Morrice 1677–1691*, 6 vols (Woodbridge: Boydell Press, 2007). See also Laura Sangha's chapter on 'Personal documents' in Part I of this volume (pp. 107–28).
28 Sharon P. Kettering, 'Patronage in Early Modern France', in Sharon Kettering (ed.), *Patronage in Sixteenth- and Seventeenth-Century France* (Aldershot: Ashgate, 2002); Linda Levy Peck, *Court Patronage and Corruption in Early Stuart England* (London: Unwin Hyman, 1990); Guy Fitch Lytle and Stephen Orgel (eds), *Patronage in the Renaissance* (Princeton: Princeton University Press, 1981).
29 The volumes published by the HMC provide a useful guide to what is available in terms of collections beyond the State Papers; see Natalie Mears' chapter for guidance on how to navigate these collections.
30 HMC, *A Calendar of the Manuscripts*, Vol. IX, p. 174.
31 Mark A. Kishlansky, *Parliamentary Selection: Social and Political Choice in Early Modern England* (Cambridge: Cambridge University Press, 1986). Plays set in Roman history frequently deal with elections and the surrounding process; see, for example, William Shakespeare, *Coriolanus*, and Kishlansky's discussion thereof, pp. 3–9.
32 Simon Adams, *Leicester and the Court: Essays on Elizabethan Politics* (Manchester: Manchester University Press, 2002), Part III.

33 For example, Angel Day, *The English Secretorie; or, Plaine and Direct Method, for the Enditing of all Manner of Epistles or Letters* (1586), available via *EEBO* and cited in Peck, *Court Patronage*, p. 15.

34 Royal progresses can be tracked through the State Papers and related collections, by looking at the movements of monarchs around the country, and also through correspondence that refers to the organization of hospitality and events that took place en route. Sometimes descriptions of the texts of the poems and masques that were staged were published. These can be accessed via *EEBO* or edited collections such as Elizabeth Goldring, Faith Eales, Elizabeth Clark and Jayne Elisabeth Archer (eds), *John Nichols's The Progresses and Public Processions of Queen Elizabeth I: A New Edition of the Early Modern Sources*, 5 vols (Oxford: Oxford University Press, 2014).

35 Felicity Heal, *The Power of Gifts: Gift-Exchange in Early Modern England* (Oxford: Oxford University Press, 2014); Natalie Zemon Davis, *The Gift in Sixteenth-Century France* (Oxford: Oxford University Press, 2000); Peck, *Court Patronage*, pp. 18–20.

36 Available via *EEBO*.

37 Brewer *et al.*, *Letters and Papers*, Vol. XIII, p. 9, no. 24. Discussed in Heal, *The Power of Gifts*, p. 95.

38 For an account of all of the buildings connected to the monarchy throughout the early modern period, see H. M. Colvin (ed.), *The History of the King's Works*, 6 vols (London: HMSO, 1963–82). For a useful series of essays, see Marcello Fantoni, George Gorse and Malcolm Smuts (eds), *The Politics of Space: European Courts ca. 1500–1750* (Rome: Bulzoni Editore, 2009).

39 Ronald G. Asch, 'The Princely Court and Political Space in Early Modern Europe', in Kümin, *Political Space in Pre-Industrial Europe*, pp. 43–60 (pp. 46–9).

40 Albert J. Loomie (ed.), *Ceremonies of Charles I: The Note Books of John Finet 1628–1641* (New York: Fordham University Press, 1987).

41 A good place to start searching for examples of architecture of all kinds is in the Pevsner Architectural Guides, published by Yale University Press and in Historic England's database of listed buildings, http://historicengland.org.uk/listing/the-list (accessed 25 January 2016).

42 A range of case studies is discussed in Kümin, *Political Space in Pre-Industrial Europe*. See also Robert Tittler, 'Political Culture and the Built Environment of the English Country Town, *c.* 1540–1620', in Hoak, *Tudor Political Culture*, pp. 133–56.

43 Asch, 'The Princely Court and Political Space in Early Modern Europe'; John N. King, 'The Royal Image, 1535–1603', in Hoak, *Tudor Political Culture*, pp. 104–32.

44 Sharpe, *Selling the Tudor Monarchy*; Kevin Sharpe, *Image Wars: Promoting Kings and Commonwealths in England, 1603–1660* (New Haven: Yale University Press, 2010); Kevin Sharpe, *Rebranding Rule: The Restoration and Revolution Monarchy, 1660–1714* (London: Yale University Press, 2013).

45 Useful starting points for these kinds of sources include national collections such as those of the National Portrait Gallery, the National Gallery, the Victoria and Albert Museum, and the British Museum in London; and the Ashmolean Museum in Oxford; as well as regional collections relating to local history. See, for examples, the Royal Albert Memorial Museum in Exeter or the Norwich Castle Museum and Art Gallery. Properties run by the National Trust and English Heritage as well as privately owned houses may also have relevant holdings, with information increasingly available online, including the National Trust Collections website, http://www.nationaltrustcollections.org.uk (accessed 25 January 2016). Published speeches and sermons can be found via *EEBO*.

46 Anna Keay, *The Magnificent Monarch: Charles II and the Ceremonies of Power* (London: Continuum, 2008), p. 190.
47 See, for example: Holinshed's *Chronicle*, available at http://www.cems.ox.ac.uk/holinshed (accessed 25 January 2016); John Hooker, *The Discription of the cittie of Excester* (1575), available via *EEBO*; Henry Manship, *The History of Great Yarmouth*, ed. Charles John Palmer (Great Yarmouth: L. A. Meall, 1854); John Stow, *A Survey of London* (1598), available via *EEBO*. A great deal of useful material for the Elizabethan period is included in Goldring *et al.*, *John Nichols's The Progresses*. David M. Bergeron, *English Civic Pageantry, 1558–1642* (London: Edward Arnold, 1971) remains the classic account.
48 Stow's account is included in Goldring *et al.*, *John Nichols's The Progresses*, Vol. I, p. 148.
49 David Underdown, *Revel, Riot, and Rebellion: Popular Politics and Culture in England 1603–1660* (Oxford: Clarendon Press, 1985); Paul Griffiths, Adam Fox and Steve Hindle (eds), *The Experience of Authority in Early Modern England* (Basingstoke: Macmillan, 1996); John Walter, *Understanding Popular Violence in the English Revolution: The Colchester Plunderers* (Cambridge: Cambridge University Press, 1999); Jason Peacey, *Print and Public Politics in the English Revolution* (Cambridge: Cambridge University Press, 2013).
50 For a useful review of the way in which this field of study took shape at the end of the twentieth century, see Annabel Patterson, 'Review: "Ideas Seldom Exist Apart from Practice": Turning over Millennial New Leaves', *Journal of British Studies*, 41 (2002), 388–401.
51 Thomas Cogswell, 'Underground Verse and the Transformation of Early Stuart Political Culture', in Susan Dwyer Amussen and Mark A. Kishlansky, *Political Culture and Cultural Politics in Early Modern England: Essays Presented to David Underdown* (Manchester: Manchester University Press, 1995), pp. 277–300.
52 See Adam Fox's work on the oral transmission of news and information: 'Rumour, News and Popular Political Opinion in Elizabethan and Early Stuart England', *Historical Journal*, 40.3 (1997), 597–620.
53 John Guy argues for a split between the political cultures of 1558–85 and 1585–1603; Collinson for two crisis points, in 1572 and 1584, both related to Parliament's stance; Simon Adams for the events of 1569 as being of critical importance. See Alford, *Early Elizabethan Polity*, pp. 2–3; Adams, 'Favourites and Factions at the Elizabethan Court', in *Leicester and the Court*, pp. 46–67 (p. 49).
54 For discussion of William Cecil's working practices and the ways in which they can be reconstructed to allow an understanding of the political culture in which he operated, see Alford, *Early Elizabethan Polity*, pp. 9–42. On 1569, see K. J. Kesselring, *The Northern Rebellion of 1569: Faith, Politics, and Protest in Elizabethan England* (Basingstoke: Palgrave Macmillan, 2010), Chapter 5. Printed copies of propaganda can be found via *EEBO* (search using keywords and dates), other relevant documents via the State Papers and local archives. See also *Depositions and Other Ecclesiastical Proceedings from the Courts of Durham, Extending from 1311 to the Reign of Elizabeth*, ed. James Raine, Publications of the Surtees Society, 21 (London: J. B. Nichols and Son and William Pickering, 1847).
55 Guy, 'The Rhetoric of Counsel', p. 310.
56 Knights, *Representation and Misrepresentation*, pp. 28–30.
57 Ibid., p. 30.

11 Popular culture

Mark Hailwood

The historical record has an inherent class bias. The majority of sources that are available to historians were created by, and reflect the opinions and experiences of, men from the upper ranks of society – the aristocracy and the gentry in our period – and to a lesser extent those of men from the professional and mercantile middling classes. The lower ranks of society, the labouring classes and the rural smallholders, leave a much lighter historical footprint. This is especially true of the pre-modern era, when the bulk of the population that these latter groups represented were not fully literate. In seventeenth-century England only 30 per cent of adult males and 10 per cent of adult females were able to sign their own names, the best indicator we have for measuring their ability to write, and those that could were concentrated in the upper echelons of the social hierarchy.[1] Most people, especially of more humble social status, lacked the ability to commit their own thoughts to paper and parchment, and to preserve them for posterity. Indeed, the great Tudor historian Sir Geoffrey Elton thought it was 'the essence of the poor that they do not appear in history'.[2]

Despite this undoubted imbalance in the historical record few historians are now as pessimistic about our ability to study the poor as Elton was, writing back in 1955. The 1960s and 1970s saw a paradigmatic shift in the priorities of the historical discipline, with a wave of social historians turning their attention away from the more traditional, political subjects of historical study – kings, aristocrats and high politics – to focus instead on the lives of ordinary men and women in the past. Historians over the past half a century have shown considerable determination and ingenuity to overcome the problems of limited source survival for the study of lower social groups, and the impulse to write history 'from below' as opposed to 'from above' remains a vibrant and central feature of the profession to this day.[3] In other words, we can study these groups, but to do so involves some particularly acute challenges when it comes to finding and interpreting sources. The aim of this chapter is to provide a guide to meeting these challenges, and in the process to highlight the considerable potential for exciting historical research that can be unlocked by doing so.

Defining popular culture

The first thing that any student embarking on a research project into 'popular culture' needs to address is the debate surrounding the definition of those terms. This chapter is not the place to rehearse that debate at length, but it is important to be aware of the fact that historians interested in the lives of ordinary men and women in the early modern period have directed a lot of thought to what exactly we might mean by the terms 'popular' and 'culture'.[4] Two crucial outcomes of these debates are worth flagging up briefly here. The first is a shift in the way the term 'popular' is understood. Early attempts to recover popular culture were criticized for trying to seek out a culture of 'the people' that was distinct and separate from the culture of 'the elite'. Historians have since come to argue that 'elite' and 'popular' cultures were not sealed off from one another: not only did they routinely come into conflict, but there were also many areas of overlap between them. This can be seen when considering the 'popular' literature of the period, such as broadside ballads. These cheap printed songs did not belong exclusively to the culture of elites or to that of the common people. Instead they could be found pasted on the walls of the cottages of rural husbandmen, as well as in the libraries of gentlemen and metropolitan elites.[5] Their appeal transcended class boundaries. In this sense then they were 'popular' in that they had a widespread appeal across society – although their attraction may have been different for different social groups.[6] This realization that the cultural worlds of the elite and of ordinary people were not hermetically sealed off from one another has redirected the attention of historians. Rather than seeking for sources that may provide access to a culture that was inhabited exclusively by ordinary people – a culture generally considered to be either beyond recovery or unlikely to have existed in such a form anyway – historians now tend to search instead for 'points of contact' between the worlds of elites and common people: to identify sources that can reveal elements of culture that were inclusive of, rather than exclusive to, lower social groups.[7] Such an approach opens up the potential of a much wider range of sources.

There have also been important developments in the way that historians think about 'culture' in the context of studying ordinary people. Pioneers of the study of 'popular culture' operated with a relatively narrow definition of culture, and sought to recover popular equivalents of what we might think of as elements of 'high culture' or 'the arts', such as songs, plays, dances and other ritualized performances. Over time this understanding of culture has been replaced with a much more capacious one: it is now taken to encompass the entire range of 'assumptions underlying everyday life'.[8] The attitudes held by common people towards issues as varied as sex, the economy, politics, marriage, the supernatural and even drinking have all now been explored in the pursuit of a better understanding of popular culture. Or, rather, *cultures*, as there is now a growing emphasis on the fact that the common people did not all think or act in the same way, and that there often existed a number of competing 'assumptions underlying everyday life', adherence to which could have been shaped by one's age, gender, occupation or local environment, amongst other things. Taken together, then, changing approaches to recovering the 'popular' dimension of an ever widening notion of 'culture' both open up a vast array of potential topics for research projects, and bring into play a wide range of sources for pursuing them. As we will see in the subsequent sections though, all of these sources must be handled with care.

Popular rituals

Let us start our consideration of the sources available for the study of popular culture in the same place as the pioneers of the subject did: by thinking about the evidence relating to popular rituals. Working with the narrower definition of culture outlined above, with its emphasis on forms of recreational performance, such scholars often identified festive occasions as the main focus of singing, dancing, drama and merry-making for the lower ranks of early modern society. The prevalence of such activities can to some extent be recovered by examining local records of expenditure, as parish or borough records often recorded spending sums of money on ale to lubricate revellers on occasions such as May Day, or to pay for model giants and dragons to be paraded through the streets at midsummer. This kind of information can be put to use to reconstruct geographical and chronological patterns in the occurrence of popular rituals, contributing to debates about their decline or survival in the face of the mounting official hostility they encountered in the early modern period.[9]

Historians' interest in popular rituals goes beyond questions of when and where they took place, though: drawing inspiration from anthropology historians have come to see rituals as expressions of the underlying values of their participants, the decoding of which can shed light on the attitudes and assumptions underpinning a culture.[10] Unlike anthropologists, historians cannot observe and analyse such rituals first hand, but there are a number of early modern descriptions of them that we can turn to. The English puritan pamphleteer Philip Stubbes, for instance, wrote extensively about lower-class festivals, dancing and even football matches, albeit from a very hostile perspective. More sympathetic were early antiquarians such as John Aubrey, who gave nostalgic descriptions of Whitsuntide festivities, in which young people 'had dancing, bowling, shooting at butts, etc., [with] the ancients sitting gravely by looking on'.[11] These accounts can help us to add more detail to our understanding of what happened on festive occasions – the games that were played, the age groups or social groups that attended them – but we must remember that they give us access to popular rituals only through 'two pairs of alien eyes': our own, and those of their contemporary observer, who was usually a literate and relatively high-status individual looking on, rather than a labourer or maidservant participating in events.[12] Moreover, such observers were rarely attempting an objective ethnographic account of these rituals. In an age when attitudes towards popular rituals correlated closely with religious and political leanings, most higher-class commentators on rituals were trying to make a point about either their inherent disorderliness or their innate wholesomeness.[13] In other words, these accounts invariably have a political edge.

Legal records

That various aspects of popular culture – from festive rituals to alehouse sociability – became hot political topics in the early modern period is in many respects a boon to historians, as the period witnessed a number of campaigns to regulate and police popular behaviour that have in turn created a significant paper trail. The records of the English Quarter Sessions, for instance, contain copious documentation relating to seventeenth-century attempts to regulate the nation's alehouses more tightly, and can be used to assess the relative success or failure of such efforts in different counties.[14] The Church courts were the main vehicle for attempts at the moral regulation of the populace, and can be examined to explore the extent of clamp-downs on, for instance, pre-marital sex among the common people.[15] These legal records can also be used to tell us much more about popular culture than just the campaigns waged against it. Historians have used court cases to explore the roles of crime and violence in the everyday lives of ordinary people – though here of course we have to be wary of the fact that it is hard to know just how representative of 'everyday life' those incidents that ended up before the courts were, and more obviously we cannot always be sure whether the events purported to have taken place in legal cases really occurred.[16]

Other scholars have attempted to get around some of these problems by reading sources 'against the grain': rather than using a murder trial to examine the history of murder, we might instead use the records created by criminal cases to reconstruct the social context in which they took place, for the records of such cases often 'inadvertently disclose to us the rhythms and routines of ... everyday existence, a world of industry, traffic and conversation in which ... contemporary interrogators were largely uninterested'.[17] These attempts to recover the rhythms of everyday life from legal records often focus their attention most closely on depositions (i.e. witness statements) that contain detailed vignettes of the day-to-day activities people were engaged in when they witnessed or got caught up in a crime.[18] Here too, of course, we are confronted with issues of truth-telling, but historians now tend to accept – following on from the influential work of Natalie Zemon Davis – that even when deponents were being untruthful, the stories they told were intended to sound like plausible accounts of everyday activity.[19] If we are less interested in passing judgement on 'whodunnit' in a given case then we can still use its records to extract information about typical patterns of everyday behaviour, such as the number of hours people worked in a day, or the composition of their social networks.[20]

It could even be argued that this kind of depositional material brings us as close as we are likely to be able to get to the actual *voices* of the common people in the early modern period (Figure 11.1). They were, in theory, the words of often relatively humble people, their own accounts of events they had witnessed or been involved in – albeit written down by a magistrate or his clerk. It is difficult to gauge how much these scribes may have filtered what was said to them. Deponents had the written account of their oral testimony read back to them before they signed it to confirm it was their own, which must have limited the scope for substantial revision. That said, legal procedures and conventions certainly shaped the questions asked and the information that was actually recorded, and power imbalances between questioner and witness no doubt conditioned what deponents were prepared to say and how they said it.[21] Such depositions do not therefore provide us with unmediated access to the 'voices of the people'. Nonetheless, they have been used in careful and imaginative ways to produce some of the most illuminating work on popular culture: the languages of insult used in defamation cases have been used to reconstruct concepts of honour among middling-and lower-class women, for instance, and witnesses' responses to questions about their 'worth' have been used to recover the ways in which ordinary people thought about work, wealth and social class.[22]

Another source that could be considered as a possible expression of the 'voices' of ordinary people are petitions. These could be sent to local magistrates or even central Government by groups making appeals on issues as

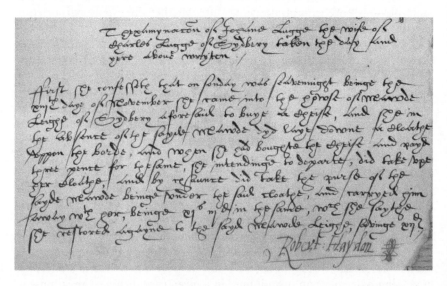

Figure 11.1 The witness statement of one Johane Lugge, who was accused of stealing a purse in a case that came before the Devon Quarter Sessions in January of 1598. Devon Heritage Centre, Quarter Sessions Bundles, Box 5, Epiphany 1598.

diverse as the granting of an alehouse licence to demands for intervention in a depressed trade.[23] They have been put to particularly effective use in explorations of poverty and poor relief, as recipients of the latter often used petitions as a way of requesting assistance.[24] Whilst they often include signatures or marks (a way of signing for those unable to write) it is not always clear who drafted them: the fact that they were often very strategic in the arguments they made could indicate the involvement of educated individuals with legal training, or alternatively a high degree of popular legal knowledge. Either way, their strategic sophistication suggests they are not a straightforward window into the values and attitudes of their signatories, but they are yet another source that can shed light on the 'points of contact' between governors and governed in early modern society.[25]

Popular politics

The most prominent way in which historians have approached 'points of contact' between rulers and ruled in early modern societies has been through the study of popular political action. The most dramatic instances of this were large-scale rebellions, which witnessed risings of the common people – usually in alliance with at least some members of the middling and upper ranks of society – that could involve tens of thousands of rebels. One source of evidence relating to such events are accounts of them given by contemporary observers, though once again they generally emanate from the pens of elites determined to condemn them.[26] They can tell us much about the way the ruling classes thought about popular politics, but to get closer to the motivations of rebels themselves we have to seek out alternative sources. Many large-scale rebellions – such as England's 'Prayer Book' and Kett's Rebellions, both in 1549, and Germany's 1525 Peasants' Revolt – produced lists of demands whose survival provides a valuable insight into the causes and aims of these uprisings.[27] Here too, though, issues of composition complicate their interpretation: they may have been composed by the most literate and educated participants in rebellion, such as the gentry, clergymen or lawyers, and whilst they no doubt drew on strong currents of popular disaffection, the issues that received the most prominent emphasis may reflect the concerns of a rebellion's leadership as much as its rank-and-file.

   In addition to studying large-scale rebellions historians of popular politics have dedicated much of their attention to smaller-scale and more localized rioting.[28] Evidence relating to these incidents principally falls within the category of legal records, as rioting was a criminal offence that leaves its traces in trial records.[29] One way of using such evidence is in reconstructing patterns of the incidence of rioting, charting variations across time and space – much like the work done on popular rituals. There are uncertainties about precisely what it is that is being counted by using such an approach though: peaks in the incidence of riot cases in the courts may reflect a growing willingness to prosecute rioters, rather than necessarily an increase in rioting itself, and many small-scale riots would have gone unrecorded if their victim had not been not wealthy enough to pursue the perpetrators through the courts.[30] Here too, then, historians have sought to go beyond recovering the fact of a riot taking place to try and uncover what it can tell us about the political culture of ordinary people and their relationship with powerful elites. Depositions from riot cases are again useful here, but they come with all the usual caveats about legal evidence, with the different parties in a suit often giving very different versions of events. The most effective work on such sources tends to take the form of closely focused case studies of particular incidents that, although they may not be able to provide certainty about exactly what happened, are often able to illuminate the complex dynamics of social relations between rioters and their opponents.[31] Once more, the study of riot has much to tell us about points of contact – or indeed of conflict – between different social groups.

There are some sources relating to popular politics that might seem to be able to take us closer again to the 'voices' of the common people. Alongside their recourse to dramatic riots and rebellions, historians have become increasingly sensitive to the fact that ordinary people routinely drew on a much wider repertoire of subtler 'weapons of the weak' in their conflict with early modern authorities.[32] These weapons included anonymous threatening letters, mocking rhymes and scathing libels, which could variously be pushed under an unpopular local lord's door, displayed in public places such as on church and alehouse doors or market crosses, and circulated in either oral or manuscript form throughout the village.[33] If the victims of such an attack chose to pursue the perpetrators for libel, a copy of the offending composition often survives in the trial papers.[34] The fact that these letters and libels were usually authored anonymously may well mean that they give us an unusual level of insight into popular attitudes: safely concealed from retribution by the cloak of anonymity the lower orders could express their true feelings about their superiors in a way that would have been highly dangerous in a public riot or rebellion.[35] On the other hand, we need to consider that these too could have a strong strategic dimension, being designed to inflict maximum shame, fear or reputational damage on their targets, and this undoubtedly shaped their form as much as any attempt to articulate cherished popular values. Again here we need to bear in mind issues about who actually composed these letters and libels – many indicate a degree of learning that suggests they were not only a 'weapon of the weak', but a weapon that could be deployed by powerful and powerless alike.[36]

Another aspect of popular politics that has interested historians is the occurrence of seditious speech: instances of the common people verbally criticizing ruling elites, often over a pot of ale in the alehouse.[37] Such expressions have been seen by some as providing a particularly privileged point of access into the political opinions and values of ordinary people, giving us an indication of what such people really thought about their superiors when they were out of ear-shot of the authorities and able to enjoy the catharsis of speaking freely.[38] They certainly provide us with a rich tapestry of popular political comment, such as the labourer Jeremy Vanhill's verdict on Elizabeth I: 'Shyte uppon your Queene; I woulde to god that shee were dead that I might shytt on her face', an opinion for which he was hanged in 1585.[39] Vanhill's fate is a crucial reminder that these verbalizations only survive in the historical record because they too were deemed a criminal offence, either of sedition or – more seriously – of treason. An unknowable quantity of such views would have gone unrecorded, but each example that did end up before the courts is also evidence that somebody who heard it decided to report it to the authorities. This raises questions about how representative such opinions were: do they reveal widely held popular sentiments that can only occasionally be glimpsed by historians, or are they evidence of more radical and outlying views that the majority of people thought worthy of punishment? Cases of seditious speech are a fascinating source, but we need to tread carefully when drawing conclusions about what exactly the sentiments expressed in them can reveal.[40]

Cheap print

In their pursuit of the attitudes and opinions of ordinary men and women historians have often directed their focus towards forms of cheap print, such as short pamphlets and broadside ballads.[41] Such sources may, on initial consideration, seem unpropitious as access points to popular culture, given what we have said about levels of literacy in early modern society: could the common people actually read such sources, or was their culture still a largely oral one? It is worth noting here that the literacy rates referred to above are much better indicators of the ability to write than the ability to read. It was common practice to learn to read before learning to write, and even many relatively humble people would have learned some reading skills in a local petty school before they started working longer hours in the family fields or workshop, a transition that halted their progression to learning writing skills.[42] In other words, it is likely that far more than 30 per cent of the adult male and 10 per cent of the adult female populations of seventeenth-century England could *read*. We also need to recognize that reading in this period was a more communal activity than it is today, with many printed works intended to be read aloud in company. One did not necessarily need to be able to read a printed product to hear it or 'consume' it. Moreover, it is important to recognize that the most prevalent printed product in the early modern period, the single-sheet broadside ballad, was designed in a multi-media format that transcended any tidy division between 'print' and 'oral' transmission. These songs were set to tunes, and were intended to be sung aloud by ballad hawkers trying to sell them – at a price cheap enough to make them affordable even to relatively poor people. Consumers then pasted them on their walls at home and attempted to learn them by heart, so that they once again moved into the oral realm. The boundary between literate print culture and illiterate oral culture was a fuzzy one, and many 'print' products could reach customers on either side of it.[43]

With this in mind, historians have mined broadside ballads in particular for what these popular songs might reveal about the attitudes and mores of

Figure 11.2   Boors Singing at a Window, by and published by John Smith, after Adriaen van Ostade, after Egbert van Heemskerck the Elder, 1706. This image of a group of singers reminds us that some early modern sources transcend the division between textual and oral cultures.

ordinary people.[44] Whilst it is accepted that they were not a cultural product consumed exclusively by lower social groups – most of our surviving examples come from collections compiled by contemporary gentlemen – they are seen as a good example of a source that highlights a cultural milieu that was at least inclusive of relatively humble people (e.g. Figure 11.2).[45] They deal with a vast array of topics, and have been used to good effect to uncover popular attitudes towards subjects as diverse as politics, marriage, economics, fashion, poverty, migration, alcohol, old age and occupational identity.[46] Question marks remain, though, about just whose attitudes are being conveyed in these ballads. They were usually authored anonymously, but what we do know about ballad authors suggests on the one hand that many of them appear to have been relatively humble individuals – men who kept alehouses, worked as shoemakers or as Thames boatmen, for instance – but on the other hand that they were literate, and demonstrate evidence of learning and education suggesting they were far from 'ordinary' or representative of the common people as a whole.[47] It seems unlikely that these ballads were penned by elites simply as attempts to shape, mould or transform popular mores better to accord with elite tastes – they were, after all, commercial products, and to have sold in the quantities that they did it seems likely that their authors and printers were tapping into pre-existing popular sentiments in the way they framed their stories and songs. They may not have been directly produced by common people, but the fact that they successfully appealed to them reveals a great deal about their world view.

Another aspect of broadside ballads that has, as yet, received rather less attention from historians, is that of the images that they included. The vast majority of cheap printed formats included a woodcut image to accompany and complement the text. Historians have often dismissed these as rather crude, and given that a limited selection of stock images tended to be used by printers – rather than images specially commissioned for each ballad – it has generally been assumed that they were purely decorative, and had little connection to the content or meaning of a ballad. They were certainly part of the attraction of the ballad product for their consumers though, and no doubt help to explain why broadsides often adorned the walls of cottages and alehouses: one ballad scholar has even described them as 'the poor man's oil painting'.[48] Careful studies of the popularity of different images, and more concerted efforts to explore possible connections between image and text, could open up the potential of these ballad woodcuts as a valuable visual source of information about popular culture to supplement or even challenge research focused on textual sources.[49] A further way of approaching early modern popular culture through visual sources would be to engage with the rich artistic tradition of painting scenes of everyday life and popular culture – especially festivals and tavern scenes – developed in particular by Dutch masters in the early modern period. Of course, such sources are once more providing the perspective of observers portraying popular culture from without rather than within, but they are a rich source to examine for evidence of attitudes towards ordinary people in early modern European society.[50]

Diaries

It would be perfectly reasonable to assume that the diary – that most privileged of sources for accessing the inner world of historical subjects – would be unlikely to feature in the tool-kit of the historian of early modern popular culture. Whilst it is certainly true that there are no surviving diaries from this period penned by the most humble of rural labourers or maid servants, there are a small number that can provide us with insight into the lives of individuals whom we could still comfortably class as 'non-elites'. Tradesmen and artisans, for instance, were much more likely to be literate than many of the lower ranks of society, as it was an important skill in running a workshop and trading. One London turner, Nehemiah Wallington, compiled over fifty notebooks between 1618 and 1654, containing accounts of his everyday domestic, working and religious life, alongside comments on national events and reflections on his own state of spiritual and mental well-being.[51] Roger Lowe, a Lancashire shopkeeper's apprentice, kept a diary in the 1660s, in which he recorded his day-to-day routines – ranging from alehouse visits to attending sermons – as well as updates and meditations on his courtship activities.[52] Adam Eyre, a Yorkshire yeoman who served in the parliamentarian army, kept a 'dyurnall' covering the years 1647–9. Although Eyre later ended up styling himself as a gentleman, his writings provide a fascinating insight into the quotidian world of an aspiring individual from within the 'middling sort', and are a particularly useful source for exploring marital life.[53] Another remarkable source is the journal of Edward Barlow, the son of a Manchester husbandman, who went on to become a mariner and travelled much of the world in a series of military and merchant voyages. During a period of captivity as a prisoner of war of the Dutch during the 1650s he taught himself to write, and went on to produce a journal that included a narrative of his life and accounts of his sea-faring, covering the years 1659–1703.[54]

These diaries and journals are remarkably rich sources, and are unparalleled in the level of detail they can provide about the everyday experiences and opinions of relatively humble people in this period. They could be used as the basis for any number of projects exploring themes as diverse as popular attitudes to love and marriage or everyday experiences of friendship, work or recreation. They too, of course, come with a number of warnings attached. Used individually they raise questions about the typicality of the opinions and experiences they reveal, and there are such a small number of diaries relating to the lower ranks of early modern society that these issues cannot be easily overcome by considering a wide range of them. Moreover, the question of typicality is complicated by the fact that the relatively humble individuals who did keep diaries were not representative of their class as a whole in important ways: they were set apart by their literacy, for one thing, and many were also distinctive in their religious beliefs – diarists were far more likely to be drawn from the ranks of 'the godly', the most committed adherents to what we might term a 'puritan' world view. Rich in detail though they may be, such diaries may have more to tell us about a distinctive subculture of literate, godly members of the lower ranks than they have about the world of the common people more generally.[55]

Conclusion

It is most certainly not the essence of common people that they do not appear in history. As we have seen here, there are a wide range of sources available for the study of popular culture in the early modern period, and an equally diverse array of possible topics that they could be used to explore. What exactly these sources reveal about popular culture is rarely straightforward however, and it may be more fruitful to think in terms of examining 'points of contact' between common people and their superiors, rather than searching for an 'authentic' and discrete popular culture. This allows us to include those issues of how sources were shaped by imbalances of power and literacy into our analysis: they can become our focus, rather than being treated as a distortion of it. Another fruitful way of approaching popular culture in this period can be to bring a number of sources together to consider a theme, providing a range of angles on a topic so that the shape of our analysis is not overly dependent on the perspective provided by one particular source type.[56] When approaching our sources with due care, then, historians can do much to recover the rich and fascinating worlds of even our most humble early modern ancestors.

Key resources

Barlow's Journal of His Life at Sea in King's Ships, East & West Indiamen and Other Merchantmen from 1659 to 1703, ed. Basil Lubbock (London: Hurst and Blackett, 1934).
Bodleian Ballads Online, http://ballads.bodleian.ox.ac.uk.
Brennan, Thomas (gen. ed.), *Public Drinking in the Early Modern World: Voices from the Tavern, 1500–1800*, 4 vols (London: Pickering and Chatto, 2011).
The Diary of Roger Lowe, ed. William L. Sachse (London: Longmans, 1938).
Early English Books Online, http://eebo.chadwyck.com/home.
English Broadside Ballad Archive, http://ebba.english.ucsb.edu.
Essex Record Office, http://seax.essexcc.gov.uk.
Fletcher, Anthony and Diarmaid MacCulloch, *Tudor Rebellions*, 5th edn (Harlow: Pearson/Longman, 2004/2008) ('Documents' section).
Old Bailey Online, http://www.oldbaileyonline.org.

Notes

1 David Cressy, *Literacy and the Social Order: Reading and Writing in Tudor and Stuart England* (Cambridge: Cambridge University Press, 1980).

2 G. R. Elton, *England under the Tudors* (London: Methuen, 1955), p. 259.

3 See Mark Hailwood and Brodie Waddell (eds), *The Future of History from Below: An Online Symposium* (2013), https://manyheadedmonster.wordpress.com/history-from-below (accessed 27 January 2016).

4 See Peter Burke, *Popular Culture in Early Modern Europe*, 3rd edn (Farnham: Ashgate, 2009); Tim Harris, 'Problematising Popular Culture', in Tim Harris (ed.), *Popular Culture in England, c. 1500–1850* (Basingstoke: Macmillan, 1995), pp. 1–27; Barry Reay, *Popular Cultures in England 1550–1750* (London: Longman, 1998), Introduction and Chapter 7; David Hall, 'Introduction', in Steven Kaplan (ed.), *Understanding Popular Culture: Europe from the Middle Ages to the Nineteenth Century* (Berlin and New York: Mouton, 1984), pp. 1–18; Martin Ingram, 'Who Killed Robin Hood? Transformations in Popular Culture', in Susan Doran and Norman Jones (eds), *The Elizabethan World* (London: Routledge, 2010), pp. 461–81.

5 Tessa Watt, *Cheap Print and Popular Piety, 1550–1640* (Cambridge: Cambridge University Press, 1991), Introduction.

6 Indeed, see the influential work of the French historian Roger Chartier, who argues that cultural artefacts such as ballads did not 'belong' to specific social groups, but were 'appropriated' or consumed by different social groups in different ways and could mean very different things to different consumers. Roger Chartier, 'Culture as Appropriation: Popular Cultural Uses in Early Modern France', in Kaplan, *Understanding Popular Culture*, pp. 229–53.

7 For an example of this emphasis on 'points of contact' see Arnold Hunt, 'Recovering Speech Acts', in Andrew Hadfield, Matthew Dimmock and Abigail Shinn (eds), *The Ashgate Research Companion to Popular Culture in Early Modern England* (Farnham: Ashgate, 2014), pp. 13–30.

8 See the introduction to Burke, *Popular Culture* for an outline of these changes; quote from p. 16.

9 For examples of such an approach, see David Underdown, *Revel, Riot and Rebellion: Popular Politics and Culture in England* (Oxford: Oxford University Press, 1985); Ronald Hutton, *The Rise and Fall of Merry England: The Ritual Year, 1400–1700* (Oxford: Oxford University Press, 1994). The most useful records for recovering this kind of information are churchwardens' accounts – used extensively by Hutton. Most of these are in manuscript form in local record offices and would require some palaeography training to use, but there are also some printed editions. See for example Alison Hanham (ed.), *Churchwardens' Accounts of Ashburton, 1479–1580* (Exeter: Devon and Cornwall Record Society, 1970). Other printed editions can be found by searching for 'churchwardens' accounts' in your university library catalogue. For more on churchwardens' accounts and where to find them see the 'Ecclesiastical sources' chapter in this volume (pp. 58–77).

10 Underdown, *Revel, Riot and Rebellion*, p. 44.

11 Philip Stubbes, *The Anatomie of Abuses* (London, 1583), available via *EEBO*; John Edward Jackson (ed.), *Wiltshire: The Topographical Collections of John Aubrey* (Devizes: Wiltshire Archaeological and Natural History Society, 1862), pp. 10–11. For other useful examples see Richard Carew, *The Survey of Cornwall* (London, 1602); and Nicholas Breton, *The Court and Country* (London, 1618), both available on *EEBO*.

12 Burke, *Popular Culture*, p. 107.

13 On these contemporary divisions see Underdown, *Revel, Riot and Rebellion*, Chapter 3.

14 See Keith Wrightson, 'Alehouses, Order and Reformation in Rural England, 1590–1660', in Eileen Yeo and Stephen Yeo (eds), *Popular Culture and Class Conflict 1590–1914: Explorations in the History of Labour and Leisure* (Brighton: Harvester, 1981), pp. 1–27; Mark Hailwood, *Alehouses and Good Fellowship in Early Modern England* (Woodbridge: Boydell and Brewer, 2014), Chapters 1–2. For more guidance on how to use Quarter Sessions records see Chapter 2 in this volume (pp. 35–57). The vast majority that survive can only be consulted in manuscript form in local record offices; they require some palaeography training to read and are in part written in Latin. The ambitious student should not be put off though: with the help of a palaeography guide such as Hilary Marshall, *Palaeography for Family and Local Historians* (Chichester: Phillimore, 2004) it is possible to focus on those records written in English, such as examinations (witness statements), which are a mine of information. There are also numerous printed editions of extracts from their proceedings: e.g. E. B. H. Cunnington (ed.), *Records of the County of Wilts: Being Extracts from the Quarter Sessions Great Rolls of the Seventeenth Century* (Devizes: George Simpson, 1932). Other printed extracts can be found by searching your university library catalogue for 'quarter sessions'. Essex has some of its Quarter Sessions records available in transcription online, and free to access: http://seax.essexcc.gov.uk (accessed 27 January 2016).

15 See Martin Ingram, *Church Courts, Sex and Marriage in England, 1570–1640* (Cambridge: Cambridge University Press, 1987). For more guidance on how to use Church court records see Chapter 2 (pp. 35–57). These, too, are mostly in manuscript form in local record offices, but there are some printed versions available, such as Jack Howard-Drake (ed.), *Oxford Church Courts: Depositions 1629–1634* (Oxford: Oxfordshire County Council, 2007); and Jack Howard-Drake (ed.), *Oxford Church Courts: Depositions 1634–1639* (Oxford: Oxfordshire County Council, 2008). Another useful selection of extracts is Paul Hair (ed.), *Before the Bawdy Court: Selections from Church Court and Other Records Relating to the Correction of Moral Offences in England, Scotland and New England, 1300–1800* (London: Elek, 1972). The cause papers of Church court cases from the Diocese of York are available online, with a searchable catalogue, and you can download images of the original documents (though you will need palaeography skills to read them and transcribe them): http://www.hrionline.ac.uk/causepapers/index.jsp (accessed 27 January 2016).

16 For a lively debate on what court records reveal about the role of interpersonal violence in early modern society see Lawrence Stone, 'Interpersonal Violence in English Society, 1300–1980', *Past & Present*, 101 (1983), 22–33; James Sharpe, 'Debate: The History of Violence in England. Some Observations', *Past & Present*, 108 (1985), 102–15; and Lawrence Stone, 'Debate: The History of Violence in England. A Rejoinder', *Past & Present*, 108 (1985), 216–24.

17 Steve Hindle, '"Bleedinge Afreshe"? The Affray and Murder at Nantwich, 19 December 1572', in Angela McShane and Garthine Walker (eds), *The Extraordinary and the Everyday in Early Modern England* (Basingstoke: Palgrave Macmillan, 2010), pp. 224–45 (p. 238).

18 These depositions can be found in both Quarter Sessions and Church court records: see nn. 14 and 15 above. Old Bailey Online represents a brilliant resource for approaching these sorts of questions for the eighteenth century, and comes complete with guides on how to interpret the trial records of the court: http://www.oldbaileyonline.org (accessed 4 January 2016).

19 Natalie Zemon Davis, *Fiction in Archives: Pardon Tales and Their Tellers in Sixteenth-Century France* (Stanford: Stanford University Press, 1987).

20 For an innovative attempt to use such records to study patterns of time-use see Hans-Joachim Voth, *Time and Work in England, 1750–1830* (Oxford: Oxford University Press, 2000). Another good example of how to use such sources is the

work of Thomas Brennan, who used depositions from eighteenth-century Parisian police records not to determine guilt/innocence or levels of crime, but to explore patterns of tavern sociability: he identifies patterns of whom people reported they were drinking with at the time a crime took place to reconstruct patterns of friendship and social networks among the common people. Thomas Brennan, *Public Drinking and Popular Culture in Eighteenth-Century Paris* (Princeton: Princeton University Press, 1988).

21 Hunt, 'Recovering Speech Acts', pp. 20–5 provides a very useful discussion of these issues.

22 Laura Gowing, *Domestic Dangers: Women, Words, and Sex in Early Modern London* (Oxford: Oxford University Press, 1996); Alexandra Shepard, *Accounting for Oneself: Worth, Status and the Social Order in Early Modern England* (Oxford: Oxford University Press, 2015).

23 Quarter Sessions records are the best place to look for such petitions.

24 See Steve Hindle, *On the Parish? The Micro-Politics of Poor Relief in Rural England c. 1550–1750* (Oxford: Oxford University Press, 2004); and Jonathan Healey, *The First Century of Welfare: Poverty and Poor Relief in Lancashire* (Woodbridge: Boydell and Brewer, 2014).

25 For further examples of the ways historians of popular culture can use petitions, see Hailwood, *Alehouses and Good Fellowship*, Chapter 1; Brodie Waddell, *God, Duty and Community in English Economic Life* (Woodbridge: Boydell and Brewer, 2012).

26 See, for example, the accounts of rebellions in Holinshed's *Chronicles* (1577 and 1587), available at http://www.english.ox.ac.uk/holinshed (accessed 27 January 2016). For a guide to interpreting the *Chronicles*, see Annabel Patterson, *Reading Holinshed's Chronicles* (Chicago: University of Chicago Press, 1994). See also Anthony Fletcher and Diarmaid MacCulloch, *Tudor Rebellions*, 5th edn (Harlow: Pearson/Longman, 2004/2008), which has a very helpful documents section that includes extracts from contemporary accounts of rebellions, as well as a range of other sources relating to rebellions that are very useful to anyone undertaking a project on this topic.

27 The English examples of these demands can be found in the documents section of Fletcher and MacCulloch, *Tudor Rebellions*. For the German Peasants' Revolt, see C. Lindberg (ed.), *The European Reformation Sourcebook* (Oxford: Blackwell, 2000), pp. 91–3.

28 For an introduction to this literature see Andy Wood, *Riot, Rebellion and Popular Politics in Early Modern England* (Basingstoke: Palgrave, 2002).

29 Riot cases appear across a range of jurisdictions, but the best way to approach them is probably through the records of Star Chamber, which was the central court with responsibility over riots: see Chapter 2 in this volume. They are held in The National Archives at Kew, and require palaeography skills to use. Old Bailey Online is an easy-to-use resource for exploring eighteenth-century London riots.

30 For examples of attempts to quantify and map patterns of rioting, and critiques of the same, see the discussion in Wood, *Riot, Rebellion and Popular Politics*, Chapter 3.

31 For example Andy Wood, 'Subordination, Solidarity and the Limits of Popular Agency in a Yorkshire Valley, c. 1596–1615', *Past & Present*, 193 (2006), 41–72; John Walter, 'Grain Riots and Popular Attitudes to the Law: Maldon and the Crisis of 1629', in John Brewer and John Styles (eds), *An Ungovernable People: The English and Their Law in the Seventeenth and Eighteenth Centuries* (London: Hutchinson, 1980); John Walter, 'A "Rising of the People"? The Oxfordshire Rising of 1596', *Past & Present*, 107 (1985), 90–143.

32 This line of enquiry has been strongly influenced by the work of anthropologist James C. Scott: *Weapons of the Weak: Everyday Forms of Peasant*

Resistance (New Haven: Yale University Press, 1985); *Domination and the Arts of Resistance: Hidden Transcripts* (New Haven: Yale University Press, 1990). See also the introduction to Michael Braddick and John Walter (eds), *Negotiating Power in Early Modern Society: Order, Hierarchy and Subordination in Britain and Ireland* (Cambridge: Cambridge University Press, 2001).

33 For an introduction to these forms see Adam Fox, 'Ballads, Libels and Popular Ridicule in Jacobean England', *Past & Present*, 145 (1994), 47–83.

34 Star Chamber records are the main repository as it was the court responsible for libel.

35 On the issue of anonymity see E. P. Thompson, 'The Crime of Anonymity', in Douglas Hay, Peter Linebaugh, John G. Rule, E. P. Thompson and Cal Winslow, *Albion's Fatal Tree: Crime and Society in Eighteenth-Century England* (London: Allen Lane, 1975), pp. 255–344.

36 See John Walter, '"The Poor Man's Joy and the Gentleman's Plague": A Lincolnshire Libel and the Politics of Sedition in Early Modern England', *Past & Present*, 203 (2009), 29–67.

37 See Andy Wood, '"Poor Men Woll Speke One Day": Plebeian Languages of Deference and Defiance in England, *c.* 1520–1640', in Tim Harris (ed.), *The Politics of the Excluded, 1500–1850* (Basingstoke: Palgrave, 2001), pp. 67–98; Hailwood, *Alehouses and Good Fellowship*, Chapter 2.

38 For the classic statement of this theory see Scott, *Domination and the Arts of Resistance*.

39 Wood, 'Poor Men Woll Speke One Day', p. 81.

40 Seditious speech cases can appear across a range of legal jurisdictions, but this does make them hard work to track systematically. They can be found in Quarter Sessions records (see above for more information on these); Assize court records (for more on these see Chapter 2 in this volume: there are a number of printed editions of their calendars, edited by J. S. Cockburn, but these do not usually contain the details of seditious words themselves); and State Papers, which are available online (see Chapter 1 in this volume (pp. 15–34)). A useful printed volume that contains numerous examples of seditious speech is James Raine (ed.), *Depositions from the Castle of York Relating to Offences Committed in the Northern Counties in the Seventeenth Century* (Durham: Surtees Society, 1861). David Cressy's *Dangerous Talk: Scandalous, Seditious and Treasonable Speech in Pre-Modern England* (Oxford: Oxford University Press, 2010) is a useful introduction to the topic.

41 For an introduction to popular literature see Bernard Capp, 'Popular Literature', in Barry Reay (ed.), *Popular Culture in Seventeenth-Century England* (London: Routledge, 1988), pp. 198–243.

42 Margaret Spufford, 'First Steps in Literacy: The Reading and Writing Experiences of the Humblest Seventeenth-Century Autobiographers', *Social History*, 4 (1979), 407–35.

43 On the complex relationship between orality and literacy in the early modern period see Adam Fox, *Oral and Literate Culture in England 1500–1700* (Oxford: Oxford University Press, 2000).

44 Ballad researchers are particularly well served by open-access online resources, and many of the surviving ballads from the period have been digitized. See, for instance, *EBBA*; and *Bodleian Ballads Online*, http://ballads.bodleian.ox.ac.uk (accessed 27 January 2016). Students with French can also explore a selection of texts from early modern French popular print culture at *Bibliothèque Bleue*, http://www.lib.uchicago.edu/efts/ARTFL/projects/BibBl (accessed 27 January 2016).

45 On ballad consumers see the introduction to Tessa Watt, *Cheap Print*; and Christopher Marsh, *Music and Society in Early Modern England* (Cambridge: Cambridge University Press, 2010), Chapter 5.

46　Angela McShane, '"Ne sutor ultra crepidam": Political Cobblers and Broadside Ballads in Late Seventeenth-Century England', in Patricia Fumerton, Anita Guerrini and Kris McAbee (eds), *Ballads and Broadsides, 1500–1800* (Farnham: Ashgate, 2010), pp. 207–28; James Sharpe, 'Plebeian Marriage in Stuart England: Some Evidence from Popular Literature', *Transactions of the Royal Historical Society*, 5th Series, 36 (1986), 69–90; Elizabeth Foyster, 'A Laughing Matter? Marital Discord and Gender Control in Seventeenth-Century England', *Rural History*, 4 (1993), 5–21; Waddell, *God, Duty and Community*; Angela McShane and Claire Backhouse, 'Top-Knots and Lower Sorts: Popular Print and Promiscuous Consumption in Late Seventeenth-Century England', in Michael Hunter (ed.), *Printed Images in Early Modern Britain: Essays in Interpretation* (Farnham: Ashgate, 2010), pp. 337–57; Patricia Fumerton, 'Not Home: Alehouses, Ballads, and the Vagrant Husband in Early Modern England', *Journal of Medieval and Early Modern Studies*, 32.3 (2002), 493–518; Hailwood, *Alehouses and Good Fellowship*, Chapter 3; Alice Tobriner, 'Old Age in Tudor-Stuart Broadside Ballads', *Folklore*, 102 (1991), 149–74; Mark Hailwood, 'The Honest Tradesman's Honour: Occupational and Social Identity in Early Modern England', *Transactions of the Royal Historical Society*, 6th Series, 24 (2014), 79–103.
47　McShane, 'Ne sutor ultra crepidam'; Bernard Capp, *The World of John Taylor the Water-Poet* (Oxford: Oxford University Press, 1994).
48　Fumerton, 'Not Home', p. 499.
49　For examples of pioneering work in this area see McShane and Backhouse, 'Top-Knots and Lower Sorts'; and Christopher Marsh, 'Woodcuts and Their Wanderings in Early Modern England', *Huntington Library Quarterly*, Special Edition: Living Broadside Ballads (June 2016). Both *EBBA* and *EEBO* (see n. 44) have recently enhanced their search functions for ballad woodcuts to encourage further work in this area.
50　The work of Tom Nichols provides a great introduction to approaching visual representations of non-elites in the early modern period: *The Art of Poverty: Irony and Ideal in Sixteenth-Century Beggar Imagery* (Manchester: Manchester University Press, 2007); and Tom Nichols (ed.), *Others and Outcasts in Early Modern Europe: Picturing the Social Margins* (Aldershot: Ashgate, 2007).
51　Only seven of these notebooks are extant, but they still represent a fascinating source. A useful modern edition of selections from the books is David Booy (ed.), *The Notebooks of Nehemiah Wallington, 1618–1654: A Selection* (Farnham: Ashgate, 2007). See also Paul Seaver, *Wallington's World: A Puritan Artisan in Seventeenth-Century London* (London: Methuen, 1985).
52　There is a printed edition of the diary: William L. Sachse (ed.), *The Diary of Roger Lowe* (London: Longmans, 1938). See also A. L. Martin, 'Drinking and Alehouses in the Diary of an English Mercer's Apprentice, 1663–1674', in Mack Holt (ed.), *Alcohol: A Social and Cultural History* (Oxford: Berg, 2006).
53　Adam Eyre, 'A dyurnall, or catalogue of all my accions and expences from the 1st of January, 1646–[7]', ed. H. J. Morehouse, in *Yorkshire Diaries and Autobiographies in the Seventeenth and Eighteenth Centuries*, Vol. I (Durham: Surtees Society, 1877), available at https://archive.org/details/yorkshirediarie01marggoog (accessed 27 January 2016). For an example of a historian using the diary see Karl E. Westhauser, 'Friendship and Family in Early Modern England: The Sociability of Adam Eyre and Samuel Pepys', *Journal of Social History*, 27 (1994), 517–36.
54　The original is held at the National Maritime Museum, Greenwich. An abridged edition has been published: Basil Lubbock (ed.), *Barlow's Journal of His Life at Sea in King's Ships, East & West Indiamen and Other Merchantmen from 1659 to 1703* (London: Hurst and Blackett, 1934). For an example of the diary's use see

Patricia Fumerton, *Unsettled: The Culture of Mobility and the Working Poor in Early Modern England* (Chicago: Chicago University Press, 2006).

55 See Chapter 6 in this volume for more on diaries (pp. 107–28).

56 For example, this approach is central to the emerging field of 'tavern studies', in which historians focus on taverns as key institutions of popular culture, and study them by using a wide range of court records, cheap print, diaries and other available sources. See, for instance, Hailwood, *Alehouses and Good Fellowship*; and B. Ann Tlusty, *Bacchus and Civic Order: The Culture of Drink in Early Modern Germany* (Charlottesville: University Press of Virginia, 2001). There is an excellent four-volume printed set of transcribed and translated primary sources relating to taverns and tavern culture, with volumes covering each of early modern France, Germany and early America. Basing a project on popular culture on these tavern sources would be a good way to proceed for students interested in working on Europe but without sufficient language skills, as finding enough resources in translation will be a challenge. It would also be a good way to approach a project on popular culture in early America. Thomas Brennan (gen. ed.), *Public Drinking in the Early Modern World: Voices from the Tavern, 1500–1800*, 4 vols (London: Pickering and Chatto, 2011).

12 Economic life

Brodie Waddell

Introduction

There is more to economic history than counting sheep, and it need not be as sleep-inducing either. That's not to say that there is no place at all for such counting. For instance, thanks to some clever statistical analysis of wool and cloth exports by a dedicated economic historian, we now know that there were over 15 million sheep in mid sixteenth-century England: about 6 for every single person. By comparison there are about 5 people for every sheep that grazes in England today.[1] But, as will be seen, there is a practically unlimited range of sources that can be used to study economic relations and material life in the early modern period, and many of these sources are not as amenable to statistical analysis as wool exports or livestock numbers.

This chapter examines some of the most important ways historians have attempted to study the economic history of this period, focusing on qualitative and quantitative approaches. It shows how richly textured descriptive sources – such as diaries, letters and printed works – can provide valuable insight into how economic changes were experienced and how attitudes towards economic issues evolved. However, these sources can also create false impressions thanks to exaggerated rhetoric and unrepresentative authors. In contrast, quantifiable sources – such as account books, taxation records and parish registers – can offer stronger evidence of the speed and magnitude of economic development, sometimes revealing counterintuitive results. However, these sources too have weaknesses, as they are often inconsistent or unsystematic in this period, making it easy to over-interpret insignificant variations. As examples from recent work show, some of the best research in this field tends to draw on both 'texts' and 'numbers' to reconstruct early modern economic life.

Qualitative sources

The vast majority of the sources discussed in the other chapters in this book provide primarily *qualitative* evidence, that is to say these sources describe events, actions or attitudes in ways that cannot be readily measured or enumerated. These sorts of records can be texts, images or objects, but what they have in common is that their value tends to come from the stories they tell. For this reason, they can be extremely useful to scholars investigating economic history, because they offer the perspective of someone who actually experienced life in the early modern period. The subjective writings of the people of this era can help us to understand their living conditions, labour relations, charitable giving, attitudes to wealth and any number of other important economic issues.

Diaries – which survive in significant numbers from the seventeenth century – and personal correspondence – which survives for earlier periods as well – can illuminate more than just family life and religion. Take, for example, the well-known mid-seventeenth-century diary of the London woodworker Nehemiah Wallington, discussed by Laura Sangha and others earlier in this volume. As Paul Seaver has shown, this marvellous document reveals much about how an undistinguished artisan managed his workshop, interacted with customers and apprentices, and interpreted his fluctuating fortunes.[2] Similarly, documentation of this kind has also been used to investigate the perceptions and practices of personal credit, of luxury consumption and of trading by religious minorities.[3] One of the chief advantages of such sources is subjectivity – they are written by the very people who were doing the buying and selling, working and lending, that historians hope to reconstruct. As such, they allow us to get a much better sense of how these practices actually worked, rather than seeing them in an abstract description or a dehumanized series of numbers. In addition, many disreputable or illicit economic activities such as smuggling or prostitution, which are unlikely to be candidly recorded in official or public sources, are acknowledged and occasionally discussed at length in more personal writings. At a more practical level, although most of this material survives only in manuscript, much of it has also been transcribed and reprinted, making it more accessible to students and overseas researchers.[4]

States and other institutional bodies have also left voluminous qualitative sources that can be used to study economic history. Perhaps the most numerous of all are judicial records. At the most obvious level, the descriptions of property offences – and their punishment – found in court documents often provide insight into who possessed certain goods, who wanted them, and how the owners sought to protect them. Even the structure and tensions within certain trades can sometimes be revealed, as with the numerous charges of embezzlement laid against the semi-independent workers in some textile industries.[5] Moreover, the spread of enclosure and other forms of agricultural 'improvement' in England in the sixteenth and seventeenth centuries was amply documented thanks to the willingness of lords and commoners to resort to the equity courts of the central government in Westminster to arbitrate their disputes.[6] Ecclesiastical records can also be informative, and these often survive from an earlier date than their secular judicial counterparts. For example, records of over 4,000 tithe disputes between clergymen and parishioners exist for the Diocese of York from the fourteenth century onwards, and these documents can provide insight into local agricultural practices or the spread of new crops long before they began to be recorded by the agronomists of the late eighteenth century.[7] However, one must not forget that the Church and the State were not the only institutions active at this time. Craft, trade and merchant guilds existed in most towns and cities across Europe from the Middle Ages until at least the eighteenth century, and their records can open a window into the lives of the skilled artisans and traders who dominated the urban economy of this period. By examining the sources produced by these 'companies' and 'corporations', one can learn how they attempted to protect their commercial privileges, lobbied about new government policies, celebrated their identity through festivities, relieved poorer members and trained the next generation of workers.[8] The sixteenth-century ordinances of the goldsmiths' guild in Nuremberg, for example, allowed widows and unmarried women to work in the craft, but set out detailed restrictions limiting their autonomy to ensure that men continued to dominate this aspect of the urban economy.[9] Unfortunately, there are no directly equivalent records for the great bulk of the workforce that laboured in the countryside. The only rural institution that is even somewhat analogous is the manor court or village commune, which potentially offered a forum for well-established tenants and their lords to organize local agriculture and arbitrate small-scale disputes. Records of these organizations are often under-studied, but are numerous for many parts of Europe.[10]

Printed works, unlike diaries or legal depositions, were intended for a potentially broad audience and thus more rarely provide much information about the economic lives of particular individuals or localities. However, what they do frequently offer is a contemporary view of the changing nature of the wider economy. From the late fifteenth century onwards, many commentators published their assessments of current living conditions, labour relations, commercial fortunes and financial affairs. In some cases, groups of authors such as those later dubbed 'mercantilists', 'political economists' or 'physiocrats' sought to determine the underlying laws that governed economic life and promoted their theories in learned treatises. Their intellectual pursuits have been studied by historians of economic thought in order to trace the roots of ideas still used by academics and policy-makers today.[11] However, most writers of the time were more likely to describe the world around them rather than attempt to work out complex theories to explain the system as a whole. William Harrison's *Description of England* (1577), for example, noted 'population expansion; the growth of internal trade, of commercial farming and more aggressive estate management by landlords; the rising domestic living standards of some and the growing insecurity of others'.[12] Moreover, many of those who described contemporary conditions did so in order to draw a moral or political lesson. Preachers, pamphleteers, ballad-writers and playwrights all published texts that can be read both as depictions of actual economic life and as rhetorical narratives designed to advance a particular moral ideal or State policy.[13] Although publications must therefore be read very closely and critically, they are now available in abundance through online collections such as *EEBO, Early European Books, EBBA* and *ECCO*. It can initially be difficult to find such sources in digital catalogues because authors often dealt with economic issues under seemingly political or religious headings. Moreover, many modern terms such as 'economy', 'finance' and 'employment' are rarely used – instead, contemporaries tended to write in a more concrete vocabulary of 'land', 'trade', 'traffick' and 'money'. That said, printed books and tracts have been used extensively to study past economic behaviour since the early twentieth century – when Max Weber and R. H. Tawney developed the idea of an early modern 'Protestant work ethic' – and they remain a valuable source for such research today.[14]

Images and objects can be much more difficult to 'read' than published texts or manuscripts. Their value to the economic historian, however, means that they cannot be ignored. The range of topics found in early modern paintings and other visual sources is uneven – images of throne rooms and battlefields are far more common than those of marketplaces or workshops – but relevant material can still be found in all of Europe's major museums (e.g. Figure 12.1). This is especially true when one includes vernacularized classical and biblical scenes such as the paintings by El Greco and Rembrandt of Christ driving the moneychangers out of the temple. Yet, as this example suggests, interpreting visual sources is a fraught process, for they are never simply straightforward depictions of actual events or settings. The butcher's stall in a Dutch genre painting may bear little resemblance to a real stall in Antwerp or Amsterdam. Art historians, who have been tackling these issues for far longer than economic historians, have developed sophisticated tools for analysing images, and their work can be very valuable when tackling these sources. Julie Berger Hochstrasser, for instance, has shown how lavish exotic commodities portrayed in Dutch and Flemish still lives can illuminate how people at the time experienced the arrival of new commodities from the East and West Indies, including human cargo in the form of African slaves.[15]

In addition to representing economic life, art and objects also contributed to it. Historians of material culture, as discussed earlier by Tara Hamling, have analysed commodities such as pottery, textiles and jewellery to understand changes in fashion and production techniques better. For instance, the long journey of eighteenth-century porcelain from a lump of clay to a desirable teapot can sometimes be glimpsed through close examination of the object itself. The many economic processes associated with this journey – consumer-oriented design, skilled wage-labour, shipping, wholesaling and retailing – are all inherent in the final product.[16] In an analogous way, surviving buildings of the era can demonstrate the spread of new materials, the development of construction methods and the living conditions of those who inhabited them.[17] A few objects, such as coins, bankers' bills and trade tokens, are even more imbued with commercial significance, revealing the changing nature of commercial transactions across the centuries.[18] So, although the

Figure 12.1 Jan Luyken, *Christelijke gevangenen worden op een plein te Algiers als slaaf verkocht* (1684). This etching by Jan Luyken depicts 'the way in which captured Christian slaves are sold in Algiers'. As a primary source, it is valuable but difficult to interpret. In one sense it shows a very real economic activity: thousands of European sailors were captured by Barbary raiders in the seventeenth century and many were sold at the large slave market in Algiers. However, the image also illuminates the culture of the artist. Luyken had likely never seen the Algiers slave market in person, so his etching is as much a product of Dutch stereotypes about north African Muslims as it is a 'realistic' portrayal of an actual event. One wonders how he would have depicted the auction of enslaved Africans in New Amsterdam.

survival of material and visual sources is extremely irregular and their interpretation is never obvious, they can also provide physical evidence of aspects of trade and labour that textual sources cannot.

Many of the qualitative sources reviewed in this section have formed the bedrock for the work of some of the most renowned scholars of economic history. Nonetheless, such material must be used with great care.By their very nature, the texts and images produced by early modern individuals are necessarily subjective and occasionally propagandistic. Sometimes this is readily apparent: a merchant who complains to the Government about the 'decay of trade' is probably exaggerating his plight and a professional surveyor is likely to over-state the profits that came with agricultural 'improvement'. However, intentional bias is not always so transparent. The authorship of printed sources is often unclear, which can obscure the fact that entrepreneurial 'projectors', paid lobbyists and zealous partisans produced many of the texts that purported to describe current economic conditions impartially. Much more pervasive is the unintentional bias that comes from the social inequality of the time. All the texts available to us have been authored – or at least mediated – by the literate, a group that was overwhelmingly likely to be wealthy, urban and male. It is not especially difficult to uncover the views of courtiers, magistrates, clergymen and merchants. In contrast, the voices of peasants, craftsmen, servants, housewives and paupers were very rarely recorded. We are often left, therefore, with the perspective of elite groups that doubtless experienced a very different economic reality from that of their less literate contemporaries. Historians must be very careful not simply to reproduce the prejudices of the privileged minority when attempting to use qualitative sources to understand the workings of early modern economy.

Quantitative sources

In an attempt to overcome the limitations of purely textual sources, many economic historians have turned to *quantitative* material. As will be seen, this does not necessarily mean relying on long lists of numbers such as account books or tax records, but it does involve focusing on sources that can be counted or measured in some way. When compared to qualitative analysis, the potential value of this approach is clear. First, it can offer a much more rigorous method for charting economic and social change. While contemporary descriptions might suggest changes in, for example, the distribution of wealth or the fortunes of trade, each text is the product of a single individual who may have little sense of long-term developments and whose view may not be comparable to those of other individuals at an earlier or later date. Sources that present a 'consistent series' of, for example, prices or wages offer a firmer foundation for reconstructing change, because they allow clear comparisons of differences across decades or even centuries. Quantifiable records also make it possible to be much more precise about magnitudes. Historians analysing textual material are often reduced to impressionistic claims, using words like 'many' or 'few', whereas numerical data enables scholars to be much more specific. Without quantification it would be impossible to know, for instance, that the urban population of Europe rose from around 6 per cent of the total in 1500 to 10 per cent in 1800, or that annual beer consumption in Holland declined from 301 litres per capita in 1622 to merely 38 litres in 1795, or that the price of bread in seventeenth-century London often doubled in times of food shortage.[19] There are real limits to counting and measuring, many of which will be highlighted in the rest of this section, but the advantages that come with such analysis should not be under-estimated by students and scholars more accustomed to relying on careful readings of textual sources. A brief survey of some of the specific types of records that can be used will reveal this more clearly.

Early modern states have provided economic historians with a wealth of quantifiable material. In some cases this was quite intentional. Many

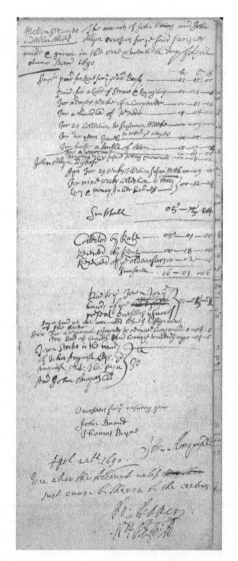

Figure 12.2 Great Melton overseers' accounts, Norfolk Record Office, EVL 645, not paginated (21 April 1690). This page shows the annual financial accounts of the overseers of the poor and highways for the village of Melton in Norfolk for the year 1689–90. In it, we can see the rudimentary book-keeping skills common at the time, but it also offers information about contemporary wages, prices and poor-relief practices. The column on the left itemizes disbursements and receipts, while the column on the right lists the sums in pounds ('li'), shillings ('s') and pence ('d') for each item: for example, the overseers' record paying 1s 8d. 'For a dayes Worke of a Carpenter' and 7s 4d. 'For halfe a Barell of beer'. They also twice list payments of 9s to a pauper named Susanna Meek for '29 Weeks Collection', which means that the overseers paid her a pension of about 18s per year, far below the level of income that would be needed to survive if that had been her sole source of support.

governments created councils, committees or offices to gather economic information, perhaps most famously in 1696 when England established a permanent Council of Trade and Plantations and an Inspector General of Imports and Exports, which collected data on the nation's overseas trade and surveyed spending on the relief of the poor.[20] However, early modern rulers were primarily interested in the economy because it was the source of their revenue. In other words, most of the officially produced quantitative records that have survived are the result of political authorities' attempts to tax their subjects.[21] One can, for example, learn a great deal about the relative prosperity or poverty of particular geographical areas within key cities or even at a national level through analysis of taxation records. They can also be employed to estimate the social distribution of wealth and thus measure the levels of economic inequality. Also, as Robert Jütte has noted, in an era before censuses, 'these sources can give us at least a rough idea about the increase or decrease of poverty' through their recording of the number of people granted exceptions as 'paupers'.[22] Yet, Jütte has also noted the many caveats that must apply to such analysis: they tend to measure difference in wealth rather than in income, the criteria for assessment and exemption often change over time, they frequently rely on indirect proxies of wealth rather than total personal assets, and ultimately they depend on the scrupulousness (or not) of the assessors.[23] England's late-seventeenth-century hearth tax, for instance, allows us to begin to reconstruct the social and geographical distribution of wealth, but we must not forget that the collectors only recorded the number of hearths in each household, not the actual wealth of the inhabitants.[24] Much the same can be said of other fiscal records. For example, nearly all of our knowledge of the levels of early modern trade comes from the tolls, dues and customs imposed on it by various governments. Such evidence survives in vast quantities during this period and without it we could say little about the rate at which global trading networks expanded or about the commercial impact of wars and other short-term events. Such records can even be used to get a sense of women's commercial roles, such as the Portuguese sardine-sellers listed in seventeenth-century tithe books.[25] Nonetheless, similar caveats apply here as well: taxes are often assessed at nominal or customary values rather than market prices, certain groups of traders or commodities could gain or lose exemptions over time, and smuggling and inconsistent administration left much trade unrecorded.

Other official documents have also been used in quantitative analysis, especially the 'vital statistics' and financial accounts produced by parishes in many parts of Europe.[26] The registers of baptisms, marriages and deaths kept by parishes may not seem especially 'economic' at first glance, but they have proved invaluable to economic historians. At the most basic level, careful statistical analysis of birth and death rates has allowed scholars to reconstruct long- and short-term demographic trends before the great national censuses of the nineteenth century. This, in turn, makes it possible to estimate rates of urbanization, levels of population pressure on the land, variations in wealth per capita, moments of 'crisis mortality' and many other measures that are all highly relevant to economic history.[27] Other scholars have used these records creatively to judge the prevalence of certain types of employment by studying the seasonality of marriage and to reassess the rise of manufacturing though analysis of the occupations of fathers included in baptismal listings.[28] The problem, of course, is that parish registers are never complete and rarely continuous. Sometimes complex calculations are required to 'reweight' samples of parish registers to account for missing records and undocumented religious nonconformists, meaning that the final figures have substantial margins of error. Parochial account books are less common than registers and thus suffer from similar deficiencies, but they too can be very illuminating when analysed quantitatively (e.g. Figure 12.2). As with the fiscal records of higher authorities, parish accounts often include tax listings that provide a basis for reconstructing the local economy and social structure. Moreover, tracking their expenditures on charity and local law enforcement can reveal the effects of economic distress and the development of early welfare systems. The voluminous poor relief records of Hadleigh in Suffolk, for example, allowed Marjorie McIntosh to trace the growth and reconfiguration of formal charity there in the late sixteenth century.[29]

The practice of keeping accounts spread well beyond 'official' institutions in this period. Religious houses were perhaps the most prominent of these in medieval Europe and they remained so in Catholic countries throughout the early modern period. Similarly, many of the nobility kept regularized financial records by the fourteenth and fifteenth centuries, sometimes also inheriting those of monasteries at the Reformation. It is thanks to these long-running accounts that economic historians have been able to trace changes in rents and tenancy across the centuries. But this era also witnessed other groups starting to record their finances. The accounts of minor gentry families and middling traders, who had previously left very few such records, begin to survive in significant numbers. For example, Jane Whittle and Elizabeth Griffiths have used the detailed disbursements and receipts of the Le Stranges, a gentry family in early-seventeenth-century Norfolk, to produce a study that examines not just the ownership of goods but how they were acquired and who managed that acquisition. It is concerned not only with durable goods, but with consumables such as food and fuel. It looks not only at goods but also at services provided in the form of labour. The focus is only sometimes on the novel and luxurious, and more often on the ordinary and everyday. And the accounts provide not just a snapshot of consumption but also a view of expenditure over the household's lifetime.[30]

Records of this sort can be even more valuable when analysed in aggregate. For over a century economic historians have used account books and similar documents to build up a picture of historical trends in wages and prices across – and beyond – the early modern period. These series can then be used to assess changes in living conditions, showing for example how seventeenth-century climatic conditions led to the price of food rising faster than wages in much of the world in the early seventeenth century, associated with a 'global crisis' stretching from Britain to Japan.[31] Figures for wages and prices derived from these sources have also been used to explain the so-called 'great divergence' in economic growth between north-western Europe and the rest of the world that has been imputed to the early modern period.[32] As these latter examples indicate, the humble account book may appear to be a rather dry and inconsequential document from a modern perspective, but in a pre-statistical age it is often one of the only sources that can be used to reconstruct economic life on both 'micro' and 'macro' scales.

Testamentary documents – wills and inventories of the deceased's goods – are another primary source that can illuminate the early modern economy when analysed quantitatively. Since the 1950s, historians have been methodically investigating the goods and money enumerated in probate documents to assess patterns of ownership across time and space. For example, W. G. Hoskins' classic study of a nondescript village in the English Midlands examined inventories and other records to demonstrate the collapse of a society based on open-field agriculture over the course of several centuries.[33] Inspired by this work, contributors to the multi-volume *Agrarian History of England and Wales* analysed vast numbers of these documents to map out striking differences among the country's various agricultural regions at this time.[34] While most of this work has focused on production by scrutinizing the crops and livestock listed in probate material, more recent studies have tended to concentrate on patterns of consumption, noting for instance the spread of clocks, mirrors, silverware and other 'petty luxuries' across the Netherlands, Britain and their overseas colonies. In fact, the now well-established argument for an early modern 'consumer revolution' primarily emerged from the statistical analysis of post-mortem inventories by Jan de Vries, Lorna Weatherill, Carole Shammas and others.[35] Wills – unlike inventories – are less obviously quantifiable, as they include only bequeathed property rather than notionally comprehensive lists of goods and their values. Yet they too have received attention from economic historians such as Amy Erickson, whose systematic investigation of these documents demonstrated that English women were not as excluded from inheritance arrangements as once assumed.[36] Given that as many as 2 million wills survive from early modern England alone, there are bright prospects for much further quantitative research on these sources. That said, such documents also contain biases that must be acknowledged. At the most basic level, both wills and inventories only rarely survive for women and the poor, making it difficult to use them to generalize about early modern society as a whole.[37] Inventories are also problematic because of their exclusion of landed property, the pre-eminent form of wealth in this period, and the apparent propensity of testators to distribute certain types of goods to family before their death, meaning that such records are far from complete surveys of the actual assets of the deceased.[38]

Tax listings, account books and probate inventories all have at least one thing in common: they all contain a clear series of monetary values that can be easily entered into a spreadsheet and statistically manipulated. Most early modern sources are not so straightforwardly quantifiable. However, that has not stopped economic historians from attempting to count or measure seemingly qualitative material. The great Ferdinand Braudel, for example, began his chapter on 'the economic dimensions of the sixteenth century' with a calculation of the speed of the circulation of information in the form of thousands of letters – the Mediterranean, it seems, was about sixty-six to eighty days long.[39] More recently, Julian Hoppit used British parliamentary records to explore the changing patterns of legislative initiatives between 1660 and 1800 relating to 'finance', 'economy' and 'communications', demonstrating both their increasing numbers and success rates.[40] Likewise, judicial sources can also be read creatively to provide insight into the often elusive world of day-to-day economic life. For example, the detailed legal depositions that survive from many European countries often record much incidental information about what witnesses and their neighbours were doing when a particular crime occurred, making it possible to investigate how much time people spent labouring in fields, workshops and markets.[41] But perhaps the current master of unexpected quantifications is Gregory Clark, who has published a book purporting to measure a remarkable lack of social mobility from the Middle Ages onwards in England, Sweden, China and elsewhere using evidence from surnames.[42] The final example ought to be a reminder not only of the vast range of possibilities opened up by inventive quantitative studies but also of the risks that accompany such research.

The potential pitfalls facing historians employing statistical analysis are many, some of which have already been noted. Perhaps the most important is the danger of equating a clear but narrow numerical series with a broader but fuzzier concept. It is certainly possible to collect data on prices and nominal wages that can be combined into an index of 'real wages' over a very long timespan, but this series *cannot* be used as general measure of 'living conditions'. As Bob Woodward and many others have shown, 'real wage' figures fail to account for changes in many other variables: the number of days worked owing to under-employment; part payment in meals or commodities; subcontracting to other workers; access to alternative sources of income through bi-employment or common land; and, of course, contributions from women and children.[43] At the other end of the spectrum is the problem of combining too much data – rather than too little – into a single measure. Wages again provide an example because these figures tend to be drawn from sources recording very diverse situations: can the payments made by a rural monastery to a stonemason over several months in 1500 really be directly compared to a one-time payment made to another mason by a metropolitan merchant in 1800? Such concerns become even more pertinent when historians attempt much higher levels of aggregation. One can, for instance, commend the efforts of statisticians to create a database of estimates of Gross Domestic Product per capita for dozens of countries across the early modern world, but such estimates are merely aggregates of hundreds of sometimes questionable sub-estimates, each of which multiplies the probability of a significant miscalculation.[44] In addition, the apparent clarity and precision that come with numerical series create the danger of over-interpretation. Not every bump or dip on a graph is pregnant with meaning – some are the result of minor errors, or simply random 'noise'. Finally, at a practical level, the rapid growth in computing power and spread of easy-to-use spreadsheet software like Microsoft Excel has undoubtedly enabled many qualitatively inclined historians to conduct rudimentary quantities analysis, but we should not over-estimate our own abilities. Much 'cliometric' research requires a diverse skill set that is best acquired through specialist training or at least careful self-directed study. Learning how to construct a random sample or run a regression successfully is sadly not part of the standard curriculum for budding historians.[45]

Conclusion

This chapter has taken as its theme the use of qualitative and quantitative sources in economic history. This is not the only theme that could have been chosen. Instead, we might have looked at the contrasting records and divergent methods used by various groups of historians: the Marxists, the *Annalistes*, the neo-classicists, etc. Alternatively, we could have surveyed the terrain chronologically or geographically, noting the rapid expansion in surviving sources associated with the spread of literacy after the Reformation, or the impressive collections created by many of Europe's early modern city-states when compared to those of expansive but weak polities such as Russia. These are important issues that will have to be tackled elsewhere. Rather than endeavouring to address them here, this chapter will conclude with a brief note on how the two main groups of sources discussed above can be used in combination.

The categorization of records as qualitative or quantitative is artificial and arbitrary. As has already been noted, seemingly 'textual' sources can often be turned into metrics that can be compared and measured. The opposite is also true. An account book might appear to be an inauspicious target for literary analysis, but the words used to describe, say, alms offered to a beggar at the accountant's door can be extraordinarily revealing. More generally, individual economic historians do not restrict themselves to only a single type of source or method. The strongest results usually emerge from a combination of textual readings and numerical calculation. This can be seen in practically all of the examples cited earlier in this chapter, so only one more need be highlighted here. Alexandra Shepard recently analysed a sample of 13,686 witness statements from the English Church courts between 1550 and 1728 in which each individual was asked to assess their own 'worth'. As she showed, their 'responses provide a rare insight into the language of *self*-description adopted by men and women of limited means', allowing us to see how wealth, poverty and employment were perceived by people of the time. The tabulation of these statements allows her to demonstrate how judgements of 'worth' were 'heavily shaped by gender and marital status', reminding us that even something as seemingly objective as personal net assets was evaluated through an intensely subjective lens at this time. Shepard drives this point home with quotations from the actual words used by respondents, for how can we 'measure' Richard Turner's claim in 1624 that he was 'just Leane Bacon'?[46] In isolation, a table of the thousands of responses or a handful of colourful witness statements would only illuminate one small facet of early modern economic life, but together they reveal a much more complex and multidimensional world.

The large quantity and wide diversity of sources available to economic historians should now be very evident. They are not distributed evenly, nor are they self-explanatory. The nature of surviving sources means that learning about the material lives and, even more, economic views of women, children, peasants and paupers is arduous and sometimes impossible. Awareness of gaps, attention to bias and, in some cases, knowledge of statistics are all important components in this type of research. Thankfully, the ability to count 15 million sheep without falling asleep is not one of the essential skills. Indeed, almost every early modernist could glean some profit from studying the sources and techniques of economic history.

Key resources

Arkell, Tom, Nigel Goose and Nesta Evans (eds), *When Death Do Us Part: Understanding and Interpreting the Probate Records of Early-Modern England* (Oxford: Leopard's Head Press, 2000).

British History Online: Economic, 173 vols, http://www.british-history.ac.uk/catalogue/economic.

Chojnacka, Monica and Merry E. Wiesner-Hanks (eds), *Ages of Woman, Ages of Man: Sources in European Social History, 1400–1750* (London: Longman, 2002), esp. Part V: 'Economic Life'.

Crawford, Patricia and Laura Gowing (eds), *Women's Worlds in Seventeenth-Century England: A Sourcebook* (London: Routledge, 2000), Chapters 3: 'Work', and 4: 'Poverty and Property'.

Darnton, Robert, 'Publishing and the Book Trade in France and Francophone Europe, 1769–1789' (2014), at http://www.robertdarnton.org.

Feinstein, Charles H. and Mark Thomas, *Making History Count: A Primer in Quantitative Methods for Historians* (Cambridge: Cambridge University Press, 2002).

Hudson, Pat, *History by Numbers: An Introduction to Quantitative Approaches* (London: Arnold, 2000).

Medema, Steven G. and Warren A. Samuels (eds), *The History of Economic Thought: A Reader* (London: Routledge, 2003).

Mitchell, B. R., *British Historical Statistics* (Cambridge: Cambridge University Press, 1988).

Records of London's Livery Companies Online (2014), http://www.londonroll.org.

Tawney, R. H. and E. Power (eds), *Tudor Economic Documents*, 3 vols (London: Longmans, Green, 1924).

Thirsk, Joan and J. P. Cooper (eds), *Seventeenth-Century Economic Documents* (Oxford: Clarendon Press, 1974).

Wilson, Charles and Geoffrey Parker, *An Introduction to the Sources of European Economic History, 1500–1800* (London: Weidenfeld and Nicholson, 1977).

Notes

1 John Oldland, 'Wool and Cloth Production in Late Medieval and Early Tudor England', *Economic History Review*, 67.1 (2014), 25–47 (p. 29, Table 1); 'Annual Statistics on the Number of Livestock in England and the UK at 1 December', Department for Environment, Food and Rural Affairs (2014), https://www.gov.uk/government/statistical-data-sets/structure-of-the-livestock-industry-in-england-at-december (accessed 13 January 2015).

2 Paul Seaver, *Wallington's World: A Puritan Artisan in Seventeenth-Century London* (Stanford: Stanford University Press, 1985), Chapter 5.

3 Craig Muldrew, *The Economy of Obligation: The Culture of Credit and Social Relations in Early Modern England* (Basingstoke: Macmillan, 1998); Linda Levy Peck, *Consuming Splendor: Society and Culture in Seventeenth-Century England* (Cambridge: Cambridge University Press, 2005); Natalie Zemon Davis, 'Religion and Capitalism Once Again? Jewish Merchant Culture in the Seventeenth Century', *Representations*, 59 (1997), 56–84.

4 See, for example, *The Notebooks of Nehemiah Wallington, 1618–1654: A Selection*, ed. David Booy (Aldershot: Ashgate, 2007), and the sources described in Chapter 6 in this volume (pp. 107–28).

5 John Styles, 'Embezzlement, Industry and the Law in England 1500–1800', in Maxine Berg, Pat Hudson and Michael Soneuscher (eds), *Manufacture in Town and City before the Factory* (Cambridge: Cambridge University Press, 1983). See also Chapter 2 of this volume on legal sources (pp. 35–57).

6 Richard Hoyle (ed.), *Custom, Improvement and the Landscape in Early Modern Britain* (Farnham: Ashgate, 2011), pp. 10–11 and *passim*.

7 'Cause Papers in the Diocesan Courts of the Archbishopric of York, 1300–1858', Borthwick Institute for Archives (2010), http://www.hrionline.ac.uk/causepapers (accessed 27 January 2016).

8 S. R. Epstein and Maarten Prak (eds), *Guilds, Innovation and the European Economy, 1400–1800* (Cambridge: Cambridge University Press, 2008); Ian Anders Gadd and Patrick Wallis (eds), *Guilds, Society and Economy in London 1450–1800* (London: Centre for Metropolitan History, Institute of Historical Research in association with Guildhall Library, 2002); Maarten Prak, Catharina Lis, Jan Lucassen and Hugo Soly (eds), *Craft Guilds in the Early Modern Low Countries: Work, Power, and Representation* (Aldershot: Ashgate, 2006).

9 Monica Chojnacka and Merry E. Wiesner-Hanks (eds), *Ages of Woman, Ages of Man: Sources in European Social History, 1400–1750* (Harlow: Longman, 2002), pp. 160–1.

10 Brodie Waddell, 'Governing England through the Manor Courts, *c.* 1550–1850', *Historical Journal*, 55.2 (June 2012), 279–315; Paul Warde, 'Law, the "Commune", and the Distribution of Resources in Early Modern German State Formation', *Continuity and Change*, 17.2 (2002), 183–211.

11 For a selection of early modern economic thinkers, see Steven G. Medema and Warren A. Samuels (eds), *The History of Economic Thought: A Reader* (London: Routledge, 2003).

12 Keith Wrightson, *Earthly Necessities: Economic Lives in Early Modern Britain, 1470–1750* (New Haven: Yale University Press, 2000), p. 3. Many further examples can be found in R. H. Tawney and E. Power (eds), *Tudor Economic Documents*, 3 vols (London: Longmans, Green, 1924); and Joan Thirsk and J. P. Cooper (eds), *Seventeenth-Century Economic Documents* (Oxford: Clarendon Press, 1974).

13 For a recent example of careful analysis of such texts, see Deborah Valenze, *The Social Life of Money in the English Past* (Cambridge: Cambridge University Press, 2006).

14 Max Weber, *The Protestant Ethic and the Spirit of Capitalism* (London: Routledge, 2001 [1905]); R. H. Tawney, *Religion and the Rise of Capitalism* (London: John Murray, 1926).

15 Julie Berger Hochstrasser, *Still Life and Trade in the Dutch Golden Age* (New Haven: Yale University Press, 2007).

16 Kate Smith, *Material Goods, Moving Hands: Perceiving Production in England, 1700–1830* (Manchester: Manchester University Press, 2014).

17 Joan Thirsk (ed.), *The Agrarian History of England and Wales*, 8 vols (Cambridge: Cambridge University Press, 1967–2000), Vol. IV, Chapters 10–11; Vol. V, Part II, Chapters 20–1.

18 C. E. Challis, *The Tudor Coinage* (Manchester: Manchester University Press, 1978). The British Museum has online images of more than 8,000 coins from the sixteenth, seventeenth and eighteenth centuries: http://www.britishmuseum.org/research/collection_online/search.aspx (accessed 13 January 2015).

19 J. L. van Zanden, 'Early Modern Economic Growth: A Survey of the European Economy, 1500–1800', in Maarten Prak (ed.), *Early Modern Capitalism: Economic and Social Change in Europe, 1400–1800* (London: Routledge, 2001), pp. 72, 84; Jeremy Boulton, 'Food Prices and the Standard of Living in London in the Century of Revolution, 1580–1700', *Economic History Review*, 53.3 (2000), 455–92 (pp. 480–3).

20 David Ormrod, *The Rise of Commercial Empires: England and the Netherlands in the Age of Mercantilism, 1650–1700* (Cambridge: Cambridge University Press, 2003), pp. 47–9. The records of these new institutions are held at The National Archives under various headings including CO 5, CO 326, CO 388, BT 6, CUST 2–3. Many of them have been abstracted in *Calendar of State Papers, Colonial*, 46 vols (London: Public Record Office, 1860–1994), available at http://www.british-history.ac.uk/catalogue (accessed 27 January 2016). For more, see Chapter 1 in this volume (pp. 15–34).

21 For more details about using English fiscal records, see M. Jurkowski, C. Smith and D. Crook, *Lay Taxes in England and Wales, 1188–1688* (Kew: PRO Publications, 1998).

22 Robert Jütte, *Poverty and Deviance in Early Modern Europe* (Cambridge: Cambridge University Press, 1994), p. 49.

23 Ibid., pp. 46–50.

24 'Hearth Tax Online: Householders in late 17th Century England', Centre for Hearth Tax Research, Roehampton University, http://www.hearthtax.org.uk (accessed 13 January 2015).

25 Chojnacka and Wiesner-Hanks, *Ages of Woman, Ages of Man*, p. 154.

26 For a list of miscellaneous printed and digital sources, see 'Parish Research', *My-Parish.org*, http://my-parish.org/research (accessed 13 January 2015).

27 E. A. Wrigley and R. S. Schofield, *The Population History of England 1541–1871: A Reconstruction* (London: Edward Arnold for the Cambridge Group for the History of Population and Social Structure, 1981).

28 Ann Kussmall, *Servants in Husbandry in Early Modern England* (Cambridge: Cambridge University Press, 1981); Martin Dribe and Bart van de Putte, 'Marriage Seasonality and the Industrious Revolution: Southern Sweden, 1690–1895', *Economic History Review*, 65.3 (2012), 1123–46; Leigh Shaw-Taylor, Tony Wrigley, Max Satchell, Gill Newton, Richard Smith, Amy Erickson *et al.*, 'The Occupational Structure of Britain, 1379–1911', Cambridge Group for the History of Population and Social Structure, http://www.geog.cam.ac.uk/research/centres/campop/occupations (accessed 13 January 2015).

29 Marjorie Keniston McIntosh, *Poor Relief and Community in Hadleigh, Suffolk, 1547–1600* (Hatfield: University of Hertfordshire Press, 2013). For a similar study of a later period, see Joan Kent and Steve King, 'Changing Patterns of Poor Relief

in Some English Rural Parishes *circa* 1650–1750', *Rural History*, 14.2 (2003), 119–56.

30 Jane Whittle and Elizabeth Griffiths, *Consumption and Gender in the Early Seventeenth-Century Household: The World of Alice Le Strange* (Oxford: Oxford University Press, 2012), p. 1.

31 Geoffrey Parker, *Global Crisis: War, Climate Change and Catastrophe in the Seventeenth Century* (New Haven: Yale University Press, 2013), p. 19 and *passim*.

32 Steven Broadberry and Bishupriya Gupta, 'The Early Modern Great Divergence: Wages, Prices and Economic Development in Europe and Asia, 1500–1800', *Economic History Review*, 59.1 (2006), 2–31.

33 W. G. Hoskins, *The Midland Peasant: The Economic and Social History of a Leicestershire Village* (London: Macmillan and St Martin's Press, 1957).

34 Thirsk, *Agrarian History*, Vols IV–V.

35 Jan de Vries, *The Dutch Rural Economy in the Golden Age 1500–1700* (New Haven: Yale University Press, 1974); Lorna Weatherill, *Consumer Behaviour and Material Culture in Britain, 1660–1760* (New York: Routledge, 1988); Carole Shammas, *The Preindustrial Consumer in England and America* (Oxford: Clarendon Press, 1990). For a recent assessment in a very different context, see Johan Fourie, 'The Remarkable Wealth of the Dutch Cape Colony: Measurements from Eighteenth-Century Probate Inventories', *Economic History Review*, 66.2 (2013), 419–48.

36 Amy Louise Erickson, *Women and Property in Early Modern England* (London: Routledge, 1993).

37 Though note the work on women and labourers in ibid., and in Craig Muldrew, *Food, Energy and the Creation of Industriousness: Work and Material Culture in Agrarian England, 1550–1780* (Cambridge: Cambridge University Press, 2011), Chapter 4. For examples of women's inventories for sixteenth-century Germany, see Chojnacka and Wiesner-Hanks, *Ages of Woman, Ages of Man*, pp. 145–8.

38 Tom Arkell, Nigel Goose and Nesta Evans (eds), *When Death Do Us Part: Understanding and Interpreting the Probate Records of Early-Modern England* (Oxford: Leopard's Head Press, 2000); Jan Kuuse, 'The Probate Inventory as a Source for Economic and Social History', *Scandinavian Economic History Review* (1974), 22–31.

39 Fernand Braudel, *The Mediterranean in the Time of Philip II*, trans. Sian Reynolds, 2 vols (Berkeley: University of California Press, 1995 [1949]), Vol. I, pp. 354–65.

40 Julian Hoppit, 'Patterns of Parliamentary Legislation 1660–1800', *Historical Journal*, 39.1 (1996), 109–31.

41 H. J. Voth, *Time and Work in England, 1750–1830* (Oxford: Clarendon Press, 2000).

42 Gregory Clark, *The Son Also Rises: Surnames and the History of Social Mobility* (Princeton: Princeton University Press, 2014).

43 Donald Woodward, 'Wage Rates and Living Standards in Pre-Industrial England', *Past & Present*, 91 (1981), 28–46.

44 Jutta Bolt and Jan Luiten van Zanden, 'The Maddison Project: Collaborative Research on Historical National Accounts', *Economic History Review*, 67.3 (2014), 627–51.

45 For introductions to these methods, see Charles H. Feinstein and Mark Thomas, *Making History Count: A Primer in Quantitative Methods for Historians* (Cambridge: Cambridge University Press, 2002); Pat Hudson, *History by Numbers: An Introduction to Quantitative Approaches* (London: Arnold, 2000).

46 Alexandra Shepard, 'Poverty, Labour and the Language of Social Description in Early Modern England', *Past & Present*, 201 (2008), 51–95.

13 Warfare

Neil Younger

What is the history of warfare? This is not as straightforward a question as it might appear. On the one hand war can be approached narrowly, through studying the central activities of the practice of warfare: battles, campaigns, command, formations, weaponry. This is the range of topics, centred on combat itself, that military history has traditionally comprised, and might be typified by regimental or campaign histories. Yet this is an approach that is often criticized now. At the risk of caricaturing, it is often regarded as tending towards the antiquarian and inward-looking; it is seen as self-referential, since it was often the preserve of soldiers or former soldiers; it is seen as excessively reverential, tending (perhaps unsurprisingly) to be nationalistic and nation-centred; and it often partook of a naive conception of history as shaped by the deeds of 'Great Men'.

It would be foolish to dismiss the scholarly efforts of this tradition; these are still important topics. Yet it would be hard to deny that recent decades have seen the historical study of warfare diversify in very interesting and very healthy ways, through the rise of what is often called the 'New Military History', or the 'war and society' approach. At heart, this approach is based on the principle that warfare, its causes, practice and consequences, simply cannot be studied in isolation from the societies that gave rise to it, and that were in turn shaped by war. All early modern people were, at some time, in some way, touched by warfare, whether they experienced it first-hand or only indirectly. Historians increasingly see warfare as a highly diverse and complex social phenomenon that can be studied from a vast range of different angles: political, social, intellectual, cultural, technological, medical. Every aspect of warfare can be seen as having a history. This is therefore a history of war that has become much more social and generally much less military.[1]

This approach has a number of real strengths. It tends to be wide-ranging and holistic. It reflects changes in broader historiography much more thoroughly. It tends to be more historicized, more sensitive to the contemporary context, judging matters by the standards of the day rather than explicitly seeking to draw practical lessons from the past or anachronistically assessing early modern practice by modern standards. This approach is also highly comparative, recognizing that early modern European states and societies were similar in many ways; warfare is by its nature very often an international pursuit, and certainly early modern European states actively sought to compare their military activity with that of their rivals, to learn from them and keep up with them.[2] As a result of these developments the history of warfare has gained a great deal more scholarly credibility, and indeed a number of universities now offer specific degrees in war studies. Military historians – or historians of warfare – can converse much more readily with their colleagues in other sub-disciplines and can borrow, adopt and adapt techniques for studying the past.

The current history of warfare is therefore a much more heterogeneous field than it was, and consequently the sources and methodologies it employs have become more varied; these new fields of study demand that historians be a little more flexible and innovative in terms of their use of sources. One important reason for this is that, as we will see, historians increasingly use sources for reasons other than those for which they were created, using them 'against the grain'. Increasingly the range of sources historians use means that it is difficult to argue that there *is* a distinctive or unique set of tools or materials that belong to the study of warfare.

As ever, the question of how war is studied and what sources are used to do so depends largely on what one is hoping to gain from the study. War is often studied, for example, as an element of the basic political narrative of national history – anyone reading a conventional history of Britain (or any other nation, or for that matter region or locality) would encounter numerous wars, both international and civil, that had significant impacts on its development. In most cases, however, the average reader is likely to be more interested in the political causes and consequences than in military topics as such. The study of the outbreak of a war or the making of a peace, for example, is often essentially a study of political processes, since, as Carl von Clausewitz famously pointed out, war can be seen as an outworking of political problems.[3] These political processes need to be studied primarily through old-fashioned archival research in State Papers, diplomatic correspondence and so on.[4] British historians are fortunate that so much of this material has been published in one form or another, and doubly fortunate that these sources are often more accessible now than ever before, owing to online access and digitization by both profit-making and non-profit-making companies.[5]

Such topics are by no means 'done'. The debate over the causes of the English Civil War/English Revolution/Wars of the Three Kingdoms, most obviously, is one of the most extensive and sophisticated in all historiography, sprawling over decades and centuries, politics, personality, ideology, religion, economics, and so on, and showing no sign of stopping.[6] There are still many excellent histories of individual wars being written, typically blending narration of events with a greater or lesser amount of thematic analysis.[7] On the other hand, some historians have treated the place of war in politics from a more cultural angle, considering contemporary perceptions of what made war legal and legitimate through looking at depictions of war in a wide range of early modern cultural products: political writings, sermons, histories, literature, plays, poetry and art.[8] It hardly needs to be stressed, for example, that early modern European monarchs and nobles often portrayed themselves as military figures in public representations or propaganda; these sources can be used to cast light on the mental worlds of early modern political figures. John Hale was a pioneer of this approach, and work by, for example, Glenn Richardson, comparing Henry VIII, Emperor Charles V and Francis I of France, adds a great deal of depth and texture to our understanding of the place of war in early modern elite culture and politics.[9]

The ostensibly simple matter of establishing the course of events in a war, or precisely what happened in a given battle or campaign – something that is methodologically fairly straightforward but in practice often not very easy – still gives plenty of scope for useful work. Any historian trying to work out the details of almost any specific event in early modern history (the earlier, the trickier) must become used to sifting through incomplete or inadequate sources: a few fragmentary references in official documents or personal letters; mentions in chronicles, perhaps ballads; adding bits of archaeological evidence ... Even extremely well-known early modern events (in my case, it was the Spanish Armada) are susceptible to quite major errors, misunderstandings and lazy scholarship, and can repay a careful review of the evidence.[10] The history of warfare perhaps suffers from the fact that the heat of battle does not provide a conducive environment for writing things down. Of course much, perhaps most, historical writing depends on the use of a broad and diverse range of sources, and certainly the range of material that is used to write the history of warfare is growing a great deal.

One area that increasingly provides genuinely new evidence is archaeology, especially when used to complement conventional documentary research. Archaeology has recently been combined with exhaustive research in chronicles, ballads and official records from both local and national sources, as well as techniques such as topography, place-name analysis and soil analysis to pinpoint convincingly the site of the Battle of Bosworth Field (1485), regrettably not in the same place as the modern visitor centre. The precise location of a battlefield might be regarded as a matter of essentially antiquarian interest, but the archaeology also cast light on the conduct of the battle itself: the weapons used, the deployment of forces and so on.[11] Equally compellingly, the bones of the most notable casualty of that battle, King Richard III, were uncovered on the site of the former Greyfriars Church in Leicester; the archaeologists were able to demonstrate that his curved spine was no Tudor myth, and to analyse the wounds that killed him.[12] Such findings are not just about the elite. Excavation of a mass grave of soldiers from Towton (1461) revealed an unexpectedly savage battle, in which fleeing soldiers were cut down and apparently mutilated by their enemies; a burial pit from Lützen in the Thirty Years War (1632) found soldiers buried almost naked, with any possessions of any value having been looted.[13]

Naval archaeology has offered remarkable material too, notably through the raising of the *Mary Rose* and the numerous underwater excavations of Armada wrecks. These have turned up masses of fascinating artefacts casting light on naval warfare and weaponry, on the sailors themselves (through the discovery of human remains), and their lives: pots, spoons, tools, games and musical instruments, religious tokens – right through to the Chinese porcelain, discovered on an Armada wreck, from which a Spanish aristocrat presumably expected to eat when ensconced as a conquering ruler in England.[14] There is a similar Swedish case of a ship overturning on its maiden voyage, the *Vasa*, which sank in Stockholm sound in 1628 and was raised again in 1961. In this case, the material remains of the ship (the hull is astonishingly well preserved) allowed historians to determine the cause of the disaster – the ship's weight sat fractionally too high in the water – but also to deduce certain facts about the essentially experimental design practices of the seventeenth-century shipwrights.[15]

These relatively traditional themes within the study of warfare remain vibrant, therefore, but the real growth areas are those that consider the wider implications of war on society, taking warfare beyond its self-referential constraints and seeing it as a facet of society as a whole. This kind of work typically falls into two broad categories: the direct and the indirect impact of warfare. The former can be defined as the 'collateral damage' inflicted by military action on civilians, which was often severe. This is often well studied using local sources to assess what happened and what it meant to contemporaries. David Potter, for example, used petitions from the local population of Picardy to assess the destruction caused by the Habsburg–Valois wars of the early sixteenth century.[16] Stephen Porter used local records from numerous towns to produce an extremely thorough survey of the material destruction inflicted on English towns and villages by the Civil War.[17] Tax assessments have been used to demonstrate the impact of military activity on Berkshire during the same wars: it dropped from fifth wealthiest county before the war to twenty-first in 1649.[18] The demographic impact of war on the local population can be assessed by using records of births, marriages and deaths, the keeping of which very much expanded in early modern Europe; Philip Benedict, for example, has used such records to assess the impact of the French Wars of Religion on Rouen.[19] The relations of soldiers and civilians can also be traced using local sources such as court records or the correspondence of local authorities, describing crime or disorder committed by soldiers, destruction of property, tension or conflict between soldiers and civilians, or the punishments imposed on soldiers.[20]

It is often difficult, however, to place such findings in context, to construct a clear-eyed assessment of the severity of the impact. It is easy to find harrowing accounts of the destructive impact of warfare on civilians: one notable example is the 1641 rebellion in Ireland: the subject of a major digitization programme, the 1641 Depositions Project. This vast body of documents records the experiences of Protestant settlers in Ireland at the time of the rebellion of 1641, in which many were attacked and lost their goods, providing sources on intercommunal violence as well as much incidental information on social and economic conditions.[21] Such events have led historians to look carefully at histories of violence and to apply concepts of war crimes and atrocities to early modern events.[22]

Yet at the same time, war was capricious in where it struck. Places such as England, Castile, Norway or large parts of France went decades, even centuries, barely seeing an army or a battle. Elsewhere, in the Netherlands, Hungary or north Italy, it was a constant. Historians need to be very careful in situating the impact of war in a world that, for ordinary early modern people, was often dangerous and unpleasant to begin with. Geoff Mortimer, for example, has examined the nature of the Thirty Years War's impact on German local society, focusing specifically on eyewitness accounts: that is, stripping out rumour, hearsay, propaganda or the sensational news typical of the period, and using only evidence specifically reported in contemporary sources as having been witnessed by the author. Mortimer found that, whilst theft of food and goods and general destruction of property were ubiquitous, more shocking crimes (the rape, torture or murder of civilians by soldiers) are very seldom mentioned. This was perhaps not the 'all-destructive fury' of German national memory.[23]

In line with the much broader efforts of the historical profession to investigate the lives of 'ordinary' people, a growing body of work looks at early modern soldiers themselves, their origins, backgrounds, experiences and fates.[24] These are difficult people to study, since they were usually illiterate and can seldom tell their own stories: they were written about by their superiors, often when they misbehaved, rather than recording their own lives. Often bureaucracy is the historian's friend: early modern armies were increasingly well organized and well documented, and they liked to keep track of their employees (or more accurately wanted to keep track of who was being paid, and how much). Surprisingly, however, the early modernist may be worse off than the late medievalist here: a major research project on 'The Soldier in Late Medieval England' has compiled a database of hundreds of thousands of pieces of data from the very detailed fourteenth- and fifteenth-century muster rolls of English forces in France.[25] Similar sources do not exist for the sixteenth century.

Documents of this kind vary greatly in the level of detail provided, but a good deal can be extracted from them. Close attention to records of enlistments, for example, can provide clues about individuals who may have been recruited several times, deserted or been punished for crimes. Town or county records often contain collections of official papers that give vivid snapshots of individual cases. Muster rolls from the county militias can also be very valuable sources, and can be found both in central and in local archives.[26] They often provide detail about individual militiamen and officers, as well as about their collective strength and organization.

These records are often very impersonal, but just occasionally an individual from the ranks of the common soldiery can be recovered from obscurity in some meaningful detail. One of the best early modern examples is a German soldier of the Thirty Years War, probably named Peter Hagendorf, who fought for twenty-five years in various armies, and whose diary survives. Marching 15,000 miles up and down Germany, to Italy and parts of France, he frequently commented on the interesting sights he saw; he was seriously wounded at times, took part in major battles including the Sack of Magdeburg and the first Battle of Breitenfeld; acquired loot and disposed of it, often for drink; engaged in some ugly encounters with civilians; and steadily received promotions. He married twice, and took his wives with him on campaign, fathering multiple children, nearly all of whom died as infants, no doubt because of the extremely unsanitary conditions in military encampments. It was an extraordinary career, a real-life Simplicissimus. He has already been the subject of scholarly work in German, and his memoirs translated, but his career is so fascinating that it seems fitting material for a play, film or opera.[27] The range of emotions experienced by early modern soldiers like Hagendorf – fear, cowardice, grief, cameraderie – is another topic increasingly attracting the attention of scholars: see for example Alastair MacDonald's study of fear and courage amongst late medieval Scottish soldiers, extracting fragments of information from contemporary chronicles and poems.[28]

The attitudes and experiences of the military elites can be accessed much more easily, of course. Warfare was an intrinsic component of noble culture, as was violence in other forms, such as the duel; this is shown in material remains (artwork, tomb monuments, buildings) as well as in literature both fictional (*Don Quixote*, for example) and non-fictional.[29] Some of the most valuable and engaging sources here are individual memoirs, written to record the course of individuals' lives, but also to pass on lessons about war or lay claim to justified reward. The best of these are informative, stylishly written, and usually highly egotistical and self-serving: the Englishmen Roger Williams and Robert Carey and the Frenchman Blaise de Monluc from the sixteenth century, and many others from the seventeenth century, with the Scottish mercenary Robert Monro perhaps the outstanding example.[30] There are also many accounts of early naval voyages published by the Navy Records Society and the Hakluyt Society, providing masses of material for the study of all aspects of life at sea as well as accounts of Europeans' early contacts with alien civilizations.

In a similar way, historians can use early modern printed matter to explore popular attitudes to warfare. Recent years have seen a great expansion of interest in the role of print and news, a trend encouraged by the increasing ability to consult printed material online. In this as in other areas, historians of warfare benefit from the fact that war has always been a topic of intrinsic interest for many observers; some of the earliest printed foreign news in England concerned matters such as the French Wars of Religion, the Habsburg–Ottoman Wars or the Siege of Malta. By the time of the Thirty Years War and the English Civil War, printed propaganda, both text and image, was commonplace.[31] Similarly, we have practical military literature: the training manuals that emerged in the early modern period, ranging from the classical Vegetius via the Renaissance Machiavelli to the most up-to-date Dutch manuals for the use of the musket or the construction of fortifications (how closely such books represent the day-to-day reality of warfare may, of course, be doubted).[32]

Print is especially helpful for the study of the Civil War period in England, especially since censorship lapsed with the breakdown of Charles I's Government; almost immediately, there was an explosion in printing of all kinds. The advent of regular news pamphlets, in particular, is useful for all sorts of purposes. Above all, access to print simply allows us to hear the voices of many more individuals, giving a huge boost to cultural approaches to early modern war studies. Mark Stoyle, for example, has used news pamphlets concerning the royalist commander Prince Rupert and his dog, Boy, to illuminate not so much Rupert's role in the war, but the witchcraft beliefs that swirled around both man and dog, and their role in the mindset of Civil War propaganda.[33] One of the most impressive attempts to recreate the experience and the mental world of early modern warfare is Barbara Donagan's study of the English Civil War. This again uses contemporary printed matter extensively to consider a wide range of attitudes to war, and is especially thought-provoking in examining the place of war within frameworks of legal and moral codes – tackling the question that is perhaps too often overlooked, of how early modern people accepted the need to inflict violent death on their countrymen on the field of battle. Again, this is a history of war that integrates seamlessly with broader social history.[34]

A broader view still of the role of war arises from looking at the indirect impact of war on states and societies. War was the most expensive and most complex thing that early modern states did, and states have indeed been described as machines for making war. Therefore the question of how, and how well, states coped with these challenges, and how they were changed by them, is one that historians of war and society have to engage with.

The most famous and influential model of how war affected State development is the long-lived thesis of the 'military revolution', proposed in the 1950s by Michael Roberts. This argued that between 1560 and 1660, changes in technology, particularly the role of gunpowder weapons, set in train a series of changes in tactics, military strategy, and the size and nature of armies. This accounted for one of the most prominent features of early modern warfare – the rapid growth in its scale – and Roberts argued that this forced the State to change and develop, to become more efficient in response. In effect one might say that Roberts was seeking to use military change to explain the rise of the modern State, or even the rise of the modern era: the transition from medieval to modern itself. This is a thesis that was later adopted and reshaped by Geoffrey Parker, in whose hands it helped explain the military dominance of European societies over much of the rest of the world.[35]

The 'military revolution' became widely accepted, and helped to stimulate a great deal of work exploring the relationship between war, politics, money and the State. There are many different angles of approach here. One is the development of the apparatus of the State – the creation of a war machine, a bureaucracy or something like it, the establishment of war offices and navy boards, dockyards and armouries. Here the records of the State itself are usually key: the central archives of State Papers and the more specialized records of particular institutions of the State.

Military logistics, for example, is a topic that is more interesting than it sounds, providing an approach to studying the detailed workings of early modern states that is often illuminating. The 'Spanish Road' is a classic case study here: the great military corridor connecting the heart of the Spanish Habsburg monarchy with the battlefields in Flanders. When researching the Spanish Road through the east of what is now France, Geoffrey Parker discovered that, thanks to the standardized archive classification system introduced by Napoleon III, he could ask for the same class of documents (EE1) in archives up and down eastern France and find the documents he wanted.[36] Archival research is seldom so convenient, however, and indeed to understand the strategic motivations that lay behind the horses and men tramping north to the Netherlands, Parker had to make use of one of the most widely dispersed archives imaginable: that of Philip II's Government, involving research in Barcelona, Besançon, Brussels, Geneva, London, Madrid, Seville, Simancas, Parma and elsewhere.[37] Matters are usually simpler for British historians; R. W. Stewart, for example, made intensive use of the reasonably well preserved sources of the Elizabethan and Jacobean Ordnance Office (plus the Exchequer, Privy Council, etc.) to study this important element of a developing military power.[38] The development of naval organization similarly depends on substantial central Government archives.[39]

Studies of early modern armies form another important category here. The ways in which military force was mobilized underwent profound change in this period, from quasi-feudal approaches largely based on the mobilization of noblemen's power to much more recognizably modern forms of troop-raising. Armies increasingly took on characteristics such as regular organization, discipline, drill, professionalism, uniforms, standardization of weapons, regular pay and so on. The New Model Army, unsurprisingly, is a central exhibit, along with the longer-term development of the English State's fiscal and military capacity in the decades after the outbreak of Civil War. In these cases, and again especially with regard to the mid seventeenth century, it is virtually impossible to disentangle military themes from political ones; what is being analysed is not simply administrative procedure, but also political intentions and consequences, and so administrative records need to be used alongside the papers of leading political figures, parliamentary debates, local accounts and so on.[40]

Furthermore, any overly simplistic view of the growth of efficient bureaucracy should be treated with caution. For one thing, English government had strong participatory (amateur) traditions too. Much of the day-to-day work of governing in the localities was carried out by members of the landed elites of nobility, gentry and yeomen. The records of such people's work, which we might now regard as official papers, routinely remained in private hands. Over time these collections may have passed to their descendants and remain in country houses, or may have been transferred to the British Library, local record offices or elsewhere (often they became dispersed in the process). Thus if one wishes to look at the war effort in early modern England, some of the best archives concern Elizabethan Kent (the papers of Sir John Leveson, now in Stafford) or early Stuart Leicestershire (the papers of the Fifth Earl of Huntingdon, mostly in San Marino, California). For this reason, studies of individual counties have tended to be popular approaches to studying all sorts of aspects of early modern warfare, government and society.[41]

Another approach that promises to be very stimulating is to consider the role of private enterprise in warfare. This is a line of thought that (intentionally or not) resists an excessively teleological focus on the development of the State at the expense of other, non-State, participants. Private businesses and entrepreneurs played important roles in warfare in a huge number of different ways, from providing provisions of clothing, equipment, munitions and food to managing the maintenance of ships or fortresses, raising troops or collecting taxes. In this way they often filled holes and bridged gaps left by the many shortcomings of the State. Like amateur local officials, such people employed their personal status and credit as much as, or more than, the authority of the State to do their work.[42] One reason why private enterprise has been neglected in favour of states, however, is that states have had continuous institutional existence down to the present day, thus ensuring the preservation of their archives, whereas most entrepreneurs and businesses have not, often making them difficult to study.

Money is of course at the heart of all of this: spending it effectively was hard enough, but getting enough of it in the first place was vastly more difficult. Successful warfare depended on mobilizing resources, and the recognition that taxmen and clerks were just as important for success in warfare as soldiers and sailors is one of the most important shifts in recent historiography, moving from purely military histories to histories of warfare. The need for money spread the impact of warfare more widely than ever, and historians have to follow. They must pay serious attention to taxation, for example, since it was predominantly raised for military purposes. There were remarkable developments in the State's ability to tap the wealth of the nation, and to mobilize finance through credit, during the Civil War and afterwards. There are highly detailed Exchequer records for income and spending, but they are not easy to use, being voluminous, incomplete, physically cumbersome and technically difficult to decipher.[43]

More broadly still, the study of tax raises some of the most fundamental aspects of the relationships between princes and their people in early modern Europe. In some ways a focus on the mechanisms of money-handling itself risks missing the point, since the administrative capacity of the organization only comes into play once the State has secured political consent: the cooperation and support from the nation (or at any rate the propertied section of it), without which no monarch, however extensive his theoretical powers, could mount warfare. Here again warfare intersects with politics, since after all warfare is essentially a means of pursuing political objectives through the use of force, and it was directed by political authorities for which the conduct of war was a prime *raison d'être*.

Within the political sphere, warfare often provoked conflicts over money that were played out in representative institutions: debates that often raised questions about fundamental constitutional matters. Taxation for war also frequently prompted resistance, opposition and rebellion in the country at large. The Civil War was itself precipitated by Charles I's need for money to repress rebellion in Scotland. A holistic understanding of the impact of war on society requires attention to all of these issues, and in practice this demands that the historian of warfare engage with and make sense of the whole political society of a nation. This is clearly an enormously challenging task, and one in which, again, historians of warfare work very closely with their counterparts in other sub-fields, most obviously in political and governmental history and indeed political ideas, straying far from the battlefield itself.[44] Early modern monarchies did not welcome dissent or free expression of political ideas, and therefore opposition to Government policy might be expressed with great circumspection or in various forms of coded language. Again, the role of news and print is helping us to investigate these matters. Records of debates in Parliament are often extremely useful in taking the temperature of the political nation's attitude to war; Conrad Russell cites an MP in the 1625 Parliament, who, hearing that £200,000 had been spent on the navy, and perhaps hardly able to conceive of such sums, wrote down instead £20,000 – a revealing slip.[45] Popular comments on war can be similarly illuminating: the Henrician State Papers contain a piquant example from a Shaftesbury man in 1521, who, in the midst of a heated and perhaps drunken altercation with a veteran of Henry VIII's French wars, exclaimed thus: 'A, sir, have ye ben with Maistre Henry Kyng? A noble act ye did ther! Ye spent awey my money and other mennys [men's], like a sort of vacabunds and knaves!'[46] One particularly creative methodology has assessed the attitude of the early Stuart political nation to warfare by tracing on a month-by-month basis how much tax they were willing to pay, and how quickly – this puts the available sources to a use for which they were never intended, but it is based on the usually reliable premise that what people do with their money is a good guide to what they really think.[47]

Work on all of these issues has blossomed in recent decades, therefore, but the master narrative that held it together has not fared so well: the 'military revolution' has come under serious attack, as grand theories often do. Whilst few historians doubt the basic propositions that early modern warfare increased markedly in scale and complexity, and the effects of this on society and the State were significant, many different historians have identified problems with specific aspects of the Roberts/Parker model. It is increasingly seen as having been an impressionistic thesis, placing too much emphasis on some, potentially atypical, armies (the Dutch under Prince Maurice; the Swedes under Gustavus Adolphus) and neglecting others.[48] It probably over-stated the importance of technology. This is a matter less of sources than of interpretation: just to give one example, one of the principal exhibits of the military revolution was the supposedly revolutionary firearms tactics pioneered by the Dutch at the end of the sixteenth century, in imitation of classical models. Yet as David Parrott has pointed out, this reputation relies more on Dutch propaganda than on objective evidence – in any case, the Dutch almost never fought pitched battles anyway. This is a remarkable example of the way in which historians can miss the mark even on points of considerable importance.[49]

The question of the role of warfare in State development has become more nuanced too. New interpretations, often describing State *formation* rather than State *building*, have arisen. Often drawing on sociological approaches, these interpretations move away from monocausal explanations of the rise of powerful states. Religious change, responses to the problems of poverty, developments in the law and the demand for a more ordered society – all these must be placed alongside warfare in our picture of State formation.[50]

The current state of the history of warfare is therefore very healthy. The field has been renewed by historians posing a wide variety of new questions, and simultaneously seeking out new sources and new methodologies to answer them. Much of this research still depends, in the traditional way, on piecing together a range of different kinds of sources, and increasingly on integrating new sources into existing narratives and methodologies; it is important not to lose sight of well-established ideas in the rush for new ones. Nevertheless, there is still a great deal to do, and many recent insights await further testing on the basis of new archives and new ways to use old archives. The modern history of warfare is still in many ways a new and a niche field, and (as the example of the military revolution showed), important revisions can still be made to many of its fundamental interpretations. Further study of many of the issues described here will undoubtedly reveal other necessary revisions to our knowledge. The notion that an understanding of war is indispensable to any full understanding of the early modern world is, however, no longer doubted.

Key resources

The 1641 Depositions project, http://1641.tcd.ie/index.php.

Aylmer, G. E. and J. S. Morrill, *The Civil War and Interregnum: Sources for Local Historians* (London: Standing Conference for Local History by Bedford Square Press, 1979). This is a guide to sources rather than a compilation.

British History Online, http://www.british-history.ac.uk.

Helfferich, Tryntje (ed.), *The Thirty Years War: A Documentary History* (Indianapolis: Hackett, 2009).

Lindley, Keith, *The English Civil War and Revolution: A Sourcebook* (London: Routledge, 1998).

Muster Books for North and East Hertfordshire 1580–1605, ed. A. J. King, Hertfordshire Record Publications, 12 (Hitchin: Hertfordshire Record Society, 1996).

The Soldier in Medieval England project, http://www.medievalsoldier.org.

State Papers Online, 1509–1714, http://gale.cengage.co.uk/state-papers-online-15091714. aspx.

State Papers Online: Eighteenth Century, 1714–1782, http://gale.cengage.co.uk/state-papers-online-15091714/state-papers-online-1714–1782.aspx.

Wilson, Peter H., *The Thirty Years War: A Sourcebook* (Basingstoke: Palgrave Macmillan, 2010).

Notes

1 On this historiographical shift, see for example Colin Jones, 'New Military History for Old? War and Society in Early Modern Europe', *European History Quarterly*, 12.1 (1982), 97–108; Peter Paret, 'The New Military History', *Parameters*, 21 (1991), 10–18.

2 See for example Steven Gunn, David Grummitt and Hans Cools, *War, State and Society in England and the Netherlands, 1477–1559* (Oxford: Oxford University Press, 2007); Jan Glete, *War and the State in Early Modern Europe: Spain, the Dutch Republic and Sweden as Fiscal-Military States, 1500–1660* (London and New York: Routledge, 2002).

3 Carl von Clausewitz, *On War*, trans. J. J. Graham, rev. F. N. Maude (Ware: Wordsworth, 1997), pp. 22–3.

4 See Chapter 1 of this volume on State Papers (pp. 15–34).

5 Examples of resources specifically designed to make historical sources available include the Institute of Historical Research's *British History Online* site, http://www.british-history.ac.uk (accessed 4 January 2016; mostly free to access); Gale Cengage's *State Papers Online, 1509–1714*, http://gale.cengage.co.uk/ state-papers-online-15091714.aspx (accessed 5 January 2016; subscription only); *State Papers Online: Eighteenth Century, 1714–1782*, http://gale.cengage.co.uk/ state-papers-online-15091714/state-papers-online-1714–1782.aspx (accessed 5 January 2016; subscription only); and TannerRitchie's *Medieval and Early Modern Sources Online*, http://www.tannerritchie.com/memso.php (accessed 28 January 2016; subscription only). Resources such as the Internet Archive (https://archive. org) and Google Books (http://books.google.co.uk) (both accessed 28 January 2016) make freely available immense numbers of digitized versions of out-of-copyright books of all kinds, amongst which are to be found numerous older printed historical sources, many very rare and themselves very difficult to access until recently.

6 A good introduction is Ann Hughes, *The Causes of the English Civil War*, 2nd edn (Basingstoke: Palgrave Macmillan, 1998).

7 Michael Braddick, *God's Fury, England's Fire: A New History of the English Civil Wars* (London: Penguin Books, 2008); Michael Mallett and Christine Shaw, *The Italian Wars 1494–1559* (Harlow: Pearson, 2012); Peter H. Wilson, *Europe's Tragedy: A History of the Thirty Years War* (London: Penguin, 2009).

8 J. R. Hale, *War and Society in Renaissance Europe, 1450–1620* (London: Fontana Press, 1985), Chapter 1; J. R. Hale, 'Sixteenth-Century Explanations of War and Violence', *Past & Present*, 51 (1971), 3–26; Steven Gunn, 'The French Wars of Henry VIII' in J. Black (ed.), *The Origins of War in Early Modern Europe* (Edinburgh: John Donald, 1987).

9 Hale, *War and Society in Renaissance Europe*; Glenn Richardson, *Renaissance Monarchy: The Reigns of Henry VIII, Francis I and Charles V* (London: Arnold, 2002).

10 Neil Younger, 'If the Armada Had Landed: A Reappraisal of England's Defences in 1588', *History*, 93.311 (2008), 328–54.

11 Glenn Foard and Anne Curry, *Bosworth, 1485: A Battlefield Rediscovered* (Oxford: Oxbow Books, 2013).

12 Philippa Langley and Michael Jones, *The King's Grave: The Search for Richard III* (London: St Martin's Press, 2013).

13 Clifford J. Rogers (ed.), *The Oxford Encyclopedia of Medieval Warfare and Military Technology*, 3 vols (Oxford: Oxford University Press, 2010), Vol. I, pp. 130–1. Christoph Seidler, 'Clues to the Thirty Years' War: Mass Grave Begins Revealing Soldiers' Secrets', *Spiegel Online*, 27 April 2012, http://www.spiegel. de/international/germany/mass-grave-from-thirty-years-war-investigated-in-luetzen-germany-a-830203.html (accessed 27 June 2014).

14 Colin Martin, *Full Fathom Five: Wrecks of the Spanish Armada* (London: Chatto and Windus, 1975); Robert Sténuit, *Treasures of the Armada*, trans. Francine Barker (Newton Abbot: David and Charles, 1972); Julie Gardiner with Michael J. Allen (eds), *Before the Mast: Life and Death aboard the Mary Rose* (Portsmouth: Mary Rose Trust, 2005); A. J. Stirland, *The Men of the Mary Rose: Raising the Dead* (Stroud: Sutton Publishing, 2005); Alexzandra Hildred (ed.), *Weapons of Warre: The Armaments of the Mary Rose* (Portsmouth: Mary Rose Trust, 2011); M. J. Rodriguez-Salgado (ed.), *Armada 1588–1988: An International Exhibition to Commemorate the Spanish Armada* (London: Penguin, 1988), p. 191.

15 Fred Hocker, *Vasa: A Swedish Warship* (Stockholm and Oxford: Medstroms Bokforlag, 2011), pp. 132–41.

16 David Potter, *War and Government in the French Provinces: Picardy, 1470–1560* (Cambridge: Cambridge University Press, 1993), Chapter 6.

17 Stephen Porter, *The Blast of War: Destruction in the English Civil Wars* (Stroud: The History Press, 2011).

18 Frank Tallett, *War and Society in Early Modern Europe 1495–1715* (London: Routledge, 1992), p. 150.

19 Philip Benedict, 'Catholics and Huguenots in Sixteenth-Century Rouen: The Demographic Effects of the Religious Wars', *French Historical Studies*, 9.2 (1975), 209–34.

20 Phillip Thomas, 'Military Mayhem in Elizabethan Chester: The Privy Council's Response to Vagrant Soldiers', *Journal of the Society for Army Historical Research*, 76 (1998), 226–48; Henry Reece, *The Army in Cromwellian England 1649–1660* (Oxford: Oxford University Press, 2013).

21 http://1641.tcd.ie/index.php (accessed 30 January 2016). The depositions are also being published in print by the Irish Manuscripts Commission.

22 Geoffrey Parker, 'The Etiquette of Atrocity: The Laws of War in Early Modern Europe', in Geoffrey Parker, *Empire, War and Faith in Early Modern Europe* (London: Penguin, 2003). David Edwards, Clodagh Tait and Padraig Lenihan (eds), *Age of Atrocity: Violence and Political Conflict in Early Modern Ireland* (Dublin: Four Courts Press, 2007).

23 G. Mortimer, 'Individual Experience and Perception of the Thirty Years War in Eyewitness Personal Accounts', *German History*, 20 (2002), 141–60.

24 Hale, *War and Society in Renaissance Europe*, Chapter 6. Charles Carlton, *Going to the Wars: The Experience of the English Civil Wars, 1638–1651* (London: Routledge, 1992). Ian Gentles, *The New Model Army in England, Ireland and Scotland, 1645–1653* (Oxford: Blackwell, 1992). Lorraine White, 'The Experience of Spain's Early Modern Soldiers: Combat, Welfare and Violence', *War in History*, 9.1 (2002), 1–38.

25 http://www.medievalsoldier.org (accessed 30 January 2016). Adrian R. Bell, Anne Curry, Andy King and David Simpkin, *The Soldier in Later Medieval England* (Oxford: Oxford University Press, 2013), pp. xi–xii.

26 *Muster Books for North and East Hertfordshire 1580–1605*, ed. A. J. King, Hertfordshire Record Publications, 12 (Hitchin: Hertfordshire Record Society, 1996). *The Montagu Musters Book, 1602–1623*, ed. Joan Wake, Publications of the Northamptonshire Record Society, 7 (Peterborough: Northamptonshire Record Society, 1935).

27 Tryntje Helfferich (ed.), 'A Soldier's Life in the Thirty Years War', in *The Thirty Years War: A Documentary History* (Indianapolis: Hackett, 2009), pp. 276–302.

28 Alastair J. MacDonald, 'Courage, Fear and the Experience of the Later Medieval Scottish Soldier', *Scottish Historical Review*, 92.2 (October 2013), 179–206.

29 On war and noble culture, see especially Roger B. Manning, *Swordsmen: The Martial Ethos in the Three Kingdoms* (Oxford: Oxford University Press, 2003); Gunn, Grummitt and Cools, *War, State, and Society*, Chapters 9–15.

30 *The Works of Sir Roger Williams*, ed. John X. Evans (Oxford: Clarendon Press, 1972); *The Memoirs of Robert Carey*, ed. F. H. Mares (Oxford: Clarendon Press, 1972); Ian Roy (ed.), *Blaise de Monluc: The Habsburg–Valois Wars and the French Wars of Religion* (London: Longman, 1971); Robert Monro, *Monro His Expedition with the Worthy Scots Regiment (Called Mac-Keyes Regiment)* (London, 1637). For other examples, see Manning, *Swordsmen*, pp. 35–7, and finding aids in Chapter 6 of this volume.

31 Lisa Ferraro Parmelee, *Good Newes from Fraunce: French Anti-League Propaganda in Late Elizabethan England* (Rochester, NY and Woodbridge: University of Rochester Press, 1996); Derek Randall, *Credibility in Elizabethan and Early Stuart Military News* (London: Pickering and Chatto, 2008); Jayne E. E. Boys, *London's News Press and the Thirty Years War* (Woodbridge: Boydell, 2011).

32 David R. Lawrence, *The Complete Soldier: Military Books and Military Culture in Early Stuart England, 1603–1645* (Leiden: Brill, 2009).

33 Mark Stoyle, *The Black Legend of Prince Rupert's Dog: Witchcraft and Propaganda during the English Civil War* (Exeter: University of Exeter Press, 2011).

34 Barbara Donagan, *War in England 1642–1649* (Oxford: Oxford University Press, 2008).

35 Michael Roberts, 'The Military Revolution 1560–1660: An Inaugural Lecture Delivered before the Queen's University of Belfast', repr. in Michael Roberts, *Essays in Swedish History* (London: Weidenfeld and Nicholson, 1967), pp. 195–225; Geoffrey Parker, 'The Military Revolution, 1560–1660: A Myth?', *Journal of Modern History*, 48 (1976), 195–214; Geoffrey Parker, *The Military Revolution: Military Innovation and the Rise of the West, 1500–1800* (Cambridge: Cambridge University Press, 1988).

36 Geoffrey Parker, *Empire, War and Faith in Early Modern Europe* (London: Allen Lane, 2002), pp. 126–7.

37 Geoffrey Parker, *The Grand Strategy of Philip II* (New Haven and London: Yale University Press, 1998), pp. 397–402.

38 Richard Winship Stewart, *The English Ordnance Office 1558–1625: A Case Study in Bureaucracy* (Woodbridge: Royal Historical Society and Boydell, 1996).

39 N. A. M. Rodger, *The Safeguard of the Sea: A Naval History of Britain, 660–1649* (London: HarperCollins in association with the National Maritime Museum, 1997); David Loades, *The Making of the Elizabethan Navy 1540–1590: From the Solent to the Armada* (Woodbridge: Boydell, 2009).

40 Gentles, *The New Model Army in England*; Reece, *The Army in Cromwellian England*. For studies of earlier English armies, see C. G. Cruickshank, *Elizabeth's Army* (London: Oxford at the Clarendon Press, 1966).

41 Thomas Cogswell, *Home Divisions: Aristocracy, the State and Provincial Conflict* (Manchester: Manchester University Press, 1998); Neil Younger, *War and Politics in the Elizabethan Counties* (Manchester: Manchester University Press, 2012).

254   *Neil Younger*

42 David Parrott, *The Business of War: Military Enterprise and Military Revolution in Early Modern Europe* (Cambridge: Cambridge University Press, 2012); David Potter, 'The International Mercenary Market in the Sixteenth Century: Anglo-French Competition in Germany, 1543–50', *English Historical Review*, 111 (1996), 24–58.
43 John Brewer, *The Sinews of Power: War, Money and the English State, 1688–1783* (London: Routledge, 1989); James Scott Wheeler, *The Making of a World Power: War and the Military Revolution in Seventeenth Century England* (Stroud: Sutton, 1999). M. J. Braddick, *Parliamentary Taxation in 17th-Century England: Local Administration and Response* (Woodbridge: Boydell, 1994); M. J. Braddick, *The Nerves of State: Taxation and the Financing of the English State, 1558–1714* (Manchester: Manchester University Press, 1996).
44 Wheeler, *Making of a World Power*; Michael J. Braddick, *State Formation in Early Modern England c. 1550–1700* (Cambridge: Cambridge University Press, 2000); Glete, *War and the State in Early Modern Europe*.
45 Conrad Russell, 'Monarchies, Wars and Estates in England, France and Spain, c. 1580–c. 1640', in Conrad Russell, *Unrevolutionary England, 1603–1642* (London: Hambledon Press, 1990), pp. 121–36 (p. 128).
46 *Letters and Papers, Foreign and Domestic, of the Reign of Henry VIII III pt I (1519–21)*, 13 February 1521, p. 437. This example found its way into the State Papers because it was deemed 'treasonous words'.
47 Simon Healy, 'Oh, What a Lovely War? War, Taxation and Public Opinion in England, 1624–29', *Canadian Journal of History*, 38 (December 2003), 439–65.
48 Jeremy Black, *A Military Revolution? Military Change and European Society 1550–1800* (Basingstoke: Macmillan Education, 1991); C. J. Rogers (ed.), *The Military Revolution Debate* (Boulder, CO and Oxford: Westview, 1995); Geoff Mortimer, 'Was There a "Military Revolution" in the Early Modern Period?', in Geoff Mortimer (ed.), *Early Modern Military History, 1450–1815* (Basingstoke: Palgrave Macmillan, 2004); Parrott, *Business of War*.
49 Parrott, *Business of War*, pp. 15–16.
50 Braddick, *State Formation in Early Modern England*; Steven Gunn, David Grummitt and Hans Cools, 'War and the State in Early Modern Europe: Widening the Debate', *War in History*, 15 (2008), 371–88.

14 Early modern science

Helen Cowie

The history of science used to be a story of progress and discovery, centred on the achievements of so-called 'great men'. Drawing predominantly on scientific treatises and other published primary sources, historians explored the genesis of key concepts and ideas to present a 'Whiggish'[1] narrative of scientific progress culminating in the 'Scientific Revolution'[2] of the late seventeenth century. Studies of natural philosophy focused on pivotal individuals such as Robert Boyle (1627–91) and Isaac Newton (1642–1727). Histories of medicine adopted a similar approach, concentrating on 'biographies, bibliographies, medical theory and the practice of physicians'.[3] Natural history, more about incremental change and cumulative knowledge than sudden conceptual breakthroughs, was largely ignored.

In the last few decades, this somewhat narrow perspective has been considerably broadened and important aspects of it challenged. On the one hand, medievalists have questioned the chronology of scientific progress, locating antecedents to many early modern 'discoveries' in earlier centuries.[4] On the other, the emphasis on individual men of science has been superseded by a growing interest in the 'invisible technicians' who facilitated their work, including servants, women and non-European people.[5] Historians are now increasingly interested in the collective and collaborative dimensions of science, and in the ways in which space and place have shaped the formation, credibility and reception of particular ideas. Making use of an extensive range of sources, from letters to museum catalogues, laboratory notes to popular natural histories, new research is illuminating the networks of exchange and expertise that underpinned scientific work and the cultural and social dynamics that shaped it. In what follows, I consider how science was defined in the early modern period, who studied it, the social and cultural contexts in which scientific knowledge was produced, and the media that facilitated its circulation and transmission.

What was early modern science?

Defining 'science' in the early modern period is difficult. The terms 'science' and 'scientist' did not exist before 1800, at least not in their current form.

It is consequently hard, and to some extent anachronistic, to determine where 'science' ended and 'magic' began; both were closely interconnected and few contemporaries drew a sharp distinction between the two. The early modern period predates the emergence of specialized scientific disciplines like entomology, botany, pharmacy or ornithology, which did not come into existence until the nineteenth century. Many scholars were polymaths, working simultaneously in fields that we would now regard as distinct. Nor was there a hard-and-fast dividing line between 'science' and 'superstition', 'professionals' and 'amateurs'; natural philosophers like Isaac Newton studied the natural world to get a better understanding of God, while a patient might consult by turns the physician, the wise woman and the priest with equal hope of a cure for his or her ailments.[6] In indicating the different branches of early modern science, we therefore need to be aware of their imprecision and permeability, and to recognize that some of our modern concepts and categories are potentially misleading and artificial.

These important caveats noted, early modern science may be divided, broadly, into two main categories: natural philosophy and natural history. Natural philosophy was concerned with laying out the principles and causes of natural phenomena. In the medieval period, natural philosophy was taught in universities and focused predominantly on deductive reasoning, based on the writings of Aristotle (384–322 bce). In the early modern period, universities remained quite conservative, but a new science founded on experiment and observation started to evolve in other sites (see 'Places', below). This new experimental approach challenged the teachings of Aristotle and, by the late seventeenth century, gave rise to a new way of doing science. In Italy, for example, Galileo Galilei (1564–1642) used the telescope to observe sun spots, contradicting Aristotle's idea that the superlunary world was immutable.[7] In Prague, Johannes Kepler (1571–1630) established the mathematical relationship between the distances of the planets from the sun and the time they take to complete their orbits.[8] In Britain Robert Hooke (1635–1703) and Robert Boyle used the air pump to prove the existence of a vacuum, while Isaac Newton devised his famous laws of motion.[9] Together, these developments transformed how the world was viewed and understood, giving rise to a 'Scientific Revolution'. They did not, however, constitute a complete break with the past, for older ways of understanding the cosmos still persisted. Kepler, for instance, practised both astronomy and astrology at the court of the Holy Roman Emperor Rudolf II (1552–1612); both were seen as equally legitimate ways of viewing and interpreting the stars.

While natural philosophy was about explaining nature, natural history was about collecting and describing it. As a form of study, natural history underwent important shifts in emphasis in the sixteenth century, thanks primarily to three key developments: the rediscovery of texts by classical writers such as Pliny (22–78 ce), Aristotle and Galen (*c*. 210–*c*. 130 ce); the discovery of the New World; and a growing desire to better understand the medicinal properties of plants. The reprinting of classical texts led to the realization that these contained factual errors, due in some cases to poor translation and copying, and in others to incorrect original observations. The discovery of the East and West Indies accentuated this concern by bringing European scholars into contact with plants and animals unknown to the Ancients. The desire to discover the curative properties of plants led to the creation in universities of chairs in botany, and botanical (or physic) gardens within their grounds (for example Pisa in 1544). In the seventeenth century, the study of natural history was further transformed by a shift towards more experimental techniques, including dissection and the analysis of plants and animals under the microscope. Though traditionally accorded less attention than natural philosophy, natural history has, since the 1990s, emerged as an important area of study, and has been seen as crucial in promoting a new sensory approach to science based on experience and collaboration. It contributed to a wider programme of study focused on observing, understanding and controlling nature.

Contexts

The history of science did not operate in a vacuum, but was intimately connected to broader social structures and processes. Historians are increasingly concerned with situating scientific developments within their broader social and political context, and thinking about the reciprocal influences of society on science and science on society. They have pointed, in particular, to some of the key social changes that facilitated advances in the fields of natural history and natural philosophy or determined the parameters within which they operated. Foremost among these were the invention of the printing press, war and the discovery of the New World.

Invented by Johannes Gutenberg in the fifteenth century, the printing press had a major impact on the practice and communication of science and medicine. Before the advent of moveable print it had been necessary to copy all manuscripts out by hand, which limited the availability of books and increased their price. With the arrival of the printing press, this laborious process was rendered unnecessary. Texts could now be reproduced quickly and in much larger quantities, and their contents standardized to a greater degree. The reproduction of illustrations also became possible, allowing botanical, anatomical and zoological images to circulate much more widely. Andreas Vesalius' (1514–64) detailed anatomical images in *De humani corporis fabrica* (1543) greatly added to the value of the work (Figure 14.1), while Conrad Gessner's (1516–65) *Historia animalium* (1563) contained 1,200 woodcuts of animals (Figure 14.2).[10] Albrecht Dürer's (1471–1528) famous engraving of a rhinoceros (Figure 14.3) sold a staggering 4,500 copies during the artist's lifetime, influencing almost all subsequent representations of the animal until the eighteenth century.[11] Historians have emphasized the close connections between the history of science and the history of the book and pointed to the vital role of printing in accelerating the dissemination of ideas.[12]

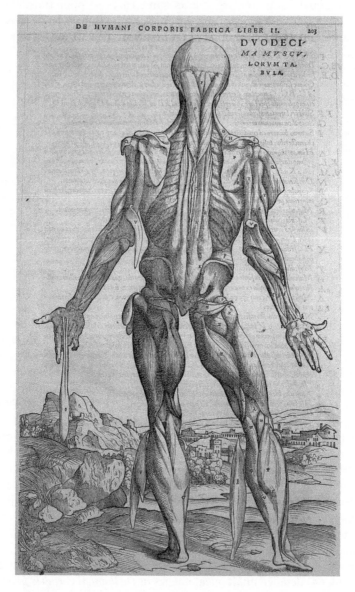

Figure 14.1 Andreas Vesalius, *De humani corporis fabrica* (Basel: Oporinus, 1543), Vol. I, p. 203.

War was another important accelerant of science in the early modern period, catalysing advances in a number of fields. The need for better weapons led to improvements in gunpowder, which demanded some knowledge of chemistry. The need for stronger defences to withstand these new armaments

Figure 14.2 'Marmot' from Conrad Gessner, *Historia animalium liber II* (Frankfurt: A Cambierus, 1602–4), p. 744.

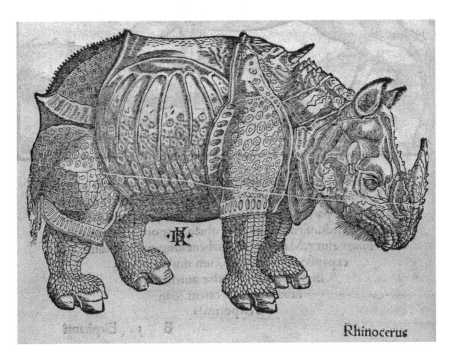

Rhinocerus

Figure 14.3 Conradus Lycosthenes, *Prodigiorum ac ostentorum Chronicon* (Basle: H. Petri, 1557), p. 18.

created employment for engineers, such as Louis XIV's (1638–1715) famous fortification designer Sébastien Le Prestre de Vauban (1633–1707). The wounds suffered during battles, meanwhile, provided the impetus for advances in surgery, exemplified by the innovations of French surgeon Ambroise Paré (1510–90). War thus furnished fertile conditions for the testing of new discoveries and provided the motivation for scholars to study (and monarchs to fund) various branches of science.[13]

Finally, the discovery of the Americas in 1492 revolutionized contemporary understandings of the world, challenging many longstanding assumptions. Conquistadors, missionaries and colonial officials in the New World were confronted with a whole host of plants, animals and natural phenomena without referents in the Bible or the writings of Greek and Roman authors. As Antonio Barrera-Osorio observes, 'there were no avocados in Pliny's pages'.[14] Unable to draw on classical precedents, travellers to the Indies and scholars back in Europe were forced to rely on their own senses and experience to describe and classify the natural world, initiating a new approach to the collection of information based on direct observation and empirical research. Discussing the medicinal properties of bezoar stones extracted from the stomachs of Peruvian vicuñas (wild alpacas), for instance, the Seville physician Nicolás Monardes (1493–1588) insisted that he would 'only put down that which I have experienced and the effects that I have understood [the stones] to have, and those that have passed through my hands, so that [my observations] may be given complete credit'.[15] This was a new departure in the history of science, and has been seen as marking the beginning of the 'Scientific Revolution'.[16]

People

The history of science once focused primarily on the contributions of so-called 'great men'. Now, however, this narrative of progress and individual genius has been replaced by a more complex approach that foregrounds the social and cultural practices of science. Instead of looking solely at the careers of major scientific thinkers, this new approach concentrates on the social interactions that facilitated their work and the 'invisible technicians' who assisted them in their experiments. It significantly broadens the definition of who may be considered a 'scientist' (a term itself not coined until the 1830s), putting much greater emphasis on the processes and social interactions of natural historians and natural philosophers. The notion that major scientific breakthroughs were predominantly the work of 'great men' sitting in their studies or laboratories no longer satisfies historians, who now seek to position such achievements within their wider social context. What qualifies as 'science' and who qualifies as a 'scientist' have undergone significant expansion, with corresponding implications for the sources historians consult and how they read them.

Studying the social dimensions of science means asking new questions and looking at old sources in new ways. First, instead of viewing science as a solitary pursuit, historians have increasingly emphasized its collaborative nature. Scholars did not collect natural history specimens or conduct experiments on their own, but usually relied on the assistance of numerous skilled and unskilled helpers. These individuals were central to the process of scientific discovery, but are often hard to identify, owing to their frequent omission from published accounts. Increasingly sensitive to their presence, historians have started to look more closely at sources such as unpublished laboratory notes to find out who these individuals were and what they did. Steven Shapin, for instance, has studied the private papers of natural philosopher Robert Boyle to demonstrate the repeated involvement of domestic servants and paid 'operators' or technicians in his famous experiments with the air pump.[17] Other historians have used travel accounts or institutional records to highlight the vital role played by African slaves and indigenous peoples in collecting natural history specimens, or the contribution of often unnamed manual labourers in transporting, preparing or stuffing them.[18] Close reading of these sources reveals that multiple individuals contributed to the study of the natural world through their physical labour, local knowledge or manual dexterity. An account book for the Royal Cabinet of Natural History in Madrid includes a payment for a range of unnamed assistants, among them a 'porter' who lugged the corpse of a dead lion from the menagerie at the Buen Retiro Palace to the museum.[19] The preface to Francis Willoughby's *Ornithology*, meanwhile, records the contribution of 'one Leonard Baltuer, a Fisherman of Strasburgh [*sic*]', who sold the naturalist 'a Volume containing the Pictures of all the Water-fowl frequenting the Rhine near that city … drawn with great curiosity and exactness by an excellent hand'.[20]

Women are another social group receiving increased attention from historians of science. Since they were almost always excluded from scientific academies, and prevented from engaging in overseas travel, women rarely wrote scientific treatises, and, as a consequence, have often been omitted from the history of science and medicine. There are a few notable exceptions to this rule, most famously the Prussian Maria Sibylla Merian (1647–1717), who visited Surinam in the early eighteenth century to study its insects, and published *Metamorphosis insectorum Surinamensium* in 1705, a beautifully illustrated work showing the lifecycle of American spiders, butterflies and other small creatures.[21] While many other women contributed to science, however, perhaps assisting with astronomical observations or producing botanical illustrations, their work is often not explicitly acknowledged in the published writings of their husbands or other male relatives, and their input has duly tended to go unnoticed. To gain an insight into female contributions to science, thus we need to look beyond published sources and analyse more personal writings such as private correspondence or self-help books. In the field of medicine, where women frequently played a crucial role in overseeing the health of their families, the analysis of surviving manuscript sources can tell us a lot about female expertise. Elaine Leong and Sara Pennell have used sources like letters, diaries and manuscript recipe books to understand domestic treatments for illness and to highlight the role of women in their compilation.[22] Women also occasionally authored midwifery manuals, such as Jane Sharp's *The Midwives' Book, of the Whole Art of Midwifery* (1671), though the majority of these texts were written by men.[23]

In thinking about the social dynamics of science in the early modern period, historians are interested not only in unearthing new contributors to science, but in showing how contemporary social structures and attitudes influenced the study of the natural world. Two issues are especially important here: patronage and credibility. Patronage was important because it provided the financial backing necessary to support aspiring men of science. In early modern Europe, royal courts and noble families offered the most reliable source of funding, often employing scholars and artists to add a cultural gloss to their rule. Rudolf II, for instance, patronized many scientists at his court in Prague, among them the astronomers Tycho Brahe (1546–1601) and Johannes Kepler. Galileo Galilei enjoyed the patronage of Cosimo II de Medici (1590–1621) in Florence. Working at the royal court often gave men of science more freedom to pursue their own research agendas than they would have had in contemporary universities, paving the way for many important discoveries. Evidence of the importance of such patronage may be found in the frontispieces of contemporary scientific treatises, which were often dedicated to the courtly patrons who had bankrolled their collections or experiments. Kepler, for instance, named his 1627 star catalogue and planetary tables *Tabulae Rudolphinae* in honour of his former patron, Rudolf II.[24]

Credibility was a more complex issue, but one that tells us a lot about the relationship between science and broader social structures. Science has sometimes been seen as operating at a remove from the politics of class and social status, impelled by an unmediated search for the truth. In reality, however, historians have shown that the mechanisms for establishing scientific authority are intimately connected to the social environment in which they emerge, and rest on existing notions of who and what can be trusted. For the early modern period, Steven Shapin has emphasized the social dimensions of truth-telling, noting how 'gentlemen' were generally held in higher esteem as witnesses on account of their independence and presumed immunity to interested bias. Shapin argues that this association between gentlemen and veracity was extended to scientific pursuits, and explains why the testimony of men of independent means, such as Robert Boyle, was given greater credence than that of women or servants.[25] Charles Perrault (1628–1703), anatomist in the Parisian Académie des Sciences (founded 1666), stated in the preface to his *Mémoires pour servir à l'histoire naturelle des animaux* that his writings could contain 'only Matters of Fact that have been verified by a whole Society, composed on Men who have Eyes to see these sorts of things', highlighting the corporate nature of science and the need, not only for direct observation, but for the sensory testimony of multiple trustworthy persons.[26] These important social dimensions all determined the form and nature of scientific 'discoveries' and were shaped themselves by longstanding (and evolving) conceptions of honour, expertise and trustworthiness. To gain an understanding of how science was done, we therefore need to analyse the language and stated methodology of practitioners – often outlined in the prefaces of their work – alongside their published findings and results. The physician Edward Tyson (1651–1708), for instance, introducing his treatise on the dissection of an orang-utan, explicitly justified the amount of space devoted to its anatomy on the grounds that this was necessary for a proper understanding of the animal:

> [T]he *Orang-Outang* (whose Anatomy I here give) being a Creature so very remarkable and rare; and not only in its External Shape, but much more in the Conformation of a great many of the inward *Viscera*, so much resembles a man, I thought I could not be too particular in my Description of it, though to some, who have not a Tast of these Matters, I may seem prolix and tedious.[27]

Places

As well as exploring the social dimensions of science, historians are also interested in the places and spaces where 'science' was done. Once, this interest would have been confined to the laboratory, the museum and the botanical garden. Now, however, it is recognized that scientific knowledge developed in a much wider range of locales, from the market, where a natural historian might purchase animals or plants from merchants, to the home, where housewives might create their own remedies for everyday illnesses.[28] Taking account of these new spaces for science, historians have broadened their area of study while paying increased attention to the social interactions and spatial configurations of more traditional scientific spaces such as the museum. Much greater emphasis is also placed on the wide geographical dimensions of science, and the networks that enabled the collection of specimens and information from the far corners of the globe.

The early modern period witnessed the emergence of several important new venues for the study of science. Most notable among these were the botanical garden, the anatomy theatre and the cabinet of curiosity. Botanical gardens came into existence in the period 1530–1600 and served both for medical research and for pleasure. Anatomy theatres emerged in the same period at universities such as Bologna, Padua and Montpellier, forming permanent sites for the dissection of cadavers. Cabinets of curiosity appeared in the years after 1500, collating both natural and man-made objects. In the sixteenth century, cabinets were mainly the preserve of private individuals, such as Ulisse Aldrovandi (1522–1605) in Bologna, Ferrante Imperato (1525–1615) in Naples or Olaus Worm (1588–1655) in Copenhagen. By the late seventeenth century, however, they were often owned by academies, who placed less emphasis on the singularity and wonder of nature, and more on order and classification.[29] Astronomical observatories, chemical laboratories and royal menageries also grew in size and number in the early modern period, providing further opportunities for studying the natural world. Surviving catalogues give us insight into the objects housed in cabinets of curiosity, while contemporary plans and engravings can illuminate the form and layout of gardens, anatomy theatres and museums. Pedro Franco Dávila's 1767 catalogue of his cabinet in Paris, for instance, lists all of the items in the collection, including a rhinoceros horn, a nine-banded armadillo from Cayenne and a monstrous pig with a single eye in the centre of its forehead.[30] A woodcut of Ferrante Imperato's celebrated cabinet in Naples (Figure 14.4) shows visitors being guided around the museum by its owner, giving us a sense of how the wonders of the natural world were displayed to a sixteenth-century audience.

Alongside these more traditional venues, science was also debated, commoditized and communicated in less formal sites. From the mid seventeenth century, coffee shops provided an important venue for exchanging and discussing scientific information. Quacks touted new medicines in the streets and itinerant showmen exhibited all manner of exotic animals. Such activities are somewhat elusive to the historian, owing to their ephemeral nature, but we can sometimes gain a sense of their content and intended audience from surviving handbills and newspaper advertisements. An advertisement in

Figure 14.4 Woodcut of the Wunderkammer room, from Ferrante Imperato, *Dell'historia natural* (Naples: C. Vitale, 1599).

the *London Evening Post* in 1739, for instance, informed 'the Curious among the Nobility and Gentry' that 'there is just arriv'd from Bengall [*sic*] in the East-Indies, alive and in good health, that strange and wonderful Creature, call'd A RHINOCEROS ... to be seen at Half a Crown each Person in Eagle-Street, Near Red-Lyon Square'.[31] A handbill from 1799 announced that the Parmesan showman Andres Raggi would exhibit a 'noble and handsome' Egyptian dromedary on the patio of a house in the Calle del Caballero de Gracia, in Madrid. Another handbill, also from Madrid, invited spectators to come and look through a microscope belonging to the French physicist François Bienvenu, under which 'the maggots that live in vinegar seem like eels'.[32] Calculated to draw crowds to their respective exhibitions, advertisements like these illuminate the commercial nature of science and underline its close association with existing sites of sociability.

Finally, it is important to remember that much scientific work took place in the home, where it required the assistance of family and servants. In more prosperous households, the study could be a place for experimentation, dissection and contemplation, while in residences lower down the social hierarchy the kitchen could be somewhere to experiment with herbs. Cabinets of curiosity were often situated within domestic spaces, blurring the boundary between public and private, while some aspiring scholars even housed more specialized equipment in their own residences; Robert Boyle had a laboratory in his house in London and Danish astronomer Tycho Brahe built an observatory at his palace in Uraniborg. These examples illustrate the complex spatial dynamics of early modern science, which, as noted earlier, were closely bound up with the social and political structures of contemporary society.[33]

Networks, circulation and reception

Historians are interested not only in the different types of spaces where science was studied, but also in the connections between these spaces. How did men of science communicate with one another? How did they obtain information about distant natural phenomena? How did they disseminate their findings, both within the scientific community and beyond? What changes did scientific knowledge undergo as it moved across space and between cultures? To answer these important questions, historians examine the correspondence networks upon which men of science relied, and the writings they produced.

First, historians are very interested in the personal correspondence networks that existed within the scientific community. The exchange of astronomical observations, books and natural history specimens was a critical part of a scholar's life. Established naturalists like Aldrovandi relied on trusted friends and associates to send them seeds, mineralogical specimens or astronomical observations from distant lands. Aspiring students of nature used letters and gifts as a way of securing their place within the scholarly community. Analysis of surviving letters can help us to reconstruct these networks of exchange and reveal the personal relationships that existed between men of science. Paula Findlen, for example, has studied correspondence networks in sixteenth-century Italy, where 'epistolary transactions were carefully crafted attempts to establish and maintain friends and patrons, obtain news, disseminate opinion and, in the case of collectors, acquire new and wonderful things'.[34] Susan Scott Parrish has examined transatlantic correspondence networks in the seventeenth century, highlighting how British colonists in North America used their familiarity with local nature to parlay their way into scientific circles in Britain.[35] By reading the private correspondence of men (and occasionally women) of science in this way, we can learn a lot about how knowledge was transmitted and uncover the unwritten rules of etiquette that governed membership of the Republic of Letters.[36]

Alongside these more informal exchanges of information, scientific knowledge was also gathered on a more formal basis by a number of corporate bodies. Government bureaucracies, religious orders (especially the Jesuits) and trading companies like the Dutch East India Company (VOC) all solicited observations and specimens from distant lands, taking advantage of existing bureaucratic and commercial networks to obtain information. From the late seventeenth century, scientific academies and institutions like the Royal Society in London and the Parisian Académie des Sciences played a similar role, requesting detailed information from correspondents across the globe. State involvement in science also grew in the eighteenth century, as governments became interested in the possibilities of controlling or appropriating valuable natural resources such as coffee or cinchona bark.[37] Given their bureaucratic origin, State, institutional and company records offer the best insight into these networks of exchange. Historians of science have used these archival sources to assess how corporate science operated in practice, examining both formal orders and instructions issued by governments or institutions, and the letters and correspondence of agents overseas. The Royal Society, for instance, circulated a list of questions to put to travellers, such as merchants and sailors, and compiled written instructions to guide their observations.[38] A series of documents housed in Spain's Museo Nacional de Ciencias Naturales and Archivo de Indias, meanwhile, record the remission of multiple botanical and zoological specimens to museums, menageries and gardens in Madrid, from 'a bat of extraordinary size' caught by the Governor of Santa Marta (New Granada) in his own house to a 'tiger cub' (probably a jaguar) dispatched from Caracas by the Governor of Maracaíbo (Venezuela).[39] These kinds of documents can help us to understand how 'scientific' knowledge was collected and how relations of trust were established. They elucidate the measures taken to ensure that distant correspondents conformed to desired modes of practice, and the difficulties and practicalities of conveying specimens and information across the globe.

If private correspondence and official documentation reveal the internal workings of the scientific community, published works constitute its public face. Scientific treatises like Isaac Newton's *Principia mathematica naturalis philosophiae* (1687), anatomical works like Andreas Vesalius' *De humani corporis fabrica*, and natural histories like George Marcgraff's and Willem Piso's *Historia naturalis Brasileae* (1648) or George Louis Leclerc comte de Buffon's (1707–88) thirty-six-volume *Histoire naturelle* (1749–88) presented the polished discoveries and observations of natural philosophers to contemporary readers and provided other men of science with foundations on which to build.[40] From the mid seventeenth century, scientific findings also started to be published in the journals of academies and societies, perhaps most notably the Royal Society's *Philosophical Transactions*, which began publication in 1665.[41] Reading published works like these, historians can gain an insight into the evolution of theories and ideas and trace shifting approaches and understandings. Book historians, moreover, are interested in assessing the circulation of works of science, looking, for example, at print runs, sales figures, marginalia (handwritten annotations made by readers) and the presence of scientific texts in contemporary libraries. They are also concerned specifically with the issue of reception: how were books read, and by whom?[42]

A second type of publication complementing the more formal and erudite scientific treatise was the popular natural history. Intended for a non-specialist readership, works of popular science became increasingly fashionable in the eighteenth century and catered for a growing interest in the sciences among the elite and emerging middle classes. Sold at affordable prices and sometimes accompanied by eye-catching illustrations, popular works of science simplified complex concepts for a broader audience and often presented them in the form a dialogue in which imaginary characters discussed the latest scientific ideas. Noel-Antoine de Pluche's (1688–1761) best-selling *Spectacle de la nature* (1732), for instance, structured lessons about nature around a series of conversations between 'a youth of quality and honour' called the Chevalier de Brevil and a local priest with a flair for natural history.[43] Bernard de Fontenelle's (1657–1757) *Conversations on the Plurality of Worlds* (1686) consisted of a series of conversations between a philosopher and a marquise in which the former attempted to explain Nicolas Copernicus' (1473–1543) heliocentric model of the universe to the latter.[44] Looking at works like this, we can gain some idea of how scientific knowledge was communicated to non-experts and trace the rise in popularity of the natural sciences, which had become common topics for books and lectures by the mid eighteenth century. We can also see how science was made to fit with contemporary religious precepts, and, where these works were translated into other languages or reprinted over an extended period, how they were adapted to different social or cultural contexts. Translating Buffon's popular *Histoire naturelle* into Spanish in 1785, for example, the Spaniard Jose Clavijo y Fajardo (1726–1806) omitted those passages in which the French naturalist challenged Catholic orthodoxy – notably his argument that the world was more than 6,000 years old – deeming these unsuitable for a Castilian readership. Clavijo likened his work as translator poetically to that of the bees, 'who collect from the stamen and the stigma of the flowers, the honey and the wax, and leave the rest'.[45]

As this last example indicates, the written word sometimes underwent significant transformations in its journey from the pen to the printed page, raising questions about authorship and intellectual property. Historians are consequently interested, not only in how scientific ideas were formed, but in the processes by which they reached their intended audience and the changes they may have undergone along the way. Take, for example, Francisco Hernández's (1514–87) manuscript work on the natural history of Mexican plants and animals. Sent to New Spain (Mexico) in 1570 on the orders of Philip II, the Spanish physician Hernández was charged with studying the medicinal properties of American plants, and, in 1576, shipped sixteen folio volumes of notes back to Spain in 1767, including illustrations of 1,200 plants by native artists.[46] Hernández hoped that the manuscript would be published. For various reasons, however, this did not happen during his lifetime, and in 1671 the naturalist's original notes were destroyed by a fire at the Escorial Palace. A version of the manuscript was published posthumously in Rome in 1651 by the Academia dei Lincei, based on an abridgement of the manuscript made several decades earlier by Nardo Antonio Recchi, but this focused almost entirely on the pharmaceutical applications of Hernández's work and omitted much of his original material. Over a century later, the Spanish Government attempted to recover Hernandez's original manuscript, re-publishing a newly discovered copy in 1790 and dispatching naturalists to New Spain to 'collect, describe, draw and illuminate all the natural productions of that Kingdom, especially those noted by Hernández'.[47] Charting the tortuous publishing history of Hernández's work, Silvia de Renzi notes the collaborative nature of the finished article, which drew on the input of multiple individuals and differed significantly from its manuscript form.[48] Other scientific works underwent similar additions and redactions, complicating the notion of the sole-authored scholarly text.

Conclusion

As Peter Dear has noted, 'the central goal of the history of science is to understand why particular people in the past believed the things they did about the world and pursued inquiries in the way they did'.[49] Historians are interested in how scientific ideas were formulated, how they were disseminated and how they were received. They study the different people who practised science and medicine; the places in which they worked; and the social networks through which ideas, books and specimens circulated. They seek to situate science within its wider social context, exploring both the impact of society on science, and the impact of science on society.

Reflecting these broad goals, the sources for the history of science and medicine are wide-ranging. Published sources such as scientific treatises, natural histories and pharmacopeia can give us an insight into the circulation and evolution of new ideas. Personal documents like letters, diaries and laboratory notes illuminate the practice of science and the social interactions that shaped it. Visual sources, such as botanical illustrations and anatomical drawings, complement written records and demonstrate the crucial role of images in early modern science. Surviving collections of surgical or scientific instruments and specimens – from astrolabes to forceps, fossils to stuffed animals – offer the opportunity to study the material culture of early modern science, and to gain a more intimate understanding of the cabinet of curiosity or the anatomy theatre. In a history of science that now encompasses servants as well as philosophers, readers as well as authors and patients as well as physicians, we need to draw on a broad cross-section of these sources to learn how early modern people interpreted the natural world and how they attempted to use and control it.

Key resources

Boyle Papers Online, http://www.bbk.ac.uk/boyle/boyle_papers/boylepapers_index.htm.
Epact, http://www.mhs.ox.ac.uk/epact. Database of early modern scientific instruments.
Hernández, Francisco and Simon Varey, *The Mexican Treasury: The Writings of Dr Francisco Hernández* (Stanford: Stanford University Press, 2000).
The Linnaean Correspondence Collection, http://linnean-online.org/correspondence.html.
The Linnaean Manuscripts Online: Sixteen Manuscripts that Re-Wrote Nature, http://linnean-online.org/linnaean_mss.html.
Marcgraff, George and Willem Piso, *Historia naturalis Brasileae* (Amsterdam: Franciscus Hackius, 1648), availabe at http://www.illustratedgarden.org/mobot/rarebooks/page.asp?relation=QH117P571648&identifier=0003.
Orta, Garcia da, *Colóquios dos simples e drogas da Índia* (Goa, 1563); Portuguese version available at http://www.bdalentejo.net/bdaobra/bdadigital/Obra.aspx?ID=295; English translation available at https://archive.org/details/colloquiesonsimp00orta.
The Royal Society Picture Library, https://pictures.royalsociety.org/home.
Sharp, Jane, *The Midwives' Book, of the Whole Art of Midwifery*, ed. Elaine Hobby (Oxford: Oxford University Press, 1999).
Topsell, Edward, *The History of Four-Footed Beasts and Serpents* (London: E. Cotes, 1658), available at https://archive.org/details/historyoffourfoo00tops.
Vesalius, Andreas, *De humani corporis fabrica* (1543); original Latin version (illustrated) available at http://archive.nlm.nih.gov/proj/ttp/flash/vesalius/vesalius.html; English translation available at http://vesalius.northwestern.edu.
Wellcome Images, http://wellcomeimages.org. See, in particular, sixteenth- and seventeenth-century engravings of anatomy theatres, botanical gardens and cabinets of curiosity, as well as contemporary botanical and zoological illustrations.

Notes

1 A 'Whiggish' approach to history is characterized by a belief that human progress is inevitable. It judges the past in light of the present.
2 There is an extensive literature on the Scientific Revolution, its origins, nature and extent. See, for example, Steven Shapin, *The Scientific Revolution* (Chicago: University of Chicago Press, 1996); John Henry, *The Scientific Revolution and the Origins of Modern Science* (Basingstoke: Palgrave Macmillan, 2002); and Peter Dear, *Revolutionizing the Sciences: Knowledge and Its Ambitions, 1500–1700* (Basingstoke: Palgrave Macmillan, 2009).

3 Mary Lindemann, *Medicine and Society in Early Modern Europe* (Cambridge: Cambridge University Press, 2010), p. 4.

4 See, for example, Edward Grant, *The Foundations of Modern Science in the Middle Ages: Their Religious Institutional and Intellectual Contexts* (Cambridge: Cambridge University Press, 1996); and Howard Turner, *Science in Medieval Islam: An Illustrated Introduction* (Austin: University of Texas Press, 1995).

5 On servants, see 'Invisible Technicians', in Steven Shapin, *A Social History of Truth: Civility and Science in Seventeenth-Century England* (Chicago: University of Chicago Press, 1994), pp. 355–408; on women, see Kathleen Perry Long (ed.), *Gender and Scientific Discourse in Early Modern Europe* (Farnham: Ashgate, 2010); on non-Europeans, see Kapil Raj, *Relocating Modern Science: Circulation and the Construction of Knowledge in South Asia and Europe, 1650–1900* (Basingstoke: Palgrave Macmillan, 2007).

6 David Gentilcore, *Healers and Healing in Early Modern Italy* (Manchester: Manchester University Press, 1998), pp. 1–2.

7 David Wootton, *Galileo: Watcher of the Skies* (New Haven: Yale University Press, 2010).

8 Peter Marshall, *The Magic Circle of Rudolf II: Alchemy and Astronomy in Renaissance Prague* (New York: Walker, 2006).

9 Steven Shapin, *The Scientific Revolution* (Chicago: University of Chicago Press, 1996).

10 Miguel de Asúa and Roger French, *A New World of Animals: Early Modern Europeans on the Creatures of Iberian America* (London: Ashgate, 2005), p. 193. Gessner's work was later translated into English by Edward Topsell and can be accessed via *EEBO*. See Edward Topsell, *The Historie of Foure-Footed Beastes* (London: William Taggard, 1607).

11 Juan Pimentel, *El Rinoceronte y el Megaterio: Un ensayo de morfología histórica* (Madrid: Abada Editores, 2010), p. 109.

12 See, for example, Elizabeth L. Eisenstein, *The Printing Press as an Agent of Change: Communications and Cultural Transformations in Early Modern Europe* (Cambridge: Cambridge University Press, 1979), pp. 520–635; Adrian Johns, *The Nature of the Book: Print and Knowledge in the Making* (Chicago: University of Chicago Press, 1998). The speed and extent of the print revolution has, however, been questioned in recent years, with medievalists arguing that texts were not necessarily as unreliable as has sometimes been assumed, and some early modernists observing that 'the stabilisation of printed texts was a long and painful business, far from completed even by the end of the sixteenth century'. See Marina Frasca-Spada and Nick Jardine (eds), *Books and the Sciences in History* (Cambridge: Cambridge University Press, 2000), p. 3.

13 Kelly DeVries, 'Sites of Military Science and Technology', in Katherine Park and Lorraine Daston (eds), *The Cambridge History of Science* (Cambridge: Cambridge University Press, 2006), pp. 306–19.

14 See Antonio Barrera-Osorio, *Experiencing Nature: The Spanish American Empire and the Early Scientific Revolution* (Austin: University of Texas Press, 2006), p. 2.

15 Nicolás Monardes, *Primera, segunda y rercera parte de la historia medicina* (Seville: Alonso Escrivano, 1574), p. 112.

16 See Barrera-Osorio, *Experiencing Nature*, p. 2; Harold Cook, *Matters of Exchange: Commerce, Medicine and Science in the Dutch Golden Age* (New Haven: Yale University Press, 2007).

17 See Shapin, 'Invisible Technicians'. Robert Boyle's papers can be accessed online at *Boyle Papers Online*, http://www.bbk.ac.uk/boyle/boyle_papers/boylepapers_index.htm (accessed 29 January 2016).

18 See, for example, Londa Schiebinger, *Plants and Empire: Colonial Bio-Prospecting in the Atlantic World* (Cambridge, MA: Harvard University Press, 2004).

19 Museo Nacional de Ciencias Naturales, Fondo Museo, Sección A – Real Gabinete, legajo 1, Libro de Cuentas.

20 John Ray, *The Ornithology of Francis Willoughby of Middleton in the County of Warwick, Esq., Fellow of the Royal Society. In Three Books, wherein all the Birds hitherto known, being reduced into a Method suitable to their Natures, are accurately described* (London: John Martin, 1678), Preface.

21 Maria Sibylla Merian, *Metamorphosis insectorum Surimanensium* (Amsterdam: Gerard Valck, 1705).

22 Elaine Leong and Sara Pennell, 'Recipe Collections and the Currency of Medical Knowledge in the Early Modern "Medical Marketplace"', in Mark Jenner and Patrick Wallis (eds), *Medicine and the Market in England and its Colonies, c. 1450–1850* (Basingstoke: Palgrave Macmillan, 2007), pp. 133–52.

23 For a modern edition, see Jane Sharp, *The Midwives' Book, of the Whole Art of Midwifery*, ed. Elaine Hobby (Oxford: Oxford University Press, 1999).

24 On the use of Habsburg heraldry in the frontispieces to seventeenth-century works of science, see William Ashworth on 'The Habsburg Circle', in Bruce Moran, *Patronage and Institutions: Science, Technology and Medicine at the European Court, 1500–1750* (Woodbridge: Boydell Press, 1991), pp. 137–68.

25 See 'Knowing about People and Knowing about Things: A Moral History of Scientific Credibility', in Shapin, *A Social History of Truth*, pp. 243–309.

26 Asúa and French, *A New World of Animals*, pp. 226–8.

27 Edward Tyson, *Orang-Outang, sive Homo sylvestris; or, The Anatomy of a Pygmy Compared with That of a Monkey, an Ape and a Man* (London: Thomas Bennet and Daniel Brown, 1699), Preface.

28 See, for example, A. A. MacDonald, 'The Renaissance Household as Centre of Learning', in Jan Willem Drijvers and A. A. MacDonald (eds), *Centres of Learning: Learning and Location in Pre-Modern Europe and the Near East* (Leiden: Brill, 1995), pp. 289–98; Pamela Smith and Paula Findlen, *Merchants and Marvels: Commerce, Science and Art in Early Modern Europe* (London: Routledge, 2001).

29 For more discussion of early modern natural history collections, see Paula Findlen, *Possessing Nature: Museums, Collecting and Scientific Culture in Early Modern Italy* (Berkley: University of California Press, 1994); and Oliver Impey and Arthur MacGregor (eds), *The Origins of Museums: The Cabinet of Curiosities in Sixteenth- and Seventeenth-Century Europe* (Oxford: Clarendon Press, 1985).

30 Pedro Franco Dávila, *Catalogue systématique et raisonné des curiosités de la nature et de l'art, qui composent le cabinet de M. Dávila*, 3 vols (Paris: Briasson, 1767), Vol. I, pp. 492–8.

31 *London Evening Post*, 14 June 1739. Many British newspapers have been digitized by the British Library. If your institution subscribes, search your library catalogue for 'British Newspapers 1600–1950'.

32 J. E. Varey, *Cartelera de los títeres y otras diversiones populares de Madrid: 1758–1840* (Tamesis: Madrid, 1995), pp. 141 and 162.

33 On the practice of science in the home, see Alix Cooper, 'Homes and Households', in Park and Daston, *The Cambridge History of Science*, pp. 224–37.

34 Paula Findlen, 'The Economy of Scientific Exchange in Early Modern Italy', in Moran, *Patronage and Institutions*, p. 8.

35 'Atlantic Correspondence Networks and the Curious Make Colonial', in Susan Scott Parrish, *American Curiosity: Cultures of Natural History in the Colonial British Atlantic World* (Williamsburg: North Carolina University Press, 2006), pp. 103–35.

36 Tycho Brahe, for example, exchanged letters with over eighty individuals during his career and published a selection of his correspondence in 1590 under the title *Epistolae astronomicae*. See Adam Mosley, 'Astronomical Books and Courtly Communication', in Frasca-Spada and Jardine, *Books and the Sciences in*

History, p. 117. The correspondence of several scholars has been digitized and is available online. Carl Linnaeus' correspondence is available at http://linnean-online. org/correspondence.html; Newton's correspondence can be accessed at http://www. newtonproject.sussex.ac.uk/prism.php?id=150 (both accessed 29 January 2016). The correspondence of the natural historian Joseph Banks has recently been collated and published. See Neil Chambers, *The Indian and Pacific Correspondence of Sir Joseph Banks, 1768–1820*, 8 vols (London: Pickering and Chatto, 2007).

37   On corporate networks, see Stephen J. Harris, 'Long-Distance Corporations, Big Sciences and the Geography of Knowledge', *Configurations*, 6.2 (1998), 269–302. On the Jesuits, see Stephen J. Harris, 'Confession-Building, Long-Distance Networks and the Organization of Jesuit Science', *Early Science and Medicine*, 1 (1996), 287–318.

38   Daniel Carey, 'Compiling Nature's History: Travellers and Travel Narratives in the Early Royal Society', *Annals of Science*, 54 (1997), 269–82 (pp. 274–5).

39   Museo Nacional de Ciencias Naturales, Fondo Museo, Sección A – Real Gabinete, legajo 171; Archivo General de Indias, Indiferente 1549. On bureaucratic specimen-gathering processes in eighteenth-century Spain, see Helen Cowie, *Conquering Nature in Spain and its Empire, 1750–1850* (Manchester: Manchester University Press, 2011).

40   Many published natural histories and scientific treatises can be accessed online via *EEBO* and *ECCO*.

41   Other important scientific journals include the *Journal des sçavans* (from 1665) and *Acta eruditorum* (from 1682).

42   See, for example, Guglielmo Cavallo and Roger Chartier (eds), *A History of Reading in the West* (Oxford: Polity Press, 1999).

43   Nöel Antoine de Pluche, *Le Spectacle de la nature* (Paris: La Veuve Estienne, 1732).

44   Bernard le Bovier de Fontenelle, *Conversations on the Plurality of Worlds* (Berkeley: University of California Press, 1990). Popular works of science were often written or translated by women. See Paula Findlen, 'Translating the New Science: Women and the Circulation of Knowledge in Enlightenment Italy', *Configurations*, 3.3 (1995), 167–206.

45   Joseph Clavijo y Fajardo, *Historia natural, general y particular, escrita en francés por el conde de BUFFON* (Madrid: Imprenta de la Viuda de Ibarra, 1791), Vol. I, p. lxxi.

46   Asúa and French, *A New World of Animals*, pp. 94–5.

47   *Noticia del descubrimiento de e impression de los mss. de Historia natural de Nueva España del Dóctor Francisco Hernández* (Madrid: Imprenta Real, 1790).

48   Silvia de Renzi, 'Writing and Talking of Exotic Animals', in Frasca-Spada and Jardine, *Books and the Sciences in History*, pp. 151–70. For a modern English translation of Hernández's work, see Simon Varey, *The Mexican Treasury: The Writings of Dr Francisco Hernández* (Stanford: Stanford University Press, 2000).

49   Dear, *Revolutionizing the Sciences*, p. 2.

15 The wider world

Margaret Small

In the period after the European discovery of the New World and the sea routes round Africa to Asia, Europeans were suddenly posed with the problem of how to process all the information about the world and its peoples that was rapidly filtering its way back to Europe. There was virtually no aspect of European thought that remained unchallenged by the geographical opening up of the world. For students of the early modern period this sudden influx of new information about the wider world presents an enormous array of sources and approaches that enable us to gain a better understanding of European attitudes to other cultures, some knowledge about those cultures themselves, and an outlook on Europe and its relationship to the wider world in the sixteenth century. Easily the most studied sources by students of the early modern period are those pertaining directly to conquest and colonization (particularly to the Spanish conquest of the New World, and the English settlement of America), but the documentation of conquest is only a small portion of the sources available to students of European conquest, colonization and contact. Everything from religious discussions, to natural history to geographical and cartographical documentation, to technology, to travel, to natural history became fields of study that were affected by the new-found knowledge of the wider world. As knowledge about the wider world grew, more and more sources became available, but this chapter will have a focus on sources written in the aftermath of encounter, with a particular emphasis on sixteenth-century sources, written in the century after the opening up of Europe to knowledge about the wider world. All the sources mentioned in this chapter are textual sources written from a European, or European-influenced, viewpoint. Every society has its own history, however, and while outsiders' outlooks can provide useful information, for the student of non-European societies the European sources need to be supplemented by indigenous material, both in written documents (where available) and in archaeological and art historical works.

Conquest and colonization

The most famous sources on conquest and colonization are Columbus's letters about the discovery of the Caribbean islands.[1] His first letter about the New

World circulated all over Europe and was published seventeen times in the space of five years.[2] This letter demonstrated an attitude of conquest from the outset – the land inhabited by the Taino was claimed by Columbus for the Spanish monarchs in a manner that clearly demonstrated Columbus's attitude to the wider world. For any student of European attitudes to lands and peoples it provides an invaluable starting point. It also, however, demonstrates how much the writer both colours his report with ideas designed to appeal to a society imbued with Renaissance ideals, and was himself affected by such ideals. The description of the lands and their pre-iron age inhabitants is reminiscent of the ancient Greek writer Hesiod's ideas of a golden age. No student should read such a letter at face value, but must consider the various conflicting preconceptions and motives Columbus had. It would be facile to say it was purely a fabrication, but it was deeply coloured by his need to gain further support from the monarchs and by his own intellectual ideas. This idea of the New World as a Hesiodic golden age found further support in the works of Peter Martyr, whose *De orbe novo* was the first great account of the New World.[3] While technically not a conquistador's account, since it was written by a humanist in the pay of the Spanish monarchy who had never himself travelled to the New World, for sixteenth-century Europeans it played a vital role in establishing their idea of the New World, its inhabitants and Spanish possession. Martyr was a key member of the Spanish Council of the Indies through which most information concerning the Spanish New World passed, and he interviewed many eyewitnesses, but his work is nonetheless influenced by his humanist preconceptions and his desire to show Spain in a good light. It remains an extremely important document for all students wishing to understand the early stages of European expansion, and European interaction with the peoples of the New World, but one of the reasons it cannot be neglected is its widespread circulation. The *De orbe novo* was published in five different countries within three decades, and was translated into seven different European languages by the end of the century.[4] It was one of the most influential texts for creating a European understanding of the New World.

As the Spanish began to infiltrate further into the New World we get more documents that portray a real knowledge of the New World and its peoples. Hernán Cortés' letters to Charles V about the conquest of the Aztecs are masterful pieces of diplomatic writing, seemingly portraying Cortés himself as a loyal servant to the Emperor willing to risk everything to further Spanish dominion and the spread of Catholic Christianity, whereas in fact, Cortés had flagrantly flouted the authority of the Governor of Cuba to whom he was subject.[5] Perhaps more important, however, are the insights the letters give us into Aztec and other Mesoamerican societies. Cortés provides a wonderful description of the city of Tenochtitlan – the tribute given, the bustling markets and the splendid buildings – that conjures up the place even to a modern-day reader. He also reports on native customs and alliances. It is the view of a frequently appalled and emotionally involved outsider, but there is much in the letters that will still help students to gain an impression of pre-conquest societies even though these views need to be augmented with archaeological and other material. The soldier Bernal Díaz, for instance, who accompanied Cortés, has left us a far less flamboyant account of the conquest that is crucial in helping students to understand the conquistadors' success and Aztec failure from a military point of view.[6] For students of non-European contact societies the Aztec sources are amazingly rich. The bulk of pre-conquest Aztec codices were destroyed, but in the post-conquest period the Spanish wished to learn more about Aztec society and ordered the creation of the Florentine Codex by the Spanish friar Bernardino Sahagun.[7] Written in both Nahuatl and Spanish, it is a twelve-volume codex documenting many facets of pre-conquest Aztec society from the training of warriors and the role of priests to marriage. There are other extant Nahuatl codices, but this is by far the most important entry point for those interested in Aztec society.

The Spanish conquest of the Aztecs provides many sources that can be used in a variety of ways to gain understanding of the politics, economics, theologies, ideas and societies of both the Aztecs and the Spanish conquistadors. The other area of conquistador encounter that provides an extremely rich body of sources for students of the early modern period is the Inca realm. Unlike the Aztecs, the Incas had no written language, and there is no Incan equivalent to the Florentine Codex. Likewise the captain of the conquistadors, Pizarro, was illiterate and produced nothing to equate with Cortés' letters. Others among the conquistadors were more eloquent, however, and we have a wealth of sources about the early period. While not necessarily the most famous, in many ways the most useful of these (at least for providing an insight into Incan society) are *Narrative of the Incas* by Juan de Betanzos, and the *Royal Commentaries of the Incas* by Garcilaso de la Vega. Betanzos was married to an Incan princess, and de la Vega was the *metizo* son of an Incan princess and a conquistador.[8] A further useful source on the ethnography and geography of the Incas is Pedro Cieza de León's *Chronicles of Peru*, which contains a wealth of geographic and ethnographic material.[9] Both of these works, though written in Spanish, are able to provide a great deal of insight into politics, warfare, marriage and hereditary customs, and Incan society in general. While there are other sources such as Zárate's *Discovery and Conquest of Peru* that are better on the conquest, these two are among the most important written sources in the early modern period for gaining an understanding of the complex Incan society.[10]

Nor are conquest and colonization narratives limited to the Spanish New World. The Spanish, as the first European invaders of the New World, provide much of the earliest ethnographic information, but by the mid sixteenth century other countries were also involved. France, for example, attempted colonies in Quebec, Brazil and Florida; all of these failed, but all spawned letters and narratives that provided detailed accounts and even images of the local lands and inhabitants.[11] We even have early maps of the lost city of Hochelaga (ostensibly Montreal, though no archaeological evidence of a settlement of such size has ever been found), which give a visual indication of a type of native city that was lost forever after French colonization began in earnest. Similarly early English colonization attempts, such as those in Roanoke and Guyana, prompted the publication of a number of narratives that included invaluable information about the lands, terrain and peoples that the English encountered.[12]

Religious commentators

In some ways this is a false category, since religion pervaded all aspects of early modern society, but the Catholic clergy and in particular the Franciscans and Jesuits did debatably more than any other institution to create a knowledge of the wider world and an understanding of extra-European peoples for a European reading public in the early modern period. They were at the forefront of European expansion and therefore were in a position to provide the clearest information for European readers about pre-contact societies. Returning to the Spanish conquest, the Franciscan Diego de Landa's account of the Maya, for instance, is one of the best-written sources on Mayan people.[13] Although abhorring the Mayan society, de Landa, in an attempt to provide an understanding of the people he had been sent to convert, recorded minute details of their society and language, which when combined with archaeological (and other textual) evidence provide our clearest knowledge of the Mayan peoples around the time of the conquest. It is true that one of the reasons that de Landa is such an important source on the Maya is because he ordered the destruction of existing Mayan codices so that historians of the written record are more dependent on European sources than they might otherwise be. De Landa's is a somewhat vitriolic account of a people he found despicably heretical, but other European Catholic sources provide a far less alienated representation of the peoples they were sent to convert. For students of the Spanish Conquest, for instance, the work of Bartolemé de Las Casas is inescapable. Horrified by what he saw of the treatment of the natives in the Spanish encomienda, he became the leading advocate of better treatment for the natives, and really started the debate about the nature of the natives.[14] There had been a prevailing idea that indigenous Americans were, in fact, natural slaves, according to the definition of Aristotle.[15] Las Casas challenged this assumption with careful argument and example, and while the encomienda system ultimately endured, he did much to challenge the existing ideas. Las Casas was a Franciscan driven by his religious convictions and his belief that all mankind were potential converts.

The Franciscans were particularly prevalent in Spanish-dominated regions, but the Jesuits travelled literally all over the known world, and Jesuit accounts are a superb source of information. The *Jesuit Relations* of the missions to the Huron and later the Iroquois in the seventeenth and eighteenth centuries, for instance, provide enormous detail on the minutiae of native life in Upper Canada.[16] The difficulties of environment; communication; the complexities of male and female relationships; the importance of stamina, strength and speech; and the inter-tribal wars are among the various aspects of First Nations life that come vividly to life in the *Jesuit Relations*, which have all been translated into English. The flip side of these accounts is that they also show the immense isolation and ill-preparedness of the European missionaries for the lands and the societies they encountered. The bulk of Europeans were still illiterate or semi-literate, and the struggle to convert illiterate societies whose languages did not hold the means to convey many of the concepts of the Christian God was a truly daunting one for these convinced missionaries.

The Catholic Church was also at the forefront of European contact with the South and East, and provided much of the most reliable and useful information on African and Asian societies back to Europe. Not all these sources are so accessible for students of the early modern period, however. All the sources so far mentioned have been translated into readily available English versions. This is not the case for all the sources on the East. The letters of the Jesuit Francis Xavier, for instance, discussing his missions to India, China and Japan, have all been translated, unlike those of his successor as Visitor to the East, Alessandro Valignano.[17] Valignano was largely responsible for arguably the most successful extra-European mission of the early modern period: the Jesuit mission to Japan, which made upwards of 300,000 converts in little over half a century. His success was based upon his policy of acculturation, which required an extremely good understanding of Japanese society and ideas. The letters remain untranslated, however, with the result that for students the best available European source on early modern Japan is João Rodrigues' *Account of Sixteenth-Century Japan*, which was published by the Hakluyt Society in 2001.[18] This is, however, a good place to begin, since Rodrigues spent much of his life in Japan and was one of the best Japanese speakers the Jesuits produced. There are several other European works (not all by Jesuits) that can supplement this account. Many of them have been brought together in Michael Cooper's volume entitled *They Came to Japan: An Anthology of European Reports on Japan, 1543–1640*.[19]

The Jesuit accounts and relations were some of the most cerebral and educated reports about the non-European lands and peoples, but not all the religious sources were so intellectual. This could have its own benefits. The Franciscan Francisco Alvares, for instance, was among the first Europeans to travel into the heart of Ethiopia, acting as chaplain to the Portuguese embassy there in the 1520s. Alvares then wrote a book that has been translated as *Prester John of the Indies*, which is lucid and interesting, but largely uncluttered by the kind of classical preconceptions that colour many of the works by better educated travellers of the period.[20] Again, it cannot replace indigenous history but as an outsider's account it is invaluable.

Embedded and captive narratives

Some of the most important narratives were from Europeans who became truly embedded in other societies. We have already mentioned the *Jesuit*

Relations from Canada, but one of the reasons they are such a useful source is because they were written by Jesuits who went out in groups of one or two and lived with the First Nations people. They were utterly dependent on their native hosts to survive, and learned a great deal about their societies as a result. One of the most interesting of these narratives is that of Cabeza de Vaca, who went on an ill-fated Spanish colonial expedition to Florida. He was one of only four to survive, and did so by becoming first a slave and then a sort of medicine man and trader, living as a captive in various indigenous societies and slowly working his way across the southern United States until he reached Spanish settlements in what is now Mexico. His account of the various native societies with whom he came into contact is neither eulogistic nor derogatory (although there were certainly some he preferred to others), and it provides a large amount of information that still has anthropological value.[21]

Not all captive accounts have the same merit. The German soldier Hans Staden spent some time as a captive of the Tupinamba in Brazil, and while captive witnessed certain terrifying and shocking episodes such as the devouring of his companions.[22] When he eventually escaped and returned to Europe he wrote an account of his captivity which circulated widely. This account emphasized the horrors but none of the shared humanity, but cannot be ignored by students of early modern European relations with the wider world. It was published alongside a series of gruesome images (which were later embellished and republished by Theodore de Bry) and did much to shape European understanding of the American peoples. When coupled with other reports, such as those of heart-eating Aztecs, and Incans who used drums made from skins, it did much to emphasize the savagery of the New World to the non-travelling European, which more tempered works like those of de Vaca could not wholly counter.

Trade

Surprisingly, one of the more overlooked set of sources on the non-European world is that of trade accounts. These are particularly important for providing accounts of European interactions with peoples to the East. Many students of the early modern period tend to forget how insular Europe was and think of encounters with new peoples as happening only in the New World. This was far from the case. By the sixteenth century Europeans had more or less lost what little first-hand knowledge they had of Asian countries and peoples outside the Ottoman empire, and even Muscovy was an alien place. Merchants, however, sought to establish new trading connections, and in the process provided a great deal of ethnographical and geographical information back to Europe. As far as English sources are concerned there are some immensely useful and surprisingly under-studied works by various English traders and ambassadors eastward. Anthony Jenkinson, for example, journeyed through Russia, down to Persia and even attempted to re-establish the Silk Road to

China.[23] The attempt was doomed to failure, but the journeys nonetheless produced detailed accounts about the people, the political dynamics and the landscapes through which he travelled. Tribal and religious loyalties and ideas are clearly portrayed in his narratives. Similarly, Ralph Fitch's account of India and South-East Asia is an interesting read in its own right and became an influential resource for the founders of the East India Company.[24] Another fascinating document, written for publication, on early Dutch trade with East India before the establishment of the Dutch East India Company, is provided by Jan Huygen van Linschoten, who also knew Ralph Fitch and wrote an account of Fitch's captivity in India.[25]

Trade documents are a very patchy source for English-speaking students of the early modern world. Infuriatingly few of them have been translated so that in many cases students interested in trade and the areas in which the merchants' primary interactions with non-Europeans took place are frequently thrown back upon the areas of English influence. Nonetheless, translations of trade narratives have helped to shed light on some poorly documented regions. The Guinea region of the west coast of Africa, for instance, played a key role in the history of European expansion, in encounter history and in the slave trade. There are no indigenous sources, however, so historians of the region are dependent on European sources to supplement the archaeological record. Despite playing a key role in the early stages of Portuguese expansion, the Portuguese sources on Guinea are paltry. The most important, particularly in providing ethnographic information, were written by traders. Easily the most widely circulated of these, and also in many ways the most impartial, was written by Alvise Cadamosto, a Venetian trader in the employ of the Portuguese, who visited the region and provided a vivid account of his travels and encounters. Cadamosto is certainly not a finishing point, but he makes a good point of departure for early modern students interested in the initial stages of European expansion, and in the history of West Africa.[26] Malyn Newitt has recently provided a useful translated set of documentary sources on the Portuguese in West Africa, some of which, such as a discussion of the Wolof kingdom at the end of the fifteenth century, give interesting insight into some of the African societies, and particularly some early accounts of the slave trade and its influence in Africa.[27] Countries and companies kept a zealous guard on trade secrets in the early modern period and this secrecy still has a legacy today. Moreover, merchant accounts are not always exciting reading, unless written in the form of travel narratives as Jenkinson and Fitch (for example) did, and publishers unsurprisingly favoured translating and publishing works that would capture the reader's attention.

Travellers

The merchants' primary purpose was economic (although one cannot help but feel that someone like Jenkinson, who persistently travelled to extremely difficult-to-reach places, was also driven by curiosity). There were, however, also a select few who may occasionally have acted as traders, but who were essentially travellers for tourism, and provided detailed accounts of the places they visited. By far the most important of these was Antonio Pigafetta, who travelled with Ferdinand Magellan around the world and seems to have acted as a translator and general assistant, but whose driving force was curiosity.[28] He was one of only eighteen men to survive the expedition, however, and his account of the journey is full of interesting ethnographic detail (including transcriptions of certain words). As a source for the voyage it is invaluable, but it also provides interesting anthropological information about the various societies that Magellan encountered at the point of contact.

A far more dubious source of this type is the *Itenerario* of Ludovico de Varthema, who travelled eastwards, ostensibly as far as Java.[29] By the time one reaches his descriptions of Java, and human flesh being sold in the market stalls in the streets, the reader realizes that Varthema has descended into the realms of pure fabrication, but some of the earlier sections are extremely important. Varthema, for instance, disguised himself as a Muslim, and entered Mecca, providing a detailed description of the city. He was the first European to have reported on it, and the description holds up to reality. His is a difficult text for students of early modern history because Varthema was a master of deceit (one of the reasons he was able to survive his travels), and his lies and fantasies filter into his narratives. It is nonetheless an important source because Varthema, pretending he was a Muslim, embedded himself in a group of Muslim traders and was able to see, and be actively involved in, much that was otherwise entirely outside European knowledge.

In many ways Pigafetta and Varthema have little in common but they demonstrate a type of information source that became increasingly important over the course of the early modern period, and that is frequently overlooked. Nobody could claim they were unbiased sources (Pigafetta, for instance, was a devoted follower of Magellan), but travellers' reports tended to be more individualistic without the party line of religious or national motivations that coloured many of the other textual sources about non-European peoples in the aftermath of the voyages of reconnaissance.

Chronicles, histories and geographies

'Chronicles and histories' provides a rather sweeping category that covers a variety of works, both by arm-chair travellers who wrote about new peoples and places from the safety of Europe, and by eyewitnesses, who set out to record the history and natural history of the places they visited. As a category, histories and chronicles are difficult to define, but for the purposes of this chapter I am considering them as works of synthesis about large regions of the world. They are an indispensable source for charting the process of encounter.

Very little was recorded about the early Portuguese expansion, for instance, and the official chronicle by Gomes Eannes de Zurara provides an important source of information although it is written from a crusading point of view and does not always provide the level of detailed knowledge about the peoples the Portuguese encountered that a student might desire.[30] Nonetheless, it is the only real source available to English speakers about the very earliest stage of the Portuguese inroads into Africa. Indeed, in part because of the dearth of translated sources, English students wanting to trace the course of Portuguese expansion and encounter history are heavily dependent on chronicles, as P. E. H. Hair has shown, although other sources, such as Jesuit records, become important later in the sixteenth century. Frustratingly, the works of one of the most important of all the Portuguese historians, João de Barros, have never been translated, but there are other significant histories for the early modern student. Castanheda, for instance, provided a hugely popular *History of the East Indies*, which was widely translated all over Europe.[31] Similarly we have seen how Peter Martyr's *De orbe novo* was the work that really made Europeans begin to think about the nature of the New World and its inhabitants.

One branch of history that evolved greatly in the period and provides an invaluable source for students is that of natural history. There was an increasing interest in flora and fauna and also in actual ethnographical interpretation. Some of the histories rolled all this in together. José de Acosta, for instance, a Jesuit sent out to Peru, wrote a *Natural and Moral History*, which discusses everything from the causes of altitude sickness to the nature of barbarian societies. His is a formidable and erudite work, greatly coloured by his humanist training, but nonetheless providing an interesting record for students interested both in early modern societies and in the origins of early modern history.[32] Similarly, Gonzalo Fernández de Oviedo wrote a *Summary of the Natural History of the New World* (available in English), and a *General and Natural History of the Indies*.[33] The latter has unfortunately never been translated in entirety, but between them they provide some very pertinent information on the flora, fauna and peoples of the New World, along with some fine pencil drawings of the flora.

The Spanish and Portuguese tended to specialize in accounts of specific regions, but other Western European nations produced whole-world geographies that can also be invaluable sources on encounter. These tended to take two forms: they could either be works of synthesis, or compilations of letters, official documents and travel narratives describing the world. Many of the more important works of synthesis have never been translated in entirety into English, and those that were have to be used carefully. For example, sections relating to the East and West Indies of Sebastian Münster's best-selling work *Cosmographiae universalis lib. VI* were translated by Richard Eden and were among the first English books on the New World to be published in the sixteenth century.[34] Ostensibly a good source of information, in reality Eden's book is more useful for demonstrating how limited and unreliable the geographical and ethnographic information about non-European societies available in sixteenth-century England was than in providing real evidence about the cultures and peoples recorded in the sections that Eden translated.

Eden's translation of Münster was issued as part of a compilation, and this is the genre that really became important in early modern England, providing an unparalleled source of information about the wider world. It was a genre that first became popular in sixteenth-century Italy, and Eden was its first English exponent, but the most important English-language compilation was that of Richard Hakluyt, closely followed by that of Samuel Purchas.[35] These two authors collected every text they could that related to English trade and travel to the far-flung reaches of the world, and published them in multi-volume collections. In these volumes students can find source material on everything from the Inuit and the Lapps to Africans, Patagonians and Indians. Not all the material is reliable (Hakluyt for instance initially believed and included the fictional tale of Sir John Mandeville's travels), but these texts form the most comprehensive body of sources from the early modern period available in English.

Images

The European age of reconnaissance spawned such a variety of sources relating to new lands and peoples that it is impossible to survey them all. For reasons of space, I am going entirely to disregard maps, technical manuals, and political and philosophical treatises, all of which have some relevance to a greater or lesser degree. In this chapter I have primarily focused on textual sources with an ethnographical content that can be used either to aid the study of non-European societies or to write encounter history. There is one body of sources that must not be forgotten, however: that of ethnographic images. The person most responsible for constructing the European idea of non-Europeans is Theodore de Bry, but he is a singularly unreliable source. An engraver and compiler from the Netherlands, he collected images from a variety of sources, embellished and classicized them, and presented them to the European public. His depictions of the Brazilian Tupinamba or the Floridan Timucua bear a closer resemblance to ancient Greek ideals and depictions than to any form of reality, but because of the pervasiveness of his engravings it is important for students interested in European ideas about the wider world to be aware of his work.[36] In many ways much more important are the travellers who returned with their own depictions of the people they encountered. Jacques le Moyne de Morgues and John White, for example, provided beautiful illustrations of the people they encountered on their ill-fated voyages to Florida and North Carolina respectively (although one has to be certain to look at the original images, since de Bry tidied up and re-engraved drawings by both these travellers).[37] Similarly voyagers to the East provided a visual record of the people they encountered. Jan Huygen von Linschoten's widely translated *Itinerario* of his voyages in India mentioned above had a large number of detailed images that have been overlooked with surprising frequency, even though they provide some fascinating information.

Conclusion

This has been a short, idiosyncratic and necessarily extremely selective introduction to the types of European sources useful for the student interested in ethnographic history and the history of encounter. All the sources chosen are widely available in English, and I have used readily available editions, although not always the most recent or the most authoritative ones. The chapter began with sources on the Spanish encounter with the New World because this is often the starting place for students, but the European encounter with the wider world in the sixteenth and early seventeenth centuries was far more extensive than merely a 'discovery' of the New World. I have tried therefore to include a selection of less obvious sources as well. Many do not realize that the opening up of the world that occurred in the sixteenth century made even peoples much closer to home more generally known to Western Europe. The first description of the Samoyed peoples and Lapp in English translations, for instance, were made as a result of the same English voyages eastward that ushered in the trade with Muscovy, and ultimately the Jenkinson voyages.[38] Muscovy was a largely unknown entity before this period. The stages for encounter reached from Northern Europe to Southern Africa, from California to Java. This chapter has focused on sources from Western European countries at the points of earliest encounter, on the ones that became big players in the rush for global trade and monopoly companies, for conquest, colonization and settlement later on in the early modern period.

Key Resources

Anderson, Arthur J. O. and Charlese Dibble, *The Florentine Codex: General History of the Things of New Spain*, 12 vols (Salt Lake City: University of Utah Press, 1950–5).

de Bry, Theodore, *Americae tertia pars memorabile[m] provinciæ Brasiliæ historiam contine[n]s, germanico primùm sermone scriptam à Ioa[n]ne Stadio Homburgensi Hesso* ... (Frankfurt, 1592) and *Brevis narratio eorvm qvæ in Florida Americæ provi[n]cia Gallis acciderunt secunda in illam nauigatione, duce Renato de Laudo[n] niere classis Præfecto: anno M D LXIIII* ... (Frankfurt, 1593).

Coleridge, Henry James, *The Life and Letters of St Francis Xavier* (London: Burns and Oates, 1881).

Columbus, Christopher, *The Four Voyages of Christopher Columbus: Being His Own Log-Book, Letters and Dispatches; with Connecting Narrative Drawn from the Life of the Admiral by His Son Hernando Colon and Other Contemporary Historians*, ed. and trans. J. M. Cohen (Harmondsworth: Penguin, 1969).

Cortés, Hernán, *Letters from Mexico*, trans. and ed. Anthony Pagden (New Haven and London: Yale University Press, 2001).

Greer, Allan, *The Jesuit Relations: Natives and Missionaries in Seventeenth-Century North America* (Boston, MA: Bedford Books and St Martin's Press, 2000).

Hakluyt, Richard, *The principal navigations, voyages, traffiques & discoveries of the English nation: Made by sea or over-land to the remote and farthest distant quarters of the earth at any time within the compasse of these 1600 yeeres*, 12 vols (Glasgow: J. MacLehose and Sons, 1903–5 [1598–1600]).

de Las Casas, Bartolomé, *A Short Account of the Destruction of the Indies*, ed. and trans. Nigel Griffin (London: Penguin, 1992).

Martyr, Peter, *De orbe novo*, trans. Francis Augustus MacNutt (New York: G. P. Putnam's Sons, 1912).

Publications of the Hakluyt Society, which aims to advance the understanding of world history through publishing scholarly editions of primary narratives of travel and exploration (so far over 200 editions in 350 volumes): for a full list see http://www.hakluyt.com/hak-soc-bibliography.htm (accessed 31.03.2016).

Notes

1 There are numerous versions of Columbus's letters in publication. The most widely available is the Penguin edition: Christopher Columbus, *The Four Voyages of Christopher Columbus: Being His Own Log-Book, Letters and Dispatches; with Connecting Narrative Drawn from the Life of the Admiral by His Son Hernando Colon and Other Contemporary Historians*, ed. and trans. J. M. Cohen (Harmondsworth: Penguin, 1969). There are also several useful websites. One very helpful site with both facsimile and translation can be found at http://oshermaps.org/special-map-exhibits/columbus-letter/iv-diffusion-columbuss-letter-through-europe-1493–1497 (accessed 17 August 2015).

2 Matthew H. Edney, 'The Diffusion of Columbus's Letter through Europe, 1493–1497', http://oshermaps.org/special-map-exhibits/columbus-letter/iv-diffusion-columbuss-letter-through-europe-1493–1497 (accessed 17 August 2015).

3 The only complete translation of Martyr's *De orbe novo* is that of Francis Augustus MacNutt (trans.), *De orbe novo* (New York: G. P. Putnam's Sons, 1912). The first volume of this can be accessed online at http://www.gutenberg.org/files/12425/12425-h/12425-h.htm; or at https://archive.org/details/deorbenovoeight-d01angh (both accessed 17 August 2015).

4 Juan Gonzalez de Mendoza, *Historia de las cosas mas notables, rites y costumbres del gran reyno de la China con un itinerario del Nuevo Mundo* (Rome: V. Accolti, 1585); Donald Lach, *Asia in the Making of Europe*, 3 vols, Vol. I (Chicago and London: University of Chicago Press, 1965), pp. 743–4.

5 The best English-language edition is Hernán Cortés, *Letters from Mexico*, trans. and ed. Anthony Pagden (New Haven and London: Yale University Press, 2001); the complete five letters in an earlier translation can be found at https://archive.org/details/lettersofcorts01cortuoft (accessed 31 January 2016).

6 The most widespread translation available for students is the Penguin edition: Bernal Díaz del Castillo, *The Conquest of New Spain*, trans. and introd. J. M. Cohen (Harmondsworth: Penguin, 1963). An online edition of John Ingram Lockhart's nineteenth-century translation of the first volume is available at http://www.gutenberg.org/files/32474/32474-h/32474-h.htm (accessed 31 January 2016).

7 Codices were manuscript books. Pre-conquest codices were written in pictograms or native languages. The complete Florentine Codex can be found online in the World Digital Library at http://www.wdl.org/en/item/10096 (accessed 31 January 2016) but this is not easy to use without some further knowledge of the source. The first English translation which is still being republished is by Arthur J. O. Anderson and Charlese Dibble, *The Florentine Codex: General History of the Things of New Spain*, 12 vols (Salt Lake City: University of Utah Press, 1950–5).

8 The standard English edition is Garcilaso de la Vega, *Royal Commentaries of the Incas, and General History of Peru*, trans. H. V. Livermore (Austin: University of Texas Press, 1987). There has been a recent abridged version of the Livermore

translation with a new, useful introduction by Karen Spalding produced by the Hackett Press in 2006. The best English-language edition of Betanzos is Juan de Betanzos, *Narrative of the Incas*, trans. and ed. Roland Hamilton and Dana Buchanan (Austin: University of Texas Press, 1996).

9 There is a partial modern-English translation: Pedro de Cieza de León, *The Discovery and Conquest of Peru: Chronicles of the New World Encounter*, trans. Alexandra Parma Cook and Noble David Cook (Durham, NC: Duke University Press, 1998). The most readily available translation is Pedro de Cieza de León, *The Travels of Pedro de Cieza de León, AD 1532–50, Contained in the First and Second Part of His Chronicle of Peru*, ed. Clements Robert Markham, 2 vols, Works Issued by the Hakluyt Society, 33, 68 (London: Hakluyt Society, 1864, 1883). They are available online at https://archive.org/details/gri_000033125008673861 and https://archive.org/details/secondpartchron00markgoog (both accessed 20 August 2015).

10 Zárate's work is widely available in an abridged Penguin edition: Agustin de Zárate, *The Discovery and Conquest of Peru ...* trans. [and partly abridged] and introd. J. M. Cohen (Harmondsworth: Penguin, 1968).

11 Jacques Cartier and Henry Percival Biggar, *The Voyages of Jacques Cartier*, Publications of the Public Archives of Canada, 11 (Ottawa: Public Archives of Canada, 1924); Charles Edward Bennett, *Laudonnière and Fort Caroline: History and Documents* (Gainesville: University of Florida Press, 1964); René Laudonnière, *A notable history containing four voyages made by certain French captains unto Florida, by R. Laudonnière [the 4th being by D. de Gourges]* ed. by M. Basanier, tr. by R. Hakluyt (London, 1587); René Laudonnière, *Three Voyages*, trans. Charles E. Bennett (Tuscaloosa: University of Alabama Press, 2001). Jean de Léry, *History of a Voyage to the Land of Brazil, Otherwise Called America*, trans. and introd. Janet Whatley (Berkeley and London: University of California Press, 1990); Roger Schlesinger and Arthur Phillips Stabler, *André Thevet's North America: A Sixteenth-Century View* (Kingston, ON: McGill-Queen's University Press, 1986).

12 For these the best source is Richard Hakluyt, *The principal navigations, voyages, traffiques & discoveries of the English nation: Made by sea or over-land to the remote and farthest distant quarters of the earth at any time within the compasse of these 1600 yeeres*, 12 vols (Glasgow: J. MacLehose and Sons, 1903–5 [1598–1600]).

13 Diego de Landa, *Maya: Diego de Landa's Account of the Affairs of Yucatán* (Chicago: J. P. O'Hara, 1975); an online translation by William Gates from 1938 can be found at http://sacred-texts.com/nam/maya/ybac/index.htm (accessed 31 January 2016).

14 A Penguin edition introduced by Anthony Pagden is available as Bartolomé de Las Casas, *A Short Account of the Destruction of the Indies*, ed. and trans. Nigel Griffin (London: Penguin, 1992); a 1689 translation can be found online at https://www.gutenberg.org/ebooks/20321 (accessed 31 January 2016).

15 On this see Anthony Pagden, *The Fall of Natural Man: The American Indian and the Origins of Comparative Ethnology* (Cambridge: Cambridge University Press, 1986).

16 A useful excerpt from the relations with introduction has been made by Allan Greer, *The Jesuit Relations: Natives and Missionaries in Seventeenth-Century North America* (Boston, MA: Bedford Books and St Martin's Press, 2000). The entire English translation made by Reuben Gold Thwaites can be found at http://puffin.creighton.edu/jesuit/relations (accessed 31 January 2016).

17 Henry James Coleridge, *The Life and Letters of St Francis Xavier* (London: Burns and Oates, 1881), available at https://archive.org/details/thelifeandletter02coleuoft (accessed 31 January 2016).

18 João Rodrigues, *João Rodrigues's Account of Sixteenth-Century Japan*, ed. Michael Cooper (London: Hakluyt Society, 2001).

19 Michael Cooper (ed.), *They Came to Japan: An Anthology of European Reports on Japan, 1543–1640* (Berkeley: London, 1981).
20 Francisco Alvares, *The Prester John of the Indies: A True Relation of the Lands of the Prester John, Being the Narrative of the Portuguese Embassy to Ethiopia in 1520*, ed. Charles Fraser Beckingham, George Wynn Brereton Huntingford and Lord Stanley of Alderley (Cambridge: Cambridge University Press, 1961 [1881]).
21 There have been numerous translations and renderings of de Vaca's account. A recent, highly readable and well-researched retelling is Andrés Reséndez, *A Land So Strange: The Epic Journey of Cabeza de Vaca. The Extraordinary Tale of a Shipwrecked Spaniard who Walked across America in the Sixteenth Century* (New York: Basic Books, 2007). A more accurate translation with a lifetime's scholarship behind it is Alex D. Krieger and Margery H. Krieger, *We Came Naked and Barefoot: The Journey of Cabeza de Vaca across North America* (Austin: University of Texas Press, 2002). A less recent but readily available translation can be found at https://archive.org/details/journeyofalvarn00nuoft (accessed 31 January 2016).
22 Neil Whitehead and Michael Harbsmeier have produced an excellent modern edition with a good introduction, particularly for those interested in anthropology. Hans Staden, *Hans Staden's True History: An Account of Cannibal Captivity in Brazil*, ed. and trans. Neil L. Whitehead and Michael Harbsmeier (Durham, NC: Duke University Press, 2008). The Hakluyt Society edition can be found at https://archive.org/details/captivityhansst00burtgoog (accessed 20 August 2015).
23 The Jenkinson narratives can be found in Richard Hakluyt, *The principal navigations*, Vol. III; a good discussion of (and excerpt from) the Silk Road section of his travels can be found at https://depts.washington.edu/silkroad/texts/jenkinson/bukhara.html (accessed 24 August 2015). E. Delmar Morgan and C. Coote also produced an edition for the Hakluyt Society entitled *Early Voyages and Travels to Russia and Persia by Anthony Jenkinson and Other Englishmen: With Some Account of the First Intercourse of the English with Russia and Central Asia by Way of the Caspian Sea* (London: Widener, 1886), which can be found online at https://archive.org/details/earlyvoyagestrav01morguoft (accessed 31 January 2016).
24 Ralph Fitch, 'The long, dangerous, and memorable voyage of M. Ralph Fitch marchant of London, by the way of Tripolis in Syria, to Ormuz, to Goa in the East India, to Cambaia, to the River of Ganges, to Begnala, to Bacola, to Chonderi, to Pegu, to Saim, &c begunne in the yeere 1583, and ended in the yeere 1591', in Hakluyt, *The principal navigations*, Vol. V, pp. 465–505.
25 Jan Huygen van Linschoten, *The Voyage of John Huyghen van Linschoten to the East Indies: From the Old English Translation of 1598*, ed. A. C. Burnell and P. A. Tiele (London: Hakluyt Society, 1885). This translation can be found online at https://archive.org/details/voyagejohnhuygh02tielgoog (accessed 24 August 2015). The original English translation from 1598 is available via *EEBO*.
26 Alvise Cà da Mosto, *The Voyages of Cadamosto and Other Documents on Western Africa in the Second Half of the Fifteenth Century*, ed. G. R. Crone (London: Hakluyt Society, 1937).
27 Malyn Newitt (ed.), *The Portuguese in West Africa, 1415–1670: A Documentary History* (New York and Cambridge: Cambridge University Press, 2010).
28 The most recent version of Pigafetta's account of the expedition is Antonio Pigafetta, *The First Voyage around the World, 1519–1522: An Account of Magellan's Expedition*, ed. T. J. Cachey (Toronto: University of Toronto Press, 2007); a version made by Lord Stanley in the nineteenth century, which was the standard text for years, is available at https://archive.org/details/firstvoyageround00piga (accessed 31 January 2016).
29 There is no recent translation but the standard Hakluyt society version is available at https://archive.org/details/travelsofludovic00vartrich (accessed 31 January 2016).

30 The standard English translation is available at https://archive.org/details/ thechronicleofth35764gut (accessed 31 January 2016). P. E. H. Hair provided a useful introduction to the early translated sources on West Africa: P. E. H. Hair, 'The Early Sources on Guinea', *History in Africa*, 21 (1994), 87–126.

31 Fernão Lopes de Castanheda, *The first booké of the historie of the discouerie and conquest of the East Indias, enterprised by the Portingales* ... (London: Thomas East, 1582) is readily available on Google Books at https://books.google.co.uk/ books?id=YkoC-kx4TAgC&pg=1&redir_esc=y#v=onepage&q&fo=false (accessed 31 January 2016).

32 J. de Acosta, *The Natural and Moral History of the Indies*, ed. Clement Markham, trans. E. Grimstone, Works Issued by the Hakluyt Society, 60, 61 (London: Hakluyt Society, 1881), available at https://archive.org/details/naturalmoralhis00markgoog (accessed 3 February 2016).

33 A translation of Book L of *Summary of the Natural History of the New World* is provided by Glen Dille, *Misfortunes and Shipwrecks in the Seas of the Indies, Islands, and Mainland of the Ocean Sea (1513–1548): Book Fifty of the General and Natural History of the Indies* (Gainesville: University Press of Florica, 2011). Nina Scott also provides partial translations of several books in Kathleen Myers, *Fernández de Oviedo's Chronicle of America: A New History for a New World* (Austin: University of Texas Press, 2008). G. F. Oviedo, *The Natural History of the West Indies*, ed. and trans. S. A. Stoudemire (Chapel Hill: University of North Carolina Press, 1959).

34 E.g. Sebastian Münster, *A treatyse of the newe India with other new founde landes and islandes, as well eastward as westward*, trans. Rychard Eden (1553), *STC*, 18244.

35 Hakluyt, *The principal navigations*. E.g. Samuel Purchas, *Purchas his pilgrimes In fiue books* (1625), *STC*, 20509.

36 For some of De Bry's images of Timucua see https://www.floridamemory.com/ collections/debry; for a selection of his Tupinamba ones, see http://oldsite.english. ucsb.edu/faculty/rraley/courses/engl165CL/early-modern.htm (both accessed 3 February 2016). The originals can be found in Theodore de Bry, *Americae tertia pars memorabile[m] provinciæ Brasiliæ historiam contine[n]s, germanico primùm sermone scriptam à Ioa[n]ne Stadio Homburgensi Hesso* ... (Frankfurt, 1592); and Theodore de Bry, *Brevis narratio eorvm qvæ in Florida Americæ provi[n]cia Gallis acciderunt secunda in illam nauigatione, duce Renato de Laudo[n]niere classis Præfecto: anno M D LXIIII* ... (Frankfurt, 1593).

37 See Jacques le Moyne de Morgues, *The Work of Jacques le Moyne de Morgues: A Huguenot Artist in France, Florida and England*, ed. Paul Hulton, 2 vols (London: British Museum Publications, 1977). The second volume is a collection of drawings and engravings by him. Kim Sloan, Joyce E. Chaplin, Christian F. Feest and Ute Kuhlemann, *A New World: England's First View of America* (Chapel Hill: University of North Carolina Press, 2007); P. H. Hulton and David B. Quinn, *The American Drawings of John White, 1577–1599: With Drawings of European and Oriental Subjects* (Chapel Hill: University of North Carolina Press, 1964). A useful website comparing the de Bry versions with the original John White drawings can be found at http://www.virtualjamestown.org/images/white_ debry_html/introduction.html (accessed 31 January 2016).

38 R. Johnson, 'The Strange Discourse of Richard Johnson Concerning the Samoeds', in Hakluyt, *The principal navigations*, Vol. II, pp. 345–9.

Index

Taylor & Francis eBooks

Helping you to choose the right eBooks for your Library

Add Routledge titles to your library's digital collection today. Taylor and Francis ebooks contains over 50,000 titles in the Humanities, Social Sciences, Behavioural Sciences, Built Environment and Law.

Choose from a range of subject packages or create your own!

Benefits for you

>> Free MARC records
>> COUNTER-compliant usage statistics
>> Flexible purchase and pricing options
>> All titles DRM-free.

REQUEST YOUR
FREE
INSTITUTIONAL
TRIAL TODAY

Free Trials Available
We offer free trials to qualifying academic, corporate and government customers.

Benefits for your user

>> Off-site, anytime access via Athens or referring URL
>> Print or copy pages or chapters
>> Full content search
>> Bookmark, highlight and annotate text
>> Access to thousands of pages of quality research at the click of a button.

eCollections – Choose from over 30 subject eCollections, including:

Archaeology	Language Learning
Architecture	Law
Asian Studies	Literature
Business & Management	Media & Communication
Classical Studies	Middle East Studies
Construction	Music
Creative & Media Arts	Philosophy
Criminology & Criminal Justice	Planning
Economics	Politics
Education	Psychology & Mental Health
Energy	Religion
Engineering	Security
English Language & Linguistics	Social Work
Environment & Sustainability	Sociology
Geography	Sport
Health Studies	Theatre & Performance
History	Tourism, Hospitality & Events

For more information, pricing enquiries or to order a free trial, please contact your local sales team:
www.tandfebooks.com/page/sales

| Routledge Taylor & Francis Group | The home of Routledge books | **www.tandfebooks.com** |